Cortina

Number Six: Fronteras Series
Sponsored by Texas A&M International University
José Roberto Juárez, General Editor

Col. Juan N. Catura

CORTINA
Defending the Mexican Name in Texas

JERRY THOMPSON

Texas A&M University Press
College Station

Copyright © 2007 by Jerry Thompson
Manufactured in the United States of America
All rights reserved
Second Printing, 2013

The paper used in this book meets the minimum requirements
of the American National Standard for Permanence
of Paper for Printed Library Materials, Z39.48-1984.
Binding materials have been chosen for durability.

Library of Congress Cataloging-in-Publication Data
Thompson, Jerry D.
    Cortina : defending the Mexican name in Texas / Jerry Thompson.
    p. cm. — (Fronteras series ; no. 6)
    Includes bibliographical references and index.
    ISBN-13: 978-1-58544-592-9 (cloth)
    ISBN-13: 978-1-62349-062-1 (paper)
    ISBN-13: 978-1-60344-451-4 (ebook)
    1. Cortina, Juan N. (Juan Nepomuceno), 1824–1894. 2. Outlaws—Mexican-American Border Region—Biography. 3. Revolutionaries—Mexican-American Border Region—Biography. 4. Mexican-American Border Region—History—19th century. 5. Mexican-American Border Region—History, Military—19th century. 6. Lower Rio Grande Valley (Tex.)—History—19th century. 7. Texas—History—Civil War, 1861–1865. 8. Texas—History—1846–1950. 9. Texas—Ethnic relations—History—19th century. 10 Mexican Americans—Civil rights—Texas—History—19th century. I. Title.
F391.C77T477 2007
322.4'2092—dc22
[B]

2006039176

I saw myself compelled in Texas to defend the Mexican name.

>   JUAN NEPOMUCENO CORTINA
>   *Prisión Militar de Santiago Tlatelolco,*
>   *Ciudad de México*
>   *August 20, 1875*

Contents

List of Illustrations	ix
Introduction	1
Chapter One: The Making of a Revolutionary	7
Chapter Two: No Night for Mexican Tears	34
Chapter Three: Flocks of Vampires in the Guise of Men	67
Chapter Four: A Frontier in Flames	96
Chapter Five: Republic in the Balance	128
Chapter Six: Tiger in the Chaparral	148
Chapter Seven: Border Caudillo	175
Chapter Eight: Predator War	200
Chapter Nine: Caudillo Vanquished	219
Conclusion	249
Notes	253
Bibliography	301
Index	319

Illustrations

Matamoros, opposite Brownsville, 1863	12
Rancho del Carmen, 1934	14
Camp of the United States–Mexico Boundary Survey, 1853	19
Market Plaza and Market House, Brownsville, ca. 1865–66	24
Miller's Hotel, Brownsville, ca. 1865	26
Brownsville, ca. 1865	38
Steamboats on the Rio Grande near Fort Brown, 1861	40
Grave of William Peter Neale	42
Heintzelman's map of Cortina's defenses, 1859	76
Juan Nepomuceno Cortina, ca. 1863	105
Cotton being ferried across the Rio Grande, 1864	107
Bagdad on the gulf, ca. 1864	108
Plaza de Hidalgo, Matamoros, ca. 1865	111
Matamoros, 1865	114
Confederates evacuating Brownsville, 1864	115
Union soldiers enter Brownsville, 1863	116
Union soldiers drilling among the ruins of Fort Brown, 1864	118
Juan Nepomuceno Cortina, 1864 (sketch)	119
Juan Nepomuceno Cortina, ca. 1864	121
Manuel Ruiz, 1864	123
Fighting in the streets of Matamoros, 1864	125
José María Cortina, ca. 1866	130
Wagons on Calle de Cesar, Matamoros, 1864	131
Imperial troops ascending the Rio Grande, 1864	138
Julián Cerda and Servando Canales, 1866	142
Tomás Mejía, ca. 1865	146
Map of Brownsville and Matamoros, 1866	151
Cortinistas attack the French gunboat *La Bellone*, 1864	156
Col. Charles Louis du Pin, ca. 1866	161

José María de Jesús Carvajal, ca. 1865	163
Hanging of *Cortinistas* Vicente Garcia, Juan Vela, and Florencio Garza, 1866	173
Imperial troops embarking from Matamoros, 1866	176
1st United States Artillery on the Rio Grande, 1866	181
Servando Canales, ca. 1866	183
Liberal camp outside Matamoros, 1866	184
Sedgwick's bridge on the Rio Grande, 1866	185
Imperial Austrian officers in Matamoros, 1865	187
Vaqueros gathering at a rancho in northern Tamaulipas, 1873	201
Cattle raid on the Texas border, 1874	203
Stolen cattle crossing the Rio Grande, 1873	210
Cortina and María de Jesús López, ca. 1886	242
Aging Juan Cortina in uniform	244
Juan Cortina's grave, Panteón de Dolores, Mexico City	246

Map

Cortina War	xii

Cortina

Introduction

> *Then came the climax of all border troubles in the person of Juan Nepomuceno Cortina . . . the most striking, the most powerful, the most insolent, and the most daring as well as the most elusive Mexican bandit . . . that ever wet his horse in the muddy waters of the Rio Bravo.*
>
> J. FRANK DOBIE

MORE THAN A CENTURY after his death in 1894, the legacy of Juan Nepomuceno Cortina remains one of considerable confusion and debate. Through the years, scholars have attempted to place his life into historical context and thereby to understand what motivated him to lead a rebellion. Whether taken as hero or villain, Cortina seems one of those historical figures whose biography elicits little compromise. In such cases, distortion and misunderstanding seem the inevitable result. A survey of how Cortina has been studied reflects his elusiveness and suggests, more generally, some of the issues underlying all historical narrative.

A useful starting point in studying Cortina is J. Frank Dobie's *A Vaquero of the Brush Country* (1929). Dobie, a renowned Texas folklorist and son of the South Texas Brush Country, refers to Cortina as "the most striking, the most powerful, the most insolent, and the most daring as well as the most elusive Mexican bandit, not even excepting Pancho Villa, that ever wet his horse in the muddy waters of the Río Bravo."[1] "Striking," though, is far from righteous. Basing his knowledge of Cortina on a long list of civil and military depositions taken in Texas, Dobie maintained that Cortina was responsible for a "reign of terror" on the border. To Dobie, Cortina was a "great bandido" who "plundered and murdered."[2] In his final analysis, Dobie's real heroes were not "great bandidos" but the high-stepping, straight-shooting Texas Rangers.

One of Dobie's distinguished colleagues at the University of Texas, Walter Prescott Webb, passed a slightly less severe judgment on Cortina in his *The Texas Rangers* (1935). Webb's characterization of Cortina is not radically different from Dobie's, but Webb does provide a far more objective backdrop of the deep-seated racism in Cameron County and Brownsville in the decade after the Mexican War, a time when blatant inequality and intolerance made possible the bloody Cortina War. "Here, indeed," Webb writes, "was rich soil in which to plant the seed of revolution and race war."[3] Still, even to Webb, Cortina was a "black sheep," someone who was "impervious to all good influences" and an individual who "inherited personal charm ... [a] flair for leadership [and the] disposition of a gambler."[4] Webb admits that the Rangers, especially those under Capt. William G. Tobin (who arrived on the border in late 1859), were "a sorry lot." The Rangers, Webb continued, were responsible for the lynching of Tomás Cabrera, a sixty-year-old Cortina lieutenant. This event instigated much of the violence that followed. In a line or two without comment, however, Webb excuses the indiscriminate execution of Mexican Texans by the legendary Rangers. In another glossing, Webb is less than critical about the senseless burning of numerous ranches and farms by the Rangers. It is no surprise then, that Webb's heroes were the same as Dobie's heroes—the larger-than-life Texas Rangers.

Fifteen years after the appearance of Webb's *Texas Rangers*, Lyman L. Woodman, a retired Air Force major, wrote a short biography of Cortina. Titled *Cortina: Rogue of the Rio Grande*, Woodman's 111-page study, though well written, draws on the same limited sources as the Dobie and Webb studies. For Woodman, like his predecessors, Cortina remains the "number one Mexican border bandit of all time ... [an] extraordinary character ... [and a] virile man [with a] sinister countenance ... unhampered by conscience."[5] Woodman's Cortina was "a ruthless belligerent ... sensuous and cruel ... [and a] selfish and merciless Robin Hood." As for scruples, Cortina "had none." However, Woodman does allow that, "for all his rascally and evil ways, Cortina did retain one commendable trait, he had a deep love for his cutthroats."[6] In the end, Woodman's work, although of some interest, remains a strange combination of history and poorly executed romantic fiction. Indeed, in a number of highly idealized scenes, one can hardly tell where the fictional Cortina leaves off and the real Cortina emerges.

Fortunately for scholars, a radically different interpretation of Cortina's life appeared in 1949—a work Woodman had evidently not seen. Charles W. Goldfinch, a graduate student at the University of Chicago, completed the first scholarly study of Cortina. Goldfinch, a son-in-law of the prominent Brownsville attorney and civil rights crusader, José T. Canales (Cortina's older half-brother's great-great-grandson), anticipated much of the reinterpretation of Mexican American history that characterized the Chicano Renaissance two decades later. In his *Juan N. Cortina, 1824–1892: A Re-Appraisal* (published in at least three editions), Goldfinch was able to trace Cortina's ancestry back to the colonial era.[7] He accomplished this task with the help of his father-in-law, who had a lifelong interest in Cortina and who had collected a number of family papers and photographs. As well, Goldfinch accessed a number of Cameron County court and land records not previously used.

Goldfinch observed accurately that a conspiracy existed in Brownsville to exaggerate Cortina's 1859 raid to secure the return of Federal troops to Fort Brown. In his analysis of the Cortina War, Goldfinch highlights that, "although Cortina had taken the law into his hands, he did not rob and steal when he had the city at his mercy as he certainly would have done had he been a bandit."[8] Minimizing the effect of Cortina's decisive defeat at Rio Grande City in late December 1859, Goldfinch's study follows much of the information gathered by the 1873 Mexican Committee of Investigation sent by President Benito Juárez to investigate problems on the border. This investigation was organized in response to a similar commission that had been dispatched to the Rio Grande by the U.S. Congress the previous year. As historian J. Fred Rippy has noted, both commissions were "unfair and inaccurate."[9] Goldfinch agrees with the Mexican commission that Cortina "had not been involved in cattle stealing but had been the victim of a smear campaign conducted by Texans with ulterior motives."[10] To defend this position, Goldfinch devotes considerable space to repudiating much of the testimony of those who testified against Cortina before the American commission.

All in all, Goldfinch's study arrived as a breath of enlightened scholarship. His use of secondary materials is critical in the best sense. Although greatly influenced by the overall interpretation of Mexican American history found in Carey McWilliams's groundbreaking *North from Mexico* (1949), Goldfinch indicts McWilliams for distorting Cortina's record and character. Goldfinch asserts that McWilliams was too dependent on sources north of the border and on almost totally neglected primary Mexican sources (at the same time, it is difficult to find in Goldfinch's study more than a dozen references to Mexican sources). In the balance, Goldfinch concludes that, "to try to make a saint of Cortina would result in [a] great distortion."[11] Regardless, Goldfinch contends that Cortina's actions put him "on the side of those whose cause was more humane than that of his opponents"—that Cortina had the "courage to stand against tyranny and oppression" and is "entitled to a great deal of admiration."[12]

Historians, especially during the Chicano Renaissance, attempted to expand Goldfinch's thesis by arguing that Cortina was a "social bandit," someone who reacted to the evils of a racist society that suppressed the Mexican Texans economically and politically, an argument that was developed by Pedro Castillo and Albert Camarillo in their *Furia y muerte: Los bandidos chicanos* (1973).¹³ Castillo and Camarillo, in turn, utilized Eric Hobsbawm's *Primitive Rebels: Studies in Archaic Forms of Social Movements in the 19th and 20th Centuries* (1959).¹⁴ The noted Tejano scholar Arnoldo De León, in his eye-opening *They Called Them Greasers: Anglo Attitudes toward Mexicans in Texas, 1821–1900*, also utilized the "social bandit" theory in his interpretation of the Cortina War, as does David Montejano in his widely read *Anglos and Mexicans in the Making of Texas, 1836–1986*.¹⁵ In his *Mexicano Resistance in the Southwest: The Sacred Right of Self-Preservation* (using a subtitle from Cortina's September 30, 1859, Rancho del Carmen *pronunciamiento*), Robert J. Rosenbaum agrees that Cortina rebelled against "gringo law officers whose arrogance rose as Anglo merchants and lawyers increased their inroads in the Valley."¹⁶ De León, Montejano, and Rosenbaum saw in Cortina a border hero in the tradition of Catarino Garza and Gregorio Cortez. Finally, California sociologist and native of the Lower Rio Grande Valley, Carlos Larralde, who has maintained a lifelong interest in Cortina, generally agrees with Goldfinch and the "social bandit" theorists. Larralde, however, goes one step further in seeing Cortina as the founder of La Raza Unida, a precursor of modern *chicanismo* who struggled to promote "unity, devotion to ... community, mutual aid, and brotherly love."¹⁷

The figure of Cortina has also surfaced in nonbiographical directions. Notable is Michael G. Webster's 1972 dissertation, "Texas Manifest Destiny and the Mexican Border Conflict, 1865–1880." Plowing fertile scholarly ground, Webster provides new insights into Cortina in the period after 1865, and was one of the first to use a number of reliable Mexican sources."¹⁸ Similarly, one of the more objective studies of Cortina is James Ridley Douglas's 1987 thesis, written at the University of Texas at Austin, "Juan Cortina: El Caudillo de la Frontera."¹⁹ Douglas's thesis is enriched by his using fifteen volumes of papers, documents, and correspondence of Benito Juárez, materials that were published in 1969 and not available to previous scholars. Douglas agrees that Cortina attempted to combat "the prejudice that had handicapped Mexicans in the United States." But he did so, Douglas contends, "for the benefit of one Mexican in particular, namely Juan Nepomuceno Cortina."²⁰ Douglas's Cortina "possessed an extraordinary aptitude for intrigue and manipulation." Although Cortina did resort to cattle stealing, Douglas maintains "such behavior was not at all unusual among the populace, both Mexican and American, along the Lower Rio Grande."²¹ Cortina was no more "evil than the other caudillos of Tamaulipas, he was just more effective at it." Douglas concludes that, "just as the Texans used the courts to take Mexicans' lands or violence to subdue them, so did Juan Cortina resort to violence to defend his dignity and rights. Simply put, Juan Cortina behaved more like the wealthy and powerful Anglos of South Texas than most observers have cared to admit. The only thing that made Cortina's activities seem so remarkable was that he was one of the few Mexicans with the temerity to challenge American domination."[22]

Another study that touched on the life of Cortina was Manuel Callahan's 2003 dissertation at the University of Texas at Austin, "Mexican Border Troubles: Social War, Settler Colonialism, and the Production of Frontier Discourses, 1848–1880." Although Callahan's Cortina is not radically different from that of Goldfinch, Webster, or even Douglas, the new study does provide a more comprehensive analysis of Cortina's influence on South Texas after 1870. While admitting that Cortina's "notoriety, his image, deeds, and motives remain ambiguous," Callahan argues that Cortina should be seen as much more than just a caudillo. To see Cortina as simply a "border caudillo," Callaghan argues, "limits a more complex analysis of the political intrigue, economic competition, and racial strife that convulsed the region."[23]

In the opening years of the twenty-first century, several well-received books elevated Cortina to new heights of historical significance. In his superbly researched and groundbreaking *Revolution in Texas: How a Forgotten Rebellion and Its Bloody Suppression Turned Mexicans into Americans* (2003), Benjamin Heber Johnson sees Cortina's appeal to "Tejano resentment of loss of land and the arrogance of the new arrivals," as inspirational to the architects of the 1915 Plan de San Diego.[24] Against the bloody backdrop of the Mexican Revolution, the Plan de San Diego sought to reclaim territory taken by the United States from Mexico in 1848, restore ancestral lands to indigenous people, create an independent republic for Latinos, and kill every Anglo male over the age of sixteen. As Johnson astutely observes, much of the inflamed rhetoric in Cortina's 1859 *pronunciamientos* is similar to the angry outcry for blood and justice in the Plan de San Diego. Similar to the Cortina War, the 1915 revolt began with a series of raids by ethnic Mexicans in South Texas and developed into a regional rebellion in which an even bloodier counterinsurgency resulted in the forcible relocation and mass execution of Tejanos by the Texas Rangers and racist vigilantes.[25]

In his forceful and critically acclaimed *Catarino Garza's Revolution on the Texas-Mexico Border* (2004), Elliott Young compares Cortina to other legendary folk heroes such as California's Joaquín Murieta. Caught in the process of colonization and nation building and seeking to redress Mexican grievances against Anglos in Texas, Cortina "expressed the frustration of a community whose displacement began when the U.S. Army invaded the region."[26] Cortina's ability to sustain his influence on the border for nearly two decades was as much a reflection of the deep-rooted resentment of Tejanos toward political and economic oppression as it was his personal leadership and charisma.

For the first time, usually without passing judgment and with little comment, Cortina's image is now prominently displayed in museums throughout

South Texas.²⁷ Moreover, he continues to spark the imagination of writers and students of Texas and Mexican history. He lives, for instance, in Larry McMurtry's epic and prize-winning *Lonesome Dove* in the character of Pedro Flores, who ran "the best armed ranch in northern Mexico" and who "had more or less held nearly a hundred mile stretch of the border . . . for nearly forty years."²⁸ In one scene in which two wayward and helpless Irish youths are stranded in northern Mexico near the Rio Grande (and somehow looking for Galveston), Capt. W. F. Call warns the Emerald Isle teenagers of Old Pedro: "He ain't a gentle man, and if he finds you tomorrow I expect he'll hang you."²⁹ In the character of Benito Garza, Cortina lives also in James A. Michener's sweeping novel *Texas*. At the end of the Mexican War, Michener portrays Benito and his brother, disillusioned with the war and Mexico's humiliating defeat, returning to the border and their homes: "As the Garzas approached the Rio Grande before turning east towards Matamoros," Michener writes, "they paused to look across the river into the still-contested Nueces Strip, and resting in their saddles, they reached the brutal conclusion . . . 'there is no chance of turning back the norte-americanos.' But in the depth of their despair they saw a chance for personal salvation and Benito, his mustache dark in the blazing sunlight, phrased their oath: 'The yanquis who try to steal that Strip from us, they'll never know a night of security. Their cattle will never graze in peace . . . they'll pay a terrible price for their arrogance.'"³⁰ Indeed, they would.

What follows is the story of Cortina's life.

Chapter One

The Making of a Revolutionary

I never signed the Treaty of Guadalupe Hidalgo.

JUAN CORTINA

BROWNSVILLE WAS STRIKINGLY HOT and sultry on July 13, 1859—the usual summer condition in South Texas—as Juan Nepomuceno Cortina spurred his pinto horse into the dung-peppered streets of the bustling community. Under indictment in Cameron County for murder and stealing livestock, Cortina came to town heavily armed. Cautiously, he rode to Gabriel Catsel's small restaurant and saloon on the east side of a busy Market Plaza, a place where he frequently went to eat and drink and socialize with friends from both sides of the border. What happened in the next few minutes stoked a firestorm of simmering racial antagonisms that evolved into a no-holds-barred, vicious guerrilla war that eventually left hundreds dead, farms and ranches in ashes, South Texas in chaos, diplomats in Austin, Washington, and Mexico City in a dither, and Texas Rangers and the U.S. Army scurrying for the border.

Although he never backed down from a fight, Cortina did not come to Brownsville that hot day in July looking for trouble. Like others, he could have easily turned away and ridden back to Rancho del Carmen, his mother's ranch some nine miles up the twisting waters of the Rio Grande or crossed on the ferry to Matamoros where racial prejudices were less pronounced. But when he saw the town marshal, Robert Shears, a former Texas Ranger, pistol-whipping an elderly Mexican—a vaquero who had once worked on his mother's ranch—Cortina became incensed. As he strode into the street to confront the "squinting sheriff" (as he called Shears), the marshal turned to curse him. Cortina responded by gunning down the lawman in the dusty street.[1] His life and that of hundreds of others living on the border would never be the same again.

Early Life

On May 16, 1824, two hundred miles up the twisting and often turbulent waters of the Rio Grande, half that distance by ox cart or wagon, Juan Nepomuceno Cortina was born in a large rock and adobe house in the small sun-baked village of Camargo, Tamaulipas, less than a block from the town's small plaza.² Called "Cheno" by his family and friends, he later recalled having spent only a few years in Camargo before "his parents moved to Matamoros where they had their interest."³ Thus it was the larger Matamoros, and not Camargo, where Cortina came of age. Long the center of frontier culture and commerce, the town was also the headquarters of the Mexican Army in the northeastern part of the country.

What little is known of Cortina's adolescence comes from John S. "Rip" Ford, who, as a frontiersman and Texas Ranger, was less than objective in recalling much of Texas history. For a large part of his life, Ford and Cortina were also avowed enemies. Ford also carried with him much of the racial prejudices that characterized Anglo attitudes toward Mexicans in nineteenth-century Texas. Cortina, Ford said, was "a wild boy," the "black sheep of the family," and someone who was "bad in school."⁴ According to Ford, Cortina was always "beating some boy terribly and getting himself expelled." As a teenager, he kept company with many of the rancheros, vaqueros, and campesinos of the lower Valley, an association that, despite his youth, brought him to an "ascendancy over this class of men."⁵ Other rumors abound explaining his spirit. One persistent story held that, as a boy, Cortina was captured by Indians and "carried off to the impenetrable mountain vastnesses of Northern Mexico." Here, the rumor continued, Cortina remained for six to eight years, thus explaining his lack of education and love of "plunder, robbery and murder."⁶

Given his adolescence, Cortina's young adult profile comes as little surprise. Jeremiah Galván, a thirty-two-year-old Brownsville Irish immigrant and well-to-do merchant who knew Cortina well, said he was "a bold and daring fellow" who spent most of his time "on horseback trading in stock, driving stock for pay," and "acting as a guide to travelers."⁷ Both Ford and Galván agreed that Cortina grew to become "an influential man among his class of rancheros on account of his recklessness." Cortina and his vaquero friends, Ford wrote, "roamed over prairies," and "threaded their way through chaparral."⁸

As a young man, Cortina was frequently seen at the lively fandangos in Matamoros and the small settlements nestled along the river. Such occasions were often a time to drink, gamble, dance, fight, and make love. At these events, people accepted that "the man who crossed Cortina courted trouble and danger."⁹ Exaggerated stories endured for decades that Cortina arrived at such festivals with a retinue of servants, carrying sacks filled with silver coins earmarked for gambling. From one monte table to another, he gambled to his limit. In gaming, so in sex: dressed in the finest border fashion, Cortina was also a noted favorite among young women. Like Ford and Galván, Stephen Powers, another less-than-objective observer and chief justice of Cameron County and mayor of Brownsville in 1860, said that Cortina "was raised in idleness" and addicted to "gambling and all sorts of vice."[10] To Powers, Cortina was a "turbulent & disorderly man, desperate . . . ignorant in the extreme, cannot even write his name; never has engaged in any industrial pursuit [and] always . . . looked upon as a great thief."[11]

And so Cortina arrived into adulthood. Although his knowledge of Cortina was colored by the heightened racial atmosphere that characterized life in Texas at the time, Ford was correct in saying that Cortina "attained manhood without being able to read or write."[12] Despite his illiteracy, Ford well noted, Cortina came to possess a "great natural shrewdness, personal bravery, and a complete knowledge of the native Mexican," by whom he was "enthusiastically admired."[13] Ford was also correct in his perception that Cortina was cunning, brave beyond question, and possessed a personal magnetism and charisma that attracted others to him. In short, he was a natural-born leader. Five-foot-six-inches in height, unusually handsome, with his mother's green eyes, a ruddy complexion, and black hair and beard, Cortina could be as charming as he was at times ruthless and unremorseful.[14]

Ancestry

At the time of Cortina's birth in Camargo in 1824, his father, Trinidad Cortina, was alcalde of the town. Trinidad had married María Estéfana Goseascochea the previous year, and it was Cortina's mother who became the moving and inspirational force in his early life. With a pretty face and sparkling black eyes, Estéfana was petite, weighing little more than 100 pounds. Illiterate, she was, nevertheless, a "lady of culture," someone who possessed a pleasing personality and politeness.[15] The Cortina household included two older children by his father's earlier marriage, José Esteban and José Eusebio de Jesús.[16] Two other half-brothers, Sabás and Refugio, both older and from his mother's first marriage, also crowded the large Cortina house, located only a stone's throw from Camargo's main plaza and La Iglesia de Santa Ana. There, along the banks of the murky Rio San Juan, the family went to worship. A brother, José María, was born in 1822 and a sister, María del Carmen, arrived later.[17] Unlike their reckless brother Juan Nepomuceno, both Carmen and José became well educated, and in time, respected members of the Matamoros and Brownsville establishment.

What Cortina knew of his ancestral lineage, he embraced with great pride. His great-great-grandfather, Blas María de la Garza Falcón, was captain of the presidio of Cerralvo, Nuevo León, on the far northeastern edge of the Spanish empire, when he was given permission by José de Escandón to establish the village of La Villa de Santa Ana de Camargo. Leading several families through the desert and mountains from Coahuila to Cerralvo and on to the Rio Grande, Captain de la Garza established Camargo on March 5, 1749, with a high mass, the singing of hymns, and as much pomp and pageantry as was possible on the rough frontier at the time.[18] Located at the confluence of the Rio San Juan and the larger Rio Grande, Camargo was the first of José de Escandon's Rio Grande settlements in what became the province of Nuevo Santander. Blas María Falcón also founded Real de Santa Petronila, the first rancho in the wilderness between the Rio Grande and the Nueces River.[19] Here on the fringes of Spain's New World empire, his maternal grandfather, José Manuel Goseascochea, a Basque from Viscaya, Spain, and an officer in the Spanish Army, came to the frontier. His fate was tragic: José Manuel was executed on April 1, 1813, in the bloody Rosillo Massacre (near San Antonio de Béxar) in the struggle for Texas independence.[20]

Cortina's destiny was more closely tied to his great-grandfather, José Saldivar de la Garza, who in 1772 was given the large Potrero del Espíritu Santo (Pasture of the Holy Ghost) land grant north of the Rio Grande. Composed of 408 square miles or 261,276 acres, the family holdings stretched up and down the winding Rio Grande for twenty-five miles and as far north as the Arroyo Colorado. The grant, including what is today the city of Brownsville, was one of the most important in all of Nuevo Santander. Bordered on the west by dense, almost impenetrable chaparral and on the east by marshes and lagoons, it was the largest grant in the area where thousands of cattle, horses, mules, sheep, and goats grazed. It was on the Espíritu Santo Grant and in the streets of Matamoros that Cortina came of age. Cortina "could handle the lariat better than any cowboy the Southwest has ever produced," a Texas Ranger told a reporter for the *New York Times* many years later. His "skill at roping was remarkable and his horsemanship was superb." In addition, the Ranger recalled, Cortina "was the nerviest and quickest man with a shooter I ever saw."[21]

Cortina's early life on the Rio Grande paralleled some of the most violent and tumultuous years of the nineteenth century. Three years before he was born, Mexico gained its independence from Spain, and Nuevo Santander became Tamaulipas. Before his tenth birthday, Cortina had witnessed a series of devastating raids by "Yndios Bárbaros" that swept over the frontier with a viciousness he never forgot. Although the small villages upriver from Matamoros bore the brunt of the attacks by the Comanches and Lipan Apaches, the ranches around Matamoros, including his family's land holding on the north bank of the river, also felt the devastating effects of the raids. In April and again in August of 1836, when Cortina was only twelve, hundreds of

Comanche warriors, with great force and fury, struck the ranches around Matamoros, killing eleven citizens and driving off thousands of livestock. Returning again from the Llano Estacado, this time in March 1837, the raiders plundered the ranches along the river, killed five vaqueros, and drove off or slaughtered hundreds of horses and cattle.[22] At one time, as many as one thousand Comanche warriors were reported to be within a few leagues of Matamoros. If the Comanches were not enough of a threat, Lipan Apaches were also reported on the Arroyo Colorado north of the Rio Grande. The Indians "wrecked the fortunes of ranchers and townsfolk alike," the *Matamoros El Mercurio* reported in October 1837.[23] Upriver at Guerrero two years later, more than six hundred feathered Lipans charged through the streets killing, wounding, or carrying off sixty citizens of the river village.[24]

Like many on the frontier, Cortina came to hate the Comanches and the other "Yndios Barbáros." In 1858, after several small bands of Taraucahuas and Tampacuas had been driven across the river by the U.S. Army and settled in northern Tamaulipas, the Indians struck Rancho la Noria, fifteen miles northwest of Brownsville, killing Gaspar Glavecke and driving off a large herd of horses. Within days, Cortina joined his older brother, José María, two of his Tijerina cousins, and several other rancheros in pursuing the raiders. Following the Indians south across the river to Rancho La Mesa, Cortina and the rancheros engaged in a vicious fight and recovered the stock. When the Indians raided into Texas a second time, Cortina again joined in pursuing them, this time for days "out on the plains" where the natives were all killed, except one female and two infants.[25] "Although absolutely ignorant of military service ... from my early youth," Cortina recalled thirty years later, "I bore arms in the difficult and dangerous struggle against Indians, defending my rancho and the interests of my family."[26]

As a teenager on the frontier, Cortina also witnessed a series of revolutions as towns and villages in Tamaulipas and Nuevo León pronounced against the centralist Mexican government and raised the flag of rebellion in the Federalist cause. In 1838, a Federalist army appeared before the gates of Matamoros, determined to seize the valuable import and export revenues of the town. Although driven off, the Federalists returned again in January 1839, only to be thrown back a second time.[27] Three years later, in 1842, Cortina was only eighteen when he watched over two hundred ragged and defeated Texans march through the streets of Matamoros on their way to prison in central Mexico. Seeking revenge for a Mexican raid on San Antonio, the Texans had appeared on the Rio Grande, only to surrender after a vicious battle upriver at Mier. The towns along the river celebrated the defeat of the Texans as bands played, bells rang, and arches of flowers shrouded the narrow and dusty streets. In Matamoros, citizens cheered as firecrackers and rockets lit up the night sky.[28]

Although born in Camargo, Juan Nepomuceno Cortina spent his formative years in Matamoros. Established in 1774 by families from Camargo, Matamoros was the hub of economic and military life on the northeastern frontier of Mexico. Sketch by L. Avery. *Frank Leslie's Illustrated Newspaper*, December 5, 1863.

In January 1844, Cortina joined the Defensores de la Patria, a company of the Guardia Nacional de Tamaulipas. Organized in Matamoros and including men from both sides of the river, the unit was charged with defending the frontier.[29] Within a year, Cortina had risen to the rank of corporal. It was yet another step toward becoming a recognized leader to many of the poor and less fortunate on both sides of the river. To the peons, or *indígenos*, he was "Cheno Cortina," a *patrón* who came to their rescue in times of trouble, lent them money, and served as *padrino* at baptisms at Matamoros's Nuestra Señora del Refugio.

Marriage

At about the same time he joined the militia, Cortina met and seduced an older Rafaela Cortéz, the widow of Juan Antonio de la Garza. Rafaela had three children of her own, and, from her union with Cortina was born a daughter, Felícita (named after Cortina's aunt), in Matamoros in 1844.[30] One year later, in Matamoros on July 1, 1845, with the approach of the Mexican War that was about to engulf the area, Cortina, then twenty-one, married a first cousin, María Dolores Tijerina. The local priest, J. M. Rodríguez, presided at the simple ceremony while two friends, Severiano Rubio and Atanacio García, acted as witnesses. Just sixteen, María Dolores was the oldest daughter of Cortina's aunt, María Feliciana Goseascochea, and Juan José Tijerina.[31] As was common for the time, the marriage may have been arranged between the two prominent and closely related families. However, the union may also have been an attempt by Cortina's mother to give her son a measure of respectability and responsibility in pulling him away from the older Rafaela. And, to some extent, Cortina must have been influenced by the marriage of his older brother, José María, who wed Concepción Alderete.

What exactly happened in Cortina's marriage with María Dolores is difficult to ascertain. There is some evidence that she died not long after their wedding vows, possibly from childbirth or from one of the deadly diseases that ravaged Matamoros and the gulf coast at the time.[32] Family legend holds that Cortina deserted his young bride, an action that greatly distressed Estéfana. Regardless of his mother's concern, Cortina continued his sexual liaisons with Rafaela, and a second child, Faustina, was born in early 1846. A baptismal record dated March 13, 1846, indicates that Faustina was "natural" (i.e., born out of wedlock).[33] Evidently, the child was not shunned by the family for Cortina's sister, Carmen, and his older brother, José María, acted as godparents at the baptismal ceremony. Later at Immaculate Concepción, a small makeshift church in Brownsville, Cortina and Rafaela eventually wed on January 30, 1850. One of the witnesses at the marriage was a family friend, Adolphus Glavecke, a Prussian-born immigrant.[34]

Sometime after the birth of his second daughter, Cortina and Rafaela went to live at Rancho del Carmen, his mother's ranch. At the sprawling ranch complex, Rafaela's three children, Elijos, Brígida, and Marcelina, along with Felicíta and Faustina, composed the family household.[35] Felicíta died young, but Faustina, who was always close to her father, lived to become Cortina's sole heir. Estéfana's share of the Espíritu Santo Grant came to consist of 44,000 acres, or one-sixth of the original grant. Although Cortina spent most of his time at the stately brick Rancho del Carmen, the headquarters of the grant on the Rio Grande that was named for Cortina's sister, he also built a ranch of his own, San José. This second ranch was not far from the river, three miles from what was then called Los Fresnos, some ten miles from Brownsville. In the dense chaparral of the lower Valley, away from the coast, Cortina came to know every footpath and every river crossing. Over time, he built his own herd of cattle and horses.[36] The 1858 Cameron County tax rolls confirm that he possessed at least twenty horses valued at $210, 110 cattle worth $660, and carts and oxen worth $230.[37] Only a few miles upriver from Rancho del Carmen, Cortina's older half-brother Sabás Cavazos also maintained a large ranch and cattle herd. In contrast to Cortina's rowdy ways, the better-educated Cavazos was elected Cameron County Commissioner,

A stately Rancho del Carmen, around which Cortina spent much of his early life, is abandoned and in the process of being dismantled, brick by brick, when this photograph was made during the depths of the Great Depression in 1934. Photograph by Bartlett Cocke. *Library of Congress.*

justice of the peace, and he became a wealthy and respected member of the region's ranching elite. Unlike Cortina, Sabás was comfortable in the social and cultural diversity of both Matamoros and Brownsville and he often found himself at odds with his younger half-brother.

A Restive Spirit

Regardless of Cortina's personal situation, events from afar engulfed the Rio Grande Valley and the life of the dashing young ranchero from San José. In February 1846, Anson Jones, the last president of the Republic of Texas, lowered the Lone Star Flag in Austin and raised the Stars and Stripes, completing the formal annexation of Texas to the United States. Never having lost hope of regaining Texas, Mexico responded by breaking diplomatic relations with the United States. With the United States inheriting the Texas claim to the Rio Grande and Mexico insisting on the Rio Nueces as the boundary, President James K. Polk, an aggressive proponent of Manifest Destiny, ordered the U.S. Army, under Gen. Zachary Taylor, to march from Corpus Christi to the Rio Grande. With a large Mexican army in wait, war clouds soon began to gather on the Rio Grande. Cortina later said that it was not ambition but patriotism that "moved him to take up arms [and] ... to fight against the invaders."[38]

Because the Defensores de la Patria were familiar with the terrain north of the Rio Grande, Cortina was employed as a scout by the Mexican commander, Gen. Pedro Ampudia. Cortina later remembered being given "dangerous duties" and sent to "scout near the enemy."[39] He might have even watched on the morning of March 8, 1846, as the blue-clad U.S. Army first came to the great river and raised their flag on a tall willow pole. When General Ampudia demanded the banner be removed from the soil of Mexico, General Taylor began digging earthen works and preparing for battle. Across the river on the outskirts of Matamoros, Ampudia, too, began to fashion breastworks. Six weeks later, with tension reaching a breaking point, two companies of U.S. Dragoons were surprised at Rancho Carricitos, just upriver from Rancho del Carmen, by five hundred cavalry commanded by Gen. Anastasio Torrejón. Eleven dragoons were killed and forty-five captured. "Hostilities may now be considered commenced," General Taylor wrote President Polk from the Rio Grande. "American blood," the president asserted, had "been shed on American soil."[40]

Leaving five hundred men to defend the earthen works the Americans called Fort Texas, General Taylor moved to protect his supply base at Point Isabel. Gen. Mariano Arista, the new Mexican commander, not only began bombarding Fort Texas but also crossed to the north bank and positioned his impressive six-thousand-man army across the main road leading from Matamoros to the coast. When General Taylor heard the sound of cannon on the Rio Grande, he wheeled his column about and began retracing his path to the river. At a water hole on the Palo Alto prairie, just north of Fort Texas, in early May in stifling humidity and heat, the two armies clashed in the opening battle of a war that came to shape the destinies of two people, two nations, and a young ranchero and *soldado,* Juan Cortina.[41] As General Taylor's army neared the Mexican lines, the eerie, frightful stillness was abruptly broken by a burst of fire from the Mexican artillery. The "unhappy war," as Cortina called it, was underway.[42] The large, unwieldy Mexican guns proved no match for the mobility and rapid-firing 6-pounder artillery of the Americans. While the Mexican gunners struggled to fire one or two rounds a minute, the Americans were firing four.

At Palo Alto, Cortina was certain to have been with the cavalry that attempted to envelop the Americans only to be driven off by the light and easily maneuverable "flying artillery" that Taylor effectively deployed to cover his flanks. The charging Mexicans paid a terrible toll, only to regroup and charge again, this time to be thrown back by the American infantry. With artillery shells bursting in the ranks of both armies, the tall, dry grass of the

Palo Alto prairie caught fire, and, within minutes, a dense smoke belched skyward, obscuring both armies. Still, the fighting continued to rage, only darkness bringing the bloodletting to a halt. Among the eerie groans of the wounded and the silence of the dead, General Arista withdrew into the chaparral while Taylor's men, after trying to mount a pursuit, slept on the battlefield.[43] It was May 8, 1846, a day that Juan Cortina would never forget.

The next morning, General Arista set up defenses along the Resaca de la Palma, a dry sickle-shaped riverbed that had once been a bend in the Rio Grande. The Mexican army watched and waited impatiently as the Americans, determined to reopen the road to the river and Fort Texas, appeared in the distance, rested, continued to advance and then charged. General Taylor first threw his Dragoons at Arista's center, and, although the Americans captured several artillery pieces, a Mexican counterattack regained the guns. As the American infantry joined the fray, great confusion prevailed in both ranks. Neither side gave ground in the hand-to-hand fighting, and, in the dense underbrush, officers on both sides lost contact with their men. But suddenly small units of the Mexican Army began to fall back toward the dry riverbed, and the tide of battle turned. With General Arista's right wing in disarray, defeat became inevitable. The Battle of Resaca de la Palma had proven even more decisive and bloody than Palo Alto. Several hundred of Cortina's comrades were killed or wounded.[44] Yet Cortina had become a combat veteran at twenty-one.

The defeat at Resaca de la Palma also doomed Matamoros. With Taylor bringing up additional supplies and reinforcements, Cortina watched as the Americans crossed the river on May 18, 1846, and entered his heroic Matamoros. Arista had decided to give up the city and move his army south into the interior. Only weeks after the Mexican retreat from the Rio Grande, Cortina was at Monterrey where he was promoted to second sergeant and then sergeant.[45] As he watched in disgust, the United States occupation of Texas and the disputed Nueces Strip turned into an invasion of Mexico.

Simmering in Defeat

Following the defeated Mexican Army south and then west, Cortina later remembered those humiliating days in the early summer of 1846. Still, he was proud that he stood and fought and offered "his blood."[46] Cortina recalled how the Mexican army gave up "ground before the superior numbers of the invaders" and how "many of his personal possessions fell into the hands of the enemy."[47] Whether this was in Matamoros, San José, Rancho del Carmen, or on the battlefield is uncertain. One thing is certain though; the life Cortina had known on the Rio Grande frontier would never be the same again.

Cortina's whereabouts in the year following the Mexican defeat at Palo

The Making of a Revolutionary

Alto, Resaca de la Palma, and the occupation of Matamoros, cannot be verified. As General Taylor moved upriver to establish a supply base at Cortina's boyhood home of Camargo, before pushing into the interior toward Monterrey, partisan irregulars remained active in the area, and Cortina may have been with them. Years later, Cortina remembered how he was forced to live a life of "proscription" and to "wander about," either fighting isolated units of the American Army or "fleeing in the deserts."[48] It was later rumored, but never confirmed, that he was wounded at the Battle of Buena Vista, southwest of Saltillo, on February 22 and 23, 1847, when General Taylor decisively defeated Gen. Antonio López de Santa Anna in a battle that determined control of northeastern Mexico.

With the fall of Mexico City in late 1847, peace came the following year with the Treaty of Guadalupe Hidalgo, a humiliating Mexican concession that Cortina came to curse and ridicule. "I never signed the Treaty of Guadalupe Hidalgo," he defiantly proclaimed.[49] Shortly after the war, probably late in 1848, Cortina returned to Rancho del Carmen and San José. Under the treaty that ended the war, he now lived on land that was part of the United States, and, for the next decade, his destiny was closely tied to the American merchants, ranchers, and lawyers who came south to the river in ever-increasing numbers. Although "it was repugnance to his patriotism to be obligated to live among the enemies whom he hated so much," he had little choice.[50] In all, the end of the war and the adjustment to an American dominated legal system proved difficult. The triumph of Manifest Destiny and the accompanying racial contempt of the victor for the vanquished at times became unendurable as the heroic and patriotic Mexican guerrilla was expected to become a docile and law-abiding citizen of Texas. At age twenty-four, Cortina realized his future was to be shaped by alien political, social, and economic forces.

Defiance and Uncertainty

Splashing across the Rio Grande, Cortina eventually returned to the saddle to ride the dense chaparral along the river, the vast open prairies to the east, and the Wild Horse Desert to the north. He watched as Rancho del Carmen became a small village of adobe and stone huts, and a chapel, all surrounding the large brick house of his mother, Estéfana. At Fort Brown, Cortina signed on with John James Dix, a contractor for the Quartermaster's Department, for $25 a month. Ironically, he came to assist the very army he had earlier fought against. Along with thirty other Tejanos and Mexicanos, Cortina was given the job of securing the equipment and draft animals that were being brought out of northern Mexico following the war. His first task was to escort seventy-five wagons and teams on their way north. Besides the six mules required for each wagon, the large caravan consisted of a herd of one thousand horses and mules.[51] Dix took command of one group of herders and placed Cortina in charge of another. At Goliad, 180 miles north of the border, as the caravan went into camp on the San Antonio River, an argument erupted between Cortina and a wagon master who wanted to take several mules from the herd but who had not acquired permission to do so. As the dispute became heated, Cortina, who understood little if any English, was struck by the wagon master, whereupon, according to Ford, a "fight began at once, and was soon in favor of Cortina."[52] By the time Dix arrived, Cortina was "astride the wagon master, and was choking him." The man's "face was black ... his tongue was protruding from his mouth [and] ... he was almost dead."[53]

Later at La Grange, on the banks of the Colorado River, Dix had no sooner left Cortina in charge of a herd of mules when another dispute broke out that may have been racial in its conception that resulted in Cortina angrily leading several of the Mexican herders out of camp. Despite Dix's friendly intervention, Cortina and five others refused any reconciliation and spurred their horses south for the border. Although the army declined at the time to pay him for his services, he was later compensated at Fort Brown. Despite his problems, Dix complimented Cortina "for strict obedience to orders and for faithful and effective discharge of his duties."[54]

Not long afterward at Rancho del Carmen, Cortina joined a friend, Juan de la Luna, who had been employed by a young Kentuckian named Somerville, to purchase eighty mules and help drive the animals north. Within days, the man from Kentucky was found dead not far from the Rio Grande. Some charged Cortina with the murder. Adolphus Glavecke, who at the time was one of Cortina's closest friends, later claimed that, after Somerville's death, Cortina drove the stolen mules to Brazos Santiago and sold them to the U.S. Army.[55] Although there is evidence that it might have been Juan de la Luna who was guilty, Cortina was indicted by a Brownsville grand jury. Even John S. Ford speculated that Cortina "may have been innocent."[56] Regardless of his guilt or innocence, Cortina was never apprehended, much less brought to trial.

A few months later near Rancho del Carmen, Cortina and two accomplices, Juan Chapa and Juan Arrocha, were said to have robbed a wagon train loaded with dry goods belonging to Charles Stillman, thereafter taking the goods to Mexico for sale.[57] Later in 1852, Cortina crossed the river from Mexico near Rancho del Carmen with a "band of robbers" and robbed the small ranches of A. T. Mason and Israel Bonoparte Bigelow, driving off sheep and more than forty horses. Cortina, it was alleged, had a habit of feasting on "fat calves ... regardless of ownership."[58] Regardless, he was only one of many individuals on both sides of the river, both Anglo and Mexican, who turned rustling into a respectable avocation in the years after the Mexican War.

The rapidly emerging community of Brownsville can be seen along the north bank of the Rio Grande in this depiction of a camp of the United States–Mexico Boundary Survey in 1853. Drawing by John E. Weyss. Engraving by James Smillie. *United States and Mexican Boundary Survey.*

The Issue of Land

After 1848, outside forces continued to shape the political future of the area north of the Rio Grande. Even before the Treaty of Guadalupe Hidalgo could be ratified, the Texas legislature moved to establish Cameron County. Elections were held in August 1848, and Santa Rita, five miles upriver from Fort Brown and four miles downriver from Rancho del Carmen, was declared the county seat. When Brownsville was established, however, Charles Stillman used his influence to transfer the county seat to the newly established community that was rapidly taking shape just west of Fort Brown. Cortina watched in amazement as a number of the merchants in Santa Rita put their small frame buildings on wheels and rolled them downriver to the new commercial center, which by 1850 boasted of a population of 519. With merchants quickly realizing that large profits could be made by shipping goods to Brownsville and then smuggling them into Mexico, outsiders came to dominate a complex trade network that developed on the river.[59] Besides the Spanish and English languages, French, and even German, could be heard on the streets of the booming community.

A series of disputes over land titles erupted between the heirs to the original Spanish land grants and the recently arrived Anglos and European-born settlers. No sooner was the ink dry on the Treaty of Guadalupe Hidalgo than the Americans and Europeans challenged the Mexican Texans for control of much of the land. In fact, Spanish and Mexican land grants, some dating back to 1767, would become the focus of dispute and controversy for decades. Although guaranteed property and civil rights under Articles VIII and IX of the Treaty of Guadalupe Hidalgo, many Mexican Texans were never informed of such rights and were deliberately kept in the dark. Moreover, in the Trans-Nueces, the State of Texas was determined to settle the titles to the lands, and Article VIII of the Texas Constitution allowed for the confiscation of land if the owner had left the land vacant or refused to participate in the Texas Revolution or aided the Mexicans in the conflict.[60] The uncertainty about the exact boundaries of many of the grants also invited litigation and acted against the natives, as did their lack of English language skills and knowledge of the American legal system. A number of individuals, including Charles Stillman, Richard King, Mifflin Kenedy, Stephen Powers, and James G. Browne built large land holdings and fortunes on the ruins of Spanish land grants.

Cortina's concern over his mother's land appears to have been the motivating factor behind his attendance at a mass meeting in Brownsville on February 2, 1850. Mexican landowners were lured to R. N. Stansbury's schoolhouse, only to sit on hardwood benches amid flickering oil lamps. There, they placed their names on a petition to create a Rio Grande Territory, "separate and distinct from Texas."[61] On the document, the name of "J. Neppomuzeno [sic] Cortinas" was accompanied by an X. Many were encouraged to attend the meeting by the demagoguery of men such as Stephen Powers, Elisha Basse, Robert H. Hord, and Samuel A. Belden, who circulated a handbill warning landowners they would be forced "into expensive and ruinous lawsuits" if the future of their lands was determined by a distant and unsympathetic government in Austin.[62] Not only would the expense of the litigation be costly, but the land, cruel as it was beautiful, would also have to be surveyed and properly deeded, all at an additional cost. "With a territorial government, land titles would at once be quieted," the Brownsville schemers promised.[63] Land speculators were clearly attempting to take advantage of the great uneasiness that existed in the minds of many Tejanos in regard to their land titles. Cortina was "taught in 1850," it was said, that "Texas had no rightful jurisdiction over that country, and that those people had too long 'tamely submitted' to her laws."[64] District Clerk W. W. Nelson was probably correct when he observed that the Separatist Movement, in which a "great many speeches and addresses were made in English and Spanish, tended to impress the Mexicans ... that Texas had no claims to the territory this side of the Nueces River."[65]

In reality, the move to create a Rio Grande Territory was conceived by greedy newcomers eager to control the vast and verdant lands of the valley. There is little doubt that Cortina and most of the 106 men who attended the meeting and whose names were recorded, almost all of them Tejano, did not realize the full ramifications of their actions. They had become unsuspecting dupes in an alien scheme of land grabbing and consolidation of power. But the Separatist Movement precipitated a countermovement whose supporters expressed confidence in the State of Texas and the idea that any land dispute could be settled fairly. In another mass meeting at Stansbury's schoolhouse on February 5, 1850, a number of leading citizens, including Israel B. Bigelow, Orlando C. Phelps, and Rice Garland, rejected the territorial movement and called for an investigation to "titles to land situated between the Nueces River and the Rio Grande, and securing to every citizen his just claims and homestead."[66]

When William H. Seward of New York presented the petition to create a Rio Grande Territory to the Senate during the debate over the Compromise of 1850, Senator Thomas J. Rusk of Texas denounced the movement as little more than a clever deception. Rusk rose to warn that individuals had "taken charge of the Mexican population and are engaged in directing their action to their own purposes."[67] He asked his colleagues to give the movement no further attention. Even when the influential and aging Senator Henry Clay of Kentucky presented a second petition, this time with the names of many of the conspirators attached, the movement came to naught and collapsed entirely when several Brownsville citizens rallied against the idea and Texas land commissioners signaled they had no intention of challenging many of the land claims in the area.

To calm concerns on the Rio Grande, the state legislature, in February 1850, established a special commission to investigate all land grants west and south of the Nueces River. The commission was to consist of two commissioners: William H. Bourland, a former Texas Ranger and Mexican War veteran; and James B. Miller, a leader in the Republic of Texas and a well-known physician. Those appearing before the commission were to submit a written description of the land they claimed along with evidence of title and rights on which the claim was based. The commission first met in Laredo on July 15, 1850, where landholders appeared suspicious of the intentions of the commissioners, but eventually submitted fifteen claims, all of which were affirmed.[68] After being coolly received in Rio Grande City, the commission continued downriver to Brownsville, where they were warmly greeted, largely as a result of the collapse of the Separatist Movement. After several weeks of hard work, Miller, seeking a respite, decided to return to Austin by way of Galveston. Two days out of Point Isabel, off Matagorda Island, Miller watched as the steamer *Anson* went down in heavy seas. On board was a trunk containing many of the original land titles from the lower Valley. By 1852, however, 234 land grants had been confirmed by the state legislature, fifty-six of them in Cameron County alone. By 1860, 350 grants had been certified in the Trans-Nueces with only a handful having been rejected.[69]

A Troubled Horizon

Cortina watched as the decade of the 1850s became one of revolution and violence on the border. After the collapse of the Separatist Movement, Brownsville's Anglo and European-born merchant elite began agitating for a revolutionary scheme to create by force a free trade zone along the border that would provide greater access to the lucrative Matamoros and Mexican trade. A few filibusters even schemed to create a Republic of the Rio Grande out of northeastern Mexico. American adventurers and zealous filibusters such as the Knights of the Golden Circle also saw northeastern Mexico as the bridgehead for a slave empire that would stretch into Central America, the Caribbean, and perhaps beyond.

The man who came to lead the revolution on the border was a forty-one-year-old well-educated schemer and adventurer named José María de Jesús Carvajal, who some thought aspired to become the George Washington of Mexico. Born in San Antonio, Carvajal was educated in Kentucky and Virginia where he became a Protestant. He was fluent in English and had become a longtime opponent of Mexican centralism. Through his De La Garza family kinship, he was also Cortina's cousin. At La Loba near Guerrero, upriver from Camargo, on September 3, 1851, Carvajal proclaimed his Plan de la Loba.[70] A Federalist government would be established, church properties confiscated, the harsh punishment for smuggling abolished, and a free trade zone created for five years. As Cortina watched from Rancho del Carmen and Matamoros, Carvajal hastily formed four hundred restless Texas filibusters into an army at Rancho de Davis near what some were calling Rio Grande City. Led by John S. Ford, many of the Texans were also motivated by Carvajal's promise to return escaped slaves to bondage in Texas, more than a thousand of whom were said to be residing in northern Mexico. Financed by prosperous Brownsville merchants, Carvajal successfully attacked Camargo in mid-September, pushed upriver to take Mier and Guerrero, and then marched downriver to overrun Reynosa. He next set his sights on Matamoros and its valuable customs house.

Although plagued by a large number of desertions, Carvajal attacked Matamoros and the Centralist Army of Gen. Francisco Ávalos on October 20, 1851, capturing Fort Paredes on the river west of town. Repulsed by artillery in his push toward Plaza Hidalgo, Carvajal continued the attack for nine days in some of the bloodiest fighting in the city's history.[71] As a young recruit in the Móvil de Matamoros, Cortina gallantly helped to defend the Plaza Hidalgo against the filibusters.[72] With Colonel Ford wounded, Carvajal eventually retreated upriver before crossing back into the United States. Invading Mexico a second time, he was decisively defeated at Cerralvo. Regrouping again on the north bank, the determined Carvajal entered Mexico yet again, only to be turned back in fighting on the San Juan River outside Camargo. With only eighty-four Mexicans and 488 Texans remaining in his army, the Plan de la Loba was dead and the "Merchants War" over. Although he had played only a minor role in helping to repulse Carvajal and his filibusters, Cortina took great pride in what he had done. Unlike 1846, an invading army could be defeated and turned back.

But the idea of a free trade zone on the Rio Grande did not die with the Merchant's War. With the Plan de Ayutla in August 1855, liberals under a Zapotec Indian named Benito Juárez toppled Antonio López de Santa Anna from power, and when a liberal army under Santiago Vidaurri drove the Centralists out of Matamoros, a free trade zone became reality in 1858. The Zona Libre was a thin ribbon of Mexican territory stretching from the mouth of the river to the border with Coahuila, above Laredo, and into the interior twenty kilometers, or twelve miles. Goods could be legally imported without payment of the exorbitant tariff duties common in the rest of Mexico. The Zona Libre proved to be a great boon to smugglers who were able to cross goods into the United States without paying duties. For decades it would complicate diplomatic relations between the two nations.[73]

Despite being embroiled in Cameron County politics and his residency at San José, Cortina remained a member of the Matamoros frontier militia. By 1851, he had risen to become a second lieutenant in the Móvil de Matamoros. Three years later, he was promoted to first lieutenant, but, by January 1855, he had resigned.[74] It was also in the 1850s that the lower Valley underwent an economic transformation that came to alter Cortina's life greatly. Cortina watched from Rancho del Carmen as hundreds of restless, land-hungry European immigrants, namely French, Irish, English, and German, as well as many Anglo Americans, flooded into the area. Free blacks, carpenters and boatmen, rough Texas frontiersmen, and schemers from as far away as New England, all crowded into Brownsville's bars, brothels, billiard parlors, and dusty streets. Several Americans who had established mercantile houses in Matamoros relocated to the bustling north bank.

Brownsville Rising

By April 1850, a Brownsville city government, with Israel B. Bigelow as mayor, had been established in the booming border town. Aldermen, all outsiders, made arrangements to celebrate the fourteenth anniversary of the Battle of San Jacinto and passed a resolution expressing "unfeigned sorrow"

For half a century, the economic heartbeat of Brownsville was Market Plaza and the Market House. It was here on July 13, 1859, that Cortina shot Marshal Robert Shears and ignited the fire that would become the bloody Cortina War. Before the conflict ended, over one hundred people lay dead and much of the Lower Rio Grande Valley was in ruin. *Frank Leslie's Illustrated Newspaper,* February 20, 1864.

at the death of the South Carolina nationalists and defender of the "peculiar institution," John Caldwell Calhoun—"a true friend of Texas and the South."[75] Laws were also enacted making it illegal to discharge a pistol in the town, "run a horse, mare, mule, ass, or gelding" in the streets, or ride animals on the sidewalks. The new city government also set out to regulate bathing in the river and control "indecency."[76] Aldermen established rules regulating and taxing goods at the local market, rented a room as a temporary jail, leased the river ferry, or *chalan,* and selected and fenced a graveyard. They also spent an inordinate amount of time attempting to control the traditionally rowdy fandangos. There was also the problem finding enough coffins for the town's deceased paupers. Despite the fact that the overwhelming majority of the town's population was Mexican, few Mexicans participated in city government during the town's pivotal antebellum years. Even when an occasional Spanish name appeared in the early historical record of the town or county, that person was always a member of the commercial or ranching elite, such as Francisco Yturria, José San Román, or Cortina's half-brother, Sabás Cavazos.

Foremost among the entrepreneurs who dominated the economy of the town and county was Charles Stillman. Stillman left home in Connecticut at the age of eighteen and came to Matamoros where he established a mercantile firm. With the approach of war in 1846, Stillman went into hiding but eventually crossed to the north bank, where he purchased title to a disputed 4,676-acre tract of land that Cortina's mother claimed. Stillman began developing and promoting a new settlement called Brownsville, which was named for Maj. Jacob Brown, who had died of gangrene after being wounded in the defense of Fort Texas. The egotistical Stillman named streets for his bride, members of his family, and even himself (St. Charles).[77] He also made a million dollars. By joining forces with other large merchants, he ran a fleet of ships from New York to Point Isabel, where goods were transported to Brownsville and Matamoros for sale in northern Mexico. The clever and cunning Stillman never learned to speak Spanish, but he did successfully bribe officials in both Texas and Mexico in the wide-scale business of smuggling that rapidly became a way of life on the river. Along with other business partners such as José San Román and Jeremiah Galván, Stillman monopolized credit services to smaller merchants and forced many of them out of business.

Cortina came to know a host of others including Stephen Powers, a New England–born lawyer who had served as U.S. consul at Basel, Switzerland, as well as chargé d'affaires for several small German states. Powers first arrived in the Valley during the Mexican War as a lieutenant in the 10th Infantry and legal aide to General Taylor. After the war, he stayed on to head one of the leading law firms in Brownsville and was elected district judge, state representative, state senator, was appointed customs collector, and became one of the most powerful political voices on the border and in the Texas Democratic Party. In 1858, Powers had been elected Chief Justice of Cameron County while he was serving as mayor of Brownsville.[78]

Another interloper, whom Cortina despised, was William Neale. Neale ran away from home in Sussex, England, at the age of thirteen and arrived in 1834 in Matamoros, where he found work as a house painter and acquired the stage line between Boca del Río and Matamoros. After the Mexican War, he moved his stages to the north bank, helped catch runaway slaves, and built nice homes on both sides of the river. He also purchased a large tract of land from Francisco Ballí Treviño twenty-five miles upriver from Brownsville at Santa María, or what he called Nealeville, near a big bend in the river. Here Neale established a ranch, a mercantile business, and built a small steamboat landing. For a time the English-born Neale also served as mayor of Brownsville.[79]

Yet another individual in Cortina's range of operations was Mifflin Kenedy. Only twenty-eight in 1850, Kenedy had already steamed the Ohio and Mississippi rivers but came to the Rio Grande during the war to captain the *Corvette* in transporting General Taylor's troops and supplies to Camargo. The Irish-Quaker Kenedy stayed on to establish his own steamboat

At Henry Miller's Hotel on Elizabeth Street in Brownsville, travelers could sleep, eat, or catch the stage for Point Isabel and Brazos Santiago. *Lawrence T. Jones III collection.*

firm with Richard King and Charles Stillman, introduce Merino sheep into the area, and marry the beautiful Petra Vela. Through ingenuity and hard work, he also became rich.[80] In a similar vein, Cortina knew Richard King. From a poor Irish immigrant family, King ran away from New York City and eventually made his way to the Rio Grande where he, too, found work with the U.S. Army. After purchasing the steamboat *Colonel Cross*, King joined Kenedy in the bustling river commerce.[81] By 1850, the two formed a partnership with Stillman to monopolize riverboat traffic on the Rio Grande. The Catholic priest in Brownsville, Fr. Emmanuel H. D. Domenech, would label many of the large merchants and capitalists on the Rio Grande as "the scum of society," men whose greed knew no ends.[82]

Other immigrants who came to the Brownsville area included men such as Alberto Campione, who arrived from northern Italy, settled at Point Isabel, changed his name to Albert Champion, and became a prosperous merchant, rancher, and farmer. Like so many outsiders who arrived during the Mexican War and in the decade that followed, Champion took a border bride, Estéfana Solís. By 1858, Champion had acquired the stage line that carried passengers and mail from Point Isabel to Brownsville. With the help of his brothers, Peter and Nicholas, who followed him to Texas, he established two ranches in Cameron County: La Florida and La Gloria.[83] Elsewhere, Francisco Yturria, of Basque heritage, turned a tailor shop he inherited from his father in Matamoros into a prosperous mercantile firm. He also married Felicítas Treviño, heiress to the San Martín Grant in Cameron County. After the war, Yturria moved most of his business interests to the north bank and became a leading political and economic force in Brownsville and Cameron County.[84] Finally, the wealthiest man in South Texas was José San Román, who left Bilbao, Spain, at the age of sixteen for New Orleans, where he remained for a decade before making his way down the coast to the Rio Grande. After opening a dry goods store in Matamoros, he established a second store on the north bank, made a fortune in commercial credit, trustee holdings, real estate, and as a cotton broker. The quiet, self-made bachelor kept a low profile yet maintained a powerful hand in the area's politics for three decades.[85]

In time, the man Cortina came to loathe the most was Adolphus Glavecke. Glavecke had broken off his medical studies in Prussia for reasons that were never disclosed and arrived on the banks of the Rio Grande in 1836, from where he summoned his two brothers, Gaspar and Charles, to join him.[86] Glavecke married Concepción Ramírez, widow of Cortina's first cousin, Casimiro Tijerina, and six children were born of the union. During the Mexican War, Glavecke served as a courier for General Taylor. Later, from his eight-hundred-acre Rancho San Pedro, a few miles upriver from Rancho del Carmen, Glavecke became influential in local politics and was elected the first tax assessor-collector of Cameron County in 1848, county commissioner in 1854, and city alderman in 1857.[87] Glavecke was so controversial and divisive, however, the city council passed a resolution calling for his removal.

Although Cortina had known Glavecke from the time he was in his teens, it was not until Cortina returned to the north bank after the Mexican War that the two became involved in rustling cattle and horses. Through his wife, Glavecke also became a major influence on Cortina's mother and brother, especially in legal and financial matters—a Rasputin-like dominance that Cortina deeply resented. Cortina was especially leery of Glavecke's intricate conflict-of-interest family dealings and his connections to the Brownsville legal establishment. In particular, Cortina was upset with the way Glavecke and County Judge Elisha Basse handled the estate of a deceased aunt, Feliciana Goseascochea de Tijerina.[88] Cortina and Antonio Tijerina, son of the deceased, charged Glavecke with mismanagement and waste, and he was removed as administrator of the estate. Cortina may also have objected to other legal proceedings in which the Espíritu Santo Grant was divided into six equal parts with Estéfana receiving the western portion and Glavecke acting as one of the witnesses in the legal proceedings.[89] In another case, *Estéfana Goseascochea de Cortina vs. Antonio Cantú,* his mother tried and successfully recovered land on the left bank of the river near the village of Santa Rita.[90] In the complicated American legal system, cases involving the lands of Mexican Texans could drag on for years.

By late 1858, Cortina and Glavecke had become bitter enemies. It was rumored the two first began quarreling over how to pay a band of rustlers they had hired to do their dirty work. In the confusion, the original owner of the cattle caught Glavecke with the animals and in an attempt to exonerate himself, the cagey Prussian claimed he had bought the cattle from Cortina. On another occasion, Cortina was said to have crossed the Rio Grande from Mexico at night and stole a herd of cattle belonging to James M. Mallet, a French-born butcher, and John S. Cross, a Louisiana planter turned rancher, and driven the cattle across the river to Rancho Mayelles, fifteen miles into the interior. Glavecke claimed he followed Cortina into Mexico in an attempt to bring the cattle back.

In the spring of 1859, with the confrontation intensifying, Glavecke rode into Brownsville and took his case before the Cameron County grand jury.[91] With Edwin B. Scarborough, publisher of the *Brownsville American Flag*, as foreman of the grand jury, three indictments were handed down against Cortina for cattle stealing. Cortina was accused of making off with a "black steer and one dun colored cow" belonging to John S. Cross and another "brown spotted frizzly haired cow ... property of one Adolphus Glavecke."[92] Ironically, the spring 1859 grand jury also indicted Glavecke for receiving stolen property.[93] Regardless of the circumstances, within weeks the dispute between Cortina and Glavecke had become a personal no-holds-barred feud. Cortina came to refer to Glavecke as "infamous and traitorous," the "author of a thousand misdeeds," an "assassin," and one whom he swore to kill on sight.[94]

Racism and Inequality

Beyond interpersonal politics, a strong indication of a troubled horizon in the Valley was the socioeconomic inequality and deep-rooted racism engulfing Brownsville. Only two years after the town's creation, the community boasted a population of three thousand and had the second busiest post office in Texas. The vast majority of the citizens were not professionals, far from "gentlemen at large," as Frank D. Stillman, brother of Charles Stillman, classified himself when the census enumerator visited Henry Miller's hotel in 1850. Rather, most were poor Mexicans who hoped to find some measure of economic security in the new town. They subsisted on the barest of necessities, cooking outdoors on open hearths while huddling in small crudely built huts, or *jacales*, on the outskirts of town or along the river.[95] The dwellings were unbearably hot in summer, and bitterly cold in winter. Called *pelados* and socially shunned, they were the poorest of the poor, the untouchables of the Rio Grande frontier. Often dressed in rags, they were easily distinguishable from the Europeans, Anglos, upper-class Mexicans, or rancheros such as Cortina who dressed in fancy and colorful garments.

Living close to the land, the poor made flour from the *colorín*, or beans, of the mesquite tree and used the sabal palms near the town for the roofs of their homes. If palms were not available, they fashioned roofs of thatch or *carrizo*, the tall cane that grew along the river and the *resacas* near the town. From the nopal of the prickly pear came jelly, wine, and *queso de tuna*, a delicious candy. Managing only a bare subsistence, they grudgingly endured the bitter discrimination that was common in Brownsville at the time. "Americans have at times committed offenses which ... have been overlooked," the *Brownsville American Flag* frankly admitted in 1856, but "if committed by Mexicans would have been severely punished."[96] A customs official in Brownsville admitted that "lawless and unprincipled Americans were much in the habit of grossly maltreating the Mexicans who visited Brownsville."[97] Many of the *pelados*, especially in the years to come, looked to Cortina for guidance and protection.

From Rancho del Carmen and San José, Cortina watched as the struggle for power and influence in Cameron County brought deep divisions to the Brownsville business and ranching elite. The powerful merchant class rallied behind Charles Stillman, Richard King, Mifflin Kenedy, and Francisco Yturria, who formed a political party called the Reds, while Stephen Powers, William Neale, Edwin B. Scarborough, Frank W. Latham, Alexander Werbeski, and a number of smaller businessmen such as James G. Browne rallied to form a rival party—the Blues.[98] Both parties were Democrats, but the Blues were said to have been more "orthodox." Weeks before an election, as tensions heightened, party loyalists wearing "badges and bearing banners" could be seen scurrying about the streets of the town. There was "scarcely a citizen ... who is not a partisan," it was said.[99] On election day, "*¡Vivan los Azules!*" and "*¡Vivan los Rojos!*" rang through the streets and at the polls. So heated was the political atmosphere on the lower border that violence seemed likely. Wild rumors abounded, including the assertion that the New Englander Powers was a "suspected abolitionist."[100]

From the beginning of municipal government, divisions also appeared. In 1850, for example, the city council invalidated the election of Israel Bigelow as mayor and ordered him dismissed.[101] But it was in county politics that the struggle for power became paramount. In an election for state senator from Cameron and Hidalgo counties in 1853, fraud and illegalities abounded. E. B. Barton, the Red candidate, accused his opponent, Edwin B. Scarborough, the Blue nominee, of manipulating the vote in the rural precincts of Santa Rosalía, Ramireño, and Las Rucias. Throughout the county, polls had been surrounded by sheriff deputies loyal to the Blue Party. With murderous looking sidearms, they intimidated and turned away anyone thought to be voting the Red ticket. At Santa Rosalía, twenty-one votes were cast before the polls officially opened. At Ramireño, a few miles upriver from Brownsville, the presiding judge took the ballot box home at the end of the day where the ballots were allegedly altered before they were tabulated. In a number of precincts, Barton charged, "a great many Mexicans fraudulently represented themselves to be American citizens," and had voted the Red ticket.[102] By this time, records indicate "open and violent hostility . . . between the Blues and Reds." In fact, by 1855, politics had become so heated that "an impartial jury could not be found in the County of Cameron or the 12th Judicial District" where "good and lawful men" were simply not available.[103]

Bringing in voters from Mexico became a time-honored custom on the Rio Grande, and Cortina was said to have been involved. Commissioners would conclude in one contested election that, of the eight hundred to nine hundred voters in Cameron County, only about two hundred were legally eligible to vote.[104] Yet the overwhelming majority of those elected to office were either European immigrants or Anglos. Rarely were Tejanos elected, and when they were, it was to a minor office and the candidate closely allied with the dominant political establishment. Only in 1853, when two Mexican Texans become county commissioners, did the majority come close to comprising a meaningful political minority. Petit and grand juries, often used as a political tool and as instrument of intimidation, rarely included Mexican Americans.

To maintain themselves politically, the European and Anglo office holders were reliant on the Tejanos to keep them in office. "When election time comes, it is wonderful to behold the friendship for the Mexican voters," the *American Flag* recorded. "Promises of all kinds are made to them, but scarcely are the promises made, when they are broken," the newspaper continued. "An hour before the election they are fast friends, 'Mexicans, my very good friends'—an hour after the election they are a 'crowd of greasers.'"[105] Thus, force, coercion, intimidation, fear, and even fraud were used to herd the majority, poor, and frequently illiterate natives to the polls on election day. Days before the election, all-night rallies were held where free food and plenty of whiskey and mescal were available. Alcohol and drunkenness became synonymous with politics in Cameron County. On election day, the potential voters, many of them still inebriated, would be taken in small groups to the polls in what was called the "corral vote."

Cortina was sometimes employed in these hotly contested elections as a "striker"—someone who was hired to herd many of the lower-class Tejanos to the polls. Cortina was said to have also served briefly as deputy sheriff and at San José and Rancho del Carmen controlled from forty to fifty votes. Anglo politicians admitted he was a "political factor of some importance."[106]

Cameron County records indicate that Cortina paid a one-dollar poll tax in 1849, 1851, 1857, and again in 1858. One Brownsville resident, W. W. Nelson, said that Cortina was "an influential man in elections" and was "treated with a great deal of leniency."[107] At one tumultuous Democratic Party convention in 1858 at the Brownsville City Hall, delegates were to choose between Henry Kahn, candidate of the Reds and the Brownsville establishment, and James G. Browne, candidate of the Blues; Cortina was said to have strolled in with about fifty followers just as the chairman was calling for a division to determine the nominee. With Cortina's backing, Browne was easily nominated.[108] By early 1859, largely because of his political influence, Cortina was appointed to the Cameron County Democratic Committee, and, despite indictments for murder and rustling that remained unresolved, he was allowed "to run at large." As a result, it was said, he "grew bolder day by day."[109]

In the contest for county tax assessor-collector in 1858, Sheriff Browne supported Cortina's brother, José María, against a local schoolteacher, Gilbert Kingsbury. In return, Cortina promised to support the Blue ticket. José María had previously served as justice of the peace in the western part of the county and was said to have been "well-respected."[110] On election day, Cortina was accused of going around to the predominantly rural Tejano precincts, reporting that Kingsbury had withdrawn from the race and that there was no alternative but to vote for José María. At the polls "where the voters were all Mexican," Kingsbury wrote, "I was represented as not being a candidate."[111] For his support, Browne befriended Cortina and apparently overlooked the indictments pending against him in district court. From his perspective, Cortina learned a valuable lesson. In South Texas, intimidation was an accepted political tactic. It was evident that the party, be they Reds or Blues, who had the most money, the most guns, and who could provide the most alcohol, and offer the most spoils, would control Brownsville and Cameron County.

The Inevitable

In addition to his feud with Glavecke, the extended legal complications over land also edged Cortina to the edge of open rebellion. Although his mother, Estéfana, was able to retain the bulk of her share of the Espíritu Santo Grant, she was forced to sacrifice a league (or 4,428 acres) to her lawyers. Heirs to the vast grant had been forced to hire the law firm of Hale and Allen to defend their title against the claims of Stillman and his partners. In January 1852, Judge J. C. Watrous declared the grant valid, which placed the heirs to the grant in possession of the land on which Brownsville had been built. The decision was so controversial that it resulted indirectly in Watrous's impeachment.[112] When the Texas Legislature confirmed the grant the next month, Rafael García Cavazos and his wife, María Josefa Cavazos (who had inherited the portion of the grant on which Brownsville stood), sold the land to Stillman's lawyers, Elisha Basse and Robert H. Hord, for $33,000, or one-sixth of its appraised value. With Adolphus Glavecke as witness, Estéfana signed away her rights to the Brownsville tract for the sum of a dollar. In a series of clever maneuvers, the land was then transferred to Stillman and the Brownsville Town Company. Cortina blamed "a multitude" of Brownsville lawyers for conspiring against the owners of the land. To Cortina, they were "vile men" in a "secret conclave" whose "sole purpose" was "despoiling the Mexicans of their land."[113] Although Sabás Cavazos, Cortina's older half-brother, seemed satisfied, Cortina deeply resented the concession and felt that his mother had been cheated. Besides the local legal establishment, Cortina also blamed Charles Stillman. To Cortina, it became increasingly doubtful that the recently arrived Americans and the Mexicans on the border could live in peace and harmony.

In 1860, a half-literate seaman from Point Isabel perhaps best captured the legal atmosphere in the Lower Rio Grande Valley when he wrote Gov. Sam Houston the following letter:

> Der Sir, Know doubt you would like to know something about [the] Cortina affair, the original difficulty is nothing more or less than a land robing affair which is carried on in a very extensive scale and that done in Judge Watros Court ... the pore Deveil of a Mexican has know chance, he is told by the rober and lawyer he has know title to his land and that another preson wants the verry land that the Mexican was borne and rased on and his father before him, and now he is told he has know title. And the very considerat Gentlman that tells the Mexican that his title is not worth any thing makes him an offer of a small amount and advises him to take it and if not there will be know alternative but law and that in Judge Watros Court they know there is know justice for them, they well know the only alternative is to get what the Robber and Lawyer think proper to give him.[114]

John L. Haynes, the dependable state representative from Rio Grande City, also understood the root causes of what became the Cortina War when he argued in the legislature and in the press that the conflict had its origins in "a settled belief on the part of the citizens of Mexican origin, that frauds were being attempted against them to deprive them of their lands."[115] When a member of the Ballí family went to inspect the family's Rancho Barreta north of the Arroyo Colorado, he was tied to a wagon wheel, whipped, and left for dead by thugs believed to be in the hire of land grabbers.[116] Other landowners were displaced when they borrowed money using their property as collateral, and unable to pay their debts, their land was seized. A few were terrorized or murdered by ruthless squatters. There is little doubt that Cor-

The Making of a Revolutionary

tina was greatly alarmed at what he saw happening in the lower Valley.[117] So was etched the scene when Cortina rode into Brownsville on that hot summer day in 1859. His mother's land was more secure than at any time since 1848. Despite indictments against him in the district court, he had not been arrested or threatened due mainly to his influence in local politics. But the treatment of Tejanos in the lower Valley had if anything grown worse since the Treaty of Guadalupe Hidalgo, not better. As Cortina slid down from his horse in front of Gabriel Catsel's small bar and cafe, armed and defiant, the history of Brownsville and the Lower Rio Grande Valley was about to change forever. Ahead lay bloodshed, atrocity, and chaos. At least one Mexican was about to fight back.

Chapter Two

No Night for Mexican Tears

*¡Viva Cheno Cortina! ¡Viva la República Mexicana! ¡Viva México!
¡Mueran los Gringos!*

CORTINISTA BATTLE CRY

THE DECADE FOLLOWING the Mexican War brought suffering and sorrow to many Mexican Texans in the Lower Rio Grande Valley and throughout the Lone Star State. In 1849, an outbreak of cholera in Brownsville took more than one hundred lives, mostly those of the poor. The cholera was followed four years later by a terrible yellow fever epidemic that took even more lives. In October 1857, a fire that started in Jeremiah Galván's two-story mercantile store on Levee Street near the river exploded ninety-five kegs of gunpowder, destroyed several nearby buildings, broke windows, and rattled doors in Matamoros. Brownsville residents reacted in a panic. Flames spread to Elizabeth Street before river steamers pumping water, soldiers from Fort Brown, and the town's citizens brought the inferno under control.[1] The following year, yet another deadly yellow fever epidemic engulfed the Valley; again, there were somber processions to the local cemeteries.

In the eyes of the Mexican Texans, one of the most pressing problems was the biting and deeply rooted racism that engulfed the state. With the bitter legacy of the Alamo and San Jacinto, coupled with the resounding triumph of the U.S. Army during the Mexican War fresh in the minds of most Anglo Texans, Tejanos became second-class citizens in a land that had once been theirs. In the bittersweet legacy of the Alamo, Tejanos inherited the bitterness of their Anglo conquerors. For Mexican Texans such as Cortina, the Alamo was a haunted house. But it was not the myth so much as how the truth came to be distorted that was so damaging to Mexicans in Texas. Mexicans were not only racially inferior, many Anglo Texans argued, they were cruel, cowardly, and treacherous. Consequently, they came to be treated cruelly, not only in the interior of the state but also in the lower Valley where they were a majority.

In September 1854, citizens of Seguin announced that all Mexican "peónes" could neither reside in nor enter Guadalupe County. Shortly thereafter, representatives from eight South Texas counties met at Gonzales to discuss the threat Tejanos posed to the institution of slavery. Many Mexican Texans, it was asserted, were assisting runaway slaves escape to Mexico by way of an underground railroad. In Bastrop, there were angry assertions that a large number of local troublemakers were veterans of "Santey Anney's army."[2] Residents of Austin followed by accusing twenty Tejanos of stealing horses and announcing that Mexican laborers could no longer reside in the capital. Two years later, authorities in Colorado and Matagorda counties went as far as to evict their Mexican Texan populations. West of San Antonio, Uvalde County prohibited Mexicans from passing through the county without a passport.[3]

In 1857, news reached Brownsville of yet another nasty racial outbreak of violence—the "Cart War." Mexican Texan teamsters, or *carreteros,* had traditionally eked out a living by hauling food and merchandise from the port of Indianola to San Antonio and into the interior of the state. When the Tejano freighters, or *fleteros,* undercut rates by rival Anglos, the latter, partly inspired by racist Know-Nothing propaganda that permeated the state, launched a terrorist campaign against their competitors. Hoping to gain control of the growing trade by accusing Tejanos of aiding runaway slaves, Anglo freighters, wearing masks fashioned from gunnysacks, not only destroyed carts belonging to Mexicans but also confiscated and pillaged their cargoes. Several Mexican Texans died in the violence when their wagon trains were robbed and destroyed. Many Tejanos fled for the safety of the Rio Grande.

Local and state authorities exerted virtually no effort to apprehend the outlaws, and it was not until the Mexican minister in Washington protested to American Secretary of State Lewis Cass that Gov. Elisha M. Pease took action. When a company of Texas Rangers was finally sent into the area to restore law and order, it became obvious their aim was more the restoration of the trade than protection of the Tejano population. At the height of the conflict, citizens in Goliad County gave notice that any Mexican caught committing a crime in the county would be swept "from the face of the earth."[4] Around Helena, in adjacent Karnes County, racial relations were said to be even worse. Although largely illiterate, Cortina was certain to have heard of the Cart War and the ethnic violence elsewhere in the state. Combined with the mistreatment of Mexicans in Brownsville, he became more and more restless.

Ethnic Intolerance

Two years after the Cart War, state representative Edward Dougherty of Hidalgo County introduced a bill in the legislature calling for the creation of a peonage system in Texas similar to what existed in Mexico. A leading and influential political figure in the Valley, the Irish-born Dougherty had fought at Palo Alto and Resaca de la Palma, taken a local bride, Marcela García, and established the small trading community of Rudyville near Relampago in Hidalgo County. In heated debate on the floor of the House of Representatives, Ángel Navarro, one of the few Tejanos in the legislature at the time, vociferously opposed the bill, saying it was "an insult to the Mexican population of the State of Texas" and that it would drag "the poor and degraded natives" into bondage and "deprive them of their liberty [and] their earnings."[5] Others in the legislature went as far as to accuse Dougherty of attempting to introduce "a system of bondage ten thousand times worse and more servile than African slavery."[6] Others opposed the bill, fearing that it would hinder the settlement of Cameron and Hidalgo counties by "as large a Caucasian population as possible." Although Dougherty claimed his bill had wide popular support, the measure went down to defeat, 42 to 32.[7]

Closer to home, a number of Mexicans were gunned down in the streets of Brownsville and their murderers were never arrested. Events were closing in on Cortina. As late as the spring of 1859, Charles Stillman claimed fifteen to twenty Mexicans of "bad character" had been driven away from the Nueces River by vigilante committees and were camped at Rancho San José, "occupied by one Cortina."[8] As well, with the Rio Grande reduced to a trickle for the first time in years and steamboats aground, a large number of ox carts came rambling down river from Roma, Rio Grande City, and Edinburg laden with wool and hides. Several carts were plundered near Rancho del Carmen, the mules and oxen driven off, and the wool and hides carried into Mexico. Many in Brownsville blamed Cortina and the men he had assembled at Rancho del Carmen.[9]

With the effect of a free trade zone, Cortina also watched commercial houses in Brownsville go out of business, and the population declined from 4,500 in 1850 to 2,300 in 1858.[10] The local economy was dealt a another blow when Gen. David E. Twiggs, the aging and infirm commander of the Department of Texas, decided to abandon Fort Brown and transfer the local garrison, mostly artillerymen, to Fort Duncan at Eagle Pass. With the blessings of the War Department, Twiggs also closed Ringgold Barracks at Rio Grande City and Fort McIntosh at Laredo and sent the troops to guard the San Antonio–El Paso wagon road and to fight Indians on the western frontier.[11] Ninety-three members of Brownsville's merchant elite and entrepreneurs from as far away as Corpus Christi and San Patricio protested Twiggs's actions to the Secretary of War, John B. Floyd, but Washington refused to countermand the orders. Unprotected by the military, "Mexican armed soldiers, highwaymen, and Indians," would invade the border, the merchants warned.[12] Twiggs bluntly replied that there never had been "any danger of the Mexicans ... crossing the river to plunder or disturb the inhabitants, and the outcry on that river for troops is solely to have an expenditure of the public money."[13] Ever since the Mexican War, the presence of the U.S. Army on the border had been a sobering symbol of power to Cortina, but, with the military gone, he realized the situation was dramatically altered.

The Moment—and Retreat

In an atmosphere of anxiety and uncertainty, Cortina rode into Brownsville on July 13, 1859, with what one observer called a "dozen desperate fellows."[14] Cortina was thirty-five at the time and in the prime of his life. Although always concerned about the indictments that shadowed him everywhere, he did not fear arrest, largely because of his political influence in the county. Moreover, law enforcement officials in Brownsville appear to have also been somewhat intimidated by Cortina.

Newly appointed City Marshal Robert Shears was also thirty-five in the summer of 1859. With a Mexican wife and child, the Kentucky-born Shears agreed to take the job of town marshal only after Mayor Stephen Powers was unable to find anyone else.[15] Shears, who did not know Cortina personally, was a carpenter by trade and a veteran of the Texas Rangers. A quiet man with a bad temper, he was known for his excessive chewing of tobacco and the rather irritating manner in which he squinted his eyes.

Powers, who was serving as both county judge and mayor, gave Shears an arrest warrant for a Mexican who was accused of abusing Gabriel Catsel, a forty-six-year-old French immigrant who ran a popular bar, coffee house, and small grocery on the east side of Market Plaza.[16] On July 13, Shears spotted the man Powers wanted apprehended on Market Plaza, and he strode forward to make the arrest. Some say the man was drunk and armed with a knife; when he resisted, Shears began pistol-whipping him while attempting to drag him off to jail. Watching from Catsel's cafe, Cortina recognized the man as having once worked at Rancho del Carmen, and he went to intervene. "Why do you ill-treat this man?" Cortina remembered asking. "He answered me insolently," Cortina responded, so "I punished his insolence and avenged my countrymen by shooting him with a pistol and stretching him at my feet."[17] Shears claimed that Cortina tried to shoot him in the back but missed; when Shears wheeled about, a second bullet ripped into his left shoulder, the bullet exiting his back.[18] While Shears lay in the street gravely wounded and bleeding profusely, Cortina swung the elderly vaquero up behind him on his pinto horse and galloped out of town—"amidst the stupor

By the time of the Cortina War in 1859, Brownsville was the fifth largest city in Texas and had the second busiest post office in the state. *Lawrence T. Jones III collection.*

of the Yankees and the enthusiastic hurrahs of the Mexicans," he would say.[19] At first, many townsmen thought Shears was mortally wounded, but, after being confined to bed for three months, he recovered.[20]

In the crucial hours following the Market Square shooting, Sheriff James G. Browne rallied twenty-five men as a posse to pursue Cortina. When the time came to ride out of town, only five men had retained enough courage to proceed, and the pursuit was called off.[21] As a result of the shooting, Cortina became somewhat of a hero to the poor and underprivileged Mexicans on both sides of the border. He had become a champion to a people who had no champion. For his daring deed, he would become the subject of endless stories and heroic border ballads, or *corridos*.[22]

On reaching Rancho del Carmen, Cortina rested briefly before splashing across the Rio Grande and riding downriver to Matamoros, where he knew he would be safe among friends. In the city, it was said, he was "received and treated with consideration and lauded as the defender of Mexican rights."[23] With a troublesome conscience and perhaps questioning the imprudence of his actions, Cortina sent a series of notes to Shears offering to settle the matter peacefully. Shears claimed Cortina even offered him money "to reconcile and compromise the shooting affair and the damages and pains" the marshal suffered.[24] Although Shears evidently considered the offer, an exact amount of money was never agreed to and negotiations were broken off. In the meantime, tensions in Brownsville intensified when Cortina was indicted by a grand jury for attempted murder.[25]

While the burning heat of the Brownsville summer passed into the gentle days of fall, Cortina remained safe in Matamoros. Fears of more violence subsided. Tired of the racism that permeated Brownsville society, the double-dealing of Cameron County public officials, the corruption of the legal establishment, and the threat of arrest if he crossed to the north bank, Cortina despaired of ever making a life for himself in Texas. Instead, he moved his family across the river and cast his future with his native Mexico. Largely through the influence of his first cousin, Col. Miguel Tijerina, commander of the cavalry in Matamoros, Cortina was able to obtain a captain's commission with permission to recruit a company of men to reinforce the Federal garrison at Tampico.[26] With growing influence on both sides of the border, Cortina had no problem finding one hundred men. Paying his recruits two dollars a week, he and his company first went into camp on the river above Matamoros, but later took up quarters in the town itself.

Thoughts of Revenge

Despite his situation, Cortina could not ignore events in Brownsville. Unforgiving and defiant, he remained adamant about killing Adolphus Glavecke, and, despite earlier attempts to reach an amicable settlement with Shears, he swore revenge on the marshal, as well as Sheriff Browne and the men who made up the posse in the wake of the Market Square shooting. Glavecke, who was at his ranch at the time of the shooting, had only recently been appointed deputy sheriff and undoubtedly feared for his life. There was little doubt Cortina was "seeking my life," Glavecke confirmed, and he did everything possible to monitor Cortina's movements.[27] In August, Glavecke wrote Colonel Tijerina and inquired whether, as rumored in Brownsville, Cortina was marching toward Tampico. Tijerina replied that Cortina had been given permission to remain in Matamoros for the traditional Diez y Seis de Septiembre celebration but would leave for Tampico the following day.[28] With the alcalde appearing on Plaza Hidalgo at midnight to cry out Fr. Miguel Hidalgo y Costilla's Grito de Dolores, September 16 was a time of great celebration in Matamoros, as it was throughout the republic. When the festivities were postponed until September 27 for unknown reasons and Cortina had still not left the border, Glavecke became even more alarmed. He also complained that Cortina was stealing cattle from the Texas bank of the river to feed his men. Colonel Tijerina assured everyone that Cortina would depart within days—but that he was being sent to Camargo, not Tampico.[29]

In early September, Cortina made a fateful decision, one that would influence the history of the border for decades and change his life forever.

Steamboats ply the Rio Grande past Fort Brown in this 1861 sketch. From 1846 until 1859, the U.S. Army maintained a strong presence on the lower border. The decision by Gen. David E. Twiggs to abandon the posts on the Rio Grande in May 1859, helped set the stage for the Cortina War. *Harper's Weekly*, March 23, 1861.

Before leaving Matamoros, he would take revenge on the hated Glavecke and his enemies in Brownsville. In the early morning hours after the Deis y Seis celebration, Cortina planned to gather as many men as possible, cross the river, and exact a deadly revenge. Glavecke later admitted that he heard rumors that Cortina had plans to attack Brownsville and that he had even approached Gen. José María de Jesús Carvajal, begging him to stop Cortina.[30]

Cortina's raid on Brownsville, which sparked the war named after him, was well planned and well executed. Taking advantage of the revelry in Matamoros, at four o'clock on Wednesday morning, September 28, 1859, Cortina and a coterie of seventy men splashed across the river into the dark and dingy streets of the slumbering town. In small parties, the men who would become known as *Cortinistas* entered the town from several directions.[31] Suddenly the crack of pistol and rifle fire echoed off the two-story wooden buildings on Elizabeth Street as shouts of "*¡Viva Cheno Cortina!*" "*¡Viva la República Mexicana!*" "*¡Viva México!*" and "*¡Mueran los Gringos!*" rang out into the night.[32] People returning from the celebration in Matamoros were shocked to see armed bands of horsemen galloping toward them and firing their pistols into the air.[33] Ironically, many of Cortina's men were equipped with rifles purchased for the state of Zacatecas in the United States but that had been distributed to the national guard in Matamoros.[34]

The sleeping town was caught completely by surprise. Clearly in command, Cortina sent one party on foot to the outskirts near the cemetery to guard the approaches to the town from the north, while another party was posted on the road leading upriver to Ramireño. "Organized resistance," wrote the French priest, Fr. Pierre Fourrier Pariot, "was out of the question."

Terror-stricken, the Americans "had only time to look for hiding places."³⁵ Bolting down Elizabeth Street, Cortina placed sentinels on the corners of the principal street with orders to shoot anyone attempting to resist or interfere. "No man could have appeared on the streets with arms without being shot down," an observer recorded.³⁶ When the nature of what was happening became evident, a number of Brownsville's poor came forth into the night to join the raiders.

Spurring his horse to the two-story Miller Hotel on Elizabeth Street, Cortina continued to divide his raiders into small parties of four or five men. Each group was given the task of finding a particular person on his death list. Among the marked men were George Morris, William D. "Red" Thomas, Peter Collins, William Peter Neale, Henry Kahn, and, of course, Robert Shears and Adolphus Glavecke. Another despised foe, Charles Stillman, had previously taken passage for New York, as he frequently did during the long, hot, and often sickly Brownsville summers. Morris, it was said, had "perpetrated many Mexican murders." Neale had gunned down a Mexican in Matamoros in a fit of jealousy and two months later killed a second Mexican in Brownsville.³⁷ Others who were "marked" were all members of Sheriff Browne's posse that had been formed following the shooting of Marshal Shears.

Fifty-nine-year-old Tomás Cabrera, second in command, was placed in charge of the *Cortinistas* along Elizabeth Street, while Cortina rode to Fort Brown, where he set up a makeshift headquarters. Disarming the lone guard in charge of the powder magazine, the raiders attempted to batter down the iron doors, hoping to explode 125 barrels of powder. Darkness thwarted their efforts; besides, the keys to the magazine were kept at the ordnance depot on Brazos Santiago. Just as dawn broke over the gulf, several of the *Cortinistas* attempted to raise the Mexican flag on the flagstaff on the parade ground but could not find enough rope to do so.³⁸

Death in the Night

In the bloody raid, one of the first to die was twenty-six-year-old William Peter Neale, mustached son of William Neale. The younger Neale had arrived in Brownsville in the early evening after driving his father's stage from Point Isabel. At first, Neale, as well as most of Brownsville's sleepy citizens, thought party revelers returning from Matamoros caused the noise. Neale was in bed with his wife and two-year-old son when several raiders raced their horses down the alley next to the Neale home, firing several shots through an open window before turning on 14th Street. Several bullets shattered the windowsill, and, when Neale rose in bed, he was fatally struck. According to the family, he was able to place his young son under the bed for protection before staggering outside into the yard and falling dead.³⁹

Son of a prominent landowner and English immigrant, twenty-six-year-old William Peter Neale was one of the victims of Cortina's bloody September 29, 1859 raid on Brownsville. *Photo by author.*

Another victim, George Morris, a blacksmith by trade and town constable, had worked for the army and was still living at Fort Brown. Hearing gunshots, Morris jumped out of bed only to see a band of men heading into the fort. Struggling to put on his pants, he grabbed a pistol, stumbled outside, and hid under the house. When Morris's wife, Luciana, persuaded the raiders that her husband was not at home, and when they turned to leave, one of the men spotted Morris under the house. Springing for safety, Morris raced across the parade ground only to be cut down by a withering rifle and pistol fire. His body was later found with several stab wounds and riddled with bullets. The raiders also cut the rings from his fingers, made off with his shoes and horse, and robbed the house of $150 and several firearms.[40]

Another party of *Cortinistas* broke down the door to Marshall Shears's house to find only his frightened twenty-two-year-old Mexican wife at home. Hearing the shouting and shooting, Shears had escaped seconds earlier to a nearby home where he concealed himself in a baking oven.[41] Using the opportunity to avenge personal grievances, some of Cortina's men appear to have exacted their own revenge. One band of raiders headed to the jail where Robert L. Johnson, the city jailer, lived on the premises, but Johnson had fled to a nearby store owned by a friend, Viviano García. When the raiders demanded the keys to the jail, García replied that Johnson was his friend, and he was determined to protect him. In answer, one of Cortina's men, Juan Vela, fatally shot García in the right side. When the mob broke into García's store, a gun battle erupted in which Johnson killed Alejo Vela, an alleged horse thief. Johnson, however, was then gunned down by Juan Vela, Alejo's brother. One report said Johnson was killed instantly, his body "pierced by several balls."[42] A grand jury later reported that Johnson had been shot in the back and in the head and that he lived into the evening, when he died. Five prisoners in the jail—four horse thieves and a murderer—were all freed. Grateful for their sudden and unexpected freedom, they joyously and unhesitatingly joined their liberators. Seven years later, Juan Vela and two of his companions, Vicente García and Florencio Garza, were apprehended and ceremoniously hanged in Brownsville before a large sullen multitude.[43]

Hearing the shooting and the name "Cortina" being shouted about, Adolphus Glavecke had no doubt about the seriousness of the moment. Racing to warn the jailer Johnson, Glavecke was spotted by several of the raiders and chased down Elizabeth Street to Levee Street, near the river, before racing toward 12th Street, only to run into a second band of *Cortinistas,* who were in the process of pillaging arms and ammunition from Frank Cummings's store. In the confusion and darkness, Glavecke made it safely to Samuel A. Belden's store on Levee Street, where he took refuge and found several other frightened citizens barricading the building.[44] Hearing that Glavecke was inside, Cortina rode up and demanded that Belden give him up. It was Cortina's respect for Belden, some say, that saved Glavecke, who had a double-barreled shotgun and was well concealed.

Shortly after daybreak, Glavecke recalled watching while Cortina reined his horse up in front of Belden's store and got down and peered in through a grated window. Glavecke took careful aim with his shotgun and came close to pulling the trigger. Many years later, he claimed the only reason he did not shoot was that he was signaled not to do so. "Although he had not been able to discover me," Glavecke wrote, "he was pretty sure I was there, for we heard him order one of his men to bring some turpentine. We expected to be burned out every minute."[45] In fact, several of Cortina's men went to the Irish-born Henry Webb's drugstore, where they took three dollars and some turpentine.[46] Although harboring thoughts of burning Belden's store and forcing Glavecke into the open, Cortina declined to do so.[47]

A fifth victim of the raiders, an unarmed Mexican *carretero* named Clemente Reyes, also fell in the violence. The exact circumstances of his death remain uncertain, but he probably was an innocent victim and was shot by accident. Although the *Cortinistas* took guns, ammunition, liquor, and several horses from private homes and stables, there was never any attempt at wholesale plunder. In fact, several times during the raid, Cortina told the Mexicans in the community not to fear him, that he came to Brownsville only to kill the bad Americans. At times he did threaten more violence, especially if Glavecke was not given up, but the killing was selective. In the midst of the raid, Cortina rode with several men to Alexander Werbiski's store and pawnshop. When Werbiski's Mexican wife answered a knock at the door and began to sob uncontrollably, fearing that her husband would be killed, Cortina calmly told her not to cry, that it was "no night for Mexican tears." When Werbiski finally did appear, Cortina demanded all the guns and ammunition in the store. The weapons distributed to his men, Cortina paid Werbiski and rode off.[48] Speaking with Cortina in the early morning hours during the raid, Francisco Yturria remembered Cortina saying that "he did not wish to trouble any of the good citizens of Brownsville; that we need not apprehend any fears, that he only wanted to revenge himself of some men who were his personal enemies."[49]

Shortly after daybreak, just as the first rays of a new day broke across the gulf, José María de Jesús Carvajal, undeniably one of the more influential men on the border and general-in-chief of the Mexican Army in Matamoros, appeared on the levee near the river and announced that he would stop the violence. Seeing Col. Miguel Tijerina, who was in charge of the customs house guards, on the Mexican bank, Carvajal signaled him to cross the river, saying he needed assistance. Crossing on horseback, Tijerina was joined by Capt. Matias Longoria, Macedonio Capistrán, Bartolo Passmento, and Manuel Treviño (the Mexican consul). Carvajal sent for Cortina, whom

Tijerina characterized as "a desperate contrary fellow." No record exists of what was said, except that Cortina was told he could expect no support from the authorities in Matamoros and that they were even likely to move against him. Whatever was discussed, Cortina agreed to leave Brownsville, and at about 7:30 A.M., he and his raiders, their numbers increased by many of the Brownsville poor on horseback and on foot, ambled slowly out of town along the levee, upriver toward Rancho del Carmen.[50]

The death of García, who "fell victim to his generous behavior," was a "lamentable occurrence," and was one of the reasons why Cortina said he agreed to evacuate the town.[51] For Neale, Morris, and Johnson, he expressed no such remorse, for they were "all criminal, wicked men, notorious among the people for their misdeeds."[52] Glavecke and Shears, in contrast, were simply lucky. "They concealed themselves," Cortina said, "and we were lo[a]th to attack them within the dwelling of others."[53]

Fire Within

With his raid on Brownsville, Cortina became one of the first Mexicans in Texas to strike back at a racist society many Tejanos considered evil. He had written his name in blood. Brownsville, a town of some 2,731 citizens, including fifty free blacks and seven slaves, had been, in the words of an army officer, "occupied by a band of armed bandits," something "unheard of in these United States."[54] Publicly in Matamoros, Ciudad Victoria, and Tampico, officials expressed shock at the disruption of "public tranquility" and Cortina's brazenness.[55] In reality, however, many Mexicans in Matamoros and along the border sympathized with Cortina and privately cheered him. In the following years, Mexicans and Mexican Texans alike flocked to his cause in untold numbers.

In the months following the raid on Brownsville, debate in Texas centered on exactly who the raiders were and where they came from. Of the seventy men Cortina had with him, fifty-four were named in indictments by a Cameron County grand jury; of these, thirty-four were thought to be from Mexico.[56] Brownsville authorities claimed the raiders were all Mexican citizens, although at least half were known to live on the north bank. Yet Gen. Winfield Scott, commanding the U.S. Army in New York at the time, concluded that "few, if any, Mexicans from the opposite side took part in the disturbances."[57] The Mexican Border Committee, sent to investigate problems on the Rio Grande in 1873, claimed the majority of the *Cortinistas* were from the United States and that many were criminals.[58] Only a few of the raiders, including Tomás Cabrera, can be identified from the Cameron County census, although a few, such as Alejo and Juan Vela, were outlaws well known in Brownsville.

Regardless, to the grand jury in the Brownsville District Court, Cortina led an "invasion of American territory by armed Mexicans."[59] Along with several of his men, he was indicted not only for murder but also for treason, one of the few times in American history that an individual has been charged by a state with sedition. Later, with the spread of violence as a backdrop, a grand jury chaired by Samuel A. Belden with Glavecke, Werbiski, Bigelow, and Yturria as witnesses, indicted Cortina and over "three hundred others" for killing Jesús Montes, George Morris, John Fox, and Robert L. Johnson.[60] Two years later, a jury in the case of *Robert Shears vs. Juan N. Cortina*, with Adolphus Glavecke as foreman, awarded Shears, who had been "grievously wounded in the left shoulder," the sum of $5,000.[61] Shears, of course, never collected his money.

On the evening after Cortina left Brownsville, Col. José Macedonio Capistrán, Col. Miguel Tijerina, Capt. Matías Longoria, along with Frank W. Latham, collector of customs at Point Isabel, rode out to Cortina's camp at Rancho del Carmen for a parley.[62] Flying the Mexican flag, Cortina had assembled two hundred men from both banks of the river, and more recruits were arriving hourly. After more than an hour of intense negotiations, Cortina asked for time to cross his personal property and stock into Mexico, and if he were allowed to do so, he said, he would not attack Brownsville again. But he remained defiant and uncompromising on one point: he would "kill those who had offended [him] when [the] opportunity offered."[63] Twice more Tijerina, Latham, and Treviño returned to Cortina's camp to negotiate, but Cortina remained adamant about killing his enemies.

A few days after the bloody raid, when Cortina appeared in Matamoros he was greeted as a conquering hero by large crowds with shouts of "Viva Cortina!" and "Death to the Gringos!"[64] One Brownsville resident remembered Cortina being "feted and lionized by principal citizens ... as a hero."[65] O. A. Carolan, a clerk at the French Consulate in the city, said Cortina was "publicly serenaded" in Matamoros where his men "come and go ... whenever they please."[66]

Very much in the Mexican tradition, Cortina issued a *pronunciamiento* from Rancho del Carmen on Friday, September 30, 1859, in an attempt to rationalize his raid. Published in the Matamoros *El Jaque* and in broadsides in Spanish and English and distributed on both sides of the river, the proclamation was addressed to the "inhabitants of the State of Texas, and especially to those of the city of Brownsville."[67] Because Cortina was illiterate, the exact author of the proclamation remains somewhat of a mystery. Speculation centered on a prominent and former Mexican army officer and well-educated revolutionary editor of *El Jaque* who was known to be a *Cortinista* partisan named Miguel Peña. Others thought the author might be one of Cortina's better-educated raiders, such as Jesús Ballí. Some suggested it might have been penned by his brother, José María, although Peña is certainly the more likely author. Regardless, the ideas expressed were certainly those of Cortina.[68]

Cortina asked the people of Brownsville and Cameron County not to be afraid. Yet he promised to "chastise the villainy of our enemies which heretofore has gone unpunished."[69] Admitting he had ridden into Brownsville to kill Adolphus Glavecke and a few other personal enemies, Cortina said he was also against the criminality of "a multitude of lawyers, a secret conclave," clearly intent on "despoiling the Mexicans of their lands." The chief villain, who was in collusion with the lawyers and who had "spread terror among the unwary, making them believe that he will hang the Mexicans and burn their ranchos," was Glavecke. But Glavecke was only part of a "perfidious inquisitorial lodge to persecute and rob us without any cause." Seeing himself as a citizen of the United States, Cortina warned that Mexicans in Texas, inspired by the "sacred right of self-preservation," would defend themselves to the death. "Our personal enemies shall not possess our lands," he continued, "until they have fattened it with their own gore."[70] To at least one Brownsville observer, the *pronunciamiento* was "the most remarkable specimen of bravado ... ever given to bombastic literature."[71] To many, such as Robert B. Kingsbury, Brownsville's postmaster, Cortina was "formally proclaiming a war of races."[72]

On the same day he issued his *pronunciamiento,* Cortina intercepted the Laredo-Brownsville mail, cut open the mail bags, opened several letters, and had the letters read to him. All the contents were then carefully placed back in the envelopes and the mail sent on to Brownsville. Cortina even dictated a letter to Kingsbury, telling the postmaster what he had done.[73] *Cortinistas* twice intercepted the Corpus Christi-Brownsville mail and would have taken the more important mail from New Orleans had it not been brought up on the Mexican side of the river.[74]

Only a few days after the Brownsville raid, Alexander Werbiski, a forty-five-year-old Polish immigrant and a Cortina ally in the rough world of Cameron County politics, rode out to Rancho del Carmen to see Cortina, only to be told the same thing that Tijerina, Treviño, and Latham had heard. Cortina wanted to take his four hundred cattle and fifty horses into Mexico, and if allowed to do so, would not attack Brownsville, but he would continue to seek revenge on his enemies. Although the "world was large," Cortina told Werbiski, he was "certain to meet them at some place."[75]

Fort Gringo

While Cortina sat in camp at Rancho del Carmen, Brownsville continued in a state of panic. Cortina's "sympathizers are to be found in every circle—no one knows who is friend or foe," and everyone was consumed with their "individual safety," Somers Kinney, the tall and slender editor of the *Brownsville American Flag*, told the *New Orleans Daily Picayune*.[76] Several leading citizens, mostly from the mercantile and ranching elite, including Powers, Kenedy, Yturria, and San Ramón, hastily formed a Committee of Public Safety for protection. One hundred men, organized into two companies, were placed under arms and, working in shifts, guarded the main arteries into the town. Fearing a second attack, the people stretched chains across the main streets. They also used eighty thousand bricks from the brickyard of J. A. Finn, a local blacksmith, to construct barricades along Elizabeth Street and in the business section of the town. At night in the central part of the town, Americans and Europeans families huddled together for protection.[77] The wife of H. E. Woodhouse, a prominent merchant, was so frightened she took flight on the steamboat *Grampus*, only to die of a heart attack at Brazos Santiago. Other prominent women in the community also fled to Brazos Santiago, where they took passage to "the states." A few crossed the river to the safety of Matamoros.[78] Merchants offered their property and entire inventory for sale for less than one-half its value only weeks earlier.

With a large part of the Mexican population in sympathy with Cortina, few besides a handful of Anglos and Europeans came forth to man the barricades and stand guard. "The town armed the best it could and placed itself in as complete a state of defense as one hundred citizens and foreigners in the midst of a large Mexican population could be expected to do," Kingsbury wrote.[79] To the American press, Brownsville had become "Fort Gringo."[80] Indeed, two days after Cortina's raid, the Committee of Public Safety, realizing that any assistance was hundreds of miles away and weeks in arriving, sent an urgent plea across the river to General Carvajal asking for assistance. In response, Carvajal dispatched a company of fifty Matamoros militia to help defend the town. Several citizens watched in awe as Mexican soldiers crossed the Rio Grande to protect United States citizens from an irregular army of Mexicans led by a man who considered himself a United States citizen and who held a commission in the Mexican military. In Austin and Washington, it was all very confusing.

Knowing that many of the Mexican militia (almost all of whom were poor) were in sympathy with Cortina, many Anglos did not trust them. One observer admitted being embarrassed "at the necessity of calling on the Mexican authorities for protection."[81] Another, George Wilkins Kendall, a well known Texas journalist, wrote from New Braunfels: "[How] humiliating it must be to the survivors of the gallant force, which in 1846 defended Fort Brown with such stubborn heroism, to see the day when a Mexican force is called from across the Rio Grande to guard the very spot. If ever a dead man's bones could rattle and rise up in rebuke, surely those of the brave Major Brown, buried at the foot of the flag-staff, would have done so when Mexican soldiery were besought for its protection."[82]

The Committee of Public Safety, headed by eleven of the town's most influential merchants and public officials, also scribbled out a petition to Gov. Richard Hardin Runnels pleading for help. Other private letters beseeched the governor and federal authorities for assistance.[83] Joined by recruits from as far away as the Nueces River to the north and Ciudad Victoria to the south, Cortina was threatening to lay the town in ashes and launch a vicious guerrilla war. "Unless these perpetrators are severely punished, the example now set, will be of incalculable evil," District Judge Edmund J. Davis told Runnels from San Antonio.[84] Desperate appeals also went north to Gen. David E. Twiggs, commanding the Department of Texas at San Antonio, and by steamer to Washington, D.C. to President James Buchanan. Men of a "very low character" had killed a number of citizens and mutilated their bodies in a "beastly manner," one Brownsville petition read.[85] With an "extraordinary influence," Cortina had "succeeded in [in]ducing into his service persons who have hitherto been regarded as good people."[86]

Although a majority of those who joined Cortina were from the small ranches and villages along the river, many arrived from the interior of Mexico. Some were almost naked. To the *Corpus Christi Ranchero*, Cortina was taking advantage of an "idle, vicious, depraved, thievish, ignorant, and fanatical population" that lived along "both banks of the Rio Grande." Many were either "escaped *peons* from the interior of Mexico, or desperadoes and escaped felons from that country as well as Texas."[87] To help arm, feed, and clothe his small army, Cortina received $6,000 in assistance from unnamed sources in Matamoros.

With every able-bodied man under arms, day and night, and "nearly worn down with fatigue," the American citizens of Brownsville were desperate for "prompt, ample, and efficient" protection.[88] In particular, they wanted federal troops back on the border. Many remained dazed at how "a single Mexican outlaw," aided by "several hundred desperate, lawless and licentious beings," could create such turmoil by holding an entire region of the Lone Star State in his grasp.[89] Prominent political figures in Austin and Washington, who did not understand the complexities of the border, also marveled at how "a man whose chief claim to distinction arose from his dexterity as a horse thief" could attract so many men to his cause.[90] For instance, in Austin, U.S. Senator John Hemphill was shocked at the news from Brownsville. How could an illiterate Mexican bandit capture an entire town? But then, General Twiggs had left the lower border defenseless, he realized. "The ravages of the marauders," Hemphill wrote, "will not be less terrible than the hostilities of the savage."[91] The senator was concerned that Cortina would capture Brazos Santiago and seize the customs house revenues and the arsenal. After receiving a copy of the petition from the Committee of Public Safety, Hemphill warned President Buchanan that an emergency existed on the lower Rio Grande and the people there must be defended. In the Texas

House of Representatives, Edward Dougherty introduced a bill calling on the governor to offer a $10,000 reward for Cortina, dead or alive.[92] The state senate urged the governor to call out at least one thousand Texas Rangers, but the lame-duck Runnels procrastinated and seemed perplexed as to exactly what to do.

Only days after learning of Cortina's raid, the State Department began pressuring Mexico to punish the "outlaws who made [an] assault upon the city of Brownsville." The American consul at Tampico, Franklin Chase, had received an extra of the *Brownsville American Flag* and a copy of the Tampico *El Prisma* with news of Cortina's raid, and he forwarded a copy to Robert McLane who headed the American legation in Veracruz. A few days later, Antonio de la Fuente, Benito Juárez's minister of foreign relations, promised to take action against Cortina.[93] But communications were slow and it was not until December that the Mexican government agreed to measures "to defend the frontier from the lawless bandits who have recently ravaged and invaded the state of Texas." Although orders went out for Cortina's arrest, the more McLane learned, the more he concluded that the people and authorities on both "sides of the Rio Grande may be responsible for much of the disorder."[94]

By the time the cry for help from the Committee of Public Safety reached San Antonio, General Twiggs had already received an urgent letter from Frank W. Latham, collector of customs at Point Isabel. Latham said Brownsville had been raided by "a well armed ... crowd of banditti" and the town was in "perfect turmoil" with many families fleeing to Matamoros for safety.[95] Although Latham made it clear the *Cortinistas* were from "a dangerous class of [the] Mexican population," Twiggs initially concluded the town had been attacked by Indians.[96] Fearing a general and coordinated offensive by Native Americans on the frontiers of Texas, Twiggs ordered one company of soldiers to the area of the upper Frio River (west of San Antonio), sent another company to take camp on the Rio Grande between Fort McIntosh and Fort Duncan, and sent a third, accompanied by a detachment of artillery, to move into the area between Fort Duncan and Fort Clark.[97] Despite the desperate pleas resonating from the border, no bluecoats, with the exception of ten men guarding the depot on Brazos Santiago, were within 250 miles of Brownsville.

A Growing Presence

Cortina's influence on the history of the border was growing in ways he could only have imagined months earlier. On October 5, 1859, after fortifying his camps at Rancho del Carmen and San José, Cortina crossed the river safely into Mexico at the head of two hundred men and went into camp at Rancho Sabinito, opposite Rancho del Carmen, some nine miles above Matamoros. Although military authorities in Matamoros promised they would arrest Cortina and disarm his small army if they appeared on the south bank, there was never any attempt to do so. Cortina's popularity in Matamoros was just as intimidating to the officials there as it was in Brownsville. In crossing the river, the long-haired Brownsville merchant Jeremiah Galván reported that Cortina not only took "his own and friend's stock but all of the other stock in the neighborhood."[98]

The bearded and serenely confident ranchero from Rancho del Carmen had defied and challenged the powerful Brownsville elite and struck a telling blow to their pride and security. In Matamoros, where he casually strolled the streets, he continued to be greeted as a conquering hero. When the Committee of Public Safety called on all "persons of Mexican origin residing in the counties of Cameron and Hidalgo to come without delay with their arms to manifest their loyalty and assist in restoring order," few stepped forward.[99] "The most striking feature in all these disturbances is the unanimity of Mexican sympathy with Cortina," Brownsville postmaster Kingsbury admitted. "I do not believe that fifty men of Mexican origin can be found on the frontier who do not sympathize with him," Kingsbury admitted.[100] "A war of blood and race is raging with a ferocity."[101] By October, the entire lower Valley, with the exception of Brownsville, Point Isabel, and Brazos Santiago, was controlled by roving bands of marauding *Cortinistas*.

At Point Isabel, where there were eighteen American and sixty Mexican Texan residents, leading citizens were sure it was only a matter of time before Cortina and his men made their appearance at the bayside community. Customs collector Latham had little doubt Cortina was preparing to attack the village and he asked the revenue cutter *Henry Dodge* that was anchored at the small port to use its guns to help protect the government warehouses.[102] Every ranch between Point Isabel and Brownsville was deserted and bands of *Cortinistas* were seen hovering around the town. Cortina's men seized a courier only a few miles from the village, quizzed him about how many Americans were in the community, and said they intended to "shake up" the place. "Helpless" and "entirely defenseless," it was "only an act of mercy that Cortina spares us," a frightened citizen wrote.[103]

On October 18, 1859, Mayor and County Judge Powers bitterly complained to President Buchanan that Cortina had taken refuge in Matamoros where persons of "consideration and influence" were protecting him. "Local authorities declare they have no power to arrest him," Powers wrote.[104] About the same time, Samuel Belden spotted Cortina purchasing supplies at a mercantile house in Matamoros and engaged him in casual conversation.[105] With Cortina in Matamoros, Brownsville authorities concluded their town was safe, and the Mexican militia could return to Mexico. On Saturday, October 8, leading citizens escorted the Mexican militia to the ferry where *abrazos* were exchanged and speeches of gratitude flowed forth. "The Mexican national guard left here for Matamoros," one citizen privately confided, "greatly to the relief of most of our people, who had great dread of them, fearing them to be more likely to turn against us than otherwise."[106]

Brownsville Tigers

The violence on the lower border might well have faded into the footnotes of history had not another nasty incident stoked the coals of the Valley's burning racial volcano. Early on the morning of October 12, a posse led by Sheriff James Browne and Deputy Adolphus Glavecke rode upriver toward Rancho del Carmen where they captured Tomás Cabrera, who was recognized from the September 28 raid as Cortina's chief lieutenant. Cabrera was brought into town and thrown into jail. The news from Brownsville once again sent Cortina into an agitated frenzy. For several years, the sixty-year-old Cabrera had been one of his closest and most trusted friends, the two having ridden together since before the Mexican War. With his wife Guadalupe, son Gerónimo, and fourteen-year-old daughter Petra, Cabrera had settled only a short distance above Rancho del Carmen. Even Stephen Powers admitted he was a man of "good character" before he joined Cortina's raiders.[107]

Within hours of Cabrera's apprehension, Cortina angrily approached the "most influential men" in Matamoros, probably Carvajal and Tijerina, asking that they relay a message to the authorities in Brownsville. If a hair on Cabrera's "head was touched and if he was not set at liberty . . . he would lay the town in ashes."[108] That night, a "prominent merchant" crossed the ferry carrying Cortina's warning while an express rider waited on the south bank to relay the town's answer. In a hastily called meeting of the Committee of Public Safety, the response was one of unbending defiance. In fact, several citizens swore they would die in the streets of Brownsville before Cabrera would be freed. Cabrera, they promised, would be tried under the laws of Texas, and if he were found guilty, he would be hanged. The next day, Cortina splashed across the Rio Grande with forty of his followers, including several Tampacuas Indians who had joined him from near Reynosa. As he returned to Rancho del Carmen, a new round in the escalating "Cortina War" promised more violence and bloodshed.

With *Cortinistas* firing shots into Brownsville in open daylight, panic once again gripped the community. Still, Cortina promised that if the Cameron County authorities would not prosecute him and release Cabrera, "he would withdraw his men and leave the country."[109] Instead, Mayor Powers obtained a 24-pounder howitzer from one of Mifflin Kenedy's steamboats and again asked authorities in Matamoros for help. In a pouring rain on October 22, 1859, sixty-five Matamoros militia pulling a 24-pounder cannon and commanded by Colonel Tijerina and Captain Longoria crossed on the ferry.

At about the same time, a sea captain named Pennington, despite warnings not to leave the coast, set out from Point Isabel to Brownsville and was captured by a band of *Cortinistas* on the Palo Alto prairie north of Brownsville. Pennington was taken to one of Cortina's camps near Rancho del Carmen. There, Cortina politely inquired who he was and what was his avocation. The captain remembered Cortina saying, "he had no cause or quarrel with any Americans save some in Brownsville."[110] The sea captain watched a cart arrive with foodstuffs for Cortina's hungry men; after a pleasant dinner, Pennington was released and sent on his way.

On October 23, the Committee of Public Safety decided there could never be peace in the lower Valley until Cortina was killed or driven into Mexico. The task of expelling him fell to twenty members of the citizen militia commanded by a thirty-seven-year-old Scottish sailor, William B. Thompson. Armed with antiquated muskets and Mississippi rifles obtained from the Matamoros National Guard, along with a few rifles donated by merchants in Brownsville, the militia called themselves the "Brownsville Tigers." Forty poorly armed Mexican rancheros led by Antonio Portillo were also recruited from the ranches between the town and the gulf. Pulling a small howitzer Kenedy took from one of his steamboats, the small army rendezvoused at Glavecke's ranch, some four miles above Brownsville, where they were joined on the morning of October 24 by seventy-five infantry of the Matamoros National Guard and a 24-pounder cannon. Slowed by heavy rains that turned the river road into a quagmire, the column moved slowly upriver until late in the afternoon when they were about two miles from Rancho del Carmen. There, they ran headlong into about twenty of Cortina's pickets concealed in the edge of the impenetrable chaparral. The Matamoros infantry, reinforced by the Brownsville Tigers, moved forward and slowly drove the *Cortinistas* back into the chaparral.[111]

Just beyond Rancho del Carmen, where the road again passed through a dense thicket of mesquite, the Brownsville Tigers spotted a number of *Cortinistas* in a "strongly fortified corral." Captain Thompson ordered an advance; again Cortina retreated, this time to another corral of upright mesquite posts some six hundred yards in the rear. To prevent any escape into Mexico, Thompson confidently sent Portillo's mounted rancheros in a flanking movement toward the river to secure several small boats that had been spotted on the riverbank.[112] At the same time, the infantry pushed forward along the main road. In what Thompson called a "severe engagement," the howitzer became useless in the thick chaparral and was dragged to the rear and the Mexican cannon brought forward. But after firing only three shots, the gun became dislodged from its carriage and had to be abandoned. Kenedy's howitzer was brought forward again, but it too became unserviceable and was abandoned. To protect the field piece from falling into Cortina's hands, Antonio Espinosa and several vaqueros hauled the gun to the riverbank and pushed it into the Rio Grande.[113]

Further confusion ensued. The Brownsville Tigers discovered their muskets would not fire in the drizzly damp weather, and, to complicate matters, not only were the Tigers low on ammunition, but also many of their cartridges were too large for their muskets.[114] Glavecke, who was with the Tigers and in charge of the ammunition, was sent scurrying back to Brownsville with an urgent plea for additional cartridges of the correct size. With the loss of both guns, darkness rapidly approaching, and Cortina and his men offering a stiff resistance, Thompson's rain-soaked men began to falter, fall back, and then flee in panic. "Our retreat was in the utmost confusion," the captain admitted.[115] Carrying four of their wounded in the rain, the Mexican guardsmen brought up the rear as the small army retreated into the darkness toward Brownsville. "Our men commenced arriving in town, some on foot, others on horses, mules, and asses, mostly double, and many of them without arms," Israel B. Bigelow reported.[116] A few who were on foot did not arrive until early the next morning. Many in Brownsville could not understand why one of the guns had been placed "under the command of Mexicans to fight Mexicans."[117]

Although Cortina was said to have three hundred men at Rancho del Carmen, few *Cortinistas* had been seen at any one time. A veteran of the U.S. Army who accompanied the Brownsville Tigers remarked that "fifty men, hid as they were, could have stampeded five hundred in a road guarding dismounted cannon."[118] In an extra on October 25 the *Brownsville American Flag* gave Cortina his due: "He has good arms, and his men are under discipline, and fight with zeal. [Cortina] shows great skill as well as courage ... he seems to wait his time and opportunity and this with self-reliance and a firmness of purpose which may well give us pause."[119] Seventeen years later, a citizen of Brownsville could find only humor in the defeat of the Brownsville Tigers at Rancho del Carmen:

> A halt was called. The "Tigers" made a firm stand, and immediately preparations were made for some movement. Much discussion ensued, and much difference of opinion prevailed among the officers ... for they were nearly all colonels, captains or majors. The sheriff—then acting in a military capacity and mounted on a beautiful white steed—in vain reiterated the words of command, "Come along, boys!" The "boys" wouldn't come. They made a firm stand—at a respectable distance too, from the enemy's line, or where they suspected the enemy line to be, for only a few straggling Mexicans could be seen, as they dodged in and out of the chaparral.

Either by intent or accident some firing commenced. The "Tigers" made a desperate charge—for home—leaving their cannon in possession of the enemy.... I was personally acquainted with one of the officers in that famous expedition, who, though a cripple, had since frequently declared to me that he got home on that occasion in less than forty minutes![120]

In the final tally, Cortina lost two men killed at the hands of the Mexican militia, along with several wounded, while the Brownsville Tigers lost one man killed and several wounded.[121] By evening, with the enemy in full retreat, Cortina's men had pulled the howitzer from the river, remounted the gun, and by the next day both the howitzer and the captured cannon were operable. In the fighting, the *Cortinistas* had also captured a large keg of gunpowder and a number of provisions.

Two days after the fighting at Rancho del Carmen and from his forward camp at Villanueva, a mile downriver from Rancho del Carmen, Cortina sent a letter written in Spanish (with "wretched spelling and grammar") to Brownsville, in which he said he did not wish to attack the town for fear of hurting "many persons who are faultless."[122] Much like a medieval knight, Cortina invited Glavecke, the "Squinting Sheriff," and "other persons who have difficulties with me," to come out from the barricades where he would meet "them on the field of battle."[123] In a position of strength, he was threatening and intimidating: "I hope you may answer me, because I am about to march upon the town and have sufficient force and artillery to batter down the houses."[124] With *Cortinistas* easily visible in the chaparral near Brownsville and the boom of the captured cannon echoing over the town every morning at exactly 6 A.M., a chilling, somewhat unnerving and eerie atmosphere settled over the town once again. In Cortina's camp there was jubilation. In Brownsville and Austin, the anxiety deepened.

A Growing Rebellion

In the days and weeks following the fight at Rancho del Carmen, recruits of all ages continued to ride and walk into Cortina's camp. Word had spread up and down the Rio Grande that Cortina was again victorious. Many men came from Mexico; others arrived from the small ranches and farms on the Texas side of the river. Some were on horseback and armed. Others arrived with only the clothes on their back. Although most shared a hatred of the gringo, they were attracted as much to the charismatic leader as to his cause. Santos Cadena rode into camp with forty men from Mier and Agualeguas.[125] Sixty men broke out of jail in Ciudad Victoria, the capital of Tamaulipas, and made their way north to the border.[126] A Mexican officer arrived from Monterrey with fifty men while a band of eleven thinly clad Tampacuas Indians walked into camp from near Reynosa.[127] Others who crossed the river were army deserters. Mexican vaqueros from the ranches around Corpus Christi were said to have ridden south to join Cortina, stealing horses while they went.[128] Called the "Eagles," Cortina's army was composed of "border ruffians of both frontiers—men ready for anything from a game of monte to manslaughter," it was said.[129]

At least three-fourths of the men who joined Cortina were from south of the border, many of them desperately poor. A few *Cortinistas* from the north bank were educated and influential in the Mexican Texan community. Teodoro Zamora, chief justice of Hidalgo County, joined early in the struggle, as did Jesús Ballí, who, like Cortina's mother, was one of the heirs to a large land grant in the valley.[130] "The whole Mexican population on both sides of the river are in favor of him," John Ford told Governor Runnels in late November 1859.[131]

With men who had served in the Mexican military in the ranks, the *Cortinistas* were drilled regularly and discipline was maintained. Weapons, provisions, and money arrived from sympathizers in Matamoros and other communities on the south bank such as Reynosa and Camargo. Even the large English mercantile firm of Hale and Company, one of the largest commercial houses in Matamoros, was said to have provided assistance.[132] The red, green, and white Mexican flag flying over their camp gave the men a sense of pride and legitimacy.

Cortina's popularity with the *pelados, labradores, vaqueros, campesinos,* and *rancheros* on both sides of the river is evident in William Neale's account of the conflict. Neale was at his Rancho Bastón near Rudyville in Hidalgo County, about thirty miles above Brownsville, when he first heard of Cortina's attack. Learning that his son, William Peter, had been grievously wounded, Neale saddled his horse and hurried downriver. After riding a short distance, he was stopped by two friendly Mexicans, both of whom confirmed that his son was dead—"that they had seen the corpse."[133] Moreover, it would be dangerous to continue along the Texas side of the river, they warned. Instead, Neale returned to his ranch, "never again to see my son or attend the last duties of burying my murdered boy," he wrote.[134]

Back at Rancho Bastón several days later, Neale received an urgent express from Mayor Powers. Also addressed to Edwin B. Scarborough and Edward Dougherty, the letter had come up the Mexican side of the river. Powers was hoping a company of loyal Mexican Texans could be raised in Hidalgo County. Realizing that Brownsville must be relieved, Neale rode out to several of the farms and ranches where he persuaded some thirty "good and picked" Mexicans, along with a few "Americans," to join him. In all, about forty men rallied and elected Justo Treviño as their captain.[135] At the same time, a second express arrived from Brownsville with news that the Brownsville Tigers were marching to attack Cortina. Certain that the Tigers would be successful, Powers said he needed assistance in arresting all of Cortina's men who were certain to flee upriver. On the morning the Tigers planned their attack, Neale rode out with Captain Treviño to muster his recruits but could only find four men. "It was useless," Captain Treviño admitted, since the men "would not fight against Cortina."[136]

Finally able to gather ten men, including three of his ranch employees, Neale rode downriver with Captain Treviño to where he could hear the rumble of cannon in the distance. While they proceeded along the river road, the small Hidalgo County contingent noticed large numbers of Mexicans galloping past them toward the sound of battle. "Their insolent manner of saluting us," Neale thought, indicated they had heard the news the "Americans had been whipped and their cannon taken from them."[137] The cannon noise, Neale learned, was shots fired by Cortina over the graves of two of his men. Still the small company continued toward Brownsville, but, nearing Rancho del Carmen, Neale ran into several *Cortinistas* who were guarding several of Cortina's wounded at a nearby ranch. Fearful of being captured or killed, Neale retreated upriver again. All along the river road, "Mexicans were continually passing down towards Cortina's camp." This proved to be too much for one of Neale's recruits, who "stole off to the enemy's camp."[138]

Back at Rancho Bastón, Neale's servants urged him to leave, saying they too would be killed if forced to defend the ranch. Using the Mexican side of the river, Neale and his wife were finally able to reach Matamoros safely. Months later, Neale returned to the ranch to find the place in ruins, his wagons and buggies gone, all the livestock driven off, and his furniture and small library destroyed. Only the burned-out shell of the brick ranch house remained. One of the workers had left to join Cortina; a second was said to be at a fandango across the river that was being held in Cortina's honor.[139]

Attack, Siege, and Conflict

On October 30, with Cabrera still in the Cameron County jail, Cortina sent thirty of his men to the outskirts of Brownsville, where they commenced firing into the town from a location near the cemetery. The shots were answered with a salvo of canister from a cannon, and citizens again scurried for the protection of the trenches and the barricades.[140]

Five days earlier, only one day after the fight at Rancho del Carmen, ten of Cortina's men captured Francis M. Campbell, a deputy sheriff who owned a small ranch and farm at Ramireño, two miles above Brownsville. A printer from Natchitoches, Louisiana, Campbell had a Mexican wife and four children, and he had been with the Brownsville Tigers in the fight at Rancho del Carmen. Brought into camp, Campbell watched Cortina distribute his horse, saddle, bridle, Sharps rifle, and pistol to his men.[141] A few days later, Campbell also watched Cortina cold-heartedly order the execution of five of his men for disobeying orders. When the firing squad asked for the honor of also shooting Campbell, Cortina told the men "that when he wanted their advice ... he would let them know."[142] Twice Cortina intervened to keep the angry *Cortinistas* from shooting Campbell, and he even allowed the Louisianan to send a note into Brownsville.

From Rancho del Carmen on October 31, 1859, Cortina sent a short letter into Brownsville addressed to Mayor Powers. Cortina said he did not want to fight, nor did he want to attack the city. At the same time, he was adamant that Cabrera be released. He was disappointed that his friends in the Matamoros militia had fought against him and that his family had been endangered in the fighting. He was treating Campbell humanely, and he expected Cabrera would also be treated with dignity.[143]

Many in Brownsville thought Campbell was seized to be exchanged for Cabrera. After being held for ten days, Campbell concluded, however, that he had been taken only to read the Laredo mail, which Cortina seized a second time. In rifling through the letters, the only ones opened were those that looked official, "to ascertain the movements of our government," Campbell recalled.[144] Once the letters were read, the envelopes were resealed and placed back in the mail pouches, and the bags left in a conspicuous place where the Brownsville authorities could find them.

While in Cortina's camp, Campbell said he was "well fed and provided for." He did notice that many of the *Cortinistas* seemed overly nervous, a few shouting, "*¿Quien vive? ¡Mexico! ¿Que regimento? ¡Cortina!*"[145] Although he was treated well, Campbell warned that if "this difficulty is not settled in some amiable manner there will be many lives lost." The deputy was sure he would not be released "until the war closes."[146] Fearing for her husband's life, Campbell's young wife, Dolores, rode out in a carriage to Cortina's camp. After listening to her emotional pleadings, Cortina released the deputy and allowed him to return safely to Brownsville, where Campbell later filed a claim for damages of $100,000 for his "imprisonment."[147]

By this time the news of Cortina's raid had spread to the outside world. On October 10, the steamer *Arizona* reached the mouth of the Mississippi River, where the startling news of Cortina's raid was telegraphed upriver to New Orleans. The next day, the *Daily Picayune* printed details of the violence.[148] At the same time, Stephen Powers sent James B. Thomas to Washington with a letter for President James Buchanan. Arriving in New Orleans, Thomas persuaded forty-four of the Crescent City's leading merchants to sign a petition calling on the government for assistance. He also convinced the president of the Southern Steamship Company, J. C. Harris, to telegraph Secretary of War John Floyd urging that the army be returned to the border.[149] In New Orleans, Thomas was also able to obtain a letter of introduction to the president from John Slidell, a prominent Democrat who had served as minister to Mexico and who had represented Louisiana in both the House and Senate.[150]

With Brownsville in a state of siege, the most alarming news from the Rio Grande came from W. A. Miller. Miller had deserted from the Brownsville Tigers and fled to Matamoros when Cortina's men began firing into the town. Arriving in Corpus Christi in early November, Miller related how on October 29, after a bitter five-hour, hand-to-hand battle, four hundred crazed *Cortinistas*—crying "death to all Americans" and "no quarter"—had overrun the barricades and seized the town. Every defender had been killed or ruthlessly executed in the wild melee. Somehow Miller came to believe, falsely as it turned out, that Mifflin Kenedy had died gallantly at the barricades, and Francis Campbell had been hanged.[151] Miller had escaped by swimming his horse across the Rio Grande to Matamoros, where he made his way through the night to the mouth of the river, recrossing to Brazos Santiago and riding up Padre Island to Corpus Christi. Miller's sworn statement appeared in a number of Texas newspapers, including the *San Antonio Herald, Corpus Christi Ranchero, Galveston Daily Civilian,* and the *Indianola Commercial Bulletin.* The typical banner headlines ran, "The Desperado Cortina Triumphant!"[152] It would take almost two weeks for the misinformation to be corrected. "Miller must have fine ears to have heard firing at Brownsville whil'st at Corpus Christi," the *New Orleans Daily True Delta* sarcastically remarked.[153] "How can our frontier people expect assistance ... if they are constantly crying wolf! wolf! wolf! even when there is no wolf?" the *San Antonio Daily Herald* asked.[154]

But the damage had been done. On the bluff overlooking the bay at the small community of Corpus Christi, there was little doubt that Cortina had overrun Brownsville and Rio Grande City. With "his band of greaser pelados," he was intending "to exterminate the gringos."[155] With the "entire Mexican population on both sides of the Rio Grande" up in arms and certain to "murder every white inhabitant and to reconquer our country as far as the Colorado River," a militia company, the "Corpus Christi Guards," was hastily recruited, and scouts, both on horseback and on foot, were sent into the countryside to detect any advance from the border.[156] By late November, Charles Lovenskiold and Henry A. Maltby had recruited ninety-eight men in Corpus Christi into a second company called the Walker Mounted Rifles.[157]

Flaming the fires of what he perceived as a genocidal racial war, Henry A. Maltby, hard-nosed editor and owner of the *Corpus Christi Ranchero*, warned that "an idle vicious, depraved, thievish, ignorant and fanatical population" was on the loose and they must be crushed.[158] "A class known as peladoes [*sic*] or labrones [*sic*]," could "be governed only by an iron rod—by force or fear," Maltby wrote. Although embarrassed by the Miller affidavit, "it matters not whether Brownsville be taken or not," the fiery editor continued.[159]

Word also reached the small village of Nuecestown, thirteen miles northwest of Corpus Christi, that Brownsville and Rio Grande City had been pillaged. It was said that Cortina was "at the head of 900 men ... swearing vengeance against every white man and declaring his intention to sweep the whole country from the Rio Grande to the Nueces and from there to the Colorado River."[160] Hearing the news, Thomas John Noakes went to sleep with a double-barreled shotgun under his bed and rushed off the next day to join a "company of defense" in Corpus Christi where he was told that Cortina had a thousand men and several cannon. Everybody was "frightened out of their wits about the Mexicans and looking for them every hour," he wrote.[161] At Banquete, a small village on the prairie twenty miles west of Corpus Christi, panicked residents formed "themselves into a minute company" and also sent scouts into the countryside.[162] To the northwest in Live Oak County at Gussettville, similar plans were made to resist Cortina's invasion from the Rio Grande.[163]

At the head of 1,500 men, Cortina was reported to be within fifteen miles of Goliad. All the Mexicans in Goliad County had joined Cortina in revenge for the ethnic violence of the Cart War, the *Indianola Courier* proclaimed.[164] In panic, riders were dispatched to the small communities and ranches in the county to sound the alarm and raise a company of volunteers.[165] Cortina "makes it a war of races; he proclaims war to the knife, and no quarter to Americans," the *San Antonio Daily Ledger and Texan* announced, certain that Cortina had at least one thousand men.[166] "We are being warred upon by atrocious savages who would as soon beat out the brains of an infant as shoot an undoubted spy. Call it by what name you please, it is a war upon the American race, and of its full extent no one knows," the *New Orleans Daily True Delta* editorialized.[167] Some even speculated that Cortina was intent on pushing the gringos all the way to the Colorado River. Flying the Mexican flag, others thought he would stop only at the Sabine.[168] Encapsulating the fears from South Texas, the *New Orleans Daily Picayune* said the pride of the entire country had been shaken by "a robber chief of a pitiful band of Mexican outlaws" who had "invaded our territory, murdered and pillaged our citizens, and spread consternation through the whole valley of the Rio Grande."[169]

Much of what W. A. Miller reported was confirmed by the border *patrón*, Henry Clay Davis of Rio Grande City. Hearing of the violence in the lower Valley, Davis fled north to San Antonio to state that the entire Rio Grande frontier was "in an uproar and that outrage and murder are the order of the day."[170] There was no doubt that Cortina, with six hundred hot-eyed "greaser *pelados*," was advancing toward the Nueces. So many men were crossing from Mexico to join Cortina, Davis said, that all the boats on the river from Edinburg to Brownsville had been seized by the *Cortinistas*.[171] All over Texas, many citizens came to envision angry serape-clad Mexicans spreading a genocidal war north from the border.

After the erroneous news of the fall of Brownsville reached Gonzales, two companies of one hundred men each were raised within forty-eight hours. In Victoria, men rushed to join a company "for the immediate assistance of the settlers on the Rio Grande."[172] In Seguin, another company of one hundred men was enlisted for action on the border. Offers of help in suppressing the rebellion came from as far away as Waco and Clarksville. In Austin, Senator Forbes Britton made a "rousing speech" pleading for volunteers. At a second meeting in the capital, zealous filibusters, including members of the Knights of the Golden Circle, condemned the chaotic situation on the Rio Grande and made plans to create a small army to invade Mexico and declare a Republic of the Sierra Madre. It was agreed that John S. Ford should lead the expedition and that men should be dispatched to New Orleans, long a hotbed of filibustering activities, to recruit more men and obtain arms and artillery. The Knights would rendezvous at Brownsville, attack Cortina, invade Mexico, and establish the desired republic. Some thought the Republic of the Sierra Madre should be proclaimed in Austin while others wanted to wait until northeastern Mexico could be occupied. Although many wanted Ford to lead the expedition, there was talk that Samuel L. Lockridge, a zealous Mississippian and filibustering veteran who had led five hundred Texans in William Walker's 1856 Nicaragua misadventure, might be more effective.[173]

On the heels of the alarming news from the border, equally frightening dispatches reached Texas from the picture-book town of Harpers Ferry, Virginia. A bearded and saintlike radical abolitionist, John Brown, had attacked the town on October 16, 1859, hoping to seize guns and spread a slave revolt down the crest of the Blue Ridge Mountains into the heart of Dixie. Somehow events in Brownsville and Harpers Ferry had to be connected, many Texans thought.[174] Taken in this muse, Cortina was really a wild abolitionist plotting with northern radicals such as William Lloyd Garrison to free the slaves in Texas and murder the slave owners in their beds. "What great difference is there between the outlawry of Opossum Brown, or whatever his name is, and that of Juan Nepomuceno Cortina?" the *San Antonio Daily Herald* asked. "None" was the answer.[175] With 1,500 men, Cortina was intent on "murdering and breaking up the white settlements, and exciting insurrection among the slaves," the *San Antonio Daily Herald* in an extra edition announced.[176] Visions of a Nat Turner–like rebellion composed of *Cortinistas* became a common nightmare in the Lone Star State. In Texas, "Cortina and John Brown got inextricably mixed up," John L. Haynes concluded.[177]

The *San Antonio Daily Herald* went as far as to assert that the Cortina War was "the result of an organized system of fanatics of the John Brown stamp, deliberately planned, and executed with a fiendish adroitness." Not only were New England emigrant aid societies supplying Cortina with arms and money, but also a series of mysterious fires in North Texas had to somehow be connected to Cortina. Accusing newspapers in Texas of exaggerating events on the border "beyond all reason," the *San Antonio Alamo Express* more accurately concluded that the conflict on the border "grew out of circumstances entirely local to Brownsville."[178] Tensions in the Alamo city were somewhat calmed when the Nuevo León and Coahuila strongman, Gov. Santiago Vidaurri, arrived to say that Cortina was not an abolitionist but an adherent to the conservative "Priest Party" in Mexico.[179]

Convinced that Cortina had murdered one hundred Americans and was on the march for the Nueces River, the aging and infirm Gen. David E. Twiggs finally decided to take action. On November 12, Twiggs telegraphed Secretary of War John Floyd that he was sending two companies of light artillery and three companies of infantry from Fort Leavenworth, Kansas, to the border. Six other companies of infantry from Fort Monroe, Virginia, were to also depart "with all speed to the Rio Grande."[180] Wiring Floyd four days later, Twiggs said that Cortina was certain to have from eight hundred to 1,500 men, and he was fearful the military warehouses on Brazos Santiago might have fallen into his hands. The 146 cannon, howitzers, and mortars, some of which were 32- and 24-pounders, as well as a vast quantity of ammunition, powder, cartridges, and gun carriages worth $125,000, "have probably been taken ... by Cortina," Twiggs told Washington.[181] After receiving additional information from the border three days later, however, Twiggs wired Washington again: "I am disposed to think the Cortina affair is greatly exaggerated."[182] Finally, on November 21, Twiggs assured Washington that the rumors from Brownsville were "mostly false" and orders sending troops to the border were being countermanded.[183]

But Texas Rangers were already scurrying for the Rio Grande. In San Antonio, in the second week in October, twenty-six-year-old Capt. William Gerard Tobin, local businessman and son-in-law of the mayor of the city, was given orders by Gov. Hardin Runnels to head for the Rio Grande to arrest Cortina and anyone else who might be "charged with the murder of peaceable citizens." Yet Tobin, who had served briefly as city marshal, was to "be prudent and refrain from disturbing unoffending Mexican & American citizens."[184] With sixty men, Tobin left San Antonio and recruited another forty men along the way. After pausing at the Santa Gertrudis Ranch of Richard King to exchange horses, Tobin's Rangers, guided by Adolphus Glavecke and an unnamed Mexican Texan compatriot who were sent north by the Brownsville Committee of Public Safety, spurred their horses south across the Wild Horse Desert. At 11 P.M. on November 10, sixteen days after leaving San Antonio, the Rangers arrived on the outskirts of Brownsville.[185]

From mail he had intercepted as well at a network of spies, informers, and sympathizers on fleet-footed horses, Cortina had known for days the Rangers were on the march and he prepared a violent reception for them in the chaparral outside Brownsville. "He knew more about what was going on outside of Brownsville than we did. He knew when the Rangers were expected," one citizen confessed.[186] Mistaking the sound of the Ranger bugle for that of the *Cortinistas,* the frightened and anxious citizens of the town fired a salvo of grapeshot at the approaching Rangers. No one was killed, but Glavecke had two balls rip into his coat and his gray horse shot from under him. District Judge Edmund J. Davis, who was accompanying the Rangers, slipped through the darkness to a small *jacal* on the outskirts of the town to within shouting distance of the barricades.[187] Suspecting a ruse, the citizens manning the defenses remained undeterred until one of the Ranger guides crossed the river to the Mexican bank and then recrossed the river to Brownsville to confirm the men in the chaparral were indeed Rangers. At long last, Tobin's Rangers entered Brownsville to be "heartily welcomed by the citizens."[188] On the morning after they arrived, several of Tobin's men climbed to the cupola of the courthouse where they spotted "Cortina with a troop ... estimated at 200 men, marching down the main road toward the city."[189] Excitedly, the barricades were hastily manned, but Cortina was only feinting an attack on the town.

A Hanging in the Night

The night after the Rangers arrived, a frenzied mob dragged the elderly Tomás Cabrera out of jail and lynched him in Market Square. "Who did it, is not known," the *Corpus Christi Ranchero* proclaimed.[190] Another source would say only that "an unknown and lawless mob" was responsible.[191] One of the Rangers, J. T. Hunter, would write years later that Cabrera was found hanged "by the neck at the market house—dead as a door nail."[192] Although the Rangers denied any involvement in the hanging, it was later revealed they had been responsible for the dastardly deed.[193] Many in Brownsville condemned the hanging, yet Ranger executions of Mexican Texans became even more frequent in the violent months that followed.

When Cortina received the word of the death of his friend, he allegedly retaliated by hanging three captives at Rancho del Carmen, including a former mail contractor named W. M. McFadden, who had been captured south of the Arroyo Colorado in early October.[194] Several Americans simply disappeared into areas controlled by the *Cortinistas* and were never heard from again. The hanging of Cabrera was without a doubt a watershed in the Cortina War. With little hope of reconciliation, the conflict would now become a vicious, no-holds-barred bitter guerrilla war that threatened to spin out of control and involve the United States and Mexico in a wider conflict.

Shortly after the San Antonio Rangers arrived on the Rio Grande, other units calling themselves Rangers reached the border. One small company of thirty men from Karnes County was commanded by John Littleton, gunfighter and sheriff of the county. Not long after taking up quarters at Fort Brown, Littleton's men were sent to meet and escort into town thirty Ranger recruits from Live Oak County. In the confusion, the Live Oak Rangers under Capt. John Donelson took a different road and entered the town without seeing Littleton. At noon the next day, after bivouacking for the night, Littleton spotted some of Cortina's men on the edge of the prairie, about a mile from Dr. Julius Verbaum's Palo Alto house. Seeing the *Cortinistas* at three hundred yards, the Rangers galloped off in pursuit.

Just south of an impenetrable bog where a dense strip of chaparral protruded out into the prairie, Cortina prepared a trap. Thinking they had the *Cortinistas* on the run, the Rangers tied their horses to some mesquite trees and plunged into the chaparral. Mounted on a beautiful paint horse, Cortina waited with one hundred of his men before springing his ambush. In a vicious, thirty-minute firefight, Cortina personally manned one of his captured artillery pieces that unleashed a deadly fire. In the fighting, three of the Rangers were killed and four others badly wounded. Lieutenant Littleton was hit with shrapnel in the right arm while John Fox was so badly injured he was unable to retreat and was apparently executed. The Rangers claimed thirteen *Cortinistas* were killed and several were wounded in the fight.[195] After the smoke had cleared and the Rangers had retreated, Verbaum complained the *Cortinistas* destroyed all the doors and windows at his Palo Alto house, as well as his fences and even his cistern.[196]

Early the next day, Captain Tobin and Nueces County Sheriff Mat Nolan rode to the scene of the bloodletting. Stripped of their clothing, the dead Rangers lay scattered about in the chaparral, one corpse in particular "shockingly mutilated." After burying their compatriots in the soft Palo Alto prairie, Tobin and Nolan took their men and rode west to the Mexican Texan village of Santa Rita, about two miles from Cortina's camp where several *Cortinistas* were thought to reside. In frenzied revenge, they drove women and children from their homes and burned the small village to the ground.

On the river, Tobin was joined by a company of thirty-nine men from Atascosa County commanded by a tough veteran of the Texas Revolution, fifty-seven-year-old, gray-haired Capt. Peter Tumlinson. The Atascosa Rangers were also joined by Mifflin Kenedy and forty rejuvenated Brownsville Tigers, dragging a 24-pounder howitzer. Fourteen men from Indianola also arrived in Brownsville, as did Lt. Loomis Lyman Langdon of the 1st United States Artillery, who had made his way downriver from Ringgold Barracks. The Rangers and Brownsville Tigers swore they would hunt Cortina and his men "down like wild beasts" or drive them into Mexico.[197]

On the morning of November 22, while Cortina waited word from his scouts and spies at Rancho del Carmen, Tobin and his Rangers, confident they could "exterminate Cortina," moved upriver to meet him in battle. Leaving sixty men at Santa Rita, the small army was past Rancho del Carmen by noon and within sight of Cortina's main camp. Here Cortina met them with a "galling fire of round shot, grape and canister."[198] Realizing the enemy was "strongly entrenched and fortified" in the dense chaparral and superior numbers of *Cortinistas* were threatening to outflank him, Tobin gave orders to fall back. In disarray and confusion, the entire force, "hotly pressed by Cortina and his followers," fled down the river road from whence they had come.[199] "The sympathies of many of [the] border inhabitants of Mexican origin on both sides of the river are with Cortina," Tobin wrote in an attempt to explain his unexpected repulse.[200] "The whole Mexican people on both sides [of] the river sympathize with him and give him 'aid and comfort,'" Captain Tumlinson wrote in blaming Mexican soldiers on the south bank for informing Cortina of the Ranger advance. During the Ranger retreat, the Mexican military on the opposite bank, "flaunted their flag before our eyes and shouted '¡Viva Cortina!'" Tumlinson complained.[201]

Back at Santa Rita, some sixty of Tobin's men returned to Brownsville, "refusing to meet the enemy in battle."[202] The next day, November 23, 1859, Tobin again moved out along the river road toward Cortina's camp and again Cortina prepared to meet him. One mile above Rancho del Carmen near San José, again in sight of Cortina's camp, Tobin lost his nerve and hesitated. In a council of war, it was determined that Cortina had between 350 and five hundred men and that it would be "imprudent to attack the enemy in his fortifications." Cortina was too "strongly fortified in and surrounded by a dense chaparral on all sides," Tobin told Governor Runnels.[203] "It was a wise decision," a regular army officer would later conclude, for in "their disorganized condition an attack would have brought certain defeat."[204] This time, Tobin retreated all the way to Brownsville. There, one hundred of his men dejectedly concluded they would fight another day and took the road out of town leading north. The remainder of the Rangers hunkered down and waited for reinforcements. Cortina had decisively repulsed the Rangers, and Brownsville remained in panic. But the U.S. Army was on the march for the border, and Cortina realized he would soon face a more formidable foe. Yet, the Cortina War, as it came to be known, which had started as a personal feud, had evolved into a struggle against racial nationalism and expansionism.

Chapter Three

Flocks of Vampires in the Guise of Men

Mexicans! My part is taken; the voice of revelation whispers to me that to me is entrusted the work of breaking the chains of your slavery.

JUAN CORTINA

WITH A PASSIONATE SENSE of survival and a thundering voice, Cortina realized he had unleashed a rebellion that stirred the conscience of all Tejanos and Mexicanos and challenged the assumption of Anglo Texan supremacy. Encouraged by his military successes, he issued a second *pronunciamiento* from Rancho del Carmen on November 23, 1859. Similar to the first proclamation, it was fiery, full of anger, and exceptionally well written. It was also inspirational to the poor and politically dispossessed who were flocking to his banner. In his *pronunciamiento*, Cortina was more confident and acutely aware he was addressing a much larger audience, even perceiving himself as the spokesman and defender of all "Mexican Inhabitants of the State of Texas."[1] The loss of land, either through legal chicanery or threats and intimidation, must be avenged, Cortina angrily announced. The impunity with which Anglos and Europeans had killed Mexicans in Brownsville and Cameron County, he continued, must not go unanswered. Moreover, the racism and arrogance of the newcomers who had arrived on the border like "flocks of vampires in the guise of men," must end. "Many of you have been robbed of your property, incarcerated, chased, murdered, and hunted like wild beasts," Cortina angrily reminded his followers.[2]

Despite its vitriol, Cortina's second *pronunciamiento* had a strange fatalism—as if Cortina sensed he might not survive the violence he had unleashed. Perceptive of his emerging place in history, Cortina spoke of being forced to lead a "wandering life" and of becoming a sacrificial lamb to the happiness of his people.[3] He was certainly aware that more powerful forces than the Rangers and the inept Brownsville militia were preparing to move against him and that his revolution on the border might be doomed.

The publication and reception of Cortina's *pronunciamiento* are telling. The document was published in Spanish in Matamoros and translated and reprinted in English, with a lengthy rebuttal by Somers Kinney in a broadside at the office of the *Brownsville American Flag*. To Kinney, Cortina was an "arch-murderer and robber" and a "Christian Comanche." His outcry for justice was little more than a "collection of balderdash and impudence." Nevertheless, Cortina had "banded together an imposing army, [was] flying a foreign flag ... on American soil," and was "levying war against the State and Union." A week later, the *pronunciamiento* was published by Henry A. Maltby in the *Corpus Christi Ranchero*.[4]

Once again, desperate pleas and ominous warnings trickled north from the border. One Brownsville resident was sure no American would be left alive south of the Nueces River.[5] Once Cortina had extended his control to the Sabine River, he was certain to free all the slaves in Texas, others speculated. "I advise you who have influence," a citizen of Brownsville wrote a friend in San Antonio, "not to wait for any action of the Legislature, but come at once at every sacrifice with sufficient force to whip and hang the traitor as high as Haman."[6]

Even before Cortina's second *pronunciamiento*, his raiders had started to pillage and destroy farms and ranches in the lower Valley, especially those of individuals known to be in sympathy with Cortina's enemies. John Graham, contractor on the Corpus Christi-to-Brownsville and Laredo-to-Rio Grande City-to-Brownsville mail routes, lost most of his horses and mules and watched his mail stations go up in smoke.[7] The all-important Brazos Santiago and Point Isabel-to-Brownsville mail route that connected the lower Rio Grande to Galveston, New Orleans, and the outside world had to be abandoned, the mail carried by Mexican couriers on the south side of the river. In a few instances, the mail was even diverted through Monterrey. In a little less than two months, Brownsville's postmaster, Robert B. Kingsbury, estimated Cortina captured twenty mail riders.

A Poisoned Wand

The toll exacted by the *Cortinistas* was amazing as Cortina's avowed enemies lost hundreds of thousands of dollars in property and livestock. Robert Shears, the "Squinting Sheriff," who was leasing a small ranch only three miles from Brownsville, lost all his horses, cows, oxen, and swine. *Cortinistas* even stole seventeen of his ducks and forty-eight of his "grown chickens."[8] Adolphus Glavecke, who sent his family to Matamoros for safety, lost 125 head of cattle, eleven horses, and three hundred bushels of corn from his ranch and farm above Brownsville.[9] Elisha Basse, a thirty-eight-year-old attorney from Maine, saw his ranch house go up in flames, his fences destroyed, his farm tools stolen, and all his livestock taken.[10] Irish-born James G. Browne lost over 250 head of cattle.[11] Gabriel Catchel, the Brownsville restaurateur, lost everything at his Rancho Sauz near Brownsville.[12] Attorney and former mayor Israel B. Bigelow claimed he lost over three hundred head of cattle and horses to the raiders.[13] Also in Cameron County, *Cortinistas* burned the farmhouse of a steamboat pilot, J. M. Ward, and took all his carpenter tools and farming implements.[14] Seven miles above Brownsville near Rancho del Carmen, at the ranch of James Johnson and Dr. Robert West, a Brownsville dentist, Cortina's men ran off goats, swine, horses, and milk cows.[15] Six miles upriver from Rancho del Carmen, *Cortinistas* burned the ranch of Hugh O'Connor, an Irish-born cattleman.[16] At Striker's Place, a farm only five miles from Brownsville, *Cortinistas* captured James Martin and A. G. Milstead and took all their livestock and weapons. Fearing they would be executed, Martin and Milstead escaped across the river and made their way to Matamoros and then Brownsville.[17] At Rancho Tío Bueno, Nathaniel White claimed he lost oxen, swine, horses, mules, and 748 head of cattle, as well as his blacksmith and carpenter tools, seventy-two bushels of "frijoles" and 1,400 pumpkins.[18] *Cortinistas* also raided the ranch and farm of Francis Campbell, destroying crops and driving off seventy yoke of oxen and ten horses.[19] In Cameron County, William Johnson lost several hundred head of cattle, swine, sheep, and goats.[20] At Los Indios, James Millett claimed Cortina's men burned his ranch house and ran off 125 head of cattle.[21] At Rancho Anacintas Altos, some twenty-four miles upriver from Brownsville, all of Jacob Miller's horses and cows disappeared.[22] At Rancho Agua Negra, James Maxwell was taken captive and watched while his small store was plundered.[23] Also in Cameron County, the raiders struck Josiah Turner's Rancho Galveston, demolishing his house and driving off over one hundred livestock.[24]

The narratives behind the plundering help fill in the story. For instance, thirty miles above Brownsville on the river at Rancho La Florida, the Italian-born Peter Champion was at home late on the evening of October 31, when three *Cortinistas* he recognized as Francisco "Chico" Milan, Francisco "Pancho" Treviño, and Enrique Medrano rode up with pistols drawn and demanded he give up all the weapons at the ranch.[25] After taking a double-barreled shot gun, a rifle, and a Dragoon pistol, Milan demanded $100 in "the name of Juan Cortina." When Champion could produce only $13.25, the men strung a noose around his neck and threatened to hang him.[26] Fearful the *Cortinistas* would indeed execute her husband, Champion's young Mexican wife, Felícitas, rushed to the nearby ranch of Isidoro Cavazos, where she borrowed $40. Galloping off with the money, the *Cortinistas* said they were determined to burn all the ranches of the *estranjeros,* or foreigners. Four days later, after Champion fled with his family and servants to Point Isabel, thirty *Cortinistas* led by Santos Cadena rode to the ranch and would have destroyed it had not Jesús Solís, brother of Champion's father-in-law, Francisco Solís, persuaded them not to do so. At the abandoned ranch, nevertheless, Champion lost his beehives and his fruit trees when they went unattended.[27] He eventually calculated his losses at 1,700 head of cattle, between forty-five and fifty horses, all his household goods, farming utensils, and "220 chickens and 6 turkeys," a net value of $16,678.[28] Nearer the coast, Champion and his two brothers lost most of the horses and mules on the Brownsville to Point Isabel and Brazos Santiago mail route.[29] Other *Cortinistas,* many of them acting independently and with little direction, plundered a train of twenty-four heavily laden carts on the way from Point Isabel to Brownsville.[30]

Others fared no better. Charles Stillman, who was in New York on business during the first three months of the Cortina War, returned to South Texas to learn his Rancho Santa Rosa, sixty miles northwest of Brownsville in Hidalgo County, had been attacked three different times. Of the ten vaqueros who worked the ranch, three had joined the *Cortinistas*.[31] Along with business partners Mifflin Kenedy and Richard King, Stillman hoped a company of Rangers, commanded by Peter Nickels, chief justice of the Hidalgo County and former sheriff of Cameron County, could be recruited in Hidalgo County to help protect the ranches in the area.[32] Elsewhere, besides taking hundreds of sheep, goats, mules, oxen, swine, and cattle at William Neale and Nestor Maxan's Rancho Bastón in southeastern Hidalgo County, Cortina's raiders destroyed a fifty-acre orange grove. Neale and Maxan would later file a claim for damages, probably exaggerated, that amounted to $33,733.[33] To Neale, Cortina "touched" the lower Valley "with his poisoned wand, and left only a blackened and scarred semblance of its former beauty."[34]

The raids continued. In late October, at Thaddeus M. Rhodes's sprawling 3,188-acre Rancho Relámpago, just west of La Bolsa and some thirty miles below Edinburg, in eastern Hidalgo County, thirty-five *Cortinistas* trampled Rhodes's garden, ran off seventeen head of cattle, thirteen horses, about ninety goats, stole his poultry, and destroyed his beehives and medical books. A physician by trade with a reputation for rustling himself, Rhodes was left "houseless, homeless and pennyless."[35] Two months after the property was abandoned, a second band of Cortina's men burned the ranch and several *jacales*. At the sprawling Rancho La Blanca, some twenty miles downriver from Edinburg in Hidalgo County, the recently widowed Salomé Ballí de Young, claimed she lost eight hundred cattle worth more than $8,000.[36]

On October 26, 1859, at Mifflin Kenedy's Rancho San Salvador del Tule, some fifty-seven miles northwest of Brownsville and seven miles west of El Sal del Rey, ranch foreman, Jacob F. George and ten Mexican vaqueros learned a band of *Cortinistas* were near and they fled into the chaparral. Kenedy would eventually allege he lost 3,135 head of cattle, 2,400 goats, and eighteen saddle horses. Many of his livestock were so badly scattered in the chaparral they were never recovered. Kenedy, however, had taken the precaution of driving most of his horses and mules north to the Nueces.[37] Although many of the Anglo farmers and ranchers piled up claims for lost livestock in the hundreds of thousands of dollars, many such as Kenedy anticipated they would be hit by Cortina's raiders and they drove their herds north.[38]

On October 31, 1859, one hundred *Cortinistas* led by Francisco Treviño and Henry Cline hit the Rancho Laguna Tío Cano of William D. Thomas and Nathaniel White, some five miles north of the Arroyo Colorado in Cameron County. Carrying the Mexican flag, the men burned the ranch and drove off several hundred horses, cattle, and swine. One of the vaqueros who worked the ranch, Juan Villarreal, joined the raiders. White and Thomas, along with Thomas's wife and two children, were able to escape into the chaparral and make their way north to Corpus Christi and safety. "The women and children of our frontier are in danger of being massacred," Thomas and White warned anyone who would listen.[39]

Retribution was rampant. On the one hand, Mexican Texans thought to be sympathetic to the Brownsville establishment and hostile to Cortina, or at odds with anyone who happened to be a *Cortinista,* suffered. On the other hand, if the small landowners were known to support Cortina, their farms and ranches were put to the torch by the Rangers. In Cameron County, Nicolas Cano, Pedro García, Manuel Dominguez, Guillermo Molina, Vicente Ramírez, and Julián Flores all lost their farms and ranch animals.[40] So did Miguel Gonzales, who had his horses, goats, and swine taken.[41] At Rancho Viejo, just north of Brownsville, Dimas Barrera also lost all his livestock.[42] In all, seventy-five individuals, including merchants such as Henry Clay Davis and John P. Kelsey at Rio Grande City, would eventually submit claims amounting to $336,879.[43]

In late November, vaqueros Santiago Solís and Cecilio Solís, along with a thirteen-year-old boy named Polinario, were herding cattle on Rancho Atascosa, about six miles west of Point Isabel, when sixty *Cortinistas* rode up and took the three men's horses. The vaqueros were taken to one of Cortina's camps at Rancho Cantú, where two hundred men were camped, "all ragged, without clothes, and no provisions but meat."[44] In desperate need of food and clothing, Cortina was heard to tell the men to prepare to march for Rio Grande City. Although he later claimed he was coerced into joining the raiders, Solís was given a six-shooter and a double-barreled shotgun and he rode off with his captors.

Soldiers in Blue

Eight days before Cortina's second *pronunciamiento*, the U.S. Army finally decided to move against Cortina. At a cabinet meeting at the Executive Mansion in early November, President James Buchanan agreed to send the army to the border and, if necessary, pursue Cortina into Mexico. On November 15, 1859, at Camp Verde in the heart of the Texas Hill Country north of San Antonio, Maj. Samuel P. Heintzelman, a hard-nosed thirty-three-year veteran of the frontier army, received orders placing him in command of what the army called the Brownsville Expedition.[45] In San Antonio two days later, Heintzelman met with General Twiggs, who urged him to hurry to the Rio Grande and chase Cortina from Texas. Not wanting to create an international incident, Twiggs urged the major, however, not to cross into Mexico unless in hot pursuit. With units of the 1st Infantry, Heintzelman departed San Antonio for Fort Merrill on the Nueces River. When Twiggs learned more of what was happening on the Rio Grande and realized that many of the rumors resonating from the border were greatly exaggerated, he issued new orders breaking up the expedition.[46] Still, with three companies, Heintzelman was to race for the Rio Grande with all deliberate speed. Some semblance of law and order must be restored.

At Fort Merrill, Heintzelman was joined by two companies of the 1st Artillery, as well as a company of the elite 2nd Cavalry. He was also met by Richard King, who offered fresh horses, guides, and words of encouragement. Passing historic Casa Blanca on the Nueces River, the army moved downriver to San Patricio before heading south for the border.[47] South of the King Ranch and north of the Arroyo Colorado, in one of the coldest northers in memory, the army began to see abandoned ranches, their first evidence of the Cortina War. While Cortina and his men shivered in the cold in their camps on the river, the army hastened south across the shifting sands of the Wild Horse Desert to the ferry on the Arroyo Colorado, which they were surprised to find had not been destroyed. Pushing on across the Palo Alto prairie, they reached Brownsville at midnight on December 6, 1859.[48]

The next morning, Heintzelman set out to obtain as much information on Cortina and his whereabouts as possible. From the beginning, he realized Cortina was far more than just a charismatic bandit. Leading citizens were interviewed and intelligence gathered, but Heintzelman could not find a reliable map of the area. The major hoped to determine the exact size of Cortina's army and the nature of his fortifications near Rancho del Carmen, but, he complained, everyone seemed "ignorant of these matters."[49] Albert Champion told Heintzelman that Cortina's men were scattered up and down the river and that the Rangers should have been able to defeat them. District Judge Edmund J. Davis promised to find a reliable spy to enter Cortina's camp and gain more information.[50] For several years, Davis had ridden the South Texas judicial circuit including Brownsville, Laredo, and Corpus Christi and knew the country and its people as well as anyone. Other Brownsville citizens insisted that Cortina had as many as 1,500 men. More reliable sources were convinced he had between three hundred and five hundred men, of whom only one hundred were mounted. Before moving against Cortina, Heintzelman also visited José María de Jesús Carvajal, the "not tall & a little stout" general who knew more about Cortina than anyone on the border.[51] Although the officers at Carvajal's headquarters in Matamoros insisted Cortina had at least six hundred men, Carvajal was inclined to think he had no more than two hundred.

Back in Brownsville, Heintzelman sent one of his officers to the Ranger camp a mile and a half from town to drill the rough and undisciplined Texans. In response, the Rangers became so inspired they galloped off in the direction of Cortina's camp to do battle, only to be abruptly halted by a hail of gunfire. One Ranger had his gun shot from his hands while another took a bullet through his hat. They all "turned and came home," Heintzelman recorded.[52] Later, when he sent the Rangers to scout Cortina's fortifications, "none of them ever got near enough to give me any information," he complained.[53]

Thorny Vastness

By early December, a band of *Cortinistas* struck a small army supply train on the Arroyo Colorado and made off with $2,000 worth of blankets and ammunition. One soldier escaped the attack and fled to Brownsville, but a second bluecoat named Featherston was stabbed and killed by Cortina's men while he slept.[54] By December 12, Judge Davis was able to provide a sketch of Cortina's position, and the army prepared to move. With 165 regulars and 125 Rangers, at midnight three days later Heintzelman marched out of Fort Brown to meet Cortina. By the time the sun rose over the Rio Grande plain, the column was within a mile and half of Cortina's position. As it happened, Cortina was not on the scene, but, with two hundred of his men at Los Indios, north of Brownsville, preparing to ambush a band of Rangers his scouts reported were on their way to Brownsville. Because the Rangers had been "so thoroughly stampeded by their previous expedition," Heintzelman was overly cautious in approaching Cortina's fortifications.[55] Two miles past Rancho del Carmen, at Rancho La Ebonal, Cortina's forward pickets waited anxiously behind well-constructed ten-foot-thick barricades of mesquite. While the army approached, Cortina's artillerymen sent a "four pound ball" down the road. In response, the regulars unleashed their own artillery but the howitzer shells from the guns sailed well beyond the fortifications and did little more than stir up clouds of smoke and dust.[56] At the same time, the *Cortinistas,* under the command of Teodoro Zamora, continued to fire grapeshot and canister at the advancing bluecoats and Rangers. One piece of canister ripped into a man's thigh while another killed a mule before slamming into an ammunition wagon that burst into flames.

Emboldened by the discipline and determination of the regulars, the Rangers dismounted and advanced on one of Zamora's flanks while the regulars moved on the other. Neither advance made much progress in the dense, almost impenetrable, chaparral. Hoping to seize the enemy's artillery, Zamora launched a "bold and fearless" counterattack while his men cried out *"¡Gringos! ¡Viva Cortina!"*[57] But the superior firepower of the bluecoats sent the *Cortinistas* reeling. At least eight of Cortina's men lay dead on the field, most of them killed by the artillery shells that burst in their ranks.[58] The exact number of dead, however, was difficult to determine because several men were blown to pieces.

Hearing the roar of artillery in the direction of the river, Cortina galloped off through the chaparral, only to find his small army in disarray and in retreat. He tried hard to rally his men, but the bluecoats and Rangers pressed him hard. After abandoning a number of arms and provisions, he was finally able to rally his men four miles up the road from La Ebonal at the ranch of Jesús de León. Here the Rangers, supported by the regular infantry and the artillery, routed his men and threw them back in confusion. Again Cortina's men fled along the river road, a few bolting for the Rio Grande and safety in Mexico.

Cortina was fearful of losing his artillery, and at a fork in the road near his Rancho San José he sent one of the cannon off into the dense chaparral. Through the night in a heavy rain, his men straggled upriver toward Edinburg, some continuing to cross the river into Mexico. Early the next morning, Cortina rallied what remained of his army only to learn that the regulars and the Rangers had retreated to Brownsville. His scouts also said the Rangers were burning the ranches and farms along the road.[59] "The Rangers were burning all—friends and foes," Heintzelman admitted.[60] But the situation would grow worse. Any Mexican Texan who was thought to have been with Cortina or even in sympathy with him was "murdered without pity, their families compelled to fly and their property stolen," a Mexican investigative committee concluded.[61]

Some of the regulars and Rangers seemed disappointed that Cortina would not stand and fight. Cortina knew he was outgunned, and he was not about to risk his small army in one decisive battle. Tobin conveyed as much to Governor Runnels: "It is not his policy to stand and receive an open attack but to draw his opponents into ambuscades, cut them off by detail, and when overpowered to slide away unnoticed into his thorny fastness." Not only were Cortina and his men "well acquainted with the various paths in the woods," Tobin continued, "they are also prepared with leather clothing which enables

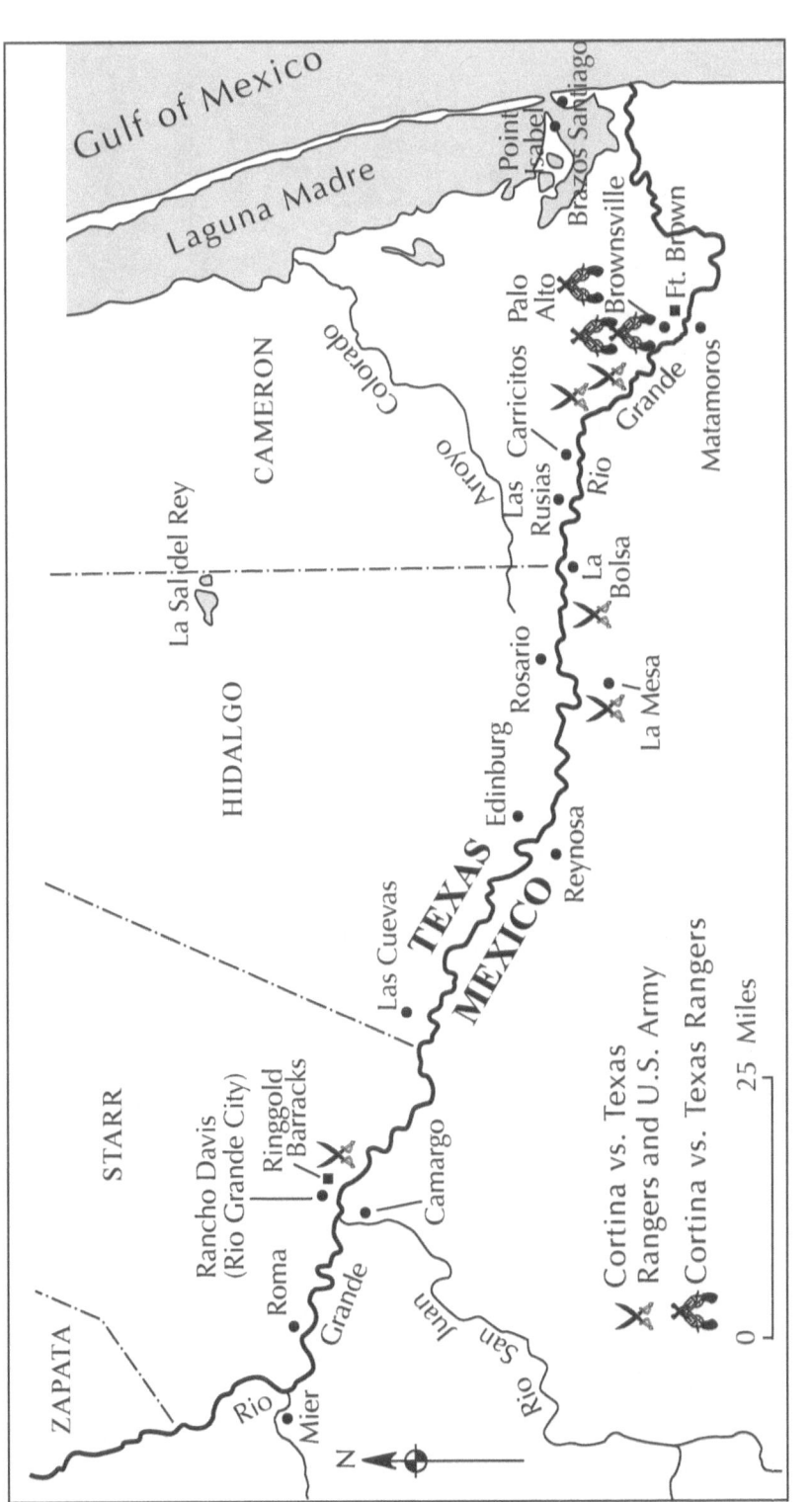

Cortina War, 1859–1860

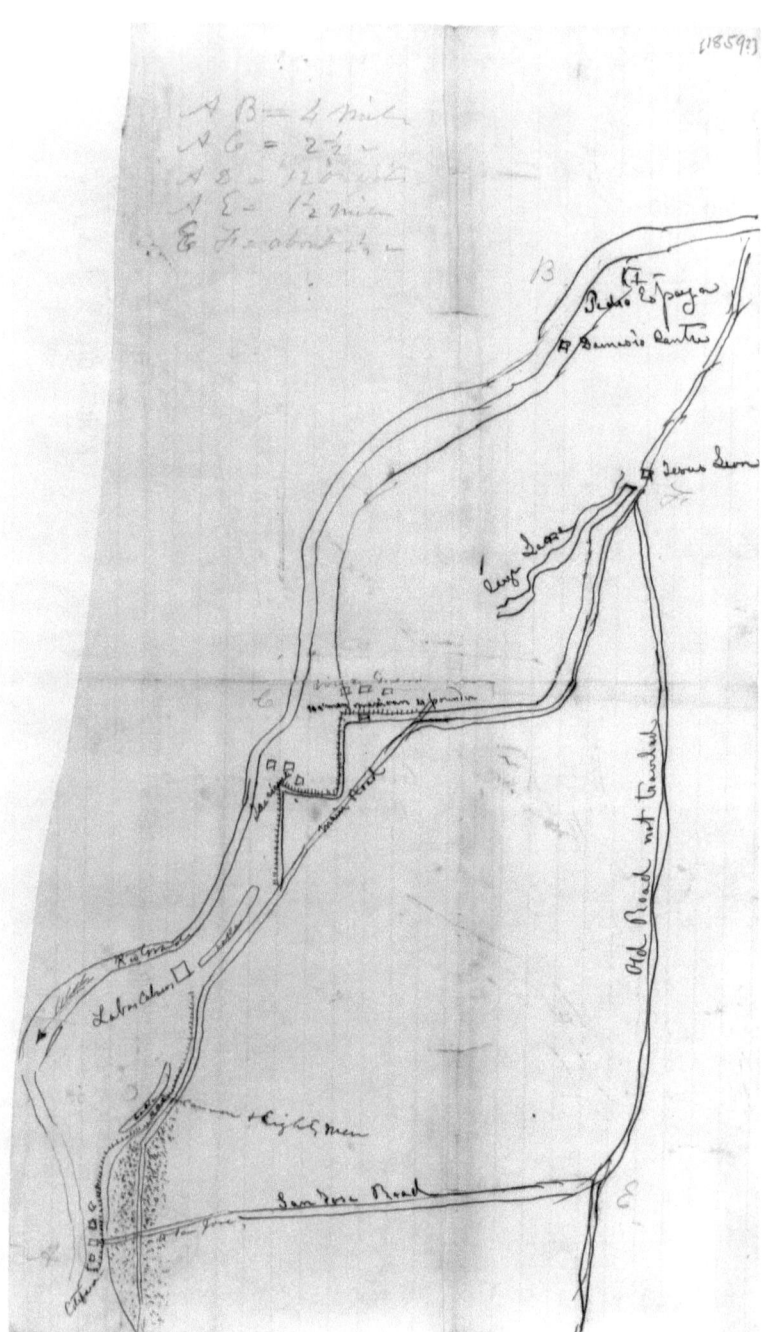

In December 1859, Maj. Samuel P. Heintzelman made this crude map of Cortina's defenses on the Rio Grande above Brownsville during the Cortina War. Rancho del Carmen can be seen on the bottom left of the map while Cortina's small Rancho San José is back in the chaparral to the northwest. *Samuel P. Heintzelman Papers, Library of Congress.*

them to traverse these woods without a scratch while we in following them bleed at every pore."[62]

Determined not to be cornered by the U.S. Army, Cortina continued to retreat upriver, many of his men burning and plundering as they went. In the rain and cold, his men rode past Rancho Carricitos near Las Rucias where the opening shots of the Mexican War had been fired fourteen years earlier, and then on to Rancho Bastón and Edinburg. Here at the county seat of Hidalgo County, only yards from the Rio Grande, the *Cortinistas* pillaged the customs house, post office, and all county offices. County Clerk William D. Thomas claimed the raiders stole $800 from his office besides taking $92.20 from the county treasurer and $114.50 from the tax assessor-collector.[63] Cortina's men also sacked many of the small dwellings in the small community and stole a number or horses.[64] With his small army again numbering as many as 400 men, Cortina pushed on to the small village of Las Cuevas and then upriver to Rio Grande City, the county seat of Starr County, where he occupied Ringgold Barracks on Christmas Day, 1859.

A Battle in the Fog

Four days earlier, at noon on December 21, with 150 regulars composed of infantry, cavalry, and artillery, along with 198 mounted Rangers, Major Heintzelman moved out of Brownsville.[65] Hoping to catch Cortina by surprise, Heintzelman pushed his small army rapidly upriver; the Rangers, meanwhile, took time to resume their burning and plundering. Any ranch or *jacal* still standing was presumed to be that of a *Cortinista*, or at least sympathizers of the crafty Cortina, and it was put to the torch. The entire countryside soon lay in ruin. "The whole country," Heintzelman wrote, "from Brownsville to Rio Grande City, one hundred and twenty miles, and back to the Arroyo Colorado, has been laid to waste."[66]

Riding with the army as a scout and guide was Henry Clay Davis, the most influential man in Rio Grande City. When the Cortina War first erupted in the lower Valley and communications were cut between Rio Grande City and Brownsville, the forty-six-year-old Georgia-born Davis raced north through the Brush Country to sound the alarm in San Antonio. Returning to Starr County, Davis mustered thirty-five men into a small defense company. Realizing that the force was too small to defend Rio Grande City, he left his young Mexican wife and four children in the town and took his small company through the chaparral to Brownsville.[67]

In the sun-baked rock and adobe village, many of Cortina's men, including fifty-four men recently arrived from Reynosa, became intoxicated. One American who fled across the river to Camargo said Cortina's men were not only drunk but were also threatening to kill all the Americans in the community.[68] Cortina tried to maintain some semblance of order but his army was unruly and difficult to control. At Ringgold Barracks, three Americans, William Robinson, John Box, and N. P. Spears, were said to have been gunned down and their bodies hacked to pieces by the drunken *Cortinistas*.[69] Badly in need of food and clothing, Cortina's men sacked several of the large mercantile houses in the riverside community, including that of the post sutler, James B. McClusky, as well as that of John P. Kelsey, a forty-two-year-old New Yorker, who later filed a claim for damages amounting to $5,000. Davis's mercantile store was also plundered, the *Cortinistas* seizing badly needed rifles and pistols. In Rio Grande City, men from the small ranches and towns in Mexico continued to join Cortina's ranks. Some speculated that in two weeks he would have an army of no less than two thousand men.

Cortina's confidence grew ever greater. "Gen'l. Houston is in favor of Mexicanizing Texas and [has placed] me over it as president," Cortina told several people in Rio Grande City.[70] When he first rode into the village, Davis's thirty-year-old Mexican wife, Hilaria de la Garza Martínez, a distant cousin of Cortina's, confronted the foxy revolutionary. Cortina said he would kill her husband on sight, but he had no intentions of harming her or her children. "You may be able to kill him, but if you do, you will have to go home and tell your folks you had to fight. . . . He told me to stay here . . . in our home and I will stay in it while one brick is on top of another," Hilaria replied. Allegedly, one of Davis's sons rushed up to Cortina during the confrontation and shouted out, "¡*Viva Tejas! ¡Muera Cortina!*" at which Cortina "laughed heartily" and reached in his pocket and pulled out a two-bit piece, which he gave to the boy.[71]

While Cortina and his men waited in Rio Grande City, Heintzelman continued to lead his army upriver. By pushing his men hard, he could catch Cortina off guard and inflict a decisive defeat, the major speculated. Leaving Las Cuevas shortly after midnight on December 27, with the Rangers riding ahead in darkened silence, Heintzelman hoped to reach Rio Grande City at daylight, outflank Cortina, and cut him off from any possible retreat. Nearing Ringgold Barracks, the Rangers plunged into the chaparral, hoping to outflank Cortina, but the underbrush was too dense and the terrain too rugged. Soon enough, they retreated to the main road.[72]

Spotting the advancing Rangers, Cortina tried to defend Ringgold Barracks but fell back toward the town where a vicious firefight erupted in the early morning fog. On the outskirts of the community, a number of the *Cortinistas* who were acting as snipers positioned themselves on top of several rock and adobe dwellings where they were able to fire on the advancing Rangers. At the same time, Cortina ordered his two artillery pieces into action; within minutes, rounds of grapeshot and canister exploded in the dry earth. One company of Rangers charged to within forty yards of the guns, but Cortina's men drove them off.

In the dense fog, with visibility little more than the length of a rifle barrel, friend became confused for foe. During the heaviest of the fighting, the Rangers were forced to dismount and lead their horses off into a mesquite motte. In the heavy morning air, Cortina ordered his bugler to sound "charge"; several of Cortina's cavalry raced out and came close to outflanking the Rangers. Several *Cortinistas,* however, were killed, with the others driven off. "Many a charger galloped off, carrying an empty saddle," as "Cortina's bold riders were left on the ground," Ford recalled.[73] Pressed on three sides, the Rangers were preparing to fall back when the white-topped wagons of the regulars appeared on the horizon. It was then that Cortina knew the battle was lost.

As Capt. George Stoneman's 2nd U.S. Cavalry galloped forward to support the Rangers, the *Cortinistas* fled through the town. Leaving provisions half-cooked, many paused only to fire their rifles or pistols at the advancing Rangers and bluecoats. In the retreat, Cortina's main camp above Rio Grande City was abandoned and overrun. Retreating along the river road toward Roma, small units escaped into the chaparral and were soon invisible in the fog. Not willing to give up entirely, Cortina sent about fifty of his men to outflank the bluecoats who were advancing along the river. Here they ran headlong into Captain Stoneman's dismounted company of the hard-riding 2nd Cavalry, and the *Cortinistas* were again forced to flee. Many of the rusty muskets of the *Cortinistas* proved to be no match for the regulars' Sharp's rifles.

Several of Cortina's men were forced to the riverbanks by the regulars, where they were systematically cut to pieces. Led by an Irish sergeant, the bluecoats commenced firing by rank. "Front rank, ready, aim fire!" the sergeant shouted in the smoke and confusion. Joined by several Rangers who rushed to the scene, the sergeant was heard to proclaim, "in place, rest ... an' we'll watch the bloody rangers hoot thim copper-skin divils."[74] Of the seventeen *Cortinistas* who were trapped by the river and who tried to swim to safety, only one survived. "While they were swimming, the boys played upon them in the water, and they sunk [*sic*] like brick-bats," a Ranger bragged.[75]

At the same time that Stoneman was doing his work, a squad of shotgun-wielding Rangers cut off and killed several other *Cortinistas.* A few of Cortina's men gained the south bank of the river but were also gunned down. In all, thirty-eight of thirty-nine *Cortinistas* were said to have been killed as they tried desperately to flee to Mexico.[76] Along the road to Roma, a second band of *Cortinistas* was attacked, and they too ran for the river after leaving ten dead comrades in the chaparral. A mile above Rio Grande City, Cortina and what remained of his small army made another gallant stand. Much as he had done on the Palo Alto prairie, Cortina concealed some of his cavalry and an artillery piece in the dense chaparral near a clearing that was crossed by the road to Roma. Here the *Cortinistas* were said to have fought "with courage and determination" against twice their number. In the thick fog and dense mesquite, much of the fighting became hand to hand a Ranger remembered. Determined not to give ground, and out of ammunition, Cortina was said to have defiantly hurled a walking stick at the charging Rangers.[77] Five miles above Rio Grande City, where the road crossed a large ravine, Cortina tried one last time to rally his men, but the Rangers charged and captured one of his guns. A mile beyond and still pressed hard, Cortina abandoned his remaining gun and all his ammunition. Within five miles of Roma, he left the main road and fled across the river with about forty of his men. For ten miles, he had been driven from every position and his army virtually destroyed.[78]

In the fighting at Rio Grande City, fifteen Rangers were wounded, some seriously, while there were no casualties in the ranks of the regulars. Heintzelman estimated that Cortina lost sixty men killed out of an army of 590. Ford was sure he lost at least two hundred. "We had no use for prisoners," one of Tobin's Rangers wrote after the battle; "therefore only three were permitted to be taken.... Today we swing a prisoner by the neck."[79] So hasty was Cortina's retreat that all his records fell into the hands of the army, including his muster rolls. Ox-carts, mules, powder, lead bullets, bridles, and saddles were also lost. Many weapons were captured, but they were mostly antiquated rifles and muskets and most of them were useless.[80]

Cortina's defeat at Rio Grande City was hailed throughout Texas as a great victory for civilization. It was San Jacinto all over again. The degenerate Mexicans had at last been defeated, and peace was certain to be restored to the Rio Grande frontier.[81] Regardless, rumors persisted that Cortina had intentions of recrossing the river to "fight till death" and "shed his blood and bury his bones on Texas soil."[82] War, after all, is notoriously hard to resolve, and both the Rangers and the regulars realized the Cortina War was far from over. Nevertheless, the "character of operations" was certain to change, Ford accurately observed. With Cortina's army broken and battered, small bands of *Cortinistas* would now "beset the roads" and "wage guerrilla warfare and murder and plunder."[83]

Fox in the Chaparral

Despite Cortina's resounding defeat at Rio Grande City, bands of *Cortinistas* did indeed remain active in Texas. There was also no waning of his support in Mexico. Only days after word of his defeat reached Matamoros, a large and noisy demonstration, complete with marching bands, was staged in the city. Several hundred people paraded and shouted, "Death to the Gringos!" and "Death to the Yankees!" These people, the American consul, Richard Fitzpatrick recorded, were "deadly hostile to every American, unless he is a Negro or mulatto."[84]

As the nature of the conflict evolved into a guerrilla war, a band of *Cortinistas* struck the Rancho de los Sauses on the river between the Rio Grande City and Roma while, at the same time, fifty *Cortinistas* raided the Rancho de Los Víboros, forty-five miles northeast of the town, seizing arms and driving off horses. The "war is not ended," Ford told newly elected Gov. Sam Houston. "Disorder, confusion, violence and bloodshed prevail everywhere and there is no telling when the end will come."[85] A mail rider on the Corpus Christi-to-Brownsville route was seized by thirty of Cortina's men north of the Arroyo Colorado. The men vowed they would kill "every American they got hold of."[86] Of the seven mail riders sent north from Brownsville, John Graham, mail contractor for the route, reported six were seized by Cortina's men. Many of the *Cortinistas* were not interested in the mail but in the horses, saddles, bridles, and equipment that were taken.

With the vast majority of the population of the lower Valley not only in sympathy with Cortina but also actively aiding and abetting him, he seemed likely to remain a threat for months, if not years. "The spirit of disaffection is wide spread among the Mexican population of this state," Ford told Governor Houston. "We have found it almost impossible to procure any correct information from them in regards to Cortina. They have furnished him with supplies and claimed the defensive plea of being robbed. They sympathize with him very generally. The only friends we have are among those who have something to lose and they constitute a very small minority."[87] There was "a feeling of deep-seated hostility in the breast of every Mexican against all *Gringos* and more particularly American *Gringos*," an unnamed resident of Rio Grande City wrote. "Even the children participate in this feeling, and in my opinion, the only way to eradicate this feeling is in the utter extermination of the stock, or the absorption of it by taking immediate possession of the whole three adjoining [Mexican] states.... The 'Greaser' and *Gringo* can never live harmoniously together, unless the latter largely predominate."[88]

After his stunning defeat at Rio Grande City, Cortina moved upriver along the Mexican bank of the Rio Grande with about forty of his men. In Texas, it was feared Roma would be attacked and burned. With a population of 562, Roma was not only the largest community in Starr County but also head of navigation on the Rio Grande and a vital trading center.[89] Built on a high bluff overlooking the river, the town seemed well situated, but Noah Cox and many of the merchants in the community were fearful that "some straggling party of Mexicans ... might attack and plunder our place."[90] Consequently, the army and the Rangers were forced to occupy the town.

Although he was known for a time to be on the Mexican bank of the river opposite Roma, Cortina's exact whereabouts in the days after the disaster at Rio Grande City are nonetheless impossible to ascertain. Two days after the fighting, small parties of *Cortinistas* entered Mier, and Cortina, with a small bodyguard, was reported to be near Ciudad Guerrero, some forty-five miles upriver. There, he had a large number of sympathizers.⁹¹ Other reports said he was near Rancho Bastón on the Texas side of the river where José María Cortina, his thirty-eight-year-old older brother, was said to be camped with three hundred men. Santiago Solís, the vaquero who had been taken captive at the Rancho Atascosa earlier and who managed to avoid the fighting at Rio Grande City, saw Cortina on the south bank of the river near Camargo five days after the battle. Cortina said he did not know how many men he lost at Rio Grande City, but he thought only about twelve to fifteen. Solís said Cortina was still adamant about driving the Americans from the border and punishing his enemies in Brownsville.⁹² By the second week of January 1860, Cortina was rumored to be on the Mexican side of he river at Rancho La Bolsa, thirty miles above Brownsville, and preparing to cross into Texas. Indeed, on January 16, twenty-five *Cortinistas* intercepted the Laredo-to-Brownsville mail near the Cameron-Hidalgo county line. Before being released, the mail rider, Pedro Mireles, was taken to Cortina's camp where he counted more than 150 well-armed and ready-to-fight *Cortinistas*.

All the small ranches from Matamoros to Camargo were said to be harboring *Cortinistas*, nearly all of them unarmed and ragged.⁹³ Others were thought to have returned to their homes in Matamoros. As for Cortina's whereabouts, Major Heintzelman perhaps put it best when he wrote, "No one knows where he has gone."⁹⁴ One thing was sure: Cortina was regrouping and remaining a dangerous threat. "His defeat at Rio Grande City," Ford admitted, "had not caused his admirers to lose confidence in him. They supposed he would retrieve his fortune and fame by some happy stroke and woo fortune to his side once more."⁹⁵ Ford was anxious to enter Mexico and kill or capture Cortina. Fearing an invasion by the Rangers and American filibusters, one hundred leading citizens of Matamoros met to protest and draft a set of resolutions that were endorsed by the city council.⁹⁶

By late January 1860, Cortina remained as elusive as ever, and many on both sides of the Rio Grande continued to worry that he would somehow manage to inaugurate a war between the United States and Mexico. In Brownsville, Major Heintzelman met with Gen. Guadalupe García, commanding the Mexican military on the Rio Grande, who said he was under orders to cooperate with the Americans in capturing Cortina. García was hoping to complete an agreement by which either army could cross the Rio Grande while in pursuit of bandits. "I told him that if he took care of his side we would of ours," Heintzelman wrote.⁹⁷ In reality, most of the Mexican military, as well as civilian authorities, quietly supported Cortina; at the same time, they were apprehensive that Cortina would provoke an invasion of their country. To appease the Americans, numerous military patrols were dispatched from Matamoros, allegedly in search of Cortina. But the news was always the same: Cortina had eluded their grasp and somehow disappeared into the chaparral. As well, one of Cortina's lieutenants was ceremoniously married in Matamoros and *Cortinistas* freely walked the streets of the city. "It is well known to everybody in this town that more than twenty of Cortina's men are in this place," the American consul reported on April 1, 1860.[98]

In fact, Cortina himself was frequently seen in Matamoros, and he continued to draw his supplies and arms from the city. A number of *Cortinistas* were also thought to be frequenting Brownsville. Well into the early spring, reports circulated that Cortina had been seen with several hundred men on the American side of the river. He also continued to recruit men from the small ranches and farms along the river, although authorities in Matamoros at one time insisted he had departed for Ciudad Victoria. With bands of *Cortinistas* roaming at large, the entire Lower Rio Grande Valley remained dangerous. On the north bank, the situation was so precarious that Jacob Thompson, Secretary of the Department of the Interior, even requested an army escort for the census enumerator for the counties of Starr, Zapata, Webb, and Encinal.[99]

Convinced Cortina was still on the border, the American military continued to pressure General García to capturing him.[100] With the bluecoat cavalry and the Rangers patrolling the river between Brownsville and Rio Grande City, and the *Cortinistas* continuing to rustle cattle on the north bank, bloody skirmishes frequently erupted.[101]

Incident at La Bolsa

Late on the evening of February 4, 1860, an excited express rider galloped into Fort Brown with news that Cortina had attacked the steamboat *Ranchero* on its way downriver from Rio Grande City. Carrying $300,000 in coin, the steamer had been fired on at La Bolsa, the big bend in the Rio Grande some thirty-nine miles above Brownsville. On board were a few Rangers who were ill, some regulars, several women and civilians, and the two cannon that had been captured at Rio Grande City.

In retaliation for the attack, Ford led forty-nine Rangers across the river to attack Cortina and one hundred of his men at Rancho La Bolsa. Expecting the Rangers would cross the river, Cortina positioned his men behind some improvised mesquite barricades. In a furious hour-long fight he was outmaneuvered and several of his men killed and wounded, despite the fact that many of the *Cortinistas* were equipped with new muskets acquired only days earlier in Matamoros. In their hasty retreat, the *Cortinistas* also lost a number of their horses and firearms. During the fighting, Cortina had hoped for reinforcements from Matamoros, but no one came to his assistance. One of those killed at La Bolsa was Faustino, a Tampacuas Indians cacique from near Reynosa.[102] In the rapidly approaching darkness, Cortina had "tried to halt his panic-stricken men," Ford remembered, and when he turned in the saddle, the Rangers opened fire. "One shot struck the candle of his saddle, one cut out a lock of hair from his head, a third cut his bridle rein, a fourth passed through his horse's ear, and a fifth struck his belt. He galloped off unhurt," Ford wrote.[103] Before crossing back to the north bank, the Rangers torched the ranch and corrals and made off with all the livestock in the vicinity. They also seized and hanged a vaquero, Cleto García, who they mistakenly thought was a *Cortinista*.[104]

Weeks later, it was learned the *Ranchero* had not been attacked from the Mexican bank of the river; much of what was being reported on the border and in the jingoistic *Brownsville American Flag* was false. The bluecoat cavalry and the Rangers had been skirmishing with a band of *Cortinistas* who had crossed the river and intercepted the mail, cut open the mail bags, and rifled through the contents.[105] In reality, the steamer had been caught in a crossfire between the *Cortinistas* who had retreated to the south bank and the Rangers and bluecoats on the Texas bank. "I have the verbal testimony of persons who stood at the time on her hurricane deck, saw the smoke, heard the reports of the guns and the whistle of the balls, as they passed over their heads," Major Heintzelman told army headquarters in San Antonio.[106] "There was no attack from the Mexican side upon our boat the *Ranchero*," Gen. Winfield Scott concluded.[107] Thirteen years later, a Mexican investigative commission went as far as to allege that the fighting had started when "people on board [the *Ranchero*] fired several shots at the ranch [La Bolsa] which was replied to." There was no doubt that the men on board the *Ranchero* had "opened hostilities," the commission went on to report.[108]

As a consequence of the Ranger invasion, "the most intense excitement has prevailed ... and the war feeling has been raised to a higher pitch than ever," a New Orleans newspaper reported.[109] When word reached Brownsville that Ford had crossed the river, the town went "wild with excitement," Major Heintzelman reported.[110] Heavily armed and frenzied filibusters, certain the news meant war between the United States and Mexico, began crossing the river to seize the ferryboats on the Mexican side when Heintzelman and his aides convinced the ruffians "of the folly of their act."[111] In Mexico, a general fear arose that Ford's Rangers would plunder all the ranches on the south side of the river.[112] There were even fears that Tobin's Rangers, who had been ordered to Brownsville to be discharged, would regroup and pillage Reynosa and Camargo, or perhaps even Matamoros.[113] However, when the Rangers were discharged, most headed north, stealing horses along the way at Rancho Viejo, north of Brownsville.[114]

Following the fighting at La Bolsa and responding to heightened threats from the Americans, General García led a small expedition upriver from Matamoros in mid-February to apprehend the elusive Cortina. García returned only a few days later to say that he "saw nothing" of the elusive revolutionary despite a rumor in Brownsville that he had actually been in Cortina's camp. Realizing that Cortina was on the verge of dragging Mexico into an unwanted war, García told the Americans that Cortina and sixty-seven of his men had been seen at Rancho La Mesa forty-five miles above Matamoros, not far from La Bolsa.[115] In response, the bluecoat cavalry and Ford's Rangers splashed across the Rio Grande. Riding into the night, the Americans hoped to secrete their horses in the chaparral and surround the ranch at daylight. Within half a mile of the ranch, however, a sentry spotted the Americans and sounded the warning. Riding into La Mesa in three columns with guns ablaze, the Americans mistakenly attacked twenty-seven men of the Matamoros National Guard. One woman was killed in the attack and a guardsman wounded. As they had done at La Bolsa, before leaving, the Rangers made off with all the livestock in the vicinity. Although the Americans were certain the Guardia Nacional was "acting in concert" with Cortina, the entire incident proved embarrassing.[116]

Reynosa

Despite his presence in Matamoros, Cortina was by the second week of March in camp near Rancho Quijano, about thirty miles south of the river on the road to San Fernando.[117] Later, he was said to be at nearby Rancho Maguey, and the Rangers and the bluecoat cavalry spurred their horses in that direction. Charging the ranch at a gallop as they had done at La Mesa, the Americans ran into a party of villagers peacefully celebrating St. Joseph's Day. One man, Elijio Tagle, fled into the brush and was killed by the Rangers. Cortina, meanwhile, was gone. After riding 140 miles in forty-eight hours, the fatigued bluecoats and Rangers and their jaded horses crossed back into Texas.[118] All were disappointed they had not killed or captured the elusive Cortina. A few days later, when Estéfana and José María informed the Americans they wanted to return to Rancho del Carmen, many on the river concluded that Cortina had decided to leave the area permanently.[119]

Despite protests by General García, Ford and his Rangers next took aim on Reynosa and Old Reynosa, the most anti-American communities on the river. While Stoneman's two companies of the bluecoat cavalry waited at Edinburg, Ford and his Rangers crossed the river in the night, hoping to surround Old Reynosa before the *Cortinistas* could escape. Failing to find any of Cortina's men in the town, the Rangers hurried downriver to Reynosa, only to be met by four hundred angry citizens, including the Mexican National Guard and men from neighboring ranches. Denying that any *Cortinistas* were in the town, the defiant and heavily armed townsmen demanded the Rangers leave Mexico immediately.[120]

So serious was the situation on the Rio Grande that one of the most respected officers in the army, Col. Robert E. Lee, was sent to the border to take command of the U.S. Army. On April 3, after joining Major Heintzelman at Ringgold Barracks, Colonel Lee sent a letter across the river to Camargo addressed to the governor of Tamaulipas, Andrés Treviño. Without mentioning Cortina by name, Lee asked the governor to "break up and disperse the bands of banditti which have ... sought protection within Mexican territory."[121] After learning that Treviño was in Tampico, Lee sent a similar letter to the civil and military authorities in Reynosa.[122] The next day the alcalde, Francisco Zepeda, replied that he was under orders to break up the *Cortinistas;* at the same time, he complained bitterly of the Rangers' invasion of Mexico. Arriving in Brownsville, Lee wrote General García, demanding the immediate arrest of all *Cortinistas* in the city.[123] While he was at Fort Brown, Lee received a letter from Governor Treviño saying that, because the American demands were diplomatic in nature, they would have to be answered by President Juárez. Treviño did ask the Mexican military and civil authorities on the river to do everything possible to prevent Cortina from crossing into Texas.[124]

On April 7, 1860, when revelers at a noisy fiesta in Reynosa fired into a camp of Rangers on the opposite bank, the Rangers returned the fire, seriously wounding two citizens. Once again, the situation on the river became volatile. The Rangers, Heintzelman wrote, "intend to make war if they can."[125] Mexican customs officials, as well as men and women from the town, were "unable to go to the river for water, since they had repeatedly been fired on from the north bank," Zepeda complained. Fearing an attack, townsmen again barricaded the plaza and pulled several cannon into position. Citizens want only to "live in peace, tranquility, and in harmony with their neighbors across the river," he continued, but they were determined to defend their homes.[126]

In the war that engulfed the Lower Rio Grande Valley in 1859–60, 151 of Cortina's men were killed and perhaps twice that many wounded. Fifteen Americans and eighty Mexicans not affiliated with Cortina also lay dead. "It will be a long time before the ill-feeling engendered by this outcome can be allayed," Heintzelman predicted.[127]

Republics on the Verge of War

Diplomatic and political reverberations from the Cortina War echoed from the valley of the Rio Grande like a tidal wave and came close to bringing on an untimely and unwanted war between the United States and Mexico. At the forefront of the question of war and peace was the newly elected governor of Texas, the legendary Sam Houston. Sworn in as governor on December 21, 1859, only days before Cortina's crushing defeat at Rio Grande City, Houston gave Cortina full play in his inaugural address: "Our entire boundary bordering upon the Rio Grande ... is in an exposed and excited condition. The utter disregard of all law and order in Mexico has communicated its unhappy influence to this side of the Rio Grande."[128] From the time he was first elected to the U.S. Senate, Houston had pushed to impose an American protectorate over Mexico, and, in the process of forging and ratifying the Treaty of Guadalupe Hidalgo, he had argued for a boundary far south of the Rio Grande. The Cortina War had served only to reinforce Houston's preconceived convictions. Moreover, Houston was contemplating throwing his hat into the race for the presidency in 1860, and he welcomed any occasion that would introduce him to a national audience.

Despite his position, Houston was sympathetic toward Mexican Texans in his inaugural address. Laws were to be "executed alike to all citizens of whatever tongue, and none need fear prejudice," he said.[129] The newly elected governor promised "a proper inquiry into the causes which have led to the recent disorders," and the implementation of measures "to prevent the recurrence of similar outbreaks."[130] Houston also set out to have all the laws of Texas translated into Spanish, and he even published a proclamation in both English and Spanish, a copy of which he sent by express to Brownsville along with a personal letter for Cortina.[131] "If the persons who have been participating in the late disturbances disperse and return to their homes and peaceful avocations, I advise ... that no arrests be attempted for the present," Houston wrote. "If a different course is pursued, it can be productive of no good, but might cause a renewal of the disorders, which I desire should cease," he continued.[132] It was not until February 9, 1860, that Ford "forwarded" the letter to Cortina. The historical record does not contain evidence of a response.[133]

Promising a full investigation, Houston pleaded with the "citizens of the Rio Grande country" to stop the wanton violence. Those displaced should "return to their homes" and resume "their lawful pursuits." Nevertheless, any persons "holding allegiance to a foreign government ... arrested with arms in their hands ... will be treated as bandits and invaders." If Cortina or anyone else had "been wronged, their cause shall be heard."[134] Houston would use all constitutional means to preserve the rights of every citizen. Mexican Texans, the governor feared, were being stereotyped as criminals and revolutionaries. In reality, they were "good and true" citizens and "should be treated as such" by "all Texians."[135]

Pushing the Border South

As promised, Houston sent two commissioners, both members of the Texas legislature, to the border "with the greatest dispatch" to "inquire into the cause, origin and progress of the disturbances on the Rio Grande."[136] Both were respected members of the Texas legislature. South Carolina–born, thirty-five-year-old State Senator Richard H. Taylor was a wealthy Mexican War veteran and slaveholder, while thirty-two-year-old José Ángel Navarro was a Harvard graduate who represented Bexar County in the Texas House of Representatives. Both were recommended by Virginia-born John L. Haynes, outspoken and farsighted state representative from Starr County who was one of the few men in the legislature to objectively view the origins of the war. "I did not wish men living on the Rio Grande, whose passions were aroused and whose prejudices would control them, to act upon an investigation like this," Haynes wrote.[137] Hurriedly making their way to Indianola by stage and down the coast by steamer to Brazos Santiago, Taylor and Navarro reached Brownsville on January 10, 1860, after only seven days.[138]

Navarro carried with him a letter from his well-known father, José Antonio Navarro, addressed to Cortina.[139] The older Navarro—a hero of the Texas Revolution—had never met Cortina in person, but he wrote as a "compatriot," someone who had fled Mexico to find happiness under the "flag of the United States." If Cortina's "unfortunate uprising" was, as rumored, indeed a result of a "local disturbance" and he had been "provoked by a few malicious and bad Americans of Brownsville," Navarro assured him that such "infamous men" had nothing in common with the "American people in general." Although a few men possessed a "crafty, evil speculative spirit" and a "thirst for the acquisition of lands," Cortina's revolution was "destitute of every hope of success and glory." Moreover, a "valiant man [should] not lose his life in a horrible and hopeless cause," Navarro went on to lecture Cortina.[140] Peace and tranquility should be reestablished in the Rio Grande Valley as soon as possible.

In Brownsville, the two commissioners were shocked by the cool reception they received. Fearing that Houston would negotiate with Cortina and make him a larger-than-life hero and embolden him further, the merchant and ranching elite rejected any peace initiative. Several "good citizens" even threatened to search the commissioner's baggage for evidence they were intending to "enter into a treaty with Cortina."[141] Their icy welcome was largely a result of Senator Edwin B. Scarborough's having inflamed local passions by writing an "incendiary" letter to Adolphus Glavecke saying the two commissioners were being sent to the border to negotiate with Cortina. Scarborough had also written Peter Champion, claiming that Houston was intending to aid Cortina. Scarborough was baffled at how the governor could send "Taylor and Navarro as commissioners to 'treat' with this desperate outlaw and to gather up material to justify his acts!"[142]

Opposition to the commissioners also spread upriver to Rio Grande City. "How long will our Chief Magistrate pretend to believe the Cortina movement [is] only a private matter for the purpose of gratifying a private pique and to revenge wrongs perpetrated on Mexicans by us Americans?

Poor Mexicans! Harmless race. They are certainly deserving the sympathy of General Houston," an angry citizen sarcastically wrote the *Corpus Christi Ranchero*.[143] The *Brownsville American Flag* also fanned the flames against Houston's peace initiative by sarcastically announcing that the governor had sent "'Ministers Plenipotentiary to the Court of Cortinas' located somewhere in those 'amiable chaparrals' of the Rio Grande."[144] In Brownsville, there was talk of "ropes" and "vengeance," not negotiations. Yet, as Haynes astutely observed, "the poisoned arrows shot at General Houston rattle harmlessly on the shield of his great reputation."[145] Both Haynes and Houston anticipated the occupation of Mexican territory, but they wanted it done "under the stars and stripes."

Navarro and Taylor were also taken aback when they learned from Major Heintzelman that the Rangers were out of control. In fact, the Rangers had "been burning ranches & hanging & shooting Mexicans without authority by law and are more dreaded than Cortina," the commissioners informed Houston.[146] It was better "to have one hundred good men than one thousand indifferent or bad ones," they concluded.[147]

Navarro and Taylor were also shocked to find hundreds of filibusters gathering in Brownsville, many of them members of the shadowy Knights of the Golden Circle (KGC), a secret, ardent, states' rights, pro-Southern, anti-Catholic organization that was hoping to create a slave empire in Mexico.[148] A few of the "notorious filibusters" such as Samuel A. Lockridge had fought with the Rangers at Rio Grande City. Arriving by land and sea, leaders of the KGC bragged they would soon have two thousand men on the border.[149] Moreover, Taylor and Navarro concluded, the Knights were inflaming the situation on the Rio Grande and the people in Matamoros feared an attack.[150]

Despite their hostile reception, the commissioners set out to gather as much information as possible. Influential men such as Stillman, Yturria, King, Kenedy, Powers, and even Cortina's hated enemies, Adolphus Glavecke and Robert Shears, came forth to testify. Typical of the testimony was that of Mayor Powers, who told the commissioners that Cortina was trying to "raise a quasi revolution . . . to cover his former misdeeds [and] make himself influential."[151] Like his colleagues, Powers was fearful Houston would negotiate with Cortina and heighten his reputation and popularity in the Valley. The two commissioners also rushed across the river to meet the authorities in Matamoros, including Gen. Guadalupe García. García promised to do everything possible to "break up the rendezvous of Cortina in Mexico," but Navarro and Taylor had little "hope of his ability to do so." Authorities in Matamoros, Navarro concluded, were only pretending to be hostile to Cortina. In reality, "they encourage him and . . . privately give him aid and assistance and wish him God speed in his enterprise."[152] Shouts of "*¡Que viva Cortina!*" were still common on the streets of the city.

Despite falling ill while in Brownsville, Taylor and Navarro were able to complete their work and forward their conclusions to Houston. The Cortina War "originally arose from private or personal feuds among parties," they concluded.[153] Moreover, there was "a great deal of animosity and hard feelings existing among the Mexicans on the opposite side of the river on account of these difficulties of Cortina."[154] Nevertheless, Cortina was a "thief and a murderer," they wrote.[155] Navarro was particularly concerned that, if drastic measures were not taken immediately, the situation could degenerate into "a war of races." In the final analysis, the commissioners told Houston exactly what he had suspected all along. Cortina "had aroused much bad feelings" among the "lower order of *rancheros*" who had "a deep seated hostility" toward "everything American." At the same time, intentional or unintentional, Taylor and Navarro fed Houston's political ambitions. There were intelligent men in Tamaulipas, they told the governor, who "regard a protectorate as the only means by which Mexico can be redeemed from the reign of outlaws and petty tyrants." Only "by taking possession of a sufficient portion of the border sections of Mexico" could Texas avoid future incursions.[156] In terms of its effectiveness as a boundary, the Rio Grande was "worse than an imaginary one," and a defensive line should be established "west of the Rio Bravo." Considering the aid Cortina had received from Matamoros, the United States and Mexico were "no longer ... neighbors in peace."[157]

While Taylor and Navarro labored in Brownsville, the legislature authorized Houston to raise a regiment of cavalry to defend the southern frontier. In need of money to equip and pay such a force, Houston sent forty-seven-year-old Corpus Christi state senator and West Point graduate Forbes Britton to Washington with dispatches for President Buchanan. "I deplore the situation of Texas. An empty treasury, the Indian troubles ... and forays from Mexico on our southern borders," the governor told the president. If necessary, Houston warned, Texas would "resort to the indefeasible right of self-defense," and muster ten thousand men "anxious ... to make reclamation upon Mexico for all her wrongs."[158]

When fighting erupted on the Rio Grande again in March 1860, Houston was even more assertive in calling for the occupation of the south bank and establishing a protectorate over northern Mexico. "The territory of Texas has been invaded [and] unless prompt measures are adopted by the Federal Government circumstances will impel a course on the part of Texas which she desired to avoid," Houston told Secretary of War John B. Floyd. "Texas cannot be invaded with impunity," he warned.[159] "There will be stirring times on the Rio Grande ere long. What are you doing?" Houston wrote Ben McCulloch in Washington.[160]

Promoting Intervention

Arriving in the capital in early March 1860, Britton rushed off to see Secretary of War Floyd, an inept Virginian, but found the secretary at a cabinet meeting. Able to meet with President Buchanan instead, the two men talked late into the night, the president asking a number of pointed questions. Did "the Constitution of Texas give Governor Houston the right to invade Mexico?" and was it the "intention of ... Governor Houston to raise a force to invade Mexico?"[161] Britton replied that the constitution gave the governor no such power but Houston wanted the frontier of Texas protected, and he "would not hesitate one moment to do so." Houston "would not raise troops for the purpose of invading Mexico but for the purpose of defending Texas," Britton continued, but the governor hoped the federal government's actions would render those by Texas unnecessary.

When Britton asked for funds to equip a regiment of Texas troops to fight Cortina and restore order, President Buchanan hesitated, saying that Congress would have to appropriate the money and only then would he authorize such a force. But the Republicans were certain to kill any such bill, the president said. When Britton met with the president a second time, Buchanan was unbending and sent him to see Floyd. Floyd responded that he had already directed Colonel Lee "to place all of his available force in Texas upon the Rio Grande."[162] This was senseless, Britton argued, because it would leave the entire western frontier of Texas defenseless against the Comanches and Kiowas.

Although Britton realized there was little hope of receiving a commitment from Washington for an all-out war against Cortina, several congressmen, including Bob Johnson of Arkansas, recommended Houston act on his own, "call out a force, cross the Rio Grande & punish Mexico." Meeting with Floyd a second time, Britton inquired how the secretary would react should Houston "deem it necessary to raise a force to invade Mexico." Such an act "would be looked upon with astonishment!" Floyd replied. "Would your department oppose by bayonetts [sic] & fight troops of Texas who would cross in such a contingency?" Britton bluntly asked. "No, sir," Floyd replied, "but I would stand upon this side & clap my hands & holler hurrah!"[163] While Britton was in Washington, Houston kept up the pressure by telegraphing Floyd that he was planning to raise five thousand Texas volunteers and was "preparing to act at a moment's warning."[164] The regular army was incapable of protecting the Rio Grande frontier, Houston argued, and as a result, Texas was left no alternative but to raise such an army itself.[165]

When army headquarters in San Antonio telegraphed Washington in mid-March 1860 that Cortina had left the border and that the war on the Rio Grande was over, Houston realized any hope of invading Mexico was gone.¹⁶⁶ Moreover, President Buchanan telegraphed saying he would not support any effort to raise five thousand volunteers, that Cortina had "retired into the interior of Mexico." Not only were there 2,651 soldiers, a large part of the American army, assigned to protect the Texas frontier, but also ten new companies of 842 men were on their way from New Mexico, Floyd said.¹⁶⁷

But Houston never took his eyes off the border. Learning the specifics about the hanging of Cabrera and other Mexican Texans, Houston demanding a full accounting.¹⁶⁸ Hearing that filibusters were still arriving on the border, Houston issued a proclamation on March 21, 1860, warning that "armed bands" were in violation of the law and that any invasion of Mexico was illegal.¹⁶⁹ As filibusters drifted north, any hope of invading Mexico faded into history with the rapidly approaching secessionist crisis.

SCHEMING AND DREAMING

Several months earlier, Secretary of State Lewis Cass secretly sent fifty-eight-year-old Duff Green to Texas as a special agent to investigate "atrocities committed by parties of armed Mexicans during insurrections in Texas." A political intriguer and champion of the South, Green was a Jacksonian Democrat turned Whig, who became a Democrat again, who had served as consul at Galveston at the time Texas was an independent republic. Long a proponent of Manifest Destiny, Green had gone to Mexico prior to the Mexican War in hopes of acquiring New Mexico and California. After the war he had helped to develop far-reaching plans for a canal that would connect the Sabine River to the Rio Grande. No one in Washington was thought to be more familiar with the situation on the border than the veteran Green. Arriving in Galveston in early December 1859, he met with several individuals who had recently arrived from Brownsville. "What we require on the Rio Grande is a person in command who has no interest in provoking a war with Mexico," Green told Cass.¹⁷⁰

Passing himself off as a railroad executive, Green reached Austin in a bitterly cold blue norther to learn from outgoing Governor Runnels that Cortina had defeated the Rangers. Austin was in a state of panic. There were even worries that Cortina's continued success would motivate bands of Indians to unite with the *Cortinistas* and launch a series of bloody frontier raids. At first, Green was convinced, as Twiggs had concluded, that affairs on the Rio Grande were greatly exaggerated and, in part, a veiled attempt to secure a greater expenditure of public money. The citizens of Brownsville were like "the fable of the boy & the wolf," he concluded.¹⁷¹

After attending Houston's inaugural, Green informed Cass of the new governor's proclamation in which Houston told the *Cortinistas* to "lay down their arms" while at the same time promising a "redress of grievances of which they complain." Then on December 31, 1859, Houston received John S. Ford's glowing report of Cortina's defeat at Rio Grande City, and everything changed. Cortina was no longer viewed as a major threat, yet Green planned to travel to Brownsville with Henry Lawrence Kinney (who spoke Spanish and who knew Cortina) and report more accurately on the "cause of the disturbances."[172]

When Rangers began returning to Central Texas from the border, both Houston and Green were shocked by the degree of devastation in the Rio Grande Valley and how the Rangers had set fire to Santa Rita and several structures at Rancho del Carmen. In Austin, there was a "multitude of rumors" emanating from the border. One held that Cortina's "beautiful wife and a daughter" had been violated and that Cortina had vowed "vengeance on the offenders."[173] In early January, Houston confided to Green his plans to invade Mexico. Although the governor openly promoted peace, Green observed, there was a desire "on the part of many in this state to involve the U.S. in a war with Mexico."[174] Long an advocate of southern expansion, Green was nonetheless concerned that the Rangers would start a war on the Rio Grande.[175] In a confidential letter dated February 10, 1860, Green told Cass to urge prudence on Buchanan. "All that prevents Gov. Houston from moving on Mexico with a major force is money and a justifiable pretext," Green concluded. There was little doubt the governor was interested in a protectorate leading to an eventual occupation of Mexico. "If Houston did move on Mexico," Green went on to say, "he would not only carry Texas & the South ... 'the Protectorate' would become the controlling issue in the next Presidential Election."[176] The crisis on the border might well propel Houston into the Executive Mansion.

Changing of the Tide

As the Mexican military began cooperating with the American military, Cortina decided to take his family into the Burgos Mountains near Ciudad Victoria, far to the south. Yet, as he rode away from the border, many of his men remained active. Three *Cortinistas* were apprehended in Texas and brought into Brownsville, where it was thought they would be hanged. The men, however, managed to bribe their Brownsville jailer and escape into Mexico.[177]

Attempting to prevent Cortina from returning to Texas, the army stationed two companies of the 1st Artillery at Fort Brown and two companies of the 8th Infantry at Ringgold Barracks. Colonel Lee also sent Captain Stoneman's two companies of the 2nd Cavalry to patrol the border between Brownsville and Rio Grande City.[178] The army was doubtful Cortina would raid Texas again, but should he do so, men from both sides of the river "would again flock to his standard," Lee speculated.[179] Not only did Cortina have American diplomats in a dither, he was still capable of igniting a war between the United States and Mexico.

By early May 1860, Cortina was reported to be back on the Rio Grande and camped at a ranch near Reynosa with forty of his men. The American military immediately send Captain Stoneman's two companies of cavalry into action. Plans called for one company to cross the river on the night of May 2 to surround Cortina's camp before daylight, while another detachment would cross the river at or near Reynosa and prevent the *Cortinistas* from escaping.[180] Just as plans were being finalized for yet another invasion of Mexico, Mexican authorities reported Cortina was downriver at Palo Blanco and that he had been seen at a *laguna* less than seven miles from Matamoros. From there, he had gone south again.[181] As it turned out, Cortina's return to the border had been an attempt to gather some of his livestock before heading into the Burgos Mountains. Mexican authorities promised the American military that any alcalde known to be sheltering *Cortinistas* would be arrested and that Cortina would be pursued "night and day."[182]

In late May, at the head of seventy to eighty men, Cortina was reported to be at Laguna de los Indios between Reynosa and China.[183] By early June, Mexican authorities spotted him with forty-five of his men at Rancho Santa Cruz, forty miles southwest of Matamoros, where it was said he was butchering beef. General García told Maj. Henry J. Hunt, who had replaced Lee on the border, that the Mexican military was determined to capture Cortina. When a military force from Matamoros and Reynosa was sent in pursuit, the *Cortinistas* dispersed, but not before one of Cortina's captains, Florencio Fernández, was wounded and executed. Another *Cortinista*, Florencio Cisneros, was taken back to Matamoros and jailed, but Cortina had slipped away.[184] Well into the late summer and early fall of 1860, rumors of Cortina's presence on the Rio Grande were common. In fact, a constant stream of misinformation came from south of the border.[185] Many in Texas were convinced Cortina was still capable of igniting a war.

Beyond the din of the *Brownsville American Flag*'s complaints that the border was in turmoil, an American officer wrote that by July 1860, everything on the Rio Grande was "perfectly quiet ... since the departure of the Rangers." Cortina had not "been heard from for a long time—and no one appears to know where he is or what he is doing."[186] Ironically, a few of the *Cortinistas* who remained on the Rio Grande were rumored to have joined with a few former Rangers and members of the Knights of the Golden Circle in stealing cattle and horses on both sides of the border.[187] Moreover, a number of outlaws were committing crimes in Cortina's name. In fact, the wily revolutionary was being blamed for crimes all the way from Rio Grande City to the Gulf of Mexico, all of which he could not have conceivably been connected. "Cortina and all who take advantage of his name are now living upon the people on the other side of the river," it was observed."[188]

Fighting the Conservatives

His shadow on the Rio Grande long and wide, Cortina joined the Liberal army of Benito Juárez in the struggle against conservatives and reactionaries led by army generals Miguel Miramón and Leonardo Márquez. Although defeated in vicious fighting in central Mexico, Miramón was installed by the conservatives as interim president on August 18, 1860. Following a series of bloody encounters around Guadalajara, Cortina saw action against the reactionaries on the high plateau in the state of San Luis Potosí. Here with a squadron of *Tamaulipecan* cavalry in March 1860, he not only drove off a large insurrectionist force that was besieging San Luis Potosí but also attacked the rear guard of the insurgents near Pozo del Carmen, northeast of the city, as they retreated into the mountains. Again on October 11, he was instrumental in defeating a reactionary force outside the state capital.[189] As "Comandante de Sección," he was with the twenty-five-thousand-man Liberal army that forced Miramón from Mexico City on December 24. Serving the republic in south central Mexico gave him the opportunity to see the capital and the great beauty of the country for the first time. Despite Cortina's valuable service to the Liberal army, many citizens on the Rio Grande frontier were sure they had not heard the last of the indefatigable Juan Nepomuceno Cortina.

Chapter Four

A Frontier in Flames

> *Let us give to the world a testimony that all are worthy successors to Hidalgo and Morelos. Long Live Mexico! Long Live Independence! Long Live the State of Tamaulipas!*
>
> JUAN CORTINA

RESTLESS AND RESISTLESS, Cortina returned to the border in early 1861 with a determination to continue his revolution and create a new sense of social justice. Although leading armed men in rebellion against the government had long been a way of life on the Rio Grande, he realized the righteous forces of indignation he had unleashed were different and could not easily be suppressed. Being harshly judged and vilified by Anglo Texans served only to incite him. He would establish his place in history and continue the struggle against those who would dispossess Mexicans of their land.

With the secession of Texas and the rapidly unfolding American Civil War, Cortina watched from the south bank of the Rio Grande as the hated Rangers returned to South Texas. The blood ran thick, as the Rangers executed anyone suspected of being a *Cortinista*. Worse, much of their killing appears to have been indiscriminate. The *Corpus Christi Ranchero* ran the following brief notice in March that proved typical: "A Mexican *vaquero*, in the employ of Sheriff Brown[e] was found shot between here and Point Isabel. The cause was traced to some of Capt. [John] Donelson's command."[1] Countless other killings went unreported. For his part, Cortina remained intrepid. Despite the numerous indictments against him in Cameron County, he crossed the river in April 1861 to visit his ranch at San José, where he told friends he would return in a few weeks with a force of Mexicans and Indians.[2] His influence with the underprivileged along the twisting and turbulent waters of the Rio Grande had not diminished following his defeat at Rio Grande City. It was upriver in Zapata County, though, where he would again etch his name in the bloody history of Texas.

With a political structure similar to other border counties, a clique of merchants and large landowners had administered Zapata County since its creation in 1856. Heading the lot was a cunning Englishman named Henry Redmond. Purchasing land on the Rio Grande as early as 1839, Redmond married into an influential local family and survived the bloody Federalists-Centralists wars that swept the area. Redmond was instrumental in establishing the county that was named after the mulatto hero of the Republic of the Rio Grande, Col. Antonio Zapata. In time, Redmond developed a lucrative trading business from his store near San Bartolo (or what was called Redmond's Ranch), just upriver from the county seat of Carrizo. He also became postmaster at Carrizo, justice of the peace, and the first county judge, as well as collector of customs at San Bartolo.[3] The political machine running the county included John D. Mussett, an articulate Arkansas lawyer who was the deputy collector of customs at Carrizo, as well as County Judge Isidro Vela, Sheriff Pedro Díaz, County Clerk Trinidad Zampano, Tax Assessor-Collector Fernando Uribe, and District Clerk Agustín Díaz. Still another player in county politics was Blas María Uribe, a wealthy merchant and rancher who controlled the votes in the small rock and adobe village of San Ignacio, upriver from Carrizo.

The degree to which the *patrón* system controlled the county was indicated by a vote of 212 to 0 in favor of secession. Prior to the election, Judge Vela had made it known throughout the county that anyone failing to vote for secession would be fined fifty cents, a considerable amount of money to many of the poor, most of them Cortina sympathizers.[4] When several individuals failed to show up at the polls, Vela ordered them arrested.

Insurrection in Zapata County

On April 12, the day before the first thunder that would shake the nation to its roots with the surrender of Fort Sumter in the far-off South Carolina harbor of Charleston, forty armed Tejanos and Mexicanos under the leadership of a thirty-nine-year-old ranchero and *Cortinista* named Antonio Ochoa, seized control of Precinct Three in the southern part of the county. Ochoa and his followers, it was said, were threatening to kill all the gringos in the county and hang Sheriff Díaz.[5] Influenced by Cortina, Ochoa and his small band were said to be "marching about the county in armed bodies threatening the lives of Tom, Dick, and John Doe."[6] Some feared Ochoa would seize the county seat of Carrizo. The men "were not only attempting to keep the county officers from taking the [Confederate] oath of office," but, the *Corpus Christi Ranchero* reported, they were also "threatening to forcibly take all public money." Moreover, they were refusing to abide by the laws of the state of Texas.[7] Ochoa and his men were confronted by Judge Vela, the well-to-do owner of Rancho Clareño, a small settlement on the river fifteen miles below Carrizo, who persuaded the men to return to their homes. Although the dissidents backed down, they denounced the Confederacy in a *pronunciamiento* they defiantly presented to Judge Vela.

From his fortified ranch near San Bartolo and realizing he was a target of the revolt, Redmond was in a state of panic; the insurrectionists, Redmond conveyed, demanded their *pronunciamiento* be "forwarded to the U.S.," which Ochoa thought was "a few miles on the other side of Bexar." It is "hard to say how far their ignorance will lead them," he continued.[8] Redmond's friend Mussett dispatched an express to Stephen Powers in Brownsville pleading for a "permanent force" for Carrizo, saying the lives of the people in the small community were in "great jeopardy." Now is "the time to save us from the cruel mercy of rob[b]ers and assassins," Mussett continued.[9]

Some in Texas saw the insurrection in Zapata County as Unionist-inspired. Ochoa and his men, it was reported, were in favor of "Old Abe, the rail splitter" and were demanding to communicate with Federal authorities in the North. With ethnic, social, and economic undercurrents, the threatened violence was, in reality, a reaction to the repressive political oligarchy and boss rule in the county. Although Ochoa owned a small ranch near Clareño, most of his followers were poor vaqueros and *labradores*, many with families and roots in Guerrero, across the river from Carrizo.[10] Some had ridden with Cortina in 1859 and 1860. One reporter from the *Corpus Christi Ranchero* could not be any clearer about his opinion: "I will tell you that that hell-hole of iniquity, Guerrero, has got to be wiped out before perfect security will be obtained for our Rio Grande settlements."[11]

Battle at Carrizo

To ensure peace in the county, Capt. Matthew Nolan—sheriff of Nueces County, Mexican War hero, Cortina War veteran, and commander of a hastily organized Confederate company of twenty-two men at Fort McIntosh—was sent downriver from Laredo. After a dusty fifty-five-mile ride, Nolan bivouacked near Redmond's Ranch on the afternoon of April 14, 1861.[12] The captain was determined to crush any resistance to state authority. Judge Vela swore out arrest warrants for Ochoa and eighty of his men. Captain Nolan, Judge Vela, and Sheriff Díaz, whom the *Cortinistas* were threatening to hang, immediately took up the line of march for Rancho Clareño, which was said to be a *Cortinista* "recruiting station" and headquarters for Ochoa.

Reaching the small village before daylight on April 15, Nolan carefully deployed his men around the ranch, and Sheriff Díaz ordered the insurrectionists, many of them still asleep, to surrender. Most were in the process of doing so when one insurgent, according to Nolan, fired at his men. One of the Confederate volunteers later confessed, however, that not a single shot was fired in defense.[13] Regardless of the truth, Nolan ordered an all-out attack. Outnumbered, caught off-guard, and surrounded, Ochoa's men never had a chance. Many were gunned down where they stood while others were killed as they fled toward the river. Although Nolan later bragged that "nine Black Republicans" were killed in the battle, several of those who died were said to have been noncombatants and might have been unarmed. Ochoa, the leader of the movement, was across the river in Guerrero at the time, but two of his lieutenants, Nepomuceno and Santiago Vela, were killed.[14] Twelve years later, a committee sent by the Mexican government to investigate border problems concluded that "inoffensive inhabitants were assassinated."[15]

In the days following the massacre at Rancho Clareño, rumors circulated that Cortina had formed an alliance with Unionists in Texas and Federal authorities in the North.[16] Hoping to avenge the victims of the Clareño Massacre, Cortina had indeed decided to reassert himself in Texas. Along with Teodoro Zamora, Antonio Ochoa, and a handful of loyal followers, Cortina set his sights on Carrizo. Hearing of his approach, Judge Vela fled with his family to the safety of Redmond's Ranch. Although the judge received assurances from Mexican authorities in Guerrero that they would do everything possible to apprehend Cortina and Ochoa, Vela was sure the promises were insincere because many citizens in the community were known to be Cortina sympathizers. It was also common knowledge that elements of the Mexican military were continuing to cooperate with the elusive revolutionary.[17] When Cortina's nemesis, Col. John S. Ford, now commanding Confederate forces on the Rio Grande frontier, received a plea for help from Redmond, he sent Capt. Santos Benavides, a seasoned Indian fighter and slave catcher who had recruited a Confederate cavalry company at Laredo, downriver to assist the Zapata County officials.

During the second week of May 1861, six heavily armed *Cortinistas* were arrested by the authorities in Camargo, but Cortina and twenty of his men rode on to Rancho Malahucea, eight miles from Mier.[18] As Cortina moved upriver, news spread by courier that he was on the march "with a considerable force." The road from Mier to Guerrero was said to be "swarming with small bands" of *Cortinistas* riding to join Cortina.[19] From Camargo, Alcalde Juan Villarreal sent expresses to Matamoros, Mier, Guerrero, and Laredo warning that Cortina was on the move. Villarreal told Henry Clay Davis there was little doubt that Cortina was determined to cross into Zapata County.[20]

By May 18, 1861, Cortina, although slowed by early summer rains, had gone into camp on the river below Guerrero. He was greeted by Ochoa, and that night Cortina rode into the town to meet with men known to be sympathetic to his cause. What he did not know was that the alcalde, Juan G. Garza, was appraising Captain Benavides of his movements.[21] Indeed, Garza dispatched twenty-five men under José María Hinojosa to the main ford on the Rio Grande, just below Guerrero, to impede Cortina's crossing. Finding another crossing, Cortina splashed across the Rio Grande into Texas. The next day, his advance guard ran into three of Captain Benavides's pickets below Carrizo, and a brief skirmish ensued. Reinforced by twenty sympathizers from Guerrero, Cortina's force was said to be growing hourly as many of the poor from Zapata County also joined his ranks.[22] Within hours, Cortina had Benavides's small band of Confederates surrounded at Redmond's Ranch. Cortina even sent two of his men under a flag of truce to the ranch in an attempt to persuade Benavides to leave and let Redmond, Vela, Mussett, and their friends defend themselves. Influential citizens from Guerrero crossed the river to assure Benavides that Cortina's only intention was to seek revenge on Redmond and those responsible for the bloodshed at Rancho Clareño. Cortina was determined, it was said, "to have Redmond's head before sundown."[23] But Benavides, who had been Webb County judge at the same time Redmond had been county judge in Zapata County, refused to forsake his friend.

As he had done when seizing Brownsville in 1859, Cortina cut all communications from Redmond's Ranch. With the cry of "Death to the Gringos!" some thought it was only a matter of time before Cortina swept the Rio Grande clean of Americans. One of Benavides's couriers was captured on the road from Roma to Carrizo, while a second rider, Ángel Jiménez, was seized on the road leading upriver to Laredo. Another messenger, however, was able to get past Cortina's pickets and reach Laredo safely.[24] Within hours, thirty-six graycoats under Refugio and Basilio Benavides, Santos Benavides's older brother and uncle, along with Lt. Charles Callahan, raced through the night to reach the besieged Confederates.

On the morning of May 22, 1861, after a fifty-five-mile ride in thirteen hours, the Laredo reinforcements ran into a party of Cortina's men near San Bartolo. A brief fight ensued. Hearing the sounds of gunfire, Santos Benavides and his men rushed to join the fray. Cortina, too, heard the sounds of battle and pushed his men forward. In a running fight that began at 1 P.M. and lasted forty minutes, Benavides completely routed Cortina's raiders. During the fighting, a number of the *Cortinistas* were caught sacking the small two-story Zapata County Courthouse. Several *Cortinistas* were shot down in the initial charge; others died when Benavides and his men pursued the partisans into the river. Six or seven *Cortinistas* were said to have drowned while attempting to swim the Rio Grande to Mexico. Eleven others appear to have been captured and were either shot or hanged by Benavides. Benavides wrote Ford, "I gave particular orders to my men that they should not take any prisoners, but kill all of the bandits that should fall into their hands; consequently I have no prisoners to report."[25]

With ten of his men, Cortina successfully "gained the opposite side of the river in safety, and in ascending its banks, faced about, took an apparent disdainful view of his recent antagonist and master, uncovered, and, with characteristic dignity, waved his hat, bidding them in the blandest tone ... a courteous temporary adieu, informing them that he would give them another call in a few days."[26] For his gallant defeat of Cortina at Carrizo, Benavides was proclaimed a hero throughout Texas.

When Confederate authorities complained to Gov. Santiago Vidaurri, powerful caudillo of Nuevo León and Coahuila, that Cortina had attacked Carrizo, Vidaurri was largely unresponsive, saying the fighting was in Tamaulipas and most of the reports of the incident were exaggerated anyway. While formally condemning the raid, the "Lion of the North" went on to say that it was only an isolated and "impotent maneuver" by Cortina who was a man "without representation."[27]

Retreating from Carrizo with a few of his men, Cortina headed downriver. From the Mexican bank of the river, a number of *Cortinistas* commenced a firefight with Confederates on the left bank at Rancho Clareño, causing Americans on the river to conclude that Cortina was again preparing to cross into Texas.[28] When two Americans were killed at Las Cuevas below Rio Grande City, Capt. John Donelson rode to the small settlement, arrested several men who were thought to be *Cortinistas,* and hanged one individual implicated in the crime.

Back in the Chaparral

Cortina suffered a serious setback when authorities in Matamoros began cooperating with Confederate authorities in Texas. At a meeting at Fort Brown, Gen. Guadalupe García agreed to not only assist the Confederates in apprehending Cortina, but also to take the field against the revolutionary himself. Permission was also given Captain Benavides to pursue Cortina into Mexico if necessary. Ford warned Benavides, however, that if he did cross the river, he should go "as a friend to Mexico, and as an enemy to the followers of Cortina and Ochoa." A force of 120 Mexican cavalrymen sent out from Matamoros in pursuit of Cortina was directed not to impede Benavides, should he be seen in Mexico.[29]

In early June 1861, Cortina crossed the Rio Grande below Las Cuevas and rode to the ranch of his lieutenant, Teodoro Zamora, where he reportedly said that in the rapidly unfolding Civil War north of the river he was for the Union. Moreover, he bragged, it was only a matter of time before he would be able to establish his headquarters at San Patricio on the Nueces River.[30] Cortina seemed always to enjoy agitating the American imagination. Many such rumors were strikingly similar to the disinformation that engulfed South Texas in 1859 and 1860. There was little doubt, nevertheless, that the vast majority of Tejanos in Hidalgo County remained sympathetic to Cortina.

In Mexico, one group of *Cortinistas* led by Zamora was concentrated south of the river at Rancho La Mesa, where they were active in stealing livestock in Texas. A smaller band of Cortina adherents under Francisco Treviño was headquartered at Rancho La Bolsa and Rancho Capote on the south bank of the river, and they, too, were crossing into Hidalgo County "killing cattle, stealing horses, and depredating in various ways." Another band of *Cortinistas* operating near Reynosa Viejo was crossing and recrossing the river at will. Unable to control the frontier, Confederate authorities were fearful that the "bands of Cortina would soon overrun and plunder the settlements."[31] Fearing an attack, Texans were forced to guard Edinburg night and day while many of the women and children fled to Reynosa for safety. Noah Cox at Roma and Henry Clay Davis at Rio Grande City, fearful that Cortina would cross the river to "rob and murder" and "burn the towns on the Rio Grande," hastened to organize local militias.[32] "We are at war with a portion of the citizens of Mexico," Ford told Gov. Edward Clark.[33]

By late June, Cortina was in camp at a small ranch twelve miles southwest of Matamoros. Rumors persisted, however, that he was near Mier with fifty to two hundred men, boasting that he held a commission from both Benito Juárez and Abraham Lincoln. Other hearsay said he had met José María de Jesús Carvajal, and the two warriors had agreed to combine their forces to again fight the conservative reactionaries in Mexico.[34] By the early summer of 1861, with his small army down to less than fifty men and the Mexican military and civilian authorities cooperating with the Confederates, Cortina's situation became more precarious. Although many of the American filibusters who had gathered on the border in the wake of the Cortina War had drifted north to join the Confederate Army, Mexicans on the northeastern frontier feared more military incursions into their country should Cortina remain active. With Gov. Andrés Treviño of Tamaulipas ordering his arrest, Cortina came to realize that, despite his popularity on the border, events had turned against him and he decided to retreat again into the interior.[35] He would say later he owed his safety to Carvajal, who provided "asylum" in the "Sierrita." The Sierrita was the Sierra de San Carlos, a small range of mountains fifty miles west of San Fernando and some 130 miles southwest of Matamoros, where Carvajal owned property near the small village of Burgos. Although forced from the border, events from afar again cast him into the forefront of Mexican history.

With Comonfort at Puebla

Just as Cortina had laid much of the Lower Rio Grande Valley to waste, the Mexican War of the Reform, the most passionate and horrifying civil war in Mexican history, had devastated much of Mexico, left the landscape dotted with burned haciendas, roads in disrepair, fields neglected, and villages sacked. Thousands of exhausted, crippled, and frustrated Mexicans drifted from village to village searching for work. Caught between the reactionary Conservatives and the uncompromising Liberals, President Ignacio Comonfort, a bureaucrat of minor importance who had been thrust into the presidency in 1855, resigned in March 1861, and Benito Juárez, a liberal anticlerical Zapotec Indian from Oaxaca, was elected. Inheriting a bankrupt nation and the French, English, and Spanish demanding repayment of overdue loans, Juárez declared a two-year moratorium on such debts. In response, the three nations agreed on a joint occupation of the east coast to collect the debts. Although England and Spain were sincere in their pledge not to seek special advantage in Mexico, Louis Napoleon Bonaparte, nephew of Napoleon I, dreamed of planting the French tricolor in the New World and, in the process, reincarnating France's lost empire in America and rescuing the church in Mexico. When Spain and Great Britain withdrew their troops from Veracruz, Cortina watched as the reinforced French army moved inland. At the conservative and proclerical city of Puebla, Gen. Ignacio Zaragoza, a Goliad-born bespectacled patriot, prepared defenses and called for reinforcements.

Zaragoza wanted to establish defenses at the eastern base of the Sierra Madre to hold the French army under Gen. Charles Latrille in the fever zone of the *tierra caliente* where the *vómito negro* and yellow fever raged, but the French army, many of them veterans of the Crimean War, took Orizaba and pushed the Liberal army from the passes leading to the more temperate central plateau. Seizing Amozoc, General Latrille reached the outskirts of Puebla to find the streets blocked and the city fortified. Zaragoza had set up defenses on the north side of the city at a convent on the Cerro Guadalupe and at the nearby fort of Loreto. Seeing the Mexicans arrayed in a long line of infantry with cavalry on the flanks, General Latrille attacked on the morning of May 5—Cinco de Mayo—only to be hurled back by the stubborn and defiant defenders. Three times Latrille advanced; three times he was repulsed with terrible losses. In a drenching rain, he ordered a retreat only to be harassed by the Mexican cavalry. Three days later, the French broke camp and retreated to Amozoc and then back down the Cumbres de Acultzingo to tropical Orizaba. Reinforced with six thousand troops from Oaxaca, Zaragoza pursued the French and attacked them at Orizaba, only to be decisively repulsed.

In February 1863, with Zaragoza dead of typhus, the French army of some 24,400 men along with two thousand Mexicans advanced from Orizaba under a new commander, Gen. Élie Frédéric Forey. Reaching Puebla—the city of red roofs, steeples, and domes—early in March, the French adopted very different tactics from those of May 5, 1862.[36] Finding the forts guarding the city to be well defended, Forey invested the city and placed his troops in position where they could attack on all sides. Bombardment began on March 23 and continued for four long days. Although one of the forts, San Xavier, fell to the attackers, the Mexicans withdrew to nearby houses and continued their resistance. Fighting from street to street, the Mexican defenders now adeptly used the churches and monasteries for defense. Desperate to defend Puebla, Juárez called on former president Ignacio Comonfort to help rescue the city and the nation. In Tamaulipas, Comonfort began recruiting an army that would eventually number seven thousand patriots.

As the fighting raged at Puebla, Cortina remained in the mountains of Tamaulipas, realizing any future at Rancho del Carmen or anywhere north of the Rio Grande was increasingly unlikely. His destiny was now with his native Mexico, not Texas. Indicative of his emerging place in history, Cortina received a commission as a major in a squadron of volunteers he called the Frontier Scouts. His small force of barefooted, badly clothed, and poorly fed *Norteños,* often eating and sleeping on the march, made their way south over primitive roads through the green-shrouded Sierra Madre Oriental to the central plateau, where Comonfort advanced to within a few miles of Puebla. Here Cortina and his Frontier Scouts commenced destroying crops and ambushing supply convoys along the route to Veracruz. As a result, General Forey was forced to detach Gen. Achille Bazaine with an army that included Gen. Leonardo Márquez's Mexican troops to deal with Comonfort and Cortina. Bazaine marched west along the road to Mexico City then cut across country toward Comonfort's army that had positioned itself on the hill of San Lorenzo, twenty-five miles southeast of Puebla. Able to push past Comonfort's sentries, Bazaine reached the vicinity of the Liberal camp on May 8 at five o'clock in the morning and immediately launched a vicious attack. Although he fought bravely, Cortina and his men were routed, many barely able to escape with their lives. In all, over one thousand of Comonfort's men were killed and wounded; another one thousand were taken prisoner.

The crushing defeat at San Lorenzo had a depressing effect on the defenders of Puebla, who had held out for sixty-two days. With little ammunition, no food, and the French ready to press the attack, General Ortega surrendered the city on the morning of May 17, 1863. His twelve-thousand-man army included Gen. Mariano Escobedo and Gen. Porfirio Díaz, both of whom later escaped. Two days later, the French army triumphantly entered the city to be joyously welcomed by the clergy and citizens who saw themselves as being saved from the godless Liberals. Religious celebrations continued for days as French and Mexican flags were hoisted to commemorate the victory.

With an army of six thousand men, Juárez realized any defense of Mexico City against General Forey's twenty-five thousand troops would be fruitless. On the morning of May 31, he addressed a hastily convened session of

Cortina's black beard was showing tinges of gray when this formal portrait was made in Matamoros around 1864. *Author's collection*

Congress, saying the government of the republic must be moved to San Luis Potosí, two hundred miles to the north. As the Mexican flag was lowered over the presidential palace, Juárez entered his carriage and rode north through the night. Cortina and what remained of Comonfort's battered army followed. On June 8, as thousands of citizens turned out to welcome them, the French army entered Mexico City in triumph. Events were moving fast. On August 8, Napoleon III sent Maximilian von Hapsburg a telegram saying that an Assembly of Notables in Mexico City was offering him the throne. Both men had been assured that opposition to the French occupation would soon end.

Back on the Border

Promoted to lieutenant colonel at San Luis Potosí, Cortina returned to Matamoros to continue the struggle to maintain the increasingly desperate republic. Control of the lower border—what with revenues from the customs house in Matamoros—was essential to help finance the operations of the government. The Matamoros to which Cortina returned in 1864 was radically different from the city he left in 1861. With the American Civil War raging north of the border, Matamoros had taken on new life. To avoid the Union naval blockade of the Texas coast, cotton traders crowded the border. To many on the Rio Grande, it was not the Civil War but La Época del Algodón, a mercantile bonanza unseen in the history of the region. In Matamoros, the American consul, Leonard Pierce Jr., said there were "ox trains, mule trains, and trains of Mexican carts, all laden with cotton" arriving from "almost every town in Texas," and from as far away as Louisiana and Arkansas. As the cotton trade expanded, the Confederacy used the opportunity to import vast amounts of tin, lead, copper, iron, nitrate of potash, quicksilver, sulfur, saltpeter, powder, and percussion caps, as well as blankets, shoes, and coffee.[37]

Matamoros had become a "great thoroughfare to the Southern States." However, as Cortina learned, it was also a hornet's nest of intrigue. Here, "cotton was exchanged for English, French, Prussian and perhaps Harpers Ferry Rifles; here the convict gray clothing of England and France found a ready market in exchange for the cotton of Messrs. King & Kennedy [sic] & Co. and here the Jew and Gentile, Gog and Magog, found their first oasis from the cotton fields of Texas, on their way to Mecca (Liverpool)." By January 1864, more than 150,000 bales of cotton had been carried across the Rio Grande, and, by the end of the war, 320,000 bales had been sent into Mexico.[38] Although the demand for Tejano and Mexicano teamsters increased, the vast profits from the cotton trade went to the speculators and corrupt government officials.

At Matamoros, much of the cotton was placed in small, shallow-draft paddle steamers and taken sixty-five miles down the twisting, tortuous, and

Due to the extensive cotton trade, both Matamoros and Brownsville prospered during the years from 1862 to 1865. Many citizens on the Rio Grande would remember the American Civil War as La Época del Algodón. Cotton bales cross the river by ferry and on the *Santa Cruz* as more cotton waits on Levy Street in Brownsville. *Frank Leslie's Illustrated Newspaper,* December 5, 1863.

shallow confines of the river to Bagdad. Here, at the mouth of the river, many of the steamers, operating as lighters, hauled the cotton to the seagoing vessels anchored in the choppy waters of the gulf two to three miles offshore. As many as 150 ships, ranging from thirty-ton schooners to two-thousand-ton steamers from ports such as New Orleans, Havana, New York, Boston, Barcelona, Hamburg, Bremen, and Liverpool waited at Bagdad to take on cotton and discharge their cargoes.[39]

In less than three years, Bagdad had evolved from a small fishing village to a bustling, vibrant port of fifteen thousand citizens. Yet the *Matamoros Daily Ranchero* referred to the community as a "sand hole on the gulf," while a correspondent for the *New York Herald* found the town to be "a dirty, filthy place" where the "streets are covered with slime and mud puddles." To the *Herald* reporter, the sickly seaside community consisted of "dirty looking buildings" where "blockade runners, desperadoes, the vile of both sexes, adventurers, the Mexican and the rebel" gather and where "numberless groggeries and houses of worse fame [where] vice in its lowest form held high carnival." The *Brownsville Weekly Ranchero* described the town as a place where "fandangos were held every night and women as beautiful as houris exhibit their charms, without the least reserve."[40]

By 1864, as many as ten stagecoaches a day departed Matamoros for the thirty-five-mile, three-hour run to Bagdad. The road along the river was also lined with wagons and carts "loaded with goods for the Texas market." Despite frequent flooding, Bagdad offered "first class hotels, boarding houses, stores well-fitted with goods ... and restaurants without number," as well as brothels, saloons, gambling houses, and a small church. Fr. Pierre Fourrier Parisot, the French-born Oblate priest in Brownsville, proclaimed Bagdad "a veritable Babel, a Babylon, a whirlpool of business, pleasure, and sin."[41]

A bustling Bagdad, Mexico, and an armada of ships in the Gulf of Mexico can be seen in this rare image of the city by the sea. Photographs of Bagdad are exceptionally rare although this engraving was most likely made from one. *Carte de visite* copy of engraving by unknown artist, ca. 1864–65. *Brownsville Historical Association.*

Octaviano Zapata

While Cortina was fighting with the Liberals in central Mexico, his *Cortinistas* remained active on the Rio Grande. Raids into Texas paralyzed Confederate operations on the border and tied down troops vital to the South's fortunes elsewhere. Beginning in 1862, Union agents called *enganchados* commenced recruiting Tejanos and Mexicanos, many of them former *Cortinistas*. One such raider was thirty-two-year-old Octaviano Zapata, who owned a small ranch near Clareño in Zapata County. A *Cortinista* associate, Zapata had escaped the Clareño Massacre in April 1861 and, with his wife and three children, taken refuge with relatives in Guerrero. Burning with a desire to strike back at his enemies in Texas, Zapata recruited between sixty and eighty *Cortinistas* from Guerrero, Mier, and the small ranches along the river.[42]

In early December 1862, Zapata and his raiders crossed the Rio Grande and attacked a Confederate supply train near Roma. Three weeks later, another train of three wagons en route from Fort Brown to Ringgold Barracks and escorted by five soldiers was attacked by Zapata's raiders at Rancho Soledad near Las Cuevas, fifteen miles below Ringgold Barracks. The *Zapatistas* killed all the teamsters except one man who escaped to Ringgold Barracks. All the wagons were taken to the riverbank and plundered, the goods then carried into Mexico.[43] In retaliation, a company of Confederates from Ringgold Barracks rode to Rancho Soledad, where "strong circumstantial evidence" implicated many of the Tejano families living in the vicinity. As a result, the soldiers burned sixteen *jacales* and rode triumphantly back to Ringgold Barracks.

On the same day as the Rancho Soledad raid, a larger party of two hundred Mexicans under Zapata crossed into Zapata County, rode to the home of sixty-two-year-old Isidro Vela at Rancho Clareño, brutally dragged the judge out of his house, and hanged him from a mesquite tree. Before leaving, the raiders "posted a placard on the body warning that they would kill any person who dared to take the body down for burial."[44] Blaming Leonard Pierce, the American consul in Matamoros, for equipping and paying the raiders, José A. Quintero, Confederate agent in Tamaulipas and Nuevo León, met personally with Gov. Albino López in Matamoros. With the frontier stripped of troops who had been sent off to fight the *Imperialistas* at Tampico and in central Mexico, López said he was "powerless to pursue the bandits."[45]

One of Zapata's zealous recruits, Guillermo Vino, was active in stealing several herds of cattle from the Texas bank as well as thirty-two horses from a Confederate company near Roma.[46] Demanding that the alcalde of Mier assist in capturing the raiders, Capt. Refugio Benavides crossed into Mexico with fifty-four of his Laredo Confederates. Able to track the *Zapatistas* to Mesquital Laleño near Camargo, the raiders were found encamped in a large corral. In the ensuing fight, eighteen of the *Zapatistas* were killed, fourteen wounded, and several taken captive. Zapata, however, was able to escape into the chaparral. The captives taken in the fray were reported to have "escaped" but were probably executed as had been the case following Cortina's defeat at Carrizo two years earlier.[47] After torching several small *jacales* in the vicinity, the Confederates returned to Texas.

In early 1863, Zapata made his way to New Orleans. Receiving a shipment of arms from the Union army, he was also promised money, uniforms, and other rewards to help end the "Confederate War."[48] Returning to Bagdad on the steamer *Honduras*, "*¡Que Viva la Unión!*" became Zapata's battle cry as additional raids on Texas were planned. Confederates were eventually able to apply enough pressure on Mexican authorities to have Zapata arrested and imprisoned in Matamoros, although he was released. Then, at Mier, Zapata was accused of assassinating Col. Jesús García Ramírez of the Mexican National Guard and a close friend of Santos Benavides. In late August 1863, Mexican troops were ambushed and routed by Zapata on the road between Guerrero and Mier. In response, Benavides, now a major in the Confederate army, rode downriver to Rancho Clareño, crossed into Mexico, and followed the trail of Zapata and his men in the direction of Mier. Early on the morning of September 2, scouts located Zapata's camp in a mesquite thicket. In the furious attack that followed, Zapata and several of his men were killed.[49]

Collaborating with the Bluecoats

Arriving on the frontier, Cortina found that Juárez had appointed Manuel Ruiz military governor of Tamaulipas. Although Ruiz was sixteen years younger than Juárez, the two had been classmates in Oaxaca, studying law together. A leading Liberal, Ruiz had served as governor of Oaxaca and as Minister of Justice under both Comonfort and Juárez, at which time he had helped author the Law of the Reform. On the border, Ruiz had little alternative but to cooperate with Cortina's Confederate enemies in Texas because the flood of cotton and goods across the river was so beneficial to the Mexican economy. To the Confederates, Ruiz was "a true gentleman and patriot, and ... a staunch friend of the Confederate States."[50] On the Texas bank, Gen. Hamilton P. Bee was concerned, however, that Ruiz would allow Cortina to seize Brownsville as he had done in 1859.

Communicating with Union officials in New Orleans, Cortina was certain that with his assistance the Confederates could be forced to evacuate Brownsville. The "confusion was indescribable" in Brownsville, it was said, simply because of Cortina's presence across the river. The Confederates were so unnerved that, on the morning of September 12, 1863, one of Bee's sentinels reported that Cortina was crossing the river with three hundred men. As a result, jittery Confederates rushed to the riverbank and opened fire on several Mexican soldiers and civilians who were peacefully bathing in the river. Bee apologized to Governor Ruiz for the "unfortunate" occurrence and even offered reparations. But Cortina was to blame for the "excited state of feeling," Bee asserted. Moreover, Bee went on to say, Ruiz should "inquire into the antecedents of Cortina," who was "notorious for the many outrages committed against the lives and property of the citizens of Brownsville."[51]

In November 1863, Cortina watched from Matamoros as Union forces waded ashore on Brazos Island and began marching on Brownsville. Commanded by Gen. Nathaniel P. Banks, 6,998 men in twenty-six ships from

By 1836, Matamoros had a population of 16,372. During the Civil War, as many as forty thousand people of various nationalities had crowded into the city. The thriving center of commerce was by far the largest, most prosperous, and cosmopolitan community on the Rio Grande. *Institute of Texan Cultures.*

New Orleans came out of the gray, cold dawn. "The flag of the Union floats over Texas today," General Banks proudly told Abraham Lincoln.[52] The bluecoats were hoping to cut the flow of cotton and strangle Texas economically. But there were other reasons for sending an army to Texas. Believing the French Imperialists to be in violation of the basic tenets of the Monroe Doctrine, Lincoln hoped to wave the Stars and Stripes at the French Imperialists and coerce them into leaving Mexico.[53]

A number of leading Texas Unionists, including Edmund J. Davis and John L. Haynes, had gone to Washington, where they told Lincoln that a Union army presence in Texas would allow Unionists who were being persecuted throughout the state a safe haven from which to join the Federal army. Moreover, from a base on the Rio Grande, Mexican Texans, many of them former *Cortinistas* with a deep-rooted contempt for authorities in Texas, could be recruited into the Union army. Few Anglos understood the Mexican population on the Rio Grande frontier as did Davis and Haynes. In Washington, Lincoln appeared impressed with their proposal to "reinaugurate the National Authority on the Rio Grande first, and probably the Nueces also." Knowing that Cortina was bitterly opposed to the Confederates, Haynes communicated with him from New Orleans, and, as a result, Cortina said he would welcome a Union presence on the frontier.[54]

Adrián J. Vidal

The expected arrival of the Union army on the Rio Grande helped to spark a violent mutiny by the unpredictable eighteen-year-old Capt. Adrián J. Vidal, Mifflin Kenedy's impetuous stepson who was in command of a Confederate cavalry company at the mouth of the river. Only later did it become evident that Vidal was under the influence of Cortina. Vidal may have also been in communication with the commander of the Union navy blockading the lower Texas coast.[55] At any rate, only days prior to the arrival of the Union Army, General Bee dispatched two young privates, Jerry Literal and D. H. Dashiell, to Clarksville to order Vidal and his company back to Brownsville to help protect the military supplies and cotton in the town.

On the evening of October 28, just as darkness engulfed Bee's headquarters at Fort Brown, rumors reached the town that Vidal and his entire company had mutinied, seized three men at Clarksville, and executed one of them. With the help of Texas Unionists from Matamoros, Vidal reportedly planned to attack Brownsville during the night. At first, Bee dismissed the report as a malicious rumor, but two hours later, Private Literal raced his horse up to Bee's headquarters with shocking news. Badly frightened and bleeding from the mouth due to a "horrid wound through the jaw," the young Confederate could not talk but motioned for a pencil and paper and scribbled out an incredible story.[56] The two Confederates had met Vidal and his company on the prairie fourteen miles east of Brownsville. They delivered the orders as directed, and the entire party continued along the road to Brownsville. After about four miles, Vidal dismounted and ordered his men to prepare a meal for the evening and asked the two privates to share a drink. Suddenly, Vidal and several of his men opened fire on the two men, killing Dashiell instantly and badly wounding Literal, who was able to mount his horse and escape in the darkness in a fusillade of bullets.[57]

With few men to defend the town, Bee was fearful that Cortina and Vidal, assisted by Unionists who had assembled on the Mexican bank of the river, would overrun Brownsville. A small patrol of ten men was sent down the road toward the gulf to locate Vidal and ascertain, if possible, his motivations and course of action. The patrol had proceeded only a few miles when they ran headlong into Vidal's entire company, which numbered more than one hundred men and who were advancing rapidly on Brownsville. In a brief skirmish, the Confederates were driven to the outskirts of town. With the "garrison and citizens thrown into a panic," Bee called a council-of-war, fearful that Vidal and Cortina would indeed sack Brownsville. Then, Bee mobilized a six-month militia company as well as three hundred men from the community who were said to be "old and young, native and foreign."⁵⁸ Bee also pulled a 24-pounder cannon and an 8-inch siege howitzer into position to guard the arsenal and the garrison at Fort Brown. He also placed his more dependable regulars on the outskirts of the town, instructing them to remain on alert through the night.

Vidal's attack on Brownsville, which he may have patterned on Cortina 1859 raid, never materialized. Crying "*¡Muerte a los Americanos!*" the *Vidalistas* passed within a mile of Brownsville about 3 A.M. in the morning darkness of October 29. Upriver, the raiders continued along the river road for about nine miles, plundering several ranches as they went and killing at least ten unoffending citizens. Some were indiscriminately murdered although a few appear to have been individuals against whom Vidal held a vendetta.⁵⁹ A Confederate company was sent in pursuit and reached the ford at Rancho del Carmen only minutes after the *Vidalistas* had ascended the south bank into Mexico. A large body of Texas Unionists was seen across the river greeting Vidal and his men.

Furious at the turn of events on the border, Bee angrily wrote Governor Ruiz claiming that Vidal was acting under orders of the American consul in Matamoros, and he demanded he be captured and returned to Texas for punishment. "I at once gave orders that all the troops on the line should unite in pursuing the insurrectionists, and from this city will immediately set forth two detachments of cavalry to reconnoiter the left bank of the Rio Grande," Governor Ruiz wrote Bee. Although Bee reported that Cortina, acting under orders from Ruiz, had captured twenty *Vidalistas* and that Vidal was in hiding in Matamoros, he soon realized that Cortina had instigated the entire affair. "A wild and reckless boy," Vidal was "daring" and a "crazy young man," the *Brownsville Fort Brown Flag* proclaimed.⁶⁰ In Mexico, the *Vidalistas* became *Cortinistas*.

Before ordering the evacuation of Brownsville, Bee ordered Fort Brown set on fire. As many as a thousand bales of cotton that could not be ferried or floated across the river were also set ablaze. Cortina watched from Matamoros as the flames spread from the fort to the town, eventually engulfing an entire block of buildings along Levee Street in front of the ferry.⁶¹ Plundering by both townsmen and soldiers added to the frightfulness of the scene. At Fort Brown, a large quantity of commissary stores and quartermaster goods were destroyed in the blaze. Adding to the chaos, 8,000 pounds of powder at the fort exploded, breaking windows and terrorizing citizens. "It was a hot and awful sight, men, women, children screaming and flying to the other banks of the river for safety," Charles Stillman wrote his wife, Elizabeth.⁶² In the mayhem, more than four hundred Unionists lined the south bank of the river to hiss and curse the panic-stricken Confederates. "Peril was around me on all sides," Bee wrote.⁶³ Finally, at midnight on November 3, 1863, Gen-

Cortina always enjoyed wide-scale support in Matamoros, especially among the poor and less fortunate. During the Cortina War, he was frequently welcomed and cheered in the city. *Lawrence T. Jones collection.*

eral Bee and his staff bid a fatigued and drunken adieu to Brownsville and headed north with a ten-man escort through the chaparral for the Nueces River. On the south bank, Cortina and the Unionists cheered.

With looting, violence, and disorder engulfing Brownsville, Judge Israel Bigelow sent an urgent plea to Cortina in Matamoros for assistance. Cortina replied that Bigelow's problems were not his problems, and he refused to intervene. Cortina did, however, prevent his men and any Unionists from Matamoros from joining the chaos on the north bank. Instead, a forty-five-year-old bandit chief and former officer in the Imperial Mexican Army, José María Cobos, stepped forward. With two hundred hastily recruited men, Cobos was able stop the plunder and restore some semblance of order. Active earlier with conservative forces in Coahuila and Zacatecas and expelled from Mexico City, Cobos had come to Brownsville, hoping to procure arms and ammunition and recruit men to seize Matamoros.[64] Along with Bishop Verea, of Monterrey, who had served in the cabinet of Miguel Miramón, Cobos had been in Brownsville for at least eight months contemplating forming a new political party. Regardless of Cobos's political affiliations, Cortina met with him, and the two agreed to cooperate in ousting Governor Ruiz. The forced removal of one of the last remaining *Juarista* governors in the republic was

Frontier in Flames

With the Confederate Army bidding a drunken farewell to Brownsville in November 1863, cotton speculators scurry to cross as much cotton to Matamoros as possible. Much of the cotton that could not be ferried or floated across the river was burned. *Harper's Weekly,* February 13, 1864.

certain to damage badly any relationship Cortina might hope to have with Juárez, but Cortina, a man of many colors, allowed his personal ambitions to overwhelm his patriotism and loyalty to the liberal cause. It is also possible that rumors were true that Cobos gave Cortina a large sum of money to assure his cooperation.

Seizing Power

Before daybreak on November 6, just hours before the Union Army entered Brownsville, Cobos, with two hundred men, crossed the river to Matamoros. With Cortina's assistance, they seized control of the city and arrested Governor Ruiz. Although Ruiz, who trusted Cortina, was heavily guarded by a cadre of supporters, a band of *Cortinistas* was able to enter military headquarters by removing some loose bricks in one of the walls, seize the governor, and even carry off some of his artillery. Cortina not only helped Cobos seize Matamoros, but he also consented to his becoming governor of Tamaulipas. At the same time, it was agreed that Cortina would head the *ayuntamiento,* or city council, and take charge of the military. Shortly

The Union Rio Grande Expedition triumphantly marches down Elizabeth Street in Brownsville in November 1863. Cortina welcomed and cooperated with the Federal army. *Harper's Weekly.*

after the coup, Cobos issued a *pronunciamiento* saying he was acting to save the citizens of Matamoros from anarchy. Although he spoke of independence and patriotism, Cobos appeared ambiguous, perhaps intentionally so, about any allegiance to the Empire. Despite his public pronouncements, the Spanish-born Cobos soon assailed the liberal constitution of 1857 and began criticizing "the accumulation of outrages" thrust on the people of Mexico by Juárez, a "tyrannical demagogue."[65] Cobos even called Cortina to his side and presented him with a copy of the *pronunciamiento*. Unable to read, Cortina had the document read to him, after which he calmly folded it, put it in his pocket, and walked away. His only comment was that that he did not agree.

In the meantime, on November 7, only one day after proclaiming himself governor, Cobos and his second in command, Rómulo Vila, a Spanish-born conservative who had been living in New York, ordered Governor Ruiz executed. Knowing that he was supported by the troops in the city, Cortina vetoed the plan and instead arrested Cobos and Vila who were summoned before a hastily called court-martial. Found guilty of treason, they were ordered executed. With a large part of the Matamoros populace looking on,

Cobos was taken to the outskirts of town near a small lagoon and shot by a squad of *Cortinistas;* Vila was allowed to "run the gauntlet, and was shot upon his flight."[66] The disorder and bedlam was so high in Matamoros at the time that Leonard Pierce feared the United States consulate might be attacked and plundered. As a result, General Banks placed a battery of artillery on the north bank and trained it on the town. "If the American flag is assailed or your person threatened," Banks promised Pierce, troops would be sent across the border.[67]

When Cortina released Ruiz, the governor surprisingly issued two *pronunciamientos,* both praising Cortina: "Long live Independence! Long live liberty! Long live the National Guard! Long live Lieut. Col. Juan Nepomuceno Cortina!" Nevertheless, Cortina refused to allow Ruiz to assume his duties as governor and sent a twenty-five-man escort to insure "his retreat from the city."[68] Realizing he could still be executed, Ruiz fled across the river with a few of his troops. In Brownsville, he wrote a lengthy letter to Juárez relating how he had become a victim of Cortina's treason. Refusing to give up hope of returning to power in Tamaulipas, the deposed governor also called on Santiago Vidaurri for assistance.

Only days after expelling Ruiz, Cortina called for the return of Jesús de la Serna as governor, arguing that he had been legitimately elected governor in 1861. Hoping to consolidate power and win the people of Matamoros to his side, Cortina issued a decree in which he lifted the state of siege that had existed in Tamaulipas for almost a year. Needing money to pay his troops, he also imposed a loan on the merchants of the city. Meanwhile, no sooner had Ruiz reached Brownsville than he rode upriver, crossed the Rio Grande, and proceeded to the old colonial town of San Fernando, eighty-five miles south of Matamoros, where he began to build an army in hopes of regaining Matamoros. Ruiz carried with him papers taken from Cobos demonstrating how the dead Spaniard had bribed Cortina with a large sum of money. The papers were forwarded to Juárez as evidence that Cortina could not be trusted.[69]

Cooperating with the Bluecoats

Less than three weeks after the Union army arrived in Brownsville, a young man crossed the ferry and appeared at the enrolling office. Identifying himself as Adrián J. Vidal, late of the Confederate Army, he declared himself prepared to raise a cavalry company for the Federals. As a result, on November 26, 1863, Vidal was mustered into the Union Army and commissioned a captain. Throughout November and December hundreds of Tejanos and Mexicanos, enticed by a bounty of $100, crossed the river to join the Union Army. Vidal's company of eighty-nine men (known simply as "Vidal's Independent Partisan Rangers") was mustered in for one year."[70] Ironically,

Confederate forces destroyed much of Fort Brown during their evacuation of the lower Valley in November 1863. In this wartime sketch by C. E. H. Bonwill, Union soldiers drill beneath the Stars and Stripes and among the blackened chimneys and ruins of the post as a steamboat anchors along the north bank of the Rio Grande. *Frank Leslie's Illustrated Newspaper*, June 11, 1864.

the Federal government recruited men the army had fought against during the Cortina War four years earlier. Only a few months after enlisting, however, Vidal, asserting he did "not understand the English language," asked to resign. Largely illiterate and frustrated with the paperwork required of a company commander, Vidal wanted to return to his family in Brownsville. Although the army agreed to an honorable discharge, the orders arrived in Brownsville too late. Impatient with army bureaucracy, Vidal fled into Mexico along with most of his men, once again to join Cortina.[71]

No sooner had Cortina taken power in Matamoros than he opened friendly relations with the Union army in Brownsville. General Banks was particularly grateful that Cortina allowed the Federals to take control of three of King and Kenedy's steamboats that had been under Mexican registry.[72] To Cortina, the Union officials were far more amenable than the Confederates they replaced. An adroit politician and pragmatist of the first order, he now became friends with the army that had defeated him four years earlier at Rio Grande City. No surprise: as a young bluecoat from Iowa wrote, Cortina was "medium in size, about 40 years of age, [with a] rather, pleasant continence . . . a genial companion of few words and no doubt . . . a daring intrepid soldier [who] inspires those under him with confidence." Cortina also "exhibited a daring, scheming, plotting, spirit of intrigue seldom surpassed by any of the human family." General Banks found Cortina to be uneducated but "of great influence with the Mexican people."[73] Only weeks after arriving on the border, Banks assembled a delegation to pay a call on Cortina in Matamoros. The party included Col. John L. Haynes and—prior to his desertion—the unpredictable Capt. Adrián J. Vidal.[74] All were warmly received by Cortina and his staff.

Cortina was rapidly emerging as a major figure in the Mexican military and in Mexican politics when C. E. H. Bonwill made this sketch of the general in March 1864. *Frank Leslie's Illustrated Newspaper,* April 9, 1864.

Well into 1864, Cortina continued his friendly relations with the Union Army. In April, for example, he sent an aide, José María Silva, to see Gen. John A. McClernand, the new commander in Brownsville, in hopes of procuring arms. Although General McClernand did not have authority to negotiate an arms deal, he asked Cortina's assistance in closing the upper reaches of the Rio Grande to Confederate cotton as well as his cooperation in arresting Rebel agents operating in Tamaulipas.[75] "I will do everything that tends to the good and prosperity of the American Union," Cortina wrote, but he did not have the authority to close the river to the Rebels.[76] Although McClernand would complain that Cortina had become "somewhat estranged" due to the influences of "rebel agents and interested cotton-traders," amicable relations continued. The destinies of the Mexican republic and the United States were inseparable, and the Union's success was closely tied to "the security of Mexico," Cortina wrote.

As the sole military power on the Mexican side of the lower border, Cortina had achieved power and influence he could only have dreamed of a few years earlier. Now not only did Union authorities seek his friendship, but also Confederates talked of making him an "offer" to assure that their cotton continued to flow freely into Mexico. Any "disbursements ... could only be made from some secret-service fund," Confederate authorities concluded, however. The "offer" was withdrawn when Gen. John B. Magruder concluded that Cortina was "bitterly opposed" to the Confederacy and could not be trusted.[77]

Defying Juárez

From the time he seized power in Matamoros, Cortina wasted no time in opening relations with Gov. Santiago Vidaurri in Monterrey. Telling the powerful caudillo he had deposed Ruiz, Cortina hoped the two men could work toward a common goal. Assuring Vidaurri of his loyalty to the liberal government, he needed the caudillo's influence to persuade Juárez "that Tamaulipas is with the nation."[78] Vidaurri responded within days that he had written to President Juárez, who was at San Luis Potosí, asking that the "affair in Matamoros" in which Cortina had seized power be recognized by the government. Vidaurri assured Juárez that Cortina was intent on preserving order and keeping Tamaulipas within the Liberal circle. On December 13, 1863, Juárez wrote Vidaurri, however, with a flat refusal. To do so, the president argued, would sanction the "ill-fated principle" that legally constituted leaders could "be removed by insurrections and not by the government or the power that nominated or elected them." Such coups had always caused the republic great pain, Juárez reiterated.[79]

Although refusing to recognize Cortina, neither would Juárez seek to have him removed. Once peace was restored to the border and Cortina and De la Serna were willing to take their directions from the central government, Juárez would reconsider recognition. However, the interests of the people of Tamaulipas, as well as the central government, could never condone an insurrection. So critical was the situation in Matamoros that Juárez decided to send a special envoy to the border to mediate the conflict between Cortina and Ruiz. But Cortina defiantly rejected any such intercession, saying that Ruiz was unpopular and could not be trusted. Moreover, at San Fernando he had ruthlessly executed six *Cortinistas* as well as several other innocent citizens. More and more, Cortina was negotiating from a position of strength, especially after he seized a shipment of ten thousand rifles and three thou-

This rare albumen print of Cortina was probably taken in Matamoros around 1864. *Robert G. McCubbin collection.*

sand pistols, along with more than a million rounds of ammunition that had been bound for the Confederacy.[80]

Hoping to mediate the situation in Tamaulipas, Vidaurri dispatched a commissioner to Matamoros to convince Cortina that it was in his best interest to cooperate with Juárez against the French interventionists. A week later, Vidaurri lectured Cortina that it was wrong "to use force to gain power and take advantage of the difficulties of the government."[81] In a play for power himself, Vidaurri established an *aduana*, customs house, at China, not far from the Tamaulipas–Nuevo León border, and lobbied Juárez to declare a free trade zone on the Rio Grande that would stretch all the way to Monterrey, thus allowing him access to the large and lucrative Tamaulipas customs receipts.

By early December 1863, Ruiz had six hundred men under arms at San Fernando and was preparing to drive Cortina out of Matamoros. Cortina barricaded the streets of the town with Texas cotton and braced for an attack. At the same time, he appealed to Vidaurri for reinforcements, saying that Ruiz was ruthless, executing people every day, even shooting people simply because they did not like him.[82] By the second week of December, the new Federal commander on the Rio Grande, Gen. Napoleon Jackson Tecumseh Dana, wrote that Matamoros was in a "great panic and confusion ... and an attack [was] hourly expected."[83] But one week later Ruiz was still at San Fernando.[84]

Not until late December 1863 did Ruiz finally arrive with his small army on the outskirts of Matamoros, where he demanded Cortina surrender the city. Although De la Serna appeared timid and considered vacating the governor's office to return to private life, Cortina was determined to fight. Before laying siege to the city, Ruiz delayed an attack for forty-eight hours to allow civilians to evacuate the city. Hundreds, including Cortina's family, crowded the ferry to Brownsville. Tons of furniture and household goods were also sent across the Rio Grande. Fearing an attack that would overwhelm him, Cortina agreed to negotiate, and he sent an emissary to see Governor Ruiz. In a series of tense discussions at a small dwelling on the outskirts of Matamoros over seven days, an agreement was finally hammered out and signed by Cortina, Ruiz, De la Serna, and their subordinates on January 1, 1864. De la Serna agreed to give up his seat as governor and retire to his ranch; Ruiz would resume the office of governor; and Cortina and Ruiz would combine their armies. Gen. José Macedonio Capistrán, a Ruiz partisan, would head the army while Cortina would be second in command. Once the agreement was fully implemented, the army would march south to meet the French at Tampico.[85]

De la Serna retired to his ranch, Ruiz assumed his seat as governor, and the soldiers prepared to march for Tampico. But Cortina reneged on the

Cortina saved Gov. Manuel Ruiz from execution in November 1863, only to expel him from Matamoros days later. A Liberal reformer from Oaxaca and close friend of Benito Juárez, Ruiz tried to retake the city in bloody street-to-street fighting in January 1864. *Frank Leslie's Illustrated Newspaper,* April 9, 1864.

agreement, and for five days he refused to move his army. To pacify him, Ruiz sent $16,000 in cash to pay Cortina's troops and contract for wagons and mules to carry supplies to Tampico. The wagons were loaded with provisions, but, according to Ruiz, Cortina hid them in the chaparral. With Cortina still refusing to depart for Tampico, Ruiz sent a messenger demanding to know why he and his army were not on the road. In a chest-pounding confrontation, Cortina replied that his men had not been paid enough, but, when arrangements were made to give the men two months' pay, Cortina raised the stakes by demanding four hundred horses and more ammunition. Realizing the horses could not be found in Matamoros, Ruiz agreed to scour the ranches around Matamoros for the animals.[86] Ruiz told Juárez, "With a thousand excuses, he avoids leaving and with enormous prudence, I suffer his presence."[87] The situation was inflamed further when Ruiz sent several warnings to Cortina that he must comply with the January 1 agreement or face attack. According to Ruiz, Cortina responded in "a most insolent manner." In addition, private conversations with Cortina's older brother, José María, and several of Cortina's subordinates went nowhere. Watching the tumultuous events from Brownsville, another American commander, Gen. Francis. J. Herron, concluded the January 1 agreement was "violated several times by both parties."[88]

CANNON IN THE STREETS

During the confrontation, Cortina's artillery commander, Col. Julio Laborda, and his infantry commander, Col. Octaviano Cárdenas, entered the military barracks on Plaza Hidalgo only to be accused of trying to "seduce" Ruiz's soldiers to Cortina's cause. Realizing that Cortina had no intention of abiding by the January 1 agreement and that he was only playing for time, Ruiz told General Herron he was "fully prepared to repel force with force."[89] During this time, a Union officer in Brownsville wrote in his journal that the *Cortinistas* were "loitered through the city with an easy nonchalance [while] ... officers rode through the streets with bravado stamped on every action."[90] He was more or less accurate: "We remain quiet and ready for anything and everything," Ruiz wrote Juárez.[91] There was little he could do to avoid a bloody showdown. Although Ruiz was sure he could hold Plaza Hidalgo against the *Cortinistas*, he pleaded with Juárez for reinforcements. On the afternoon of January 12, 1864, violence erupted when Colonel Cárdenas rode up to Governor Ruiz's headquarters and insulted the governor by shouting "Death to Ruiz!"[92] He was grabbed by the governor's guards, dragged into an inner courtyard, and summarily executed.[93]

Three hours later, with Cortina vowing revenge, a fierce artillery duel erupted. In the impassioned fighting that followed, Cortina brought forth six hundred men and six artillery pieces while Ruiz had eight hundred men and four pieces of artillery.[94] Cortina held the western part of the city while Ruiz and his men clung to the area around Plaza Hidalgo and the eastern half of the city. Without pause, the fighting continued through the night and into the early morning of January 13 with as many as 250 artillery rounds exchanged. "The roar of artillery and the almost constant volleys of musquetry [sic] indicated a most bloody fight," a Union soldier wrote from Brownsville.[95] Although the damage to the sturdy rock and adobe buildings in the city was slight, broken glass from doors and windows lay everywhere. At the one-story American consulate near the plaza, Leonard Pierce was panic-stricken: "A battle is now raging in the streets of this city," he wrote General Herron in Brownsville. "My person and family are in great danger, as the road between here and the ferry is said to be infested with robbers. I have

The ferocious fighting in the streets of Matamoros between the forces of Cortina and Gov. Manuel Ruiz captured the imagination of the noted Civil War artist C. E. H. Bonwill. *Frank Leslie's Illustrated Newspaper,* February 20, 1864.

also about $1,000,000 in specie and a large amount of other valuable property under my charge in the consulate, and from the well-known character of Cortina and his followers, I fear the city will be plundered." Pierce asked Herron to intervene "at the earliest possible moment" to save his family and carry the specie to Brownsville.[96]

At the height of the fighting in the early morning darkness, Cortina penned an urgent dispatch and sent it by one of his most trusted aides, José Treviño, to Vidaurri in Monterrey. Complaining of great fatigue and his inability to write well, he blamed the violence on Ruiz. Unsure about the outcome of the fighting, Cortina contemplated a "catastrophe" and asked Vidaurri for asylum should it be necessary for him to flee Matamoros. It was essential, Cortina said, that Vidaurri not only send reinforcements but also use his influence with Juárez to persuade the president not to support Ruiz.[97] Only hours after Treviño reached Monterrey, Vidaurri responded that he would write Juárez, who was in Saltillo, and explain the urgency of the situation, but Cortina would be more effective if he would contact the president himself. Not only were there no reinforcements in Monterrey, while Treviño was in the city he had also been arrested for theft.[98]

As the fighting raged in Matamoros, Cortina slowly gained ground. As a result, Governor Ruiz sent an urgent appeal to General Herron in Brownsville saying that he could not protect the American consulate or the property of the numerous foreign businessmen.[99] With his fortunes fading fast, Ruiz realized the Federal army was all that could save him, and he reminded General Herron that only a few years earlier Mexican troops had been sent to Brownsville in the early stages of the Cortina War. Realizing the seriousness of the situation, Herron put three regiments under arms, sent forty men to seize the ferry, and dispatched four companies—along with an artillery battery—across the river to the American consulate.[100] At the same time, he sent notes to both Ruiz and Cortina, saying the Americans were crossing the river but only to protect the American consulate and that they would "take no part in the fight."[101] Amid confusion, chaos, and artillery thunder, the U.S. military arrived at the American consulate to find Pierce, the British consul, and representatives from Ruiz and Cortina wanting to know what American soldiers were doing on Mexican soil.[102]

Fighting from house to house and street to street and supported by Colonel Laborda's artillery, the *Cortinistas* steadily gained ground until they reached Plaza Hidalgo. Here, some of Ruiz's soldiers who had taken up defenses in and around the large cathedral and its twin towers were overrun and killed. With more artillery and superior weapons, Cortina clearly had an advantage over Ruiz's army, which was equipped with older, antiquated weapons, many of which became inoperable during the fighting. The turning point came when a number of *Cortinistas* gallantly charged and seized Ruiz's artillery. Low on ammunition and his artillery gone, Ruiz and what remained of his demoralized army fell back, then fled in panic. With the enemy on the run, Cortina's cavalry "dashed through the streets striking down the fleeing fugitive[s]." By mid-morning, Cortina had successfully routed Ruiz and was in control of the city. Scores of Ruiz's men lay dead, some "shockingly butchered or murdered in cold blood," an American soldier recorded.[103] In the aftermath of the fighting, the *Cortinistas* sacked the homes and businesses of anyone thought to have aided Ruiz. At least two hundred of Ruiz's men and officers escaped by swimming the Rio Grande to Brownsville while many others were captured. Leaving his personal belongings and his archives behind, Ruiz, along with most of his cavalry and a number of his officers, crossed the river below Matamoros only to have their weapons seized by Herron's bluecoats. After eighteen hours of carnage and mayhem, the battle for Matamoros was over. As many as three hundred men lay dead. Included were all Ruiz's artillerymen, who gallantly fell at their guns. Among the dead was ex-governor Albino López, a prominent Ruiz partisan. Ruiz himself had been slightly wounded in the head and chest. "We have lost everything except our honor," he dejectedly told Juárez. Cortina was "now the absolute master of Matamoros."[104]

Within hours of the cessation of hostilities, Cortina proclaimed himself governor of Tamaulipas and issued two fiery *pronunciamientos*, both of which Ruiz denounced as lies and insults to his "honor and dignity." Cortina had fallen into a dark "abyss of bad deeds [from which] no one could save him.[105] To Cortina, Ruiz was an "enemy of peace" who could not be trusted and who had "cruelly and cowardly" executed Cárdenas "inquisition style," thus perpetrating the violence. Cortina had tried to contain his raging impulses, but he was compelled to respond to Ruiz's "barbarism." Cortina's paramount objective, he said, was to maintain peace and guarantee personal liberties. As a result, he agreed to pardon anyone who had fought against him. Not only did he pardon prisoners taken in the fighting, but also Ruiz's officers who had fled to Browsville. Even General Capistrán could return to his ranch in peace. "Forget forever the resentments," Cortina wrote, "let us give to the world a testimony that all are worthy successors to Hidalgo and Morelos. Long live Mexico! Long live independence! Long live the State of Tamaulipas!"[106] Self-righteous and stubborn, with deeply rooted revolutionary inclinations, he was well on his way toward achieving what he perceived as greatness.

Chapter Five

Republic in the Balance

Your screams of war should be: Long live the Supreme Constitutional Government! Long live Independence! Long live the State of Tamaulipas!

JUAN CORTINA

IN FEWER THAN FIVE YEARS, through sheer bravado, cunning determination, and a lot of luck, Juan Cortina had risen from a near illiterate Cameron County ranchero to the pinnacle of power in Tamaulipas. Power had its price, however, and, a few months after proclaiming himself governor, two Frenchmen tried to assassinate him. Although both would-be assassins were immediately seized and executed, the incident served notice that Cortina's biography would be ultimately etched in blood.[1]

Although continuing to strive for recognition from the Liberal government, Cortina realized the republic was on the verge of collapse. Regardless, he was determined to hold on to power in Tamaulipas. He faced a new crisis in late January 1864, when Juárez accepted the resignation of Ruiz but again refused to recognize him. Cortina was at fault for breaking the January 1 agreement with Ruiz, and the president was appointing a military commission headed by Andrés Treviño to govern the state. On January 27, Cortina informed Vidaurri he had no intentions of acquiescing to Juárez's decree. Not only did he refuse to recognize Treviño, he viewed him "with horror." Treviño was the worst person Cortina could think of to govern the state because he did not understand the affairs of Tamaulipas any more than Ruiz. "Give up all hope" should be inscribed on the doors of the National Palace, Cortina proclaimed in disgust, taking a line from Dante's *Inferno*.[2] Whether Italian literature or affairs south of the border, the stories would have more than a little in common.

A Whirlwind of Change

A few days after his crushing defeat of Ruiz, Cortina wrote Vidaurri, playing on the old caudillo's vanity. *Tamaulipecos* were deeply indebted to Vidaurri, Cortina said, and the two should renew their efforts to expel the *Imperialistas*. "In a life so new to me," Cortina continued, he was counting on Vidaurri for protection, especially because the two had developed a "true friendship."[3] Cortina told the caudillo he was sending a three-man delegation headed by his brother, José María, to Juárez in Saltillo, and they would be stopping in Monterrey. What Cortina did not tell Vidaurri was that José María carried with him over $20,000 in customs receipts, money the Liberal government needed for its depleted treasury and to pay its badly demoralized army. If Cortina could not win Juárez's allegiance by seizing power in Matamoros, he would purchase it. José María also carried a letter in which Cortina pledged himself as a "patriot and loyal servant to the Supreme Government."[4]

Despite Cortina's ascendancy to power, the struggle among the Liberals for control of Tamaulipas remained intense. No sooner had Ruiz reached Brownsville than he sent one of his lieutenants and sixty cavalry to Camargo to recruit troops and begin rebuilding his army. Underestimating or deliberately misconstruing Cortina's popularity on the frontier, Ruiz told Juárez that no one was willing to follow Cortina, and it was only a matter of time before his regime collapsed. All Ruiz needed was one thousand reinforcements and more artillery and he would drive Cortina out of Matamoros. But the reinforcements and artillery never arrived.[5]

While the fortunes of the republic continued to fade, Cortina nurtured friendly relations with Vidaurri, seeing the wily Monterrey caudillo as the key to power and success in northeastern Mexico. To placate Vidaurri, Cortina sent one hundred rifles to Monterrey, promising more arms if he could find them. But he refused to relent to Juárez. While promising additional funds, he wrote the president thanking him for warmly receiving José María in Saltillo. However, as a subtle warning, he told Juárez that as soon as he found additional weapons he would double the size of his army in Matamoros to 1,500 men. A number of Americans had even joined his small army, volunteers whom Cortina considered dubbing "Texas Volunteers."[6] The next day, Cortina wrote the president again to say he was sending José María with another $25,000 and that more money would follow as soon as he was able to bring the customs houses at Reynosa, Camargo, Mier, and Nuevo Laredo under his control. At the same time, Cortina received news that Gen. Guadalupe García, who had previously commanded the military on the Rio Grande and who was at Ciudad Victoria with two hundred men, had formed an alliance with former governor De la Serna, and they had pronounced

José María Cortina was one of the few Tejano office holders in Cameron County prior to the Cortina War. Although he did not initially join his younger brother in the war, the did become a colonel in the Mexican military in the war against the *Imperialistas*. South of the border, he rendered valuable service to his brother as a loyal courier, surrogate, recruiter, and field commander. *Brownsville Historical Association.*

Supply wagons bound for Piedras Negras load on Calle de Cesar in Matamoros during La Época del Algodón. *Frank Leslie's Illustrated Newspaper,* February 20, 1864.

against him. Cortina wanted the president to issue orders placing García and all the military in Tamaulipas under his control.[7]

Before leaving for Bagdad, Cortina dictated and sent a letter to Vidaurri on February 20, 1864, urging the old caudillo to join in helping to defeat the "despotic Napoleon." Vidaurri had written asking for money, but Cortina said he could "not spare a single centavo," that all the revenues must go to support the government. The struggling republic was experiencing the worst of times, and any hope of winning the war with the French was fading rapidly.[8] Continuing to pledge his allegiance to the national government, he sent Juárez another $40,000. At the same time, it was widely rumored on the border that Cortina amassed a personal fortune from the Matamoros customs revenues, a fortune that included thousands of dollars in gold in New Orleans.[9]

A Beleaguered Republic

The showdown between Cortina and Juárez was muted when the government became engulfed by events of greater magnitude. With the *Imperialistas* on the offensive, events in northern Mexico were moving fast. While Cortina was struggling for control of Matamoros, the beleaguered armies of the republic remained on the defensive throughout the country. Morelia had fallen to the French on November 30. The *Juaristas* evacuated Guanajuato on December 9, and, on December 23, Gen. Tomás Mejía seized San Luis Potosí. In many ways, Juárez needed Cortina more than Cortina needed Juárez. The loss of Tamaulipas at this time would have seriously damaged the fading hopes of the Liberals in northern Mexico.

In Monterrey, Vidaurri began to sway in the wind. Fiercely independent and arrogant, Vidaurri continued to be a nuisance to Juárez by defying the president's demand to relinquish money from the customs house at Piedras Negras (revenues that amounted to between $40,000 to $50,000 a month).[10]

As Juárez and his small army dropped the 3,500 feet along the sixty miles of winding, narrow, and twisting mountain road from Saltillo to Monterrey, Vidaurri remained defiant. On February 12, Juárez entered Monterrey and occupied the statehouse; Vidaurri barricaded himself with his troops in the *Ciudadela,* a heavily fortified section of the city. Two days later, Vidaurri came out to negotiate, his *Norteño* partisans lining the streets and cheering him wildly. In a heated exchange, Vidaurri's son drew a pistol and threatened Juárez as the president fled through the streets in a stagecoach, an angry mob in pursuit.[11] Never had the fortunes of the Liberal government been so low.

Back in Saltillo and in ill health, Juárez declared Vidaurri in open rebellion. In addition, he issued a decree separating the states of Coahuila and Nuevo León and declared both in a state of siege. Moreover, he ordered Vidaurri to appear in person in Saltillo. When Vidaurri failed to respond and began negotiations with the French, the president declared him a traitor and ordered him arrested. Hearing the shocking news from Monterrey, Cortina responded by issuing a *pronunciamiento:* "Today the question is to be or not to be," he said, borrowing a line from Shakespeare's *Hamlet,* and reaffirmed his loyalty to the republic.[12] At this crucial time in Mexican history, Cortina could have wavered as did Vidaurri, but he chose instead to stand with Juárez and the republic. On the evening of February 27, Cortina called his officers and all the municipal officials of Matamoros to a meeting in the city hall. There, he explained at length the shocking news from Monterrey about how Juárez had entered the city but was forced back to Saltillo, after which Vidaurri had declared himself in open rebellion. Certain the "Lion of the North" had designs on Matamoros and Tamaulipas, Cortina said he was fearful Vidaurri would seize the city and annex Tamaulipas to Nuevo León and Coahuila. Vidaurri was immoral, evil, and power-hungry, and Cortina swore he would keep Tamaulipas free of his influences. On March 4, 1864, Cortina's loyal supporters in Matamoros presented him with an elegantly engraved, silver-mounted sword that was inscribed, "*Presentado de honor al intrépido Coronel de Caballería J. N. Cortina por los fronterizos amigos de la Justicia.*"[13]

Yet the political situation in northeastern Mexico grew chaotic by the day as Cortina refused to recognize Andrés Treviño as governor and gave notice he would resist any invasion of the state. With little alternative and desperate for support, Juárez was forced to recognize Cortina. As the governors of Chihuahua and Sonora wavered in their support, the president could not afford to lose Tamaulipas. In early March, the president sent two commissioners, Francisco Mejía and Blas Balcarcel, to Matamoros with a letter for Cortina recognizing him as military governor of Tamaulipas. After thanking Juárez for his trust and confidence, Cortina responded that he would send José María with part of his army to Linares as the *Juaristas* moved against Vidaurri in Monterrey. Cortina also told the president that a French frigate along with three small barks had arrived off Bagdad, and the commander had inquired if Vidaurri was in possession of Matamoros. Cortina was convinced the ships were little more than a distraction, however. Should a single Frenchman step ashore, Cortina promised, he would drive them into the sea.[14]

While Cortina was preparing another letter for Juárez, the news reached Matamoros on the evening of March 29 that Vidaurri had fled Monterrey, and Juárez was preparing to enter the city with seven thousand troops. Escorted by a small army of his loyal *Norteños* and with eighteen pieces of light artillery and the state treasury and archives, Vidaurri fled for the border. Halfway to the Rio Grande, on a barren plain near the foothills of the Sierra Gomas in the desert at the settlement of Villa Aldama, Vidaurri's army was overtaken and crushed by 1,600 pursuing Liberals. Vidaurri raced on for the border at Laredo to find refuge with his friend, Col. Santos Benavides, before going on to San Antonio. By the second week of April, Juárez had established his government in Monterrey.[15]

While Juárez huddled with his ministers in Monterrey, the French imperialists continued on the offensive. On January 7, 1864, French troops under Gen. François Achille Bazaine occupied Guadalajara. A month later Gen. Félix Douay occupied Zacatecas and on May 17, a large Republican army under Gen. Manuel Doblado suffered a crushing defeat at Matehuala. On May 28, after a trip of four thousand miles by sea, Ferdinand Maximilian Joseph and Marie Charlotte Amélie Léopoldine arrived at Veracruz to establish a monarchy on the ruins of Juárez's failed republic. Within a month, Acapulco had fallen to the French and on July 3, forces of the Empire entered Durango. By this time, the Imperialists had moved north into Coahuila and Nuevo León. In early August, Republican forces evacuated Monterrey, and Juárez sent his family to New York by way of Matamoros and New Orleans. "The dark little Indian in worn black clothes and riding in old carriages with a few friends, followed by a wagon with the nation's archives, and escorted by a few horsemen, disappeared into the deserts of the north," a Juárez biographer would write.[16] As the beleaguered president and his small entourage moved from village to village in the vast arid expanses of northern Mexico, the republic again appeared on the verge of collapse. When Juárez arrived at El Paso del Norte on the sandy banks of the Rio Grande on the northern fringes of the republic, many in Mexico and the United States were sure the republic was finished. Everywhere the French and Imperial arms appeared successful, except, that is, for Tamaulipas.

Holding Power

As Cortina held on to power on the border, Union authorities in Brownsville continued friendly relations with the unpredictable border jefe and aspiring caudillo. "Cortina informs me that he will do anything we want," Gen. Francis J. Herron told Washington in January 1864. Cortina "is on very friendly terms with us," the general confirmed ten days later.[17] An example of the amicable diplomacy existing on the Rio Grande came in early 1864, when Juárez sent his Minister of Justice and Finance, José María Iglesias, to Matamoros to see Cortina. Learning that Iglesias was in Matamoros, General Herron invited him to Brownsville and sent his coach to meet the minister at the ferry. At Fort Brown, Iglesias was wined and dined and the Mexican flag hoisted in his honor.[18]

In Matamoros, Cortina interceded with Union authorities to assure that Mexican Texans were treated fairly. When Matías Hinojosa, who owned a small farm and ranch at Paso de los Tamales near Rancho del Carmen, complained that Federal soldiers had seized his boat and one of his servants, Cortina bluntly told Herron that the small craft was a "Mexican boat" under Mexican authority seized in "Mexican Territory" and that it should be returned to its owner. Many Mexican Texans along the river were being treated "like they were Confederates," Cortina complained. Federals were trampling on their fields and cutting mesquite on their property without permission or compensation. Another badly treated Tejano, Justo Hernández, who Cortina said was a good and honest man, complained that he was being prohibited from grazing his cattle at Villanueva, Las Norias, and Rancho Anacintas Altos.[19] Another *Cortinista*, whom Cortina wanted released, had been arrested while carrying a pistol at Rancho del Carmen. Yet another Tejano, Benito Cipriano, had been arrested but never charged with any crime. Cortina sent other men who complained of stolen livestock to Herron.

Cortina also complained that the small ferry his mother used to transport goods back and forth across the river at Rancho del Carmen had been destroyed; on April 21, Cortina sent one of his officers, Lt. Col. Miguel Echazarrete, in person to see Herron to complain of "abuses committed on his rancho" in Texas.[20] The same day, Cortina dispatched Col. Ignacio Navarro to obtain the release of three *Cortinistas* who were being held by the Federals. Cortina also wrote Herron to say that a party of Americans commanded by a sergeant had been apprehended in Mexico and were being held in Matamoros and he was not sure if they were Confederates or Federals.[21] At the same time, Herron made several requests that Cortina apprehend men who had committed crimes in Texas and who had fled to Mexico.

Well into the spring of 1864, Cortina complained to General Herron that soldiers were trampling on the rights of Tejanos, at least one of whom the Brownsville provost marshal asserted had burglarized a home and stolen two hundred pounds of lard. Another Cortina supporter, Ramón Garza, whom the Federals were holding in Brownsville and Cortina wanted released, was a "decrepit ... poor, honest old man."[22] With one of the worst droughts in memory in South Texas and hunger plaguing many of the poor, Cortina requested permission from Federal authorities for Tejanos to drive their cattle into Mexico.

Although the Union Army held Brownsville and the lower Valley, the bluecoats rarely ventured upriver beyond Ringgold Barracks, and the Confederate flow of cotton continued at Laredo and Eagle Pass. With the borders of Tamaulipas reaching upriver beyond Nuevo Laredo, Cortina was forced to maintain relations with the Confederates in Texas. In May 1864, he received a petition from the citizens of Guerrero complaining of "excesses" by soldiers from the "so called Southern Confederacy." Col. Santos Benavides had once again crossed his forces into Mexico, and Cortina told Herron the Federals should stop such "oppressions."[23] After the repulse of the Union forces in a cotton raid on Laredo in March 1864, however, there was little Herron could do, although he had once hoped to link up with the Union Army in far West Texas.

In Matamoros, when *Cortinistas* deserted and fled into Texas, Cortina requested they be apprehended and returned to Mexico. Maritime diplomacy on the Rio Grande also proved to be time-consuming and troublesome. In May 1864, when Union authorities seized the English schooner *Maggie Jane* near the mouth of the river after it had tied up on the north bank while the crew searched for a deserter, Cortina complained of the Americans' heavy-handedness. He was fearful that, if the Union navy persisted in seizing neutral vessels, all foreign commerce would be endangered and grind to a halt.[24]

Collaboration with Federal authorities outweighed any discord and was reflected in a secret extradition treaty Cortina negotiated with Gov. Andrew Jackson Hamilton, whom Lincoln had appointed as provisional governor of Texas. As a result, on March 27, 1864, General Herron seized Manuel G. Rejón, Santiago Vidaurri's secretary of state who had fled to Brownsville. Accusing Rejón of "engaging in contraband with Rebels ... particularly furnishing them [with] lead and other munitions of war," Herron extradited him to Matamoros. The next day, Cortina ordered him executed by firing squad at high noon.[25] When José A. Quintero, Confederate agent in northern Mexico, learned that he too might be charged with treason for being an accomplice of Governor Vidaurri, he rushed to see Juárez, who assured him that rumors of an extradition treaty between his government and the United States was without foundation and that Quintero could peacefully reside in Mexico without fear.[26]

In early April 1864, Gen. John A. McClernand took command of the Union army on the Rio Grande. He asked Cortina to use his influence with Juárez to seize all the cotton and property in Mexico belonging to the Confederacy and expel anyone aiding and abetting the rebellion in the United States.[27] On hearing that Cortina had agreed to meet with Confederate cotton speculators, McClernand rushed across the river to meet with him in person. The success of the Union army in Texas, Cortina told McClernand, "was necessary to the security of Mexico, not only against trans-marine nations but against the ambitious aims and aggressive spirit of the so-called

Confederate government." McClernand was excited by what he heard in Matamoros. Cortina not only professed friendship but also issued a *pronunciamiento* that amounted to "little less than a declaration of war against the rebels."[28] As a reward, the Federals officially gave Cortina ten artillery pieces in a formal ceremony on Plaza Hidalgo in Matamoros. On the occasion, McClernand also presented Cortina with an elegantly engraved sword. Hearing of the events in Matamoros, Gen. John B. Magruder, commanding the Confederate forces in Texas, angrily asserted that the Federals were in violation of the "laws of nations by openly furnishing the Mexican troops with arms with which to carry on [a] war against the French."[29] Magruder was particularly miffed that Governor Hamilton and Cortina had "walked arm in arm through the streets of Matamoros" during the ceremony.

Diplomatic reverberations resulting from the cooperation between Cortina and Federal authorities echoed forth from the Valley of the Rio Grande all the way to Washington, where L. de Geofroy, the French chargé d'affaires, vehemently complained to Secretary of State Seward that the Union army was not only supplying Cortina with arms but also helping him recruit men.[30] De Geofroy was also perturbed that an organization had been formed in New Orleans made up of Mexican refugees and federal officers called the "Defenders of the Monroe Doctrine." The "D.M.D.," as it was known, had the stated objective of acquiring arms and shipping them to Cortina and the Liberals. In response, Seward had Gen. Nathaniel Banks, overall commander of Union forces on the Texas gulf, investigate the situation. Banks admitted that arms had been shipped to Mexico, but every effort would be made to "avoid any unlawful interference with the affairs of Mexico."[31]

Continuing to consolidate power in Matamoros, Cortina also courted the friendship of a few of his former Confederate enemies in Texas. In a strange turn of events, he wrote a letter that was intended for Colonel Ford but somehow ended up in the hands of Col. Santos Benavides. Cortina said he was sending an aide, José María Silva, upriver to Reynosa and Camargo to facilitate the flow of cotton across the river.[32] Hearing that an agreement had been reached to protect the cotton crossing at Laredo, General Magruder wrote to thank him for his cooperation.[33] But events far from the Rio Grande also required great effort. Despite the deadly effects of the yellow fever and the *vómito negro*, the French had reoccupied Tampico in August 1863.[34] After the Liberals under Carvajal seized Tuxpan, Col. Charles Louis du Pin and three hundred contra-guerrillas arrived to help defend Tampico. On April 18, after four hours of bloody fighting, much of it hand to hand, Carvajal's Fieles de Tamaulipas Battalion, which was made up of a large number of Americans, was routed by Du Pin and thrown back across the Rio Pánuco.[35] The defeat, Cortina wrote from Matamoros on Cinco de Mayo 1864, was due to Carvajal's "lack of judgement and prudence." Because of "fatalism, misfortune, or some other cause," the troops of Carvajal always manage to "end up in disaster," he continued.[36] By the early summer of 1864, however, Cortina and the Liberals took the offensive against the French at Tampico. After skirmishing with the contra-guerrillas in a series of running encounters around Ciudad Victoria, Cortina rushed back to the Rio Grande when he heard the French were preparing to seize Bagdad.

Circle of Bayonets

Just as Cortina was arriving in Matamoros, the Union army abandoned Brownsville, and Cortina's old antagonist, Col. John S. Ford and his Confederate "Cavalry of the West," occupied the town. Although preoccupied with the French, Cortina was now forced to devote more attention to his Rebel neighbors. The bulk of the Federal army on the Rio Grande was transferred to Louisiana, but they continued to hold Brazos Island while Cortina maintained contact with them. Even before entering Brownsville in late July, Ford crossed the river to Camargo to meet with José María Silva, Cortina's aide and secretary of state, who offered to sell the Rebels thirty pieces of artillery, most of it rifled cannon, along with a large amount of small arms, all having been procured in the United States. Ford also discussed with Silva an "arrangement to detach the Mexicans from the Yankee service." Learning that large numbers of Tejanos and Mexicanos were deserting into Mexico with their weapons, Ford sent agents to Matamoros to purchase the arms.[37] Yet Cortina did not trust Ford, whom he associated with the forces of oppression in Texas. Although many of the southern sympathizers in Matamoros were hostile to Cortina, he was said to have "treated them kindly and honorably."[38] The Confederates "hate me" he would write from Mexico City years later, "a hatred in which I glory."[39]

On June 18, with the Federals still on the coast, Cortina wrote General Herron saying the *Imperialistas* were advancing rapidly from Tampico toward Ciudad Victoria and it was only a matter of time before they landed at Bagdad and marched on Matamoros. "I am counting on help from you with your forces ... it case it is needed," Cortina wrote.[40] If Imperial forces did land at Bagdad as expected, he was hoping the Union navy in the gulf could attack the French navy. And if forces of the Empire were able to occupy Matamoros, he was prepared to take his army and all their arms and equipment across the river into the Union lines.[41] On August 22, the French landed four hundred marines at the mouth of the Rio Grande, seized Bagdad, and, while waiting for reinforcements, immediately began fortifying the town with Texas cotton. With Cortina absent in San Fernando, José María issued a *pronunciamiento* calling on the citizens of Matamoros to rally to the republic and drive the *Imperialistas* out of Tamaulipas.[42] Although now on the defensive, Cortina was able to capture the French steamer *Ark* on the Rio Grande.[43]

Imperial troops ascend the Rio Grande on the steamboats *Alamo* and *Mexico* while the gunboat *Luisa* follows. Confederate soldiers can be seen welcoming the *Imperialistas*. *Le Monde Illustré*. Courtesy of Gerard Mignard.

With four armies operating in the lower Valley, the military situation and the twisted international diplomacy that followed was to become even more intriguing. In the beginning, the Confederates were uncertain what to expect from the *Imperialistas*. They were especially concerned that the Empire would curtail, if not halt, the flow of supplies to the Rebel army in Texas. Consequently, as soon as the French arrived at Bagdad, Colonel Ford dispatched two officers as emissaries. "Will you respect persons and property covered by the flag of the Confederate States of America?" Ford inquired.[44] The commander of the French expeditionary forces responded by sending an emissary of his own to Brownsville. "If the exigencies of war should take me to Matamoros you may rest assured that I shall see that all persons and property covered by the flag of your nation are duly respected," the French commander told Ford.[45] Not to be outdone, Col. Henry Martyn Day, the Union commander on Brazos Island, also sent a delegation to see the French. But the forces of the Empire would always remain closer to the Confederacy.

As the French began moving against him from the coast and Monterrey at the same time, Cortina's situation became precarious. With their rear protected by Colonel Du Pin's dreaded contra-guerrillas, Gen. Tomás Mejía advanced rapidly from Monterrey and San Fernando. Cortina tried desperately to make a stand along the San Fernando River, hoping to hold the Imperialists off with his artillery firing grapeshot. Outflanked and unable to maneuver his artillery into position, Cortina gave the order to retreat toward Matamoros, abandoning a large quantity of ammunition, which Du Pin threw into the river.[46] Cortina had hoped to concentrate his forces at San Fernando but the road was now open to Matamoros.

Cortina seemed doomed; "shut up in a circle of bayonets," he would later say. In Matamoros he "could not communicate with his government, neither could he hope for aid."[47] Cortina did respond by raising the import tax on cotton, enacting a passport fee, and ordering a forced loan of $200,000 on the wealthy merchants of the city. When thirty merchants resisted, he ordered them jailed.[48] As the French juggernaut rolled toward Matamoros, wild rumors were rampant that Colonel Day, commanding the small Federal garrison on Brazos Island, was promising to make Cortina a brigadier general in the U.S. Army, providing he capture Brownsville.[49] Cortina held "an old and deep-seated grudge against Brownsville," Ford complained. He "hates Americans, particularly Texans." If Cortina could only "force his way through our lines, plunder our people and get within the Yankee lines, it would be a finale he would delight in," the Confederate colonel concluded.[50]

Affairs in both Matamoros and Brownsville rapidly descended into fear and uncertainty when Cortina stopped the passage of forage from the Mexican side of the river and began tying up the ferries on the south bank of the river at night. Ford responded by complaining that he was impeding free navigation on the river. "I shall claim and exercise the right to navigate said river without any interference from any quarter," the Rebel colonel tersely warned.[51] Cortina calmly responded that the boats had always been controlled by Mexico and tied up at night on the south bank. He also expressed a desire to meet Ford to discuss the violation on the frontier "of the laws of neutrality and good neighborly conduct." Cortina was particularly miffed that Confederates had been firing on his men while they were skirmishing with the French near Bagdad. He was sure Ford knew of these outrages and he demanded that he take steps to prevent such occurrence in the future.[52]

In late August 1864, it was Ford's turn to complain when Cortina's men began sniping at Confederate forces at Freeport, just upriver from Brownsville: "I shall cordially act in concert with you in speedily arranging a plan to check these outrages," Ford tersely wrote.[53] Cortina responded by again complaining that any time his forces engaged the French near Bagdad they had been fired on from across the river. Moreover, when French steamers began to penetrate the river, they were preceded by Confederate soldiers scouting along the north bank who reported on the location of his pickets. When the French seized the village of La Burrita, upriver from Bagdad, a French steamboat tied up at a Confederate camp on the north bank, where the Rebels gave them a hardy cheer. Afterward, the entire force of Confederates followed the French steamer up the river. With the French now in control of a large part of the river, the Confederates had even received a shipment of arms, Cortina complained, in return for which the Rebels had driven a herd of beeves across the river.

With the situation on the river quickly intensifying, *Cortinistas*, this time with artillery and small arms, opened fire on Confederates camped at Palmito Ranch, killing several of the Rebels. To Ford, the attack was "unprovoked and unwarranted."[54] To Cortina, it was obvious the Confederates had formed an alliance with the French to drive him out of Matamoros.[55] As a result, Cortina moved six hundred men and an artillery battery into position on the river above Matamoros. He also ordered eight cannon pulled into position overlooking Brownsville.

The Confederates were certain they were to be attacked by Cortina from across the river, while at the same time, the Federals moved in from the coast. "Troops under your command are patrolling the banks of the Rio Grande," Ford curtly told Cortina in a panic, "your artillery is bearing upon the City of Brownsville, you stopped communications with this bank. I would respectfully inquire, if by these acts you intend to indicate that war exists between your government and that of the Confederate States?" Failing to receive a conclusive answer, Ford turned to the French at Bagdad for assistance, but Commander Vernon responded that his position was one of "perfect neutrality towards the United States as well as towards the Confederacy," and he refused to assist the Rebels.[56] If, as Ford surmised, Cortina was intent on attacking Brownsville, the Confederates had no alternative but to strike at Matamoros first. In so doing, Ford had no doubt he might provoke an international incident that would result in President Lincoln sending a large army to the Rio Grande to again cut the flow of badly needed supplies into Texas.

With the Union Army

Although Cortina had some 1,500 men in his Cortina Brigade and twenty guns and could undoubtedly put up a bloody fight, his eventual demise appeared inevitable. At a hastily called council-of-war at the old *cabildo* on the plaza in Matamoros in late August 1864, he took the floor to say that the cause and future of Mexico was closely tied to the United States and the Federal Army. "Surrounded on all sides by hostile forces" and a major assault on Matamoros only days away, he said, every effort must be made to save the artillery and munitions of war. Cortina continued that, as a result, he had undertaken negotiations with Leonard Pierce, the crafty American consul, and he was sure that Colonel Day in Brazos Santiago would welcome the "Cortina Brigade" into his lines. He also believed that, if necessary, the Federals would join him in attacking the French.

In the tense meeting, Maj. José A. Puente rose to urge caution, saying that any such agreement was unprecedented, and he wondered if Pierce was authorized to make such an accord. Cortina responded that he would never do "anything which might compromise or dishonor" the army, but they must confide in his patriotism and good faith. At this point, several officers retired to a separate room and drafted a proposal to be presented to Pierce. The

Cortina Brigade would assist the Federals, even in attacking Brownsville, providing Colonel Day attack the town simultaneously. Once the artillery and munitions of war had been crossed to the north bank, all officers in the Cortina Brigade, including Cortina, must retain their rank and privileges. Although the agreement was endorsed by a majority of those attending, several officers, including Col. Servando Canales, Col. Julián Cerda, Lt. Col. Mario G. Hidalgo, and Major Puente, remained apprehensive.[57] Nevertheless, that evening Major Puente translated the document into English for presentation to Pierce. A few days later, at a meeting between Pierce and Cortina, in which Puente acted as interpreter, the American consul frankly said that neither he nor Colonel Day was authorized to sign such an agreement, but he was sure the Cortina Brigade would be welcomed by the American army and that Cortina could retain control over his artillery and weapons. With Cortina's plan in place, Pierce dispatched a messenger to Colonel Day on Brazos Island, asking the Federals to push back the Confederates camped on the river below Brownsville, thus allowing Cortina to cross the Rio Grande into Texas.

Once they were in the United States, Pierce thought the *Cortinistas* could serve "as beef hunters or muster in as rangers." However, exactly "how this matter will end no one can tell," he admitted. In the end, Canales, Cerda, and Hidalgo concluded they would not "take a single step in the hair-brained measures proposed by Cortina."[58] Still, they did not have the nerve to challenge their commander openly. As such, on the evening of September 3, Cortina gave orders for his brigade to move downriver the next morning to attack the French near La Burrita. In reality, the advance was only a feint that would allow the Cortina Brigade to ford the river and join the Federals, who by design should be advancing from Brazos Island. At the same time, Cortina's brother, José María, would cross above Brownsville and fight his way toward Brazos Santiago. If possible, Cortina would assist the Federals in driving the Confederates out of Brownsville, whereupon Cortina could cross the rest of his artillery and munitions of war.[59] Arriving near La Burrita on September 5, Cortina's artillery opened fire on the French, but it soon became evident that he had no intention of seriously attacking the *Imperialistas*. Many of the officers wanted to assault the French lines, but Cortina, after only a few shots, ordered the artillery and his cavalry to the rear. By noon, Cortina and his staff had followed with the infantry. Three hours later, he ordered his artillery to open fire on the Confederates, who were spotted on the opposite bank of the river. Realizing the ramifications of their commander's orders, Canales, Cerda, Hidalgo, and Puente became indignant. Learning that Cortina had sent his cavalry across the river and that they had already joined the Federals who were skirmishing with the Confederates, they became even more defiant. As a result, Canales huddled with Cerda,

Cols. Julián Cerda and Servando Canales were outspoken critics of Cortina's plan for crossing his army into Texas in September 1864. When 303 *Cortinistas* joined the Union Army on the north bank, it touched off a firestorm of diplomatic protests that reverberated across North America and all the way to Paris. Cortina remained in Matamoros and eventually went over to the French Imperialists. Although he would later return to the Liberal cause, his credibility in the eyes of most *Juaristas* was largely destroyed. *Harper's Weekly,* November 17, 1866.

and the two concluded that "Cortina had taken a wild and criminal measure" and they would not cross the river.

That evening at La Burrita, Canales confronted Cortina, demanding to know why he had not attacked the French. Cortina responded that his intention, as he had said at the council-of-war in Matamoros, was to cross his forces into the United States. Canales responded that what Cortina was trying to do was "not only insane but criminal, that the people of Tamaulipas would never forgive him, and that it was a treacherous deed to set aside his own flag in order to array himself against a people fighting for its independence." If Matamoros must be given up, Canales and Cerda and several other officers concluded, it seemed logical to join the Confederates rather than the Federals. Cortina angrily responded that he was determined to cross his army into Texas, that he was in command, and that he would not change his plans. "Other words, of more or less bitterness were exchanged" by the two "without either altering in any degree the determination of the other," it was said.[60] As Cortina began crossing his army and artillery into Texas, Canales led his men upriver to Matamoros. It was a parting of ways between the two cagy warriors, a disagreement that would grow into bitterness and hatred and endure for decades and profoundly influence the course of events in Tamaulipas.

On the evening of September 8, Colonel Day dispatched a detachment of the 1st Texas Cavalry to the Rio Grande to provide safe passage for Cortina's men. He also scribbled out a note to Cortina saying that he and his men would be welcomed into the United States but his arms must be surrendered.[61] Pushing upriver from White's Ranch to a few miles above Palmito Ranch, the Federals found that Col. Miguel Echazarreta was already across the river with three hundred of Cortina's *Exploradores del Bravo* and three 6-pounder brass cannon. No sooner had the Union forces began negotiating with Colonel Echazarreta to disarm than Col. George Giddings's Confederates attacked them. Outnumbered, the Union commander quickly rearmed the *Cortinistas*, who in the fighting that ensued, fought bravely.[62] The Mexican artillery was particularly effective in repulsing the Rebel advance. But when Confederate reinforcements arrived, Colonel Giddings ordered a second attack on the Union center. When this, too, failed, a third attack finally succeeded in forcing the Federals and the *Cortinistas*, who were short of ammunition, downriver some two miles. In the confusion of battle, a few of the *Cortinistas* fled back across the river. The Confederates, with their backs to the river, were now able to establish a line of pickets that stretched from Brownsville to the Gulf of Mexico.

Fearing that Canales would assume command of what remained of his army in Mexico, Cortina retreated back to Matamoros himself. Any hope of escaping into Texas was gone.[63] Afraid that Colonel Giddings would be reinforced and that his small army and the *Cortinistas* would be overrun and the Mexican artillery captured, Colonel Day led two hundred men and two pieces of artillery from Brazos Island across Boca Chica to White's Ranch before he fell back toward Brazos Island. When the Rebels followed, Day said he "routed" them with his artillery.[64] Nevertheless, on the morning of September 12, along with what remained of the Exploradores del Bravo, Day crossed Boca Chica to the safety of the Federal guns on Brazos Island.

In the fighting along the river, Colonel Ford claimed over one hundred Mexicans and Union soldiers were either killed or wounded. Colonel Day reported that none of his men were killed, although one Union soldier and twelve *Cortinistas* were captured. Day was certain "the killed and wounded of the enemy must have been great."[65] Yet Ford reported a loss of "two or three killed, a few wounded, and three missing."[66] Whatever the numbers, the French were furious with Colonel Day and the Federals for assisting Cortina. As soon as the commander of the Imperial forces at Bagdad, A. Veron, realized what was happening, he dispatched his aide-de-camp to Colonel Day to complain. "I am bound to consider the forces of Gen. Cortina as troops belonging to the United States," Veron wrote.[67] The French commander warned that he had better not encounter Cortina, "on my road, either now or later."[68] When Maj. Gen. John G. Walker, a Missourian in command of the Confederate District of Texas, learned the *Cortinistas* had crossed the river into Texas and had joined the Federals, he sent orders that if Cortina could be captured, he was not to "be treated as a prisoner of war, but as a robber and murderer, and executed immediately."[69] General Walker was not the only Texan who wanted Cortina dead.

A week after the fighting, Colonel Ford sent a flag of truce to Brazos Island to inquire if the Mexicans he had captured were indeed in the service of the United States as they claimed.[70] Colonel Day replied by explaining that the *Cortinistas* were indeed "in the service of the United States and fighting under the U.S. flag," and they should be treated as prisoners of war.[71] On Brazos Island, Colonel Day confiscated all the *Cortinistas'* muskets, Enfield rifles, horses, mules, and their artillery. Nevertheless, Day reported all 303 of Cortina's men were pleased with their treatment. Several even enlisted in the U.S. Army, although most eventually returned to Mexico, many to serve Cortina again.[72]

The presence of the *Cortinista* army in the United States touched off a firestorm of diplomatic protests from the French that reverberated across North America and all the way to Paris. Writing from Montreal, L. de Geofroy, the French chargé d'affaires to the United States, demanded that the *Cortinistas* be disarmed. Moreover, if Cortina had crossed himself, he should "never leave the American territory to make some incursion with his men upon the right bank of the Rio Grande."[73] Seward responded by asking for an explanation from General Banks, who ordered Gen. Edward Richard Sprigg Canby to investigate. In turn, General Canby asked Colonel Day for details. In the process, Canby assured Banks that an "armed enemy of France" would not be tolerated in the United States and that Day would be directed to treat such a force as "enemies of the United States."[74] But what Seward told the French and what was happening on the distant Rio Grande frontier were two very separate and distinct things.

Desperate for artillery of any kind and anxious to purchase Cortina's guns that remained in Matamoros, Rebel authorities in Brownsville, despite the fighting in early September, once again opened relations with Cortina. Gen. Thomas F. Drayton, in temporary command on the river, even signed an agreement with Cortina calling for the resumption of "free and unrestricted intercourse of persons and the passage of merchandise across the Rio Grande." Yet to General Walker, Cortina was little more than "a successful robber, who finds himself accidentally in possession of a city."[75]

In late September 1864, Cortina appeared at the ferry to invite Ford to "come over and hold a friendly talk." Although his comrades warned the Rebel colonel that Cortina was certain to kill him, Ford went anyway. "We needed artillery and knew Cortina would be glad to sell his," Ford recalled, so the "Mexican and the Texian agreed to do business."[76] A variety of proposals were presented, none of which Cortina found acceptable. Yet Ford was in the process of inspecting the guns when a rider galloped up to say that lead columns of General Mejía's *Imperialista* army were entering the city. Consequently, Ford "left in some haste and made Brownsville in good time." He would later conclude, "the whole thing was fixed up by Cortina to let General Mejía find Ford in the hall where the artillery was," thus embarrassing him and damaging future relations with the *Imperialistas*.[77]

With the Empire

As the Imperial army neared Matamoros, General Mejía sent a courier to see Cortina, requesting a meeting the following day. Realizing he had no alternative, Cortina reluctantly agreed. With the Imperial forces certain to enter the city, Cortina made a decision that would haunt him for the rest of his life. He declared for the Empire and gave up his hold on Matamoros. Many years later, in an attempt to salvage his reputation, he would argue that at the time he had no alternative, that cooperation with General Mejía was the only way he could keep his army intact and save his artillery. It was widely rumored at the time that Mejía gave Cortina a large sum of money to buy his allegiance.[78] Rather than surrender or sign on with the French, Col. Servando Canales and most of his men fled to Brownsville where Ford granted them asylum, provided Canales disarm and disband his regiment.

Commanding the Imperial forces on the Rio Grande, Gen. Tomás Mejía, who was honorable and never unnecessarily cruel, was criticized for his lenient treatment of Cortina. A reactionary defender of the Church and dreaded opponent of the Liberal government, Mejía had fought the republic for a decade. For his dedication to the conservative cause and his gallant defense of Matamoros in 1865, Maximilian awarded him the grand cross of the newly created Order of the Mexican Eagle. As Cortina stood by on June 19, 1867, the Indian from Guanajuato was executed at Querétaro along with Maximilian and Miguel Miramón. *Lawrence T. Jones collection.*

On September 26, with flags flying and drums beating, General Mejía triumphantly entered Matamoros, and Cortina put on the uniform of the Empire. Three days later, Confederate authorities in Brownsville rushed across the river to congratulate the *Imperialists* and assure General Mejía of their friendly intentions toward Maximilian and the Empire.[79] Mejía graciously embraced the Confederates, saying he would reciprocate by crossing to Brownsville for a visit in a few days. The little general told the gray-clad Rebels that the flag of the Empire meant "peace and progress." The appearance of "Gen. Tomás Mejía upon the Rio Grande was viewed with pleasure by [the] Confederates," Ford declared. To the gray-clad Rebel colonel, Mejía was "honest, sincere, and truthful," and someone "who had fought his way up from a low position to the top of the ladder."[80] Despite the deep-rooted corruption in the Imperial Mexican army, where everyone regarded "state property as a milch cow," Mejía was "widely regarded as one of the best and most honest citizens."[81] Yet he was seen by at least one French marine as a womanizer and, ergo, somehow to die at an early age.[82] In Matamoros, Mejía began a series of redoubts and forts that eventually encircled the city from the river on the east to the river on the west. Work that had begun earlier on a major fortification, Casa Mata, was also completed. Principal architect for the construction was Maj. Felix A. Blucher, Prussian-born engineer in the Confederate army.[83]

Suspicious of Cortina and his motivations, General Mejía wasted no time testing his mettle when he sent him in pursuit of Canales who had crossed his army back into Mexico. Knowing his antipathy for the Confederates in Texas and fearing that Cortina unleashed might again raid Texas, General Slaughter wrote General Mejía to protest, but there was little the Rebel commanders could do but maintain a vigil on the river. Upriver near Guerrero, Cortina encountered the rag-tag army of his former friend and decisively drove him from the field. In the fighting, he was said to have commanded his small army with "considerable skill."[84]

From the time Cortina went over to the Empire, he seemed to exert more and more independence, and Mejía and the French seemed mystified as what should be done with him. By the time Mejía was called to Mexico City for consultations in March 1864, Cortina had become very much of an independent war lord, and many on the river were sure it was only a matter of time before he switched sides again.[85] Cortina is "in the service of the Empire, but recruiting fast, and when the time arrives will be found in the right place," Union authorities reported from Brazos Santiago.[86] The result seemed inevitable. Scurrying about through the chaparral, Cortina, a complex and enigmatic man of many lives and convictions, was certain to again declare for the republic.

Chapter Six

Tiger in the Chaparral

I hope General Grant will not recognize the traitor and bandit Cortina... I have him where I want him, between two fires.

JOSÉ MARÍA DE JESÚS CARVAJAL

ON APRIL 1, 1865, at San Fernando on the coastal plain, some eighty-five miles south of Matamoros, Cortina reasserted his loyalty to Juárez and the Mexican republic.[1] Consistently plotting to deliver Matamoros to the Liberals, his heart had never been with the Empire. Besides, he had never been given the money Mejía had promised when he originally gave up Matamoros. Cortina's decision to cast his fate with the Liberals proved to be a serious blow to the Imperial cause and a decisive factor in turning the tide against the Empire in Tamaulipas. Telling Minister of War Miguel Negrete that he was "determined to resume" his "natural character," Cortina was eager to be back in the Liberal cause.[2]

Only days after pronouncing against the Empire, Cortina cut the telegraph from Bagdad to Matamoros and took four hundred cavalry and a company of infantry and advanced on Matamoros in hopes of securing the artillery he had previously secreted in the city. Finding no guards on the outskirts of the city and only a few soldiers patrolling Plaza Hidalgo, he raced into the city with forty of his best men late on the evening of April 11. In a running gun battle on the plaza, Cortina killed an Imperialist colonel and several of his men while losing only one of his sergeants. "I held the streets for more than two hours," he bragged. After securing his artillery, stealing some horses, and persuading several citizens to join him, Cortina courageously galloped out of town. He retreated to Santa Rosalía, six miles upriver from Matamoros, then moved his brigade to China. There, he was able to pay his men for the first time in months. He also sent José María to Juárez with a full report of his actions, hoping again to ingratiate himself with the president.

Although never fully trusting Cortina, the struggling Republican government was relieved to have him back in their ranks. Juárez "is pleased with General Cortina's protests of patriotism," Foreign Minister Sebastián Lerdo de Tejada reported from Chihuahua.³ Despite his renewed loyalty, Cortina remained politically and militarily autonomous, frequently refusing to follow orders from his Liberal superiors. Yet he remained on the offensive and attacked Matamoros on May 1, only to be bloodily repulsed.⁴

More than anyone else, Cortina could sniff the changing tide in Tamaulipas. Retaining control of several hundred loyal soldiers, he sent his older brother José María to Camargo. Although forces of the Empire frequently held Camargo, Cortina had always been popular in the town. He was also hoping men from Reynosa, Mier, and Guerrero would rally to his cause. After all, they had done so in the past. As José María rode upriver, he carried a manifesto from Cortina asking all the villages and towns along the Rio Grande help him in expelling the invaders. Continued French intervention would result in the "death of our nationality and the extermination of the [Mexican] family," Cortina warned. He promised to fight to the death the Empire and all the Mexican traitors who supported it. Tamaulipas must be pacified at all costs.⁵

With fifty soldiers, José María seized the customs house at Camargo and $30,000 in revenues. Here on the banks of the San Juan River, only a stone's throw from the Cortina family home near the plaza, Liberal forces began to gather. The same afternoon José María rode into town, Francisco de León arrived with 408 well-equipped cavalry. That night, Juan Cortina, a cousin of Gen. Juan Cortina, arrived from upriver with another 150 men.⁶ Within three weeks, Cortina had more than doubled the size of his army. From distant Chihuahua, the president seemed pleased that he was making progress against the *Imperialistas* on the lower Rio Grande.

Realizing his success in Mexico was closely tied to events in the United States, Cortina met with Union officers outside Matamoros, urging them to advance on Brownsville, saying the sooner they took the city the sooner he could seize Matamoros. He also asked for the return of the artillery he had sent across the river in October 1864.⁷

In a meeting at Bagdad as late as May 26, General Mejía, who was leery and suspicious of a large American military presence on the frontier, told Union authorities that, despite the surrender of Confederate forces east of the Mississippi, the "Rebels in Texas were a recognizable power."⁸ Despite Mejía's wishes that the Confederacy live on, Cortina watched as the Rebel Army on the Rio Grande disintegrated into disorder and confusion in the late spring of 1865. With the accompanying chaos, violence in Texas became even worse than before the Civil War. From Eagle Pass to the gulf, a general breakdown in law and order led to highway robberies, murders, kidnapping, and general thievery. One prominent individual who fell victim to the violence was Ramos Larrache, a wealthy merchant from San Luis Potosí. Along with three other men, Larrache was killed by Cortina partisans near Rio Grande City in July 1865.[9]

Both Cortina and Juárez cheered the end of the Civil War and the arrival of the Federal army on the Rio Grande. "We will have our backs covered" and a "fresh breath of air," Juárez wrote from Chihuahua.[10] With the arrival of the Union army, the president seemed excited that arms and ammunition could flow across the Rio Grande into Republican Mexico. Upriver in Coahuila, nine hundred new rifles and four pieces of artillery were crossed on the ferry at Piedras Negras.[11]

Affairs Beautifully Mixed Up

With the collapse of the Southern Confederacy, as many as eight to ten thousand gray-clad, unrepentant Rebels, fearing they would be imprisoned or hanged for treason by an unforgiving Union army, fled to Mexico. Those crossing the Rio Grande included generals Edmund Kirby Smith, John B. Magruder, and Joseph O. Shelby. Texas governor Edward Clark, as well as former governors from Louisiana, Kentucky, and Missouri, along with the last Rebel governor of the state, Pendleton Murrah, all fled into Mexico. In late May 1865, while Confederates made their way into Mexico and Union forces arrived in Brownsville, relations with the *Imperialistas* became increasingly volatile. As Cortina huddled in the chaparral outside Matamoros, Gen. Frederick Steele, a New York–born hero of the Vicksburg Campaign, set up army headquarters on Brazos Island and then at Fort Brown.[12] Steele was especially interested in capturing Magruder and Smith, who were said to have crossed the river at Eagle Pass.[13] With orders to seal off the border to Confederate refugees and bandits, Steele and a large part of the black 25th Army Corps prepared to reoccupy the posts upriver from Brownsville.

Despite their lack of sufficient cavalry, Federal officers hoped to join forces with Cortina to apprehend as many Rebels as possible. When it was learned that General Shelby was already in the Mexican interior with a large quantity of rifles and two pieces of artillery, Steele wrote Mejía demanding that he be arrested and turned over to Federal authorities, along with all his arms and ammunition.[14] As Steele learned, Mejía was not about to make any such arrests. Not only had he received Confederate arms and artillery in Matamoros, but he also was openly recruiting the defeated and wayward southerners into his Foreign Legion.

At this time, Melinda Rankin observed, "a man with a 'blue coat' could pass Cortinas' camp unhurt, while a 'gray coat' would uniformly come up missing."[15] One former Confederate who did not fare well in Mexico was

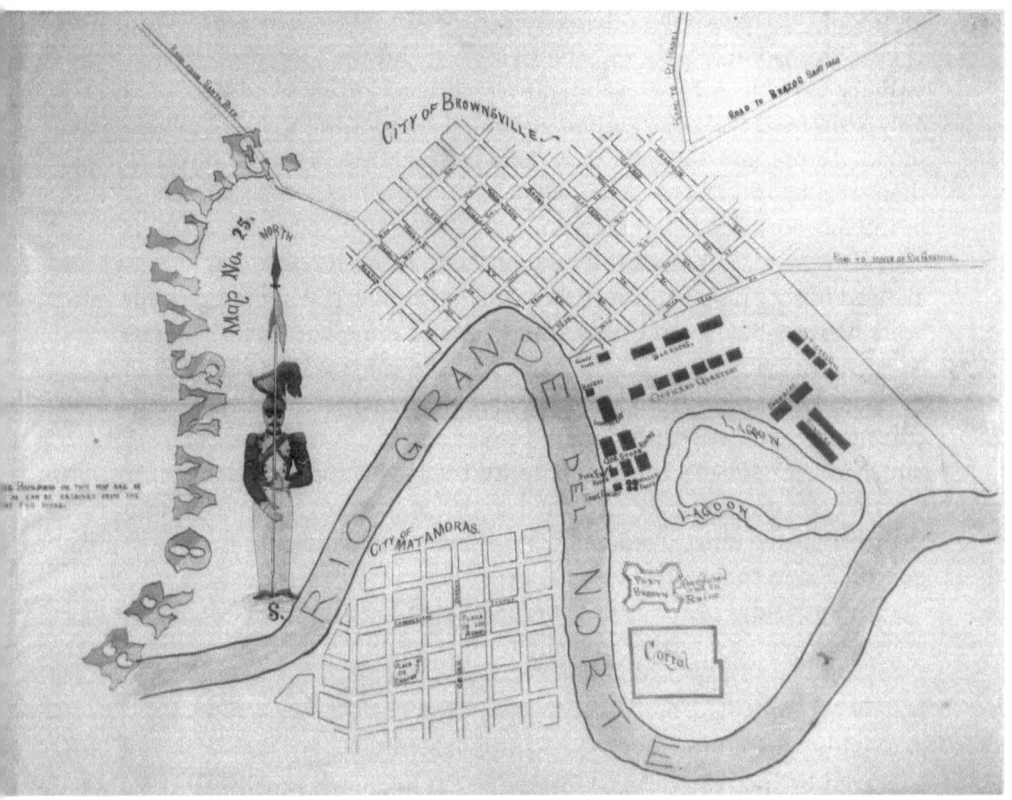

Shortly after the Civil War, the U.S. Army made this map of Fort Brown and the twin cities of Brownsville and Matamoros. *National Archives.*

Mosby Monroe Parsons, a Confederate general from Missouri. After obtaining a passport from Mejía in Matamoros, Parsons and several members of his staff and their families headed south only to be robbed and brutally murdered by a band of Cortina's cavalry led by Col. Dario Díaz at a ranch seven miles from China, Nuevo León, on the road from Camargo to Monterrey. Another Confederate fatality was Governor Murrah who died of tuberculosis in Monterrey.[16]

After crossing the Rio Grande a few miles from Roma, another party of Confederates including generals Alexander Watkins Terrell, William P. Hardeman, and Clay King, as well as colonels George Flournoy, M. T. Johnson, and Peter Smith, were surrounded in the chaparral not far from the river by twenty-five heavily armed *Cortinistas*. Cortina's men gave the men in gray some green corn for their horses but demanded they surrender their weapons. Fearing if they did so they would be shot, Terrell and his men refused but agreed to be escorted into Mier where they were met by an angry mob and the alcalde who demanded they surrender their arms. With little choice, the Confederates reluctantly did so and were escorted to the town's military barracks for the evening. Fearful that Cortina would arrive and not only keep their weapons and horses but also order the Rebels before a firing squad, Terrell and his men were able to bribe several local officials, regain their weapons and horses, and gallop off into the night to an uncertain future in the interior of the country.[17]

With the U.S. Army firmly established on the Rio Grande, Cortina was allowed to set up a recruiting office in Brownsville. It was the first time in six years he was able to freely walk the streets of the town. Besides Tejanos and Mexicanos, many of those who came forth to enlist were recently discharged African Americans. With lingering and bitter memories of the Cortina War, citizens of the town were dismayed to see bands of *Cortinistas*, some of them under indictment in Cameron County, freely walking the streets of the city. Cortina's men were easily identified from the six-guns strapped to their hips, their bright red shirts, and ribbons in their hats indicating the company or guerrilla band to which they belonged.[18]

On both sides of the lower border it was a well-known fact that the Federals were openly courting and sheltering Cortina and his guerrillas. "There is a perfect mystery why this notorious assassin and outlaw has not been picked up by the law loving authority of the United States," moaned Henry A. Maltby, the editor of the pro-Imperial *Matamoros Daily Ranchero*. Encouraged by the Americans, Cortina began to launch raids against Imperial supply lines from camps in Texas.[19] Well aware of Americans' complicity in the raids, French authorities complained bitterly to Secretary of State William Seward that Cortina was not only using Brownsville as his headquarters but also crossing the Rio Grande at will.

Bluecoats Again

To confirm his legitimacy with the Federals, Cortina sent Lt. Col. Domingo López de Lara to the Americans with a letter saying he had been appointed by Juárez to defend Tamaulipas against the *Imperialistas*. As such, he wanted to cross merchandise he was seizing in Mexico into Texas, sell it, and use the money to purchase arms and pay his men.[20] Hoping to obtain as many weapons in the United States as possible, he went out of his way to befriend the American military, even granting them permission to cross into Mexico should they find it necessary.

At a festive 1865 Fourth of July celebration in Brownsville, Cortina and a number of his richly attired officers appeared as guests of the Federal Army.[21] Although no liquor was served at the function, a number of officers became "decidedly mellow," and one of Cortina's men loudly pronounced that he did not like the American music. At the same time, he also demanded that a certain "señorita not dance with the Yankees." In a fracas that followed, one of the Federal officers drew a pistol and struck the officer over the head. "A general muss came very near ensuing, but it ended in loud and long-drawn curses, without further demonstration of a knock-down character," Maltby wrote in the *Ranchero*.[22] Despite the altercation, three weeks later Cortina invited the American officers to a convivial fandango at Rancho del Carmen.[23] About this time, a correspondent for the *New York Herald* found Cortina comfortably quartered in Brownsville:

> I found the chief at a small house belonging to him. He was seated in a room floored with brick, and containing a small table, covered with a red cloth. A few chairs made up the rest of the furniture of the room. Cortina is a man of about 50 years of age. He is of the middle size and strongly made. There is nothing at all noteworthy about his face. His black hair and beard are now tingeing with gray. As to dress, the chief wore simply a light black coat and pantaloons of a gray color. In everything he looked the quiet citizen.[24]

Exaggerating, as he was prone to do, Cortina told the reporter he had three thousand men and could be in Matamoros in a few days. With the defeat of the Empire, the people of Mexico and the United States could live in peace and harmony, he said.

From his headquarters at Rancho del Carmen, Cortina brazenly seized two steamboats, the *Señorita* and the *Belle*, and forced the steamers to tie up on the Texas bank of the river.[25] "Affairs on the Rio Grande frontier are getting beautifully mixed up," Gen. Philip H. Sheridan telegraphed Washington from New Orleans.[26] In July, Cortina seized a third steamer, the *Camargo*, and forced it to the Texas bank.[27]

A Growing Uneasiness

Although the French complained endlessly and vociferously about Cortina, Federal authorities on the frontier did little to curtail his activities in Texas as he continued to strike at the Imperialists in Matamoros. "Cortina is giving the *Imperialistas* a great deal of trouble," General Steele wrote from Brownsville. General Mejía and the Empire held Matamoros, but Cortina "appears to have full sway everywhere else on the Rio Grande, interrupting their communications both by land and water," Steele observed.[28] Although he initially cheered Cortina's seizure of the *Señorita*, General Grant eventually concluded the Federals were becoming too cozy with Cortina, and orders went out to curtail his activities in Texas. Moreover, the attack on the *Señorita*, Grant pointed out, had come from the Texas side of the river. Permitting such actions was "entirely inexcusable on the part of the commander at Brownsville."[29]

As the Americans listened politely to French protests, they intensified their diplomatic pressure to force the Imperialists out of Mexico. Particularly upsetting was talk in Mexican Imperial circles that Texas should be returned to Mexico as a protectorate. A confrontation seemed inevitable. At the same time the Americans were quietly aiding Cortina, they attempted to calm Mejía's concerns and trepidations relative to the growing American military presence on the border. "In the conflict we take no part," Gen. Egbert Benson Brown told Mejía, reflecting official State Department policy. "We practice absolute non-intervention and non-interference." Although Mejía initially "presented a feeling of kindness towards the government of the United States," he could not be trusted, Brown concluded, although the Mexican general was allowing the Americans to purchase beef and horses in Matamoros.[30]

With the American officers and their black soldiers decidedly in sympathy with Juárez and the liberal cause, tensions continued to intensify in the hot and humid summer of 1865. In a war of words, Mejía went as far as to complain that Brownsville had become a haven for enemies of the Empire and that American soldiers were firing on his troops on the south bank of the river.[31] Black soldiers were reported to have secured temporary leaves-of-absence to join Cortina. In Brownsville, it was said, men could receive up to $50 a month to enlist as "bodyguards" to assist unnamed parties having "business" in Mexico.[32] In fact, both Cortina and the Imperial army, especially the contra-guerrillas, were recruiting Americans, many of them former Confederates or discharged Federals.[33] Cortina not only recruited large numbers of African Americans but also men with experience in the artillery.

While on a tour of the Rio Grande frontier in the summer of 1865, General Sheridan met with Cortina in Brownsville and reported him in "good spirits." With an additional four hundred men, Cortina could take Matamoros, Sheridan told General Grant. Still hoping to go after the Confederates who had fled to Mexico and chase the French out at the same time, Sheridan wanted to intervene in Mexico himself. "I feel certain that with 6,000 to 8,000 cavalry I can stir up the whole of Northern Mexico," the little general bragged.[34] Later, when Cortina sent an agent to army headquarters in New Orleans, Sheridan confided to Grant that Juárez was "stupid." Nevertheless, he hoped to meet with the Mexican president at Fort Duncan or somewhere on the upper Rio Grande to coordinate a strategy to expel the forces of the Empire.[35] Grant, too, wanted the French kicked out of Mexico.

As the bluecoats waited anxiously for orders that would send them into Mexico, President Andrew Johnson and the Radical Republicans were busy waging a political war in Washington. In the meantime, Secretary of State Seward remained hesitant about interfering in the internal affairs of Mexico or creating any hostile action that might provoke the Mexican Imperialists into an armed conflict. As far as Seward was concerned, the Mexican Empire could not sustain itself and the French should be given time to evacuate the country. American intervention would only prolong the occupation, Seward theorized.

Orders soon arrived in Brownsville to "prevent aid or supplies being given from the United States to either belligerent." Yet war materials, overtly and covertly, continued to flow across the river to support Cortina and his struggling and beleaguered *guerrilleros*. Smuggling, long a way of life on the Rio Grande, became more rampant and lucrative than at any time in the recent past. Nevertheless, "troops under my command," General Brown repeatedly told Imperialist and Liberal alike, "will not be permitted in any manner to interfere in the present relations of Mexico."[36] What Brown and the Federals were saying in public and what was happening on the river at night were very different, however.

A major confrontation developed when Federal authorities demanded the return of the artillery Mejía had purchased from the Confederates in the final weeks of the Civil War. Until the guns are given up, "annoy the French authorities as much as you can ... without provoking actual hostilities," General Sheridan suggested to Steele.[37] Juárez hoped the showdown would lead to American intervention. Regardless, Mejía was diplomatically cornered, the president astutely calculated. "If Mejía surrenders the pieces, he will be left weak and Cortina will be able to attack him with success; and if he does not surrender them, he will be attacked by the Americans," Juárez surmised.[38] After weeks of heated rhetoric and missives flying back and forth across the Rio Grande, the French finally acquiesced in early July 1865, when an express arrived from Emperor Maximilian directing Mejía to give up the guns.[39] Tensions continued, nevertheless, when the Federals "quietly" returned to Cortina the artillery and arms he had sent across the river in October 1864, including three rifled brass 12-pounder artillery pieces.[40]

Lurking in the Chaparral

On the south bank, General Mejía's three-thousand-man Imperial Army, only three hundred of whom were French and Austrian, remained securely entrenched in Matamoros. Yet they were under almost constant attack from Cortina's rag-tag guerrillas who lurked in the chaparral on the outskirts of the city. Although outnumbered ten to one, Cortina successfully cut communications between Matamoros and Bagdad and by August was in control of the roads leading upriver and into the interior of the country. Only by purchasing supplies from across the river were the Imperialists able to sustain themselves. "Guerrillas continue to swarm about Matamoros," a correspondent for the *New York Herald* reported in July 1865; three hundred *Cortinistas* "circle about the city, killing or capturing every living thing which moves."

Cortina's guerrillas attack the French gunboat *La Bellone* on the Rio Grande near La Burrita. *Le Monde Illustré. Courtesy of Gerard Mignard.*

When pursued by Mejía's cavalry, "they flee to the chaparral—low thick, tangled woods whose devious winding paths they are perfectly familiar, and where it is impossible to pursue them."[41] A fifth column of *Cortinistas* even tried to assassinate Tómas Pauda, the editor of the conservative newspaper *Monitor de la Frontera*.[42]

Fearing that Cortina would launch an all-out attack on the city, General Mejía confiscated arms from anyone in Matamoros thought to be sympathetic with the republic, declared martial law, and armed several hundred French, German, Spanish, and English citizens, including one company of two hundred men commanded by Francisco Yturria.[43] As tensions heightened, frightened citizens fled to Brownsville. "A general exodus of women, children and parrots to Brownsville, began yesterday morning and is still going on," one newspaper reported.[44] During the exodus, Mejía even gave permission for Rafaela and the Cortina family to leave the city, although he refused their request to carry $30,000 in specie with them.[45]

With orders to take Cortina "dead or alive," the *Imperialistas* had commenced a major campaign to defeat him as early as May 1865. Twenty-five miles upriver shortly thereafter, one of Cortina's captains and several of his men were captured and summarily executed on the spot.[46] Continuing upriver, the *Imperialistas* seizing Reynosa in May 1865. At Camargo, Cortina made a gallant stand but was thrown back across the San Juan River.

One of the victims of the vicious war on the river was the colorful and impulsive Adrián J. Vidal. In June 1865, Vidal was captured by the *Imperialistas* while hiding on the steamer *Alamo* at Camargo. Said to have been on his way downriver to confer with Cortina, he was tried as a guerrilla spy, found guilty, and ordered shot.[47] Although Vidal's wealthy and influential stepfather, Mifflin Kenedy, used "powerful means," evidently bribes, to save his stepson, on the morning of June 14, 1865, Vidal was executed. "I write with a heavy hand, as my boy has been shot at Camargo," Kenedy vividly recorded. "As bad as he is, I would have saved him if [I] could, but my efforts have failed.... He died at 20 years, one month and five days old, and to all appearances less concerned than any one present. He took the bandage from his eyes, and faced the guard, requesting them not to shoot him in the face, which was not complied with. He requested his body be sent to his mother. My brother being at Camargo at the time with the *Alamo,* he has brought him down, and [he] is buried here in Matamoros."[48] The young captain had served both the blue and the gray, deserted from both, joined a third army, and was shot by a fourth. Vidal's short and violent life was perhaps symbolic of the tumultuous times along the Rio Grande at this pivotal time in history.

Empire Rejuvenated

The Matamoros merchant elite, who had watched their trade decline with the end of the American Civil War, cheered as Mejía took the offensive against Cortina and successfully reestablished communications to Camargo.[49] For the first time, stages arrived from Monterrey and Bagdad without being robbed.[50] With Cortina and the *Juaristas* on the defensive for the first time in months, the future of the Empire on the border looked bright. General Steele, who had been approached by an agent of the Liberal government with the idea of selling mules in Texas to raise money for the *Juaristas,* was convinced the republic was on the verge of collapse.

A festive mood returned to Matamoros. Each week, large crowds gathered on the plaza in the heroic city to hear the martial airs of the Imperial band. In early August, Maximilian's agent, Luis Robles, along with General Mejía and other officers from both the Federal and Imperial armies, gathered for a grand ball in Matamoros.[51] A month later, the Diez y Seis de Septiembre celebration included an elaborate banquet where red and green streamers decorated the hall. The gathering was said to have been the most splendid ceremony ever held in the city. A few days later, Robles invited the Americans for a steamboat excursion and a dance in the evening.[52] A week later, officers of the American military crossed the river again for a festive ball to celebrate General Mejía's forty-fifth birthday.[53] There was one dinner after another, a young Austrian officer wrote from Matamoros: "I do not believe that in my whole life altogether I have enjoyed so much champagne, Rhine wine, claret and all sorts of delicacies as in the five weeks of my stay here." At one gala there was "3,000 elegantly served places at tables in the open in the great square" where "every man [had a] bottle of claret, masses of English beer and champagne ... stewed fruit and roasts and pieces of ham, in a word everything imaginable."[54] Contemplating a visit by Emperor Maximilian and Empress Carlota, Mejía constructed a magnificent opera house, El Teatro del Imperio, to entertain the royal couple. Although Cortina continued to hover on the outskirts of the city, it appeared to many in Matamoros and throughout Mexico as if peace would at last be restored to the troubled land.

As Cortina failed to drive the enemy out of Matamoros, the fighting shifted to the interior of the state. He recaptured Camargo and harassed the fleeing Imperial garrison as they retreated toward Monterrey. In July, he also attacked a convoy containing a large quantity of specie on the way from Matamoros to Monterrey, but was bloodily repulsed with heavy losses. Several *Cortinistas* who were captured in the attack were executed as bandits on the spot.[55] Barely able to escape himself, Cortina fled across the river to regroup at Rancho del Carmen. A few weeks later, an Imperial night patrol out of Matamoros surprised Cortina's pickets some sixteen miles upriver from Matamoros, overran his camp, captured saddles and weapons, and even took an elegantly engraved sword Ignacio Comonfort had presented Cortina in Ciudad Victoria in 1863.[56]

In typical guerrilla fashion, small bands of *Cortinistas* remained active, often robbing wagon trains and stages on the roads to Monterrey and Bagdad. The dedicated Protestant missionary, Melinda Rankin, recalled how the stage she was riding in was stopped in the night by a band of *Cortinistas* halfway between Monterrey and Matamoros. "It has become extremely hazardous to travel through [Cortina's] dominions," she wrote, "and every stage attempting to pass met with portions of his command, and passengers were dispossessed of every thing they had, escaping only with their lives."[57] Informed they were prisoners, the passengers were taken to a camp in the chaparral where a lieutenant said Cortina was not far away. "Our carriage was driven into the center of a large space, around which were stationed vast numbers of armed men, some on foot and some on horses [and] several men lying around on the grass evidently sick."[58] After about five hours, a band of martial music heralded Cortina's arrival. He was, Rankin recalled, "the complete personification of a guerrilla chief." For several minutes, Cortina sat on his horse in silent contemplation, as the terrified passengers watched silently. Suddenly he placed his hand on his stomach, looking earnestly at the passengers and said, "*Yo tengo hambre*," and with his staff at his heels, he retired to a small *jacal*. After about thirty minutes, he emerged, looking very much nurtured, spoke with the stagecoach driver, gave him a pass, and bade to passengers to "go in peace."[59]

In response to the interruption of commerce, thirty-four of the leading merchants in Matamoros protested to General Steele that "armed bands of men who, under pretext of carrying on a civil and foreign war, limit themselves almost entirely to the perpetration of outrages by plundering private property and murdering innocent travelers." Merchants such as José San Román, Jeremiah Galván, and Samuel Beltrán could not understand how bandits committing "foul deeds and nameless outrages," could be allowed to "cross into the State of Texas for an asylum against punishment." The merchants were perplexed that "the property of Americans doing business in Mexico" was "subjected to pillage by raids fitted out under the protection of the flag of their own country."[60] Despite such protestations, General Steele paid the merchants little attention. Indeed, merchants at Reynosa, Camargo, and Mier—towns that frequently changed hands during this turbulent period of Mexican history—suffered from both the *Imperialistas* and the *Juaristas*. With the customs receipts from Matamoros and Bagdad flowing into the Imperial coffers, the only money to feed, clothe, and equip the struggling *Juarista* army in Tamaulipas and Nuevo León came from forced loans on businesses and prominent citizens.

In late July, with the ringing of church bells in Matamoros, it was reported that Cortina had suffered a resounding defeat at Rancho del Brazil, upriver from Matamoros. Several *Cortinistas*, including African Americans, were said to have been captured and hanged by the banks of the Rio Grande. But hours later, the *Imperialistas* came limping back into Matamoros carrying their wounded and pulling their artillery. "If Cortina has been beaten, then he is plainly not pursued," one newspaper reported.[61] Every month, a few of Cortina's guerrillas were caught and executed. Often as not, many of those who died were only thought to be Cortina partisans. Yet by late summer, Cortina had become even more active than before. In September, for example, he captured a *conducta* carrying $100,000 in specie between the Rio Grande and Monterrey.[62]

To complicate matters, General Mejía continued to complain that *Cortinistas* on the Texas bank of the river were sniping at his pickets. As a result, Steele warned Cortina to desist and withdraw his forces. Cortina responded by asserting that the incident had come when Mejía's soldiers seized several peaceful citizens and burned Rancho Sabinito. Saying he was "aware of the neutrality of the United States in the political affairs of Mexico," Cortina related how the *Imperialistas* had fired on several innocent citizens while they were swimming the river to safety, even continuing to shoot at them after they had reached the Texas shore.[63] By September, General Steele was complaining that Cortina's men, particularly Andrés Olguín, Rafael Rodríguez, and Ramón Cantú, were stealing cattle in Texas and driving the livestock into Mexico. Such cattle raids must stop, Steele warned. Although Cortina promised he would do everything possible to apprehend the raiders and turn them over to the American authorities, he pointed out that the three men had never been in his army or were deserters.[64]

Hyena of Tamaulipas

Frustrated with their inability to defeat Cortina, the swashbuckling, cigar-chomping Col. Charles du Pin and his dreaded battalion of contra-guerrillas were sent into Tamaulipas.[65] Based at Ciudad Victoria and Matamoros, the contra-guerrillas were superbly mounted, well paid, and well equipped. They were feared all over northeastern Mexico. Under orders to eradicate the *Cortinistas* and the guerrillas infesting the primitive roads in the region, Colonel Du Pin's cavalry "fought fire with more fire," gaining a reputation for their unrepentant brutality against combatants and civilians alike.[66] Called the "Hyena of Tamaulipas" the sombrero-crowned Du Pin, who recruited a number of Americans in Matamoros, was accused of hanging "invalids and cripples" and sacking entire towns.[67] In large areas of northeastern Mexico, especially the Huasteca, the guerrilla war reached new heights of savagery and ruthlessness. This rugged, water-blessed region of the Sierra Madre Oriental included southwestern Tamaulipas, southern Nuevo León, and northern parts of Veracruz and San Luis Potosí. With choking tropical cloud forests, spectacular waterfalls, secluded caves, and rugged, verdant canyons, large parts of the Huasteca were virtually inaccessible. Here native dialects were common and the pursued took refuge. In the valley of Rio Blanco in the Huasteca, south of Monterrey, the contras executed civilians, hanged captives, pillaged homes, burned crops, destroyed the municipal archives, drove off all the animals in the vicinity, and even "killed all the hogs and chickens," besides "throwing ... offal into the streets and public squares till the smell was intolerable."[68] To the east in the area around Ciudad Victoria, Du Pin and his contra-guerrillas were said to have stripped the land bare and "left the inhabitants exposed to starvation."[69]

Individuals thought to be guerrillas or in sympathy with Cortina were summarily shot by Du Pin. Hoping to avoid his unbridled wrath, thousands of destitute villagers fled into the mountains. In the unending violence, Cortina and his guerrillas were equally brutal. "Every prisoner, upon either side, after going through the form of a trial—a mere mockery—is taken out and shot," one newspaper reported.[70] Suffice it to say that never in its long history had Mexico seen a war as vicious as the war of the *guerrilleros* in Tamaulipas.

A serious problem for the Liberals in Tamaulipas was the constant, often bloody, and almost fratricidal internal struggle for power. In early August, Francisco de León arrived at army headquarters in Brownsville asking to be recognized as the legitimate governor of Tamaulipas. Cortina had become, De León asserted, a "murderer, robber & mean scoundrel," someone without principle who had been "stealing from his countrymen & everybody else to enrich himself." Cortina was not only illiterate, he had "betrayed everybody that ever trusted him."[71] Juárez was being repeatedly deceived by Cortina

In command of the Imperial contra-guerrillas, Col. Charles Louis du Pin used savage means to suppress Cortina and his guerrillas. A painter, intellectual, and writer who spoke several languages, Du Pin was physically broken by his service in Mexico and died in poverty at Montpellier, France, in 1868. *Author's collection.*

who had killed "good liberals who were defending the cause of independence."[72] It was only a matter of time, De León told the Americans, before Cortina went over to the Empire again.

Hoping to bring some semblance of unity to the Liberal army in Tamaulipas, Juárez sent Gen. Mariano Escobedo to the frontier to command the Army of the North. The bespectacled Escobedo, who looked more like a schoolteacher than a soldier, had begun life as a farm laborer in Nuevo León. A dedicated Liberal, he had fought against the Americans in 1847 and gallantly at Puebla on Cinco de Mayo, 1862, after which he was promoted to brigadier general. Later he was captured by the Conservative forces of General Mejía at Rio Verde in San Luis Potosí but released. Arriving on the Rio Grande, one of the first things Escobedo did was meet separately with Cortina and Servando Canales at Camargo. If the Imperial army were to be driven out of Tamaulipas, the two warriors would have to put the past behind them and unite under his command. Without hesitating, Cortina said he would serve the republic anywhere duty called him, but Canales hesitated, saying only that he would help drive the *Imperialistas* out of Tamaulipas.

Coming to play a large role in the war in Tamaulipas at this time was the old warrior José María de Jesús Carvajal, who had been sent by Juárez to New York to procure arms, munitions, and raise money and volunteers for an expeditionary force to Mexico.[73] In October 1865, after General Escobedo learned that Carvajal was likely to succeed, he prepared to move on Matamoros. He also issued two *pronunciamientos* from his headquarters at Santa Rosalía. The first was an attempt to rally as many troops to the Liberal cause as possible, saying he would lead them in casting off "the yoke of the so-called empire." He also hoped to persuade the Imperial Mexican troops in Matamoros to throw down their arms and join the Liberals.[74]

Battle for Matamoros

By October 20, 1865, Escobedo and his Army of the North arrived at the gates of Matamoros where they began to entrench. From his headquarters at the Albino Peña ranch, Escobedo send an ultimatum into the city giving General Mejía two hours to surrender. Mejía promptly replied that he had sufficient men and arms to defend the city, and he invited Escobedo to "commence your operations as soon as you think convenient."[75] Expecting an onslaught for months, Mejía had strengthened the cordon of forts guarding the city, even clearing the chaparral and tearing down several small *jacales* in front of the defenses. He also declared Matamoros and Bagdad in a state of siege.[76]

In the early morning darkness of October 25, Escobedo's army, including numerous black Americans, was in line of battle in front of the fortifications guarding the heroic city.[77] The assault was to begin at 3 A.M., but a cold north

One of the few men to enjoy as much power and influence on the Rio Grande as Cortina was José María de Jesús Carvajal. Related to Cortina by blood, Carvajal persuaded Cortina to evacuate Brownsville in 1859. Although the two men were once close, they became bitter rivals in the struggle for power in Tamaulipas. *Carte de visite by Mathew Brady. Lew Wallace collection, Indiana Historical Society.*

wind with pounding rain swept in from the north and delayed the attack for three hours. Shortly before daybreak, Cortina led the left wing of the army while Gen. Pedro Hinojosa attacked on the right. At first, only small parties of thinly clad soldiers could be seen approaching the city in the grayish dawn, but then a much larger party attacked one of the artillery redoubts along the southeastern defenses. Hinojosa overran one fort, advancing as far as Plaza de Independencia before he was halted. On the far left, Cortina silenced the guns from one fort and overran a second. Hearing that part of his fortifications had been overrun, Mejía heroically galloped out at the head of five hundred Imperial cavalry and drove the *Juaristas* from the captured works.[78] As other attacks slammed against the breastworks closer to the river, many of the foreign citizens of the city, especially the European merchants and their employees, helped barricade the streets with cotton bales near Plaza Hidalgo. Hundreds of frightened citizens crowded the banks of the Rio Grande awaiting passage to Brownsville.

In the midst of battle, the Imperial gunboat *Paisano* steamed onto the scene and began shelling the attackers. As the *Juaristas* fell back, several companies of Imperial troops with fixed bayonets pursued them into the chaparral. At the same time, the *Antonia*, a steamboat that had been sold to the French by King and Kenedy and converted into a gunboat, also approached the city from downriver. With sixty French marines on board, the vessel was fired on from the American side of the river. Realizing the French had orders not to fire on individuals on the north bank, several Mexicans, said to be *Cortinista* sympathizers, shouted obscenities and pelted the marines with rocks. The French noticed that two individuals on horseback who fired on the *Antonia* were warmly greeted in a camp of the American army.[79]

General Mejía and the captain of the *Antonia*, as well as the commander of the French fleet in the Gulf of Mexico, all wrote Gen. Godfrey Weitzel protesting the attack on the *Antonia* as a "flagrant violation of neutrality."[80] The tone of one letter was so disrespectful that Weitzel, who was suffering from dengue fever, angrily returned it without comment. Any communication, he said, should be in a "proper tone and couched in proper language." He excused the incident by saying that he did not have enough men to patrol the river properly and that to do so would require "all the cavalry of Europe and America combined." The Liberals, by their gallant "fight for freedom," Weitzel asserted, had "awakened the warmest sympathies in every American breast."[81] With Escobedo's officers and hundreds of *Cortinistas* using Brownsville to rest and take their meals while the siege progressed, the French went as far as to proclaim the city "the headquarters of the *Juaristas*."[82]

For sixteen days in late October and early November, Matamoros remained under attack. As daily skirmishes erupted in the rain and mud, the trenches and fortifications around the city came to resemble those of Verdun and the Somme a half century later. Matamoros is so closely "besieged that no one dares to stir an inch beyond the fortifications," the *New York Herald* reported.[83] The Liberals occasionally lobbed an artillery shell into the city, scaring an already frightened populace. Completely isolated, the only means by which the *Imperialistas* could communicate with Bagdad was by gunboat or by couriers on the American side of the river.

On the morning of November 9, a small Imperial reconnaissance rode out to find Escobedo's trenches deserted and only a few broken firearms and blankets scattered on the bare earth. With their rag-tag army, Escobedo and Cortina had retreated into the chaparral like hungry wolves, regrouping to fight another day. Using Cortina's cavalry as his rear guard, Escobedo moved his army slowly upriver.[84] The "enemy 'folded their tents like the Arabs and silently stole away,'" the *Ranchero* observed.[85] Matamoros, the "heroic city of a hundred sieges," the American commercial agent Lucious Avery wrote, had withstood yet another bloody assault.[86]

In the battle for Matamoros, as many as five hundred *Juaristas* were killed or wounded and fifty-eight captured. Imperial losses were placed at fewer than twelve. As many as one hundred of the wounded Liberals were carried across the river and cared for in makeshift hospital tents erected by the U.S. Army.[87] It was later revealed that during the siege a plot had been undertaken by former Confederate officers in the Imperial Army to assassinate General Mejía and turn the city over to the Liberals. One of the conspirators, Capt. W. W. Gholson, who had commanded Fort Matanzas during the fighting, was arrested, tried, found guilty, and executed within hours.[88]

Attack and Counterattack

Although defeated, Cortina remained determined to drive Mejía out of Matamoros. On November 10, seven miles upriver from Matamoros, the steamer *Antonia*, carrying a detachment of French marines and two field pieces, was attacked by Cortina and his men from both banks of the river and when the boat ran aground, several marines were killed and wounded.[89] A week later, a detachment of contras was ambushed and surrounded by a band of *Cortinistas* in the same area. The unfortunate captives had ropes tied around their necks and were dragged off into the chaparral. "Pieces of clothing, blood, and other signs of the dragging of their victims, appeared for several miles," the pro-Imperial Matamoros press reported.[90] Three days later, a second detachment of contras was ambushed and cut to pieces by a band of *Cortinistas* in the same location.

In and around Matamoros, anyone found with arms and not in the Imperial army was assumed to be a *Cortinista* and executed. In late September 1865, three of Cortina's men, two of them Americans, were shot on the outskirts of Matamoros.[91] Believing that Juárez had given up and fled the country and that Mexico was close to being pacified, Maximilian issued a controversial decree in October 1865, making the death penalty mandatory for all *Juaristas* caught bearing arms. Moreover, the Liberals were to be shot without appeal within twenty-four hours of their capture. Two years later, the infamous decree would come to haunt the emperor.

In late December 1865, *Cortinistas* attacked a supply train between Matamoros and San Fernando, only to be bloodily repulsed by the contras. Eleven of Cortina's guerrillas were killed in the attack while seventeen were captured. When Mejía ordered the captives executed, General Weitzel vehemently protested, saying the executions would be an infamous and "horrible act of barbarity." To "execute Mexicans, fighting in their own country, and for the freedom of their country against [a] foreign power, is an act which at this age will meet with universal execration." Mejía fired back that the captives were "bandits and highway robbers." It was strange, he said, that such barbarians should receive comfort from the "civilized world."[92]

SQUABBLES WITHOUT END

When Escobedo first arrived on the Rio Grande, he was concerned that Cortina was too independent and that he would not follow orders. Indeed, when he ordered Cortina to Monterrey, the wily caudillo, despite what he had promised Escobedo, flatly refused, saying he was needed on the Rio Grande to protect the ranches and towns. After the attack on Matamoros, however, Escobedo wrote Juárez that Cortina was solidly in the Liberal fold and that he was following orders. "I do not have the slightest reason to complain ... his conduct could not get any better," Escobedo told the president from Camargo.[93] Still, Cortina and Canales refused to cooperate. In fact, Cortina, Canales, De León, and Carvajal were all claiming to be governor of Tamaulipas at the same time. Disillusioned at the disunity in the Liberal ranks, Escobedo blamed much of the disorder on the merchants of Matamoros who were dupes of General Mejía and more interested in making money than in sustaining the republic. In Tamaulipas, "all classes of society are composed of bandits," he told Juárez.[94] Despite the burning patriotism of many *Tamaulipecos*, it was all Escobedo could do to keep Cortina and Canales from attacking each other.[95] Most of Cortina's guerrillas were scattered in the small villages and ranches along the river, while Canales and his seven hundred men occupied the principal towns such as Reynosa and Camargo.

In late December 1865, General Escobedo seized Monterrey, but within weeks seven hundred Imperial cavalry drove him out. The Liberals, nevertheless, were emboldened by his daring as well as a successful offensive in the southern part of the state.[96] But what happened at Bagdad caught the attention of everyone in northeastern Mexico. From the time the *Imperialistas* first occupied the community, they had struggled to maintain a small garrison in the town. A reporter for the *New York Herald* found the soldiers poorly armed, demoralized, and bedraggled. The garrison, he wrote, was "devoid of spirit, seemed indolent, and were positively little better than a pack of... ragamuffins."[97]

At Clarksville on the north bank, a small band of American filibusters, led by a grandiose dreaming William D. St. Clair, in cooperation with Francisco de León, made plans to seize the steamboat *Rio Grande*. Shortly after midnight on November 5, St. Clair and three men paddled across the river in a small skiff and pulled up beside the *Rio Grande,* which was docked at the wharf just upriver from the seaside community. Only one guard was on duty at the time, and the steamer was easily taken. Although the boat was "hard aground" in low tide, fifty filibusters, using ropes, were able to pull the vessel across the river. Claiming the *Rio Grande* in the name of the Mexican republic, St. Clair announced he would turn the steamer into a gunboat: "She is a fine vessel and I think after she is properly fitted, I shall force Matamoros to surrender," he boasted. "I have already challenged the *Antonia* to a fight."[98] The incident, he gloated, had "created great excitement in Bagdad as well as Clarksville."[99] As it turned out, the steamer, which was seized by American authorities in Clarksville, belonged to a maritime entrepreneur from New Orleans and not the Empire.

Disgraceful in the Extreme

A much more serious challenge to Imperial authority on the Rio Grande came at Bagdad a month later. Encouraged and carrying orders from the scheming Mexicophile Lew Wallace, a blustery adventurer and former Tennessee Unionist and captain in the 5th Tennessee Infantry (Union) named R. Clay Crawford conceived a plan that went beyond St. Clair's: he would seize the entire town.[100] In Brownsville, Crawford and another filibuster, Arthur F. Reed, obtained commissions in the Liberal army, and, with tacit approval of the Federals, opened a recruiting office where they offered $50 a month in gold and all expenses for anyone who would join in an invasion of Mexico.[101] Recruits included army deserters, outlaws, adventurers from Galveston, and border riffraff.[102] Crawford, who claimed to be a major general in the Republican army, sent one of his recruits to spy on the Imperial forces in Bagdad. He was particularly interested in knowing the size of the town's garrison, the number of artillery pieces in the community, and the size and nature of the vessels anchored at the port.[103]

In Brownsville, Crawford persuaded Cortina to make a demonstration on Matamoros at the same time he attacked Bagdad, thus preventing Mejía from rushing reinforcements to the coast.[104] On January 4, a number of Crawford's recruits had crossed the river from Clarksville and quietly gathered at the Globe Hotel. In the early morning darkness the next day, the "promiscuous crowd of adventurers" sprang their surprise.[105] Imperial soldiers guarding the ferry, part of the 180 Mexicans who garrisoned the town, were easily subdued. At the same time, more than 150 men, many of them black soldiers in blue uniforms, crossed from Clarksville.

As the assault continued, the Imperial gunboat *Antonia*, which was anchored at the docks and lined with cotton bales, raked the raiders with an incessant fire, killing two and wounding two others. The raiders, however, were able to pull a captured cannon into position and rake the gunboat with a deadly fire.[106] Several shots pierced the pilot house, killing an Austrian cadet and a French noncommissioned officer, while other shots ripped into the boat just above the waterline. Although battered, the *Antonia* was able to gather enough steam to limp off into open water.

The garrison commander and the captain of the port were taken prisoners in their beds. After two hours of sporadic fighting, the Imperial garrison surrendered.[107] Stores, warehouses, saloons, and even private residences were ransacked as a terrified populace fled into the sand dunes for safety. "Every species of movable property was crossed from Bagdad to Clarksville," one newspaper reported.[108] As many as fifty lighters loaded with plunder crossed the Rio Grande. For days, "mules, asses and carts" laden with stolen goods could be seen on the road from Clarksville to Brownsville.[109] In the raid, the raiders lost four men killed and eight wounded while the Imperial losses were placed at eight killed and twenty-two wounded.

Although Cortina was in on the planning, the raid caught Escobedo and the other Liberals by surprise. Hearing the news from Bagdad, Escobedo initially told Weitzel that his forces had seized the town, but within hours he was asserting the Americans had done so without his approval.[110] When Col. Enrique A. Mejía, who Escobedo designated to command Bagdad, arrived on the scene, Crawford refused to turn over command and even arrested him, although within hours the colonel was released.[111] Also arriving in Bagdad, Francisco de León sent an urgent plea across the river asking the American military for help in "restoring order and protecting American citizens."[112]

Shortly after De León arrived, Cortina galloped into Clarksville with forty men, having raced down the American side of the river. His motivation in occupying the town was to acquire "abundant resources and power to act independently," Escobedo surmised, as he refused to recognize Cortina.[113] When Colonel Mejía also refused to recognize him and turn over command, Cortina scoffed, saying the colonel was not from the border and did not have the support of the troops. Mejía angrily replied that he was a loyal Mexican and, wherever the enemy was to be found, he would fight them.[114] Realizing he did not have Escobedo's support or enough men to hold the town, Cortina, as De León had done, asked the American military for help. Rebuffed, he headed back to Brownsville and to his headquarters on the river above Matamoros.[115]

On the evening of January 25, without a shot being fired, a combined force of contras, French marines, 120 Austrians, one hundred *Rurales*, and three hundred Mexican Lancers—some arriving on the *Camargo* and *Antonia*—chased the *Juaristas* out of Bagdad.[116] The town was "completely empty and pillaged, abandoned both by the enemy as well as by all its inhabitants."[117] The entire population, perhaps as many as seven thousand citizens, had dwindled away. When the evacuating *Juaristas* fled to Clarksville on the *Prince of Wales*, Americans seized all their arms and artillery, along with the steamboat. Although the *Juaristas* claimed the arms and artillery had been lawfully captured, Mejía demanded they be returned to Mexico.[118] If the Americans did not comply with his demands, some said, the French were preparing to blockade Brazos Santiago. Although General Sheridan compared Emperor Maximilian to a lowly Caribbean pirate, he issued orders returning the weapons to Mejía.[119] The *Imperialistas* even persuaded the American customs officials in Clarksville to return some of the plunder they had confiscated following the January raid on Bagdad.

Far from the Rio Grande, diplomatic reverberations from the Bagdad Raid continued for months. In Washington, Matías Romero, able and energetic Mexican minister to the United States, received a letter from Col. Enrique A. Mejía protesting the American decision to turn the arms and artillery over to Gen. Tomás Mejía, "chief of the traitors in Matamoros."[120] Romero wrote Secretary of State Seward asking for an explanation of how arms and artillery taken from a Republican officer who sought refuge in the United States could be given to an enemy of the Mexican Republic the United States did not diplomatically recognize.[121] In Washington diplomatic circles, it all seemed very confusing. Secretary of War Edwin M. Stanton, along with General Grant and Secretary Seward, did not have an answer for Romero. At Bagdad, a "delicate matter" and an embarrassment had transpired, Grant admitted, and everyone in Washington was anxious to put the incident in the past. In the final analysis, General Weitzel perhaps put it best: "The whole affair was disgraceful in the extreme from beginning to end."[122]

On the night of January 21, 1866, not long after the Bagdad Raid, a band of *Cortinistas* crossed the river and plundered a ranch on the river below Matamoros, mortally wounding the ranch owner, Cristobal Rosa. Cortina's men continued to attack any steamer on the river bound for Matamoros. In an increased effort to control Cortina, authorities in Texas arrested thirty of his partisans.[123] The continued violence along the river provoked the *Ranchero* to sarcastically editorialize that "thugs and thieves, ruffians and robbers, pickpockets and pillagers, filibusters and free niggers, burglars and bandits, Mexican outlaws and midnight assassins ... hold complete sway ... over the greenback side of the lower Rio Grande Valley."[124]

Shocked at the audacity of the Bagdad Raid and fearful that Matamoros, too, would be attacked by filibusters, more than 150 merchants charged the United States with not enforcing its neutrality laws. The petitioners called on the military to "check the arbitrary interference of its officers in Mexican affairs." Moreover, the U.S. Army was protecting "the traitor Cortina and his banditti from the vengeance of the Imperial Government."[125] Embarrassed by the raid, Gen. Horatio Gouverneur Wright, commanding the Department of Texas, arrived on the Rio Grande with orders to enforce the neutrality laws and arrest those implicated in the raid.[126] But Wright got nowhere when every officer he questioned denied any complicity. A few of the filibusters were arrested, but most fled to New Orleans.[127] A military commission that investigated the raid concluded only that the port had been sacked and that American soldiers, employed by leading filibusters, had been involved.[128]

In the Bagdad affair, Escobedo told Juárez, Cortina had exhibited "crass ignorance" and "bad faith" and he could no longer be trusted. He was simply too "ambitious and wholly lacking in patriotism."[129] If the Liberals in Tamaulipas persisted in quarreling and fighting among themselves, the war might well be lost and Cortina and Canales would be to blame. To unify his command in Tamaulipas, Escobedo realized he must confront both men and use force, if necessary, to "get rid of their ambitions and foolishness."[130]

Intrigue in a Time of Crisis

Further complicating affairs on the Rio Grande was the vain and ambitious Jesús González Ortega, who as chief justice of the Supreme Court, claimed the presidency in conformance with the Constitution of 1857 when national elections could not be held. As the former governor of Jalisco and a general in the Liberal army who represented the more radical wing, Ortega had been in the United States in 1865, visiting with President Johnson, touring Niagara Falls, and raising money for the Liberal cause. Rumors on the frontier swirled that Cortina was preparing to swear allegiance to Ortega and attack Escobedo.[131] In Washington, Juárez's diplomat, Juan A. Zambrano, was convinced that Cortina could not be trusted and that he was likely to ally himself with the *Orteguistas.*

Zambrano feared that Cortina was becoming too cozy with Miguel Negrete. Negrete had supported peasant uprisings and had opposed Liberal land privatization efforts. He had allied himself with Juárez who had made him a general and promoted him to minister of war over other officers. Cortina was a "bandit" and a "worm," Zambrano told Juárez. Negrete had, indeed, written Cortina, arguing that Juárez was an enemy of the people and that he was in the process of destroying the constitutional government and the federal system. Negrete even sent an envoy to Cortina rather than meeting with him in person. "It is necessary for the Motherland and for you that we talk," Negrete wrote.[132]

Although he had a large following in northern Mexico, Ortega had no army, and he feared Escobedo would have him arrested. Crossing the river, he made his way to Brownsville, hoping to find passage to New York. But on the evening of November 3, 1866, while on board the steamer *St. Mary*, General Steele had him arrested.[133] Sent to New Orleans but eventually released, Ortega returned to Mexico, where he issued a *pronunciamiento* reasserting his claim to the presidency and protesting his treatment in the United States only to be arrested and imprisoned.[134]

In Tamaulipas, Carvajal continued to influence Liberal politics. Traveling to New York where he passed himself off as "Joseph Smith, Esq.," Carvajal hoped to recruit ten thousand Americans for the Republican army, secure loans and arms, and finalize plans for a railroad across the country before returning to Tamaulipas to assist Escobedo in expelling the *Imperialistas* and uniting the Liberals. In the United States, Carvajal warned anyone who would listen that Cortina could not be trusted. "I hope Gen. Grant will not recognize the traitor & bandit Cortina," Carvajal wrote Gen. Lew Wallace. Cortina could not "be trusted in any capacity," Carvajal went on to say. The "people will not trust him and besides he is no officer."[135]

One possible solution for the quarreling Liberals, both Escobedo and Carvajal agreed, was for Gen. Juan José de la Garza to assume power as military governor. De la Garza was said to be "a man of conviction and valor," someone who was well educated, "animated with patriotism" and could "get along with anyone," even Cortina and Canales.[136]

In the meantime, the Liberal bickering and fighting continued. In March 1866, Cortina attacked one of Canales's partisans, Jesús Palacios, at San Fernando and had Palacios and his two sons executed. Fearful of being attacked himself, whether by Canales or the contras or both, Cortina signaled he was willing to cooperate with Carvajal by recognizing De la Garza as governor and commander of the Liberal forces in Tamaulipas.[137] Saying he was making a great sacrifice in giving up his claim as governor, Cortina said, nevertheless, he could be at the gates of Matamoros within days. At the same time, he wrote Leonard Pierce, who was busy procuring arms for him in Brownsville, promising to pay for the weapons as soon as he arrived on the river. Before he could march for the Rio Grande, however, Cortina received a setback when Colonel Du Pin and his contras overran one of his camps near San Fernando.[138]

Death by Hanging

As Cortina struggled for power in Tamaulipas, events in Texas were never far from his mind. He had watched with trepidation in April 1861, as one of his men, Evaristo Rómulo, was apprehended and hanged by the Texans for his role in the 1859 Brownsville Raid. The lingering and deadly ramifications of the raid came to haunt him again in the summer of 1866, when three *Cortinistas*, Vicente García, Juan Vela, and Florencio Garza, were apprehended near Brownsville. Like Rómulo and Cortina himself, they had been indicted by a Cameron County grand jury in 1859 for murder. Juan Vela was convicted in District Court on May 15, 1866, and Vicente García and Florencio Garza four days later, after which District Judge Franklin Cummings sentenced the three to be publicly hanged on June 22.[139]

Even though their murder convictions were under the criminal laws of the State of Texas, the doomed men were held in the military prison at Fort Brown. From early morning on the day they were scheduled to die, a large crowd of citizens from both sides of the river gathered near the prison and the gallows.[140] Many were Cortina sympathizers and said to be unruly—so much so that the Cameron County sheriff, fearing mob violence, deputized two hundred men. As more and more Mexicans poured across the border and made their way toward the prison, it was feared a rescue attempt would be made. The situation was so tense that the sheriff appealed to the military for assistance, and Gen. George Getty agreed to call out the entire garrison at Fort Brown.

As the hour for their execution approached, Fr. Pierre Fourrier Parisot, the thirty-nine-year-old Oblate priest in Brownsville, took the confessions of the three men.[141] The condemned trio had been kept in leg irons since their convictions, and, with the execution set for 3 P.M., a blacksmith was brought to their cells an hour earlier to remove their manacles. He worked hurriedly and awkwardly with a cold chisel and severely gashed the ankles of the men. The prisoners, accompanied by Father Parisot, then limped from their cells to a waiting wagon while heavily armed deputies and black troops with bayoneted rifles surrounded them.

On the cart were three coffins, on which the condemned men were made to sit as they slowly rolled toward the gallows in the one-hundred-degree heat and stifling humidity of the Brownsville summer. There, Father Parisot guided them in the recitation of the Rosary. One of the prisoners shouted to the crowd that he knew he was going to die, but that it was all right because Cortina would have the blood of those responsible for his death.[142] All three men displayed coolness and bravado as they nimbly mounted the ten steps to the top of the scaffold. Before their arms were bound, García and Vela waved their hats at the large multitude that had gathered. An entire regiment of

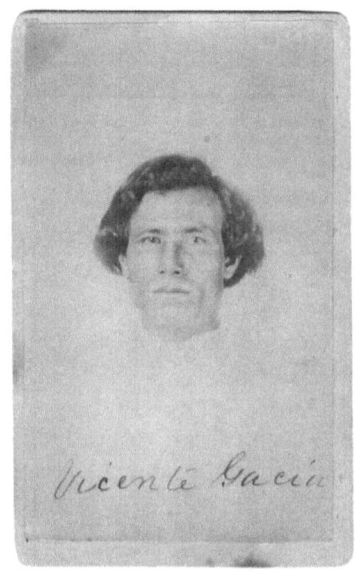

Vicente Garcia

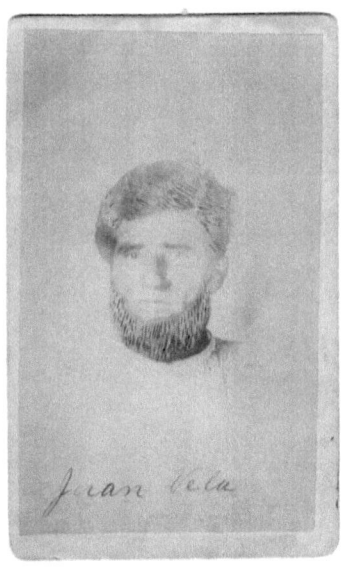
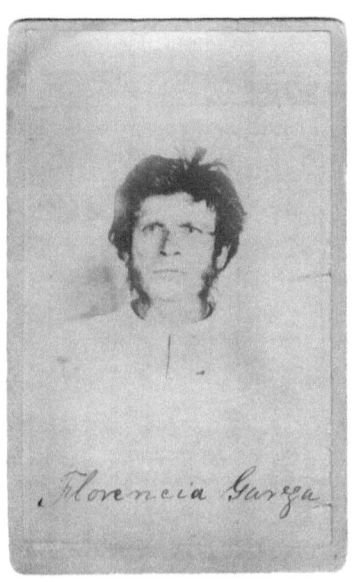

Juan Vela Florencio Garza

Three *Cortinistas,* Vicente Garcia, Juan Vela, and Florencio Garza, were convicted of murder as a result of Cortina's 1859 raid on Brownsville and were hanged before a large sullen crowd on the prairie east of Brownsville on June 22, 1866. Noted photography expert, Lawrence T. Jones III, has concluded the portraits of the three doomed men were probably taken in their jail cells where the lighting was poor, thus explaining why the images were retouched. *Lawrence T. Jones III collection.*

black troops surrounded the gallows on two sides. In the rear of the gallows was a battalion of mounted cavalry. Four pieces of artillery were placed on the front side, facing away from the gallows toward the civilians. As the men's arms and legs were bound and the nooses adjusted around their necks, one of the condemned men bellowed out an allusion to an American who had been hanged a few days earlier on the same scaffold: "When Americans come to be hung, they cry and behave like babies. Mexicans die like men and I intend to show it."[143]

What followed was downright macabre. After a final prayer, the "drop" was released, the men falling four feet. Vicente García and Juan Vela died quickly and easily, but Florencio Garza struck the edge of the platform and the jerk on the rope around his neck was weakened. Because their hands had been secured only at the elbows, Garza made a superhuman effort and raised one hand and then the other to the rope above his head, slowly lifting himself up as the throng of onlookers groaned and gasped in amazement and horror. The executioner was forced to lie down on his stomach on the platform, reach down, and, after a severe struggle, wrench the dying Garza's hands from the rope. He literally pulled Garza up, readjusted the noose, and then let him drop again. It took another minute or two for Garza to die, his torso twisting to and fro beneath the platform. Cut down from the gallows, the three *Cortinistas* were hastily buried in unmarked graves in the Brownsville Cemetery. The event was unsettling, but such was life along the turbulent and bloody waters of the Rio Grande in the summer of 1866 where life transcended international boundaries.

Chapter Seven

Border Caudillo

*At last the republic was restored . . . and the Empire which only
depended on the fictitious aid of foreign troops, died in a lake of blood.*

JUAN CORTINA

WITH CORTINA AT THE CENTER of the vortex, the struggle for power in Tamaulipas between the Empire and the republic raged throughout 1866 and into 1867. After occupying Bagdad, the *Imperialistas* began constructing a "splendid little redoubt" they christened Fort Carlota. On March 23, 1866, however, the Imperial garrison was battered by a storm that swept over the town from the gulf and demolished the army's two-story barracks.[1] The community was ravaged again by a four-day storm in late July that inundated the town, damaging four vessels that were at anchor and capsizing several smaller craft.

In the wider scope of Tamaulipas and Nuevo León, large areas of the coastal plains and the Huasteca remained intensely hostile to the Empire. Although Cortina remained active, stagecoach connections between Matamoros and Monterrey were reestablished. In Matamoros, a grand review was held on Plaza Hidalgo as the Austrian Corps, the Mejía Division, the *Rurales*, and the contras paraded and formed in line of battle. Thousands of citizens poured forth to witness the "grand and imposing spectacle," at which time General Mejía was presented with the Grand Cross of the Order of the Mexican Eagle by a representative of Emperor Maximilian.[2]

As the liberal cause remained fractured and fragmented, hopes for the Empire appeared promising. In a region with a long history of failed federalism, the national interest of the Republican government continued to be plagued by the virtual autonomy of the different generals and aspiring jefes and caudillos such as Cortina. A correspondent for the *New Orleans Crescent* perhaps best summarized the situation on the Rio Grande: "Canales outlaws

On June 23, 1866, with considerable pomp and pageantry, the remnants of General Mejía's Imperial forces embark on the *Antonia* for Bagdad and Veracruz. *Carte de visite* attributed to Louis de Planque. *Lawrence T. Jones III collection.*

Cortina, Escobedo & Co. outlaw both, and Mejía outlaws the whole gang."[3] Isolated from the central government and operating largely on his own, Cortina remained irresolute and uncooperative.

Although Cortina was seen as an intrepid fighter by a large percentage of the population on the Rio Grande frontier, others saw him as an outlaw and opportunist who had once served the Imperial army. He was repeatedly assailed by Servando Canales, who began promoting his brother, Tristán, as governor of Tamaulipas. On the north bank, the American military continued to curtail his activities, even seizing three cannon he had secluded in the dense chaparral near Rancho del Carmen. The military was forced to take action when a captain was killed, possibly by *Cortinistas,* only a few miles upriver from Brownsville. About the same time, a courier on his way from Brownsville to Brazos Santiago was also murdered.[4]

Leaving Matamoros in the early morning darkness on April 27, 1866, Gen. Rafael Olvera, with 350 Imperial infantry and a sizeable cavalry force composed of Austrians and Mexicans, caught Cortina off-guard at Palo Blanco, twenty-five miles above Matamoros, and routed his small army of two hundred men. Brandishing swords, the Imperial cavalry galloped into the camp before Cortina's pickets could sound the alarm. Within minutes, Cortina's encampment was overrun. At the time of the attack, the *Cortinistas* were said to be "lying around, sleeping, smoking, and card playing."[5] Scrambling for their lives, many were shot or sabered by the *Imperialists*. Within hours, rumors reached Matamoros that Cortina had died of wounds received in the attack. Other hearsay said he had been taken prisoner and shot. Yet others reported he had been captured and was being brought to Matamoros to be publicly executed. In reality, Cortina had mounted a bareback horse and raced off in a hail of bullets in yet another one of his amazing escapes. His personal effects—including his horse, saddle, pocket book, watch, money, official correspondence, and a sword he had been presented by the Americans—were seized. Fifty-six prisoners, 137 horses, and a large amount of armaments were also taken.[6]

Encouraged by General Olvera's success, Mejía ordered a second expedition the next day that overran a second camp of *Cortinistas* at Rancho Sabinito. Fifty of Cortina's men were killed while a 6-pounder cannon, more than one hundred rifles, twenty boxes of ammunition, and fifty horses and mules were taken. Among the dead *Cortinistas* were several Americans who had been in charge of the artillery.[7] With cathedral bells ringing, thousands of citizens crowded the streets and lined the rooftops as 118 of Cortina's men were paraded through the streets. The prisoners were in a wretched condition, one observer wrote, "dirty, ragged—some more than half naked—bareheaded, barefooted, and really looking as if they felt it would be a kindness to shoot them at once, and put them out of their misery."[8] Writing Juárez from Camargo three weeks later, Cortina admitted his small army had been decisively defeated.[9] Hoping to regroup, he wanted to go in person to see Juárez, but he did not know where the government was located.

Still struggling to bring some semblance of unity to the Liberal army in Tamaulipas, Escobedo contemplated joining Cortina in destroying Canales and then turning on Cortina himself, if necessary. Cortina, he realized, was the only individual in Tamaulipas who had wide-scale public support and the motivation to eliminate Canales. Another problem was the growing popularity of González Ortega. To Escobedo and Juárez, Cortina could serve as a deterrent to the rise of Ortega and the *Orteguistas*. In the final analysis, Escobedo was forced to admit that the government had no alternative but to placate Cortina.[10]

Waterloo of the Imperial Army

Despite optimism among supporters of the Empire, the summer of 1866 would see the undoing of Mejía's army on the Rio Grande. At daylight on June 7, a huge column consisting of two hundred large wagons pulled by two thousand mules departed Matamoros for Monterrey with three million dollars in merchandise.[11] Commanded by General Olvera, the six-mile-long caravan was guarded by 290 Austrians and 1,110 Mexicans, including companies of contras, *Rurales,* and *Zapadores* (engineers), along with eight pieces of artillery.[12] Moving through the thick chaparral without adequate water, the march turned into a nightmare. On the first day in the scorching heat and stifling dust, five men died of sunstroke. On the second day, three more succumbed. To quench their thirst, many of the men began eating the *tuna* of the prickly pear cactus and consequently suffered with uncontrolled diarrhea.[13] To complicate matters, the *Juarista* cavalry sporadically harassed the column, although grapeshot fired into the chaparral by the artillery frequently sent the guerrillas scurrying for cover. The heavily laden wagons were slowed by the deep arroyos along the route that frequently had to be filled in by the Mexican engineers.

Learning the convoy would be departing Matamoros and that another column of French and Mexicans would be riding out from Monterrey to meet it, General Escobedo ordered his scattered armies into action. From his headquarters at Linares, the bespectacled general positioned a division of infantry at China, a cavalry brigade at Paso del Zacate, and another cavalry brigade on the road between Monterrey and Cerralvo. At the same time, Gen. Gerónimo Treviño, the Philip Sheridan of Mexico, was sent to impede the column leaving Monterrey. Treviño effectively threw up obstacles and poisoned the watering holes with rotting debris and animal carcasses. Although the column from Monterrey reached Cerralvo on June 12, Escobedo learned from a captured messenger that the French would not move again until the column from Matamoros reached Mier. As a result, he changed plans and ordered his scattered armies to march for Camargo.

By June 15, Escobedo was in position southeast of Camargo, just west of Mesa de Santa Gertrudis, along the Matamoros-Camargo Road.[14] Here he carefully positioned his army, effectively blocking General Olvera's access to water. As the *Imperialistas* and *Juarista* scouts came in contact, both armies bivouacked for the night. Lt. Ernst Pitner, a young Austrian in the Imperial Army, remembered being "greeted with a veritable volley from the shrubberies running alongside the camp."[15] Hungry and without water, many of the *Imperialistas* slept with their firearms. To quench their burning thirst, some pillaged the wagons for wine but the wine only intensified their dehydration. Realizing their impending peril, one veteran officer warned Lieutenant Pitner, "Tomorrow there will be confusion the like of which one will not often witness."[16]

Escobedo deployed his army into five attacking columns with a sixth in reserve. At 4 A.M. in the early morning darkness of June 16, the slumbering Imperial column slowly went into motion. Two Austrian rifle companies led the way as wagons in groups of four were placed in the middle of the column. Seeing large numbers of *Juaristas* on the horizon, General Olvera sent the two companies forward with an artillery battery. A company of Mexican *Zapadores* was then brought up followed by the cavalry, with the contras guarding the rear. For half an hour, the Imperial Army crawled forward toward the crest of the mesa as the artillery fired on Escobedo's men in the distance.

On the opposite side of the mesa, Escobedo had concealed his cavalry in a thicket of mesquite while his infantry were ordered to lie flat on the ground. The *Juaristas* waited until the front of Olvera's army reached the crest of the mesa and were within rifle shot before they launched a ferocious attack. "The enemy," Lieutenant Pitner wrote, "broke out of a woodlands and in close order advanced offensively towards us." When the Imperial forces regrouped and advanced on the *Juarista* left, Escobedo sent General Treviño's cavalry into action. With the rattle of spurs and the crack of pistols, Treviño's horsemen turned the Imperial flank and sent the *Imperialista* cavalry scurrying for cover. In the meantime, the fighting became hand to hand among the ranks of the infantry. "It was a moment of the most frightful small-arms fire," Pitner remembered, "and the men in their ranks fell down dead in droves."[17] With no alternative, the Austrians fixed bayonets and gallantly charged the *Juaristas,* only to be attacked by a second column of Escobedo's infantry, most of the men screaming "*¡Viva la Libertad!*" With half their men killed or wounded and supported only by a company of *Zapadores,* the Austrians ran for the safety of the wagons. Surrounded by both infantry and cavalry and realizing their situation was hopeless, 350 men of the Sierra Gorda Imperial infantry stuck their rifles in the ground with the point of their bayonets, threw their arms into the air, and also cried out "*¡Viva la Libertad!*" "The combat with side-arms was of short duration, having ended at seven in the morning with the complete destruction of the austrio-traitor forces," General Escobedo reported.[18]

Besides millions of dollars in merchandise, Escobedo's *Juaristas* seized more than a thousand muskets, the eight pieces of artillery, and a large amount of ammunition and military equipment, including gun carriages, lances, and sabers. Even the Imperial band—cornets, clarinets, drums, and all—was grabbed. The Imperial army was badly hurt: 396 men were killed, 165 wounded, and hundreds taken prisoner. Only a few officers in the Imperial Mexican cavalry managed to escape the slaughter. The "miserable cowards," Escobedo wrote, "had not the courage to brave death on the field of battle, but trusted their lives and safety to the fleetness of their horses."[19] Some of those who fled into the chaparral were able to reach the Rio Grande and arrive safely in Texas. In the Republican ranks, Escobedo had 155 men killed.[20] "The fighting was very severe and the slaughter fearful on both sides," Lucius Avery, the American commercial agent in Matamoros, recorded.[21] Shortly after the battle, several of the Mexican Imperial officers and contras were singled out as having previously executed *Juaristas,* so they were dragged off and shot. The wounded from both sides were hauled in wagons to a makeshift hospital on the plaza in Camargo. Placed on mud and stone floors in the oppressive June heat with little medical care, many expired within days. It was a disaster, an episode, the *Brownsville Daily Ranchero* wrote, that signaled "a death blow to the reign of [the] Empire in Northern Mexico."[22] The "national arms are once more crowned with glory," Escobedo reported in triumph. "Let us hasten onward, fellow soldiers and capture Matamoros; then we can have time to rest."[23] Cortina would always regret he had not been at Santa Gertrudis, which proved to be the Waterloo of the Imperial Army on the Rio Grande.

Three days after the disaster, General Mejía evacuated Bagdad in the night. In Matamoros, the morale of Mejía's six-hundred-man garrison was badly shaken by the news from upriver. With desertions intensifying, he realized the city could no longer be defended. Only six days after the news from Santa Gertrudis reached him, he concluded an agreement with the newly proclaimed governor of Tamaulipas, José María de Jesús Carvajal, who had arrived from New York, to evacuate the city within forty-eight hours.[24] Happy to see the *Imperialistas* gone from the frontier, the military at Fort Brown agreed that Mejía could use steamers flying the American flag to evacuate his men to Bagdad.

Many of the merchants and leading citizens were vehemently opposed to surrendering the city to Carvajal, preferring Escobedo instead, but there was little they could do. While drums beat and flags flapped in the summer breeze, Mejía marched his Imperial Army to the riverbanks. Laden with their arms, ammunition, baggage, two 6-pounder artillery pieces, the *Imperialistas* headed downriver on the steamers *Colonel Holcomb, Eugenia,* and *Colonel Benedict.* No sooner were the steamers out of sight than citizens rushed into the streets to celebrate.[25] At noon on June 24, the first of Escobedo's Army of the North entered Matamoros to the "ringing of bells, firing [of] national salutes, and a general rush of people to the streets."[26] With the evacuation of Matamoros and Bagdad, no Imperial armies remained on the Rio Grande frontier. Across the mountains and deserts of northern Mexico the tide of battle had changed. The only Imperial force left in northeastern Mexico was at Tuxpan, Tampico, and Monterrey.

During the height of the fighting between the Liberals for control of Matamoros in 1866, Capt. A. M. Randall's battery of the 1st U.S. Artillery point ominously across the Rio Grande in this image by noted Civil War and Reconstruction artist A. R. Waud. A well-defended Casa Mata can be seen in the distance on the far left as well as Fuerte Colegio on the far right. The Mexican gunboat *Chinaco* plies the Rio Grande. *Harper's Weekly*, November 17, 1866.

Within weeks, over a thousand Liberals were at the gates of Tampico. The dreaded Colonel Du Pin was dispatched from San Luis Potosí to help defend the city, but he was defeated and turned back at Tula. One month after the fall of Matamoros, on August 8, 1866, after 350 Mexicans in the Imperial ranks went over to the Liberals, Tampico surrendered.[27] Tuxpan, too, fell to the Liberals. Fed by mounting support from the north, long the hotbed of Republican rule in Mexico, the Liberal cause everywhere gathered momentum. As Juárez won the hearts and minds of more and more Mexicans, the war, which had been seen for many years as a dispute between conservative and liberal Mexicans, increasingly became a war against the foreign invader. During the summer of 1866, Republican forces recaptured Monterrey, Saltillo, Guaymas, and Oaxaca. The Empire was on the ropes.

A Struggle Within

In Matamoros, Carvajal remained as unpopular as ever. Citizens of the heroic city, Lucius Avery recorded, "hold in fresh remembrance that on three different occasions he has fought against the city laying a large portion of it in ashes and causing the destruction of an immense amount of property."[28] Supported by Canales, Carvajal did everything possible to make himself unpopular; loans were levied and property confiscated from anyone who was thought to have aided Mejía and the *Imperialistas*. Resentment festered. There "are movements on foot of a revolutionary nature for the purpose of displacing Carvajal in favor of Cortina," Avery wrote.[29]

Learning that General Mejía had been allowed to escape unscathed,

General Escobedo was furious. From distant Chihuahua, President Juárez declared Carvajal's actions "null and of no force, because those who made it on the part of the Republican government had not the proper authority."[30] Moreover, Carvajal and Juan José de la Garza, his chief lieutenant whom Escobedo had previously praised, were ordered court-martialed. To complicate matters, at Camargo on August 21, Cortina issued a *pronunciamiento* reaffirming himself as governor.[31] Before Escobedo could reach Matamoros, Canales, assisted by Gen. Pedro Hinojosa, turned on Carvajal in a bloodless coup d'état. Carvajal was "not fit to govern," Canales announced, and he proclaimed himself military governor.[32] Hearing of the coup, Ford, who was on Carvajal's staff, dashed into headquarters yelling, "A revolution is on foot. In ten minutes we may have our throats cut!"[33] In the confusion, Carvajal shot the officer who tried to arrest him and along with his friend and advisor, Lew Wallace, who seemed to somehow always be involved in Mexican affairs, fled to Brownsville. Ironically, just as Carvajal was fleeing to Brownsville, "literally at the lance's point," Wallace would write, a King and Kenedy steamer arrived in Matamoros loaded with arms he had secured in the United States for the Liberal cause.[34]

Hoping to consolidate power in the city, Canales issued a *pronunciamiento* promising "independence and liberty" and asking the citizens to lay all "animosities aside."[35] Hearing of the events in Matamoros and echoing Juárez's philosophy, Foreign Minister Sebastián Lerdo de Tejada gave orders nullifying Canales's actions. No hope for the "salvation of the country can be entertained, if a stop is not put to military revolts," he concluded. Moreover, Gen. Santiago Tapia, a loyal Liberal, was announced as military governor and Canales and Hinojosa were ordered to Chihuahua "to answer for their actions."[36] But in Matamoros, Canales had Tapia arrested and Hinojosa was appointed in his place.[37] While Cortina watched from the chaparral, political chaos remained the order of the day.

At last, Escobedo saw an opportunity to destroy Canales, even if he had to use Cortina—whom he mistrusted—to do it. In Tamaulipas, which was infested with bandits and caciques with questionable loyalties and varying constituencies, Cortina was the only person who could compete with Canales for the hearts and minds of the people. Thirsting for power, Canales was not about to give up Matamoros or report to Chihuahua. Considered by many to be far more ruthless than Cortina, he was determined to hold the city at all costs, yet he possessed little influence beyond Matamoros. "The city is at the mercy of a reckless and irresponsible man," the American consul reported.[38] When the garrison manning one of the forts guarding the city dared to declare against him, he had the soldiers arrested and ordered six of the officers hanged.[39] A larger yet unsuccessful coup d'état against Canales on September 23, possibly inspired by Cortina, resulted in the death of at least

Servando Canales was Cortina's bitter rival for power in Tamaulipas. From a politically astute and prominent family, Canales questioned Cortina's leadership while defending Matamoros in September 1864 and denounced his decision to join the *Imperialistas*. As governor of Tamaulipas in 1877, Canales came within hours of executing Cortina and would have done so had not Porforio Díaz intervened and whisked him off to prison in Mexico City. *Carte de visite* by Louis de Planque, ca. 1866. *Brownsville Historical Association.*

A camp and sentinel of the Liberal forces of Cortina and Escobedo are depicted in this sketch on the outskirts of Matamoros prior to the bloody September 27, 1866 attack on the forces of Servando Canales. *Harper's Weekly,* November 17, 1866.

eighty individuals.[40] In the confusion, a small force of Americans who had been fighting with the Liberals attacked Plaza Hidalgo but were driven off. Fleeing to a steamer in the river and then to Brownsville, they were quickly disarmed by the American military. Canales began paying his men daily to avoid such revolts. And, to avoid assassination, he also organized a large and loyal bodyguard.[41] Assisted by his brother Tristán, whom he continued to promote as governor, Canales had men whipped for minor disciplinary discretions and threatened them with execution should they attempt to desert.

As Canales struggled to solidify power, Cortina, now backed by Escobedo and Juárez, held Bagdad and controlled the roads leading into Matamoros. Guards refused to allow any merchandise through to Monterrey without assessing heavy duties.[42] To help pay his soldiers, Cortina levied *préstamos,* forced loans, of $100 each on the merchants who had reoccupied Bagdad.

During Cortina's attack on Matamoros in December 1866, U.S. troops under Gen. John Sedgwick crossed the Rio Grande on a hastily constructed pontoon bridge to defend the American consulate. Sedgwick had been persuaded to intervene in the fighting by leading Matamoros merchants and was later reprimanded for his actions and removed from command. *Harper's Weekly*, January 5, 1867.

When several refused or could not come up with the money, the *Cortinistas* helped themselves to their merchandise. A few of the merchants fled to Brownsville. In late November, Cortina feigned an attack on Fort Monterrey and then assaulted Casa Mata near the Plaza de Independencia at the northwestern gates to the city.[43] Canales, however, was able to reinforce the defenses and the *Cortinistas* were bloodily repulsed.[44] Later in the month, Escobedo joined Cortina in front of the city with several thousand men, demanding that Canales surrender.

Once again the American military became involved in the internal affairs of Tamaulipas. After enjoying breakfast in Matamoros with a number of influential merchants, many of them Americans, Col. Thomas D. Sedgwick, commanding the garrison at Fort Brown, agreed to intervene. Sedgwick was encouraged by rumors that Canales was unable to pay his troops and that they were threatening to sack the city.[45] The next day in Brownsville, several small boats were hauled to the riverbank and floated into position, creating a pontoon bridge the newspapers dubbed "Sedgwick's Bridge." Despite explicit written instructions not to intervene in Mexican affairs, on November 23, 1866, Sedgwick sent 118 men of the 4th U.S. Cavalry across the river. Officially, the men were to protect "American citizens and their property" and "guard the city and prevent bloodshed between the two contending parties." Backed by artillery, the Americans occupied the Plaza Hidalgo where they raised the Stars and Stripes.[46]

The next day, Canales agreed to recognize the authority of the Liberal government but on the condition that his men could retain their weapons and continue to hold the city, but Escobedo refused such overtures. In hopes of avoiding bloodshed while at the same time protecting the merchants and their goods, Sedgwick helped arrange for negotiations. But when Canales arrived at the Liberal camp outside the city, Escobedo refused to see him and swore "like a Turk."[47] After several hours, the two men met in the corner of a room. Voices were raised, and the two became so angry observers feared there would be a fight. When tempers finally calmed, Canales said he would surrender the city only if Escobedo would compensate the merchants for the funds they had previously given him, said to be as much as $600,000. When Escobedo flatly refused, the meeting ended in "bickering and recrimination."[48]

Buckets of Liberal Blood

Before daylight on November 27, 1866, Escobedo prepared to attack the fortifications with 1,500 men. With Cortina feigning an assault on the southern and eastern defenses with his Tamaulipas Brigade, Escobedo launched an all-out attack from the west. In the attack, forts Guadalupe, San Fernando, Monterrey, and the fortifications opposite Freeport all came under heavy artillery fire. But the fourteen guns guarding the forts and Casa Mata took a terrible toll on Escobedo's men. At Fort Monterrey, one thousand men approached to within thirty yards before the defenders opened a devastating fire. The fighting was particularly fierce because Escobedo's men were forced to charge across the murky waters of the moat guarding the low earthen parapets. One company of Austrians, who had joined the Liberals after the disaster at Santa Gertrudis, were said to have lost half their men in the attack.[49] One observer thought Escobedo's men were close to carrying the fortifications, but reinforcements appeared and the charging columns began to waver. Canales's "infantry and cavalry joined in the firing, and the columns of Escobedo were rolled back, leaving the ground strewn with the dead and dying."[50] In the assault, many of the bridges constructed to span the moat proved to be too short, and scaling ladders were not available. Once the attack faltered, Canales, who commanded Fort Monterrey in person, ordered his infantry and cavalry in pursuit. About five hundred yards from the fort at a spot where a lagoon was spanned by a narrow bridge, the fighting was hand to hand. In less than thirty minutes, Escobedo lost 250 men killed

Imperial Austrian officers in Matamoros pose for the camera of Louis de Planque. Large numbers of Austrians were killed or captured at Santa Gertrudis near Camargo on June 16, 1866, in what proved to be the Waterloo of the Imperial Army on the Rio Grande. *Carte de visite* by Louis de Planque. *Lawrence T. Jones III Collection.*

and 150 taken prisoner. One of those killed in the bitter fighting was Canales's brother, Modesto.[51]

At Fort San Fernando on the eastern outskirts of the city, Cortina's eight-hundred-man Tamaulipas Brigade formed in a long line, much in the European tradition, and marched on the fortifications. Certain they would carry the works, the men were given the watchword of "Oaxaca" and the countersign "Durango." To distinguish themselves from the defenders because they did not have uniforms, the men stuck "a green leaf of any kind of plant" in their hats.[52] Here also, Canales's defenders waited until the advancing column was within twenty yards before opening a devastating small arms and artillery salvo. "No set of men ever made a more gallant display of valor, and no set of men were ever more suddenly defeated, dispersed, annihilated," an American officer wrote of the Tamaulipas Brigade.[53] Retreating with heavy losses, Cortina's men fell back into the chaparral. Several unsuccessful attacks were also made on Fort Paredes on the river, opposite Freeport, but the fighting here subsided quickly.

Many of Escobedo's wounded officers were carried across the river for medical care in Brownsville. In three hours of bloody fighting, Escobedo lost several hundred men killed, four hundred wounded, and between three hundred and four hundred taken prisoners. The defenders lost seventy-five men killed.[54] Matamoros had seen bloodshed before, but nothing quite as bad as that of late November 1866. Not deterred, Escobedo and Cortina promised they would renew the attack.

With orders not to fire on Escobedo's forces should they enter the city, the Americans continued to occupy Plaza Hidalgo and the ferry at Santa Cruz during the fighting.[55] In the midst of battle, the Americans sent a flag of truce to Escobedo, asking that he not fire on the American troops in the city. Escobedo responded by inquiring what the American troops were doing in Mexico. At the height of the fighting, Sedgwick placed all his forces in a state of readiness to cross the river should the Americans come under attack. In addition, 250 men under "Rip" Ford were hastily organized in Brownsville, including Confederate and Union veterans, citizens, and even "strangers."[56]

At the height of the bloodletting, Sedgwick received a telegram from Gen. Phillip Sheridan in New Orleans ordering him to withdraw. Leaving fifty men to guard the plaza and a few men at the ferry, the Americans recrossed the river to Brownsville. Just as quickly as it had been constructed, the pontoon bridge was dismantled. "The object of the occupation," General Sheridan explained, "was for the alleged purpose of protecting American citizens." Yet Sheridan concluded that Sedgwick had been "made the cat's-paw [by the] shrewd merchants of Matamoros, who wanted to secure the liabilities which were due to them from Canales before he was obliged to give up the city to the liberal forces."[57] In Sheridan's mind, there was little doubt the Matamoros "merchants were at the bottom of all the troubles over there."[58] Colonel Sedgwick was not a "strong man" and he had "been simply outwitted by a combination of military and civil influences," the *Brownsville Rio Grande Courier* concluded.[59] Consequently, Secretary of War Stanton ordered Sedgwick relieved of command and placed under arrest.[60]

His army badly battered and demoralized, Escobedo called for reinforcements and began digging parallel trenches in front of the city. Cortina's Tamaulipas Brigade entrenched in the chaparral in front of Fort San Fernando.[61] Learning that Gen. Gerónimo Treviño would be arriving from Monterrey to reinforce Escobedo, Canales realized his hold on Matamoros was slipping, and he immediately entered into discussions with Colonel Sedgwick, who was still in command at the time, about the possibilities of crossing his army to Brownsville and surrendering to the Americans. Because the

United States and Mexico were not at war, this idea made no sense to Sedgwick. In the end, negotiations were renewed with Escobedo, and, despite the bloodletting and mistrust between the two, it was agreed that Escobedo and Cortina would march into the city to unite with Canales and then fight the *Imperialistas* elsewhere. "The terms of surrender are unconditional and still conditional," the *Ranchero* remarked.[62] Early on the morning of December 1, 1866, Escobedo and Cortina slowly moved into the city and took possession of the upper forts. Still popular with the people of Matamoros, Cortina was widely cheered by many in the city. "The troops of both armies are now parading through the town ... and apparently upon the most friendly terms," the *Ranchero* reported.[63]

Hoping for access to the lucrative funds of the Matamoros customs house, both Cortina and Canales continued to jockey for power. Escobedo contemplated calling for elections, but he knew the popular Cortina would emerge victorious. Carvajal, too, wanted to be governor, but he remained unpopular, and few in the city trusted him. It was also rumored that Canales, who was still under orders to report to Juárez, would insist on his brother, Tristán, or his other brother, Antonio, as governor. Disregarding both Canales and Cortina, Escobedo left his trusted adjutant, Gen. Felipe Berriozábal, in command and struck out for Monterrey and central Mexico and the epic events that would unfold at Querétaro. Cortina and Canales were ordered to follow, but, with no money to pay their men, the two hesitated. Neither wanted to march first and leave the other to displace Berriozábal.

Prowling around the Villas of the North

Claiming he would obey Escobedo but not Berriozábal, Cortina moved upriver to occupy the towns and villages on the river, recruiting and levying *préstamos* and protesting Berriozábal's occupation of Matamoros as he went. At Reynosa, he entertained Maj. Charles H. Graves, commander of the American forces at Ringgold Barracks, and even sent his horse and an escort to the river to usher the major into the town.[64] At the same time, he called on Juárez to name him governor of Tamaulipas. The president, though, had received too many complaints of Cortina's independence and callousness to agree.[65] Besides Escobedo, Manuel Gómez, whom Juárez had appointed governor of Nuevo León, had written the president, saying that Cortina was "an untrusting fox" and that "ignorance and malice made him distrust everyone."[66]

Returning to the lower Valley, Cortina lingered about Matamoros, proclaiming himself loyal to Juárez yet threatening to attack the city. With General Berriozábal, who had previously lost the city of Morelia to the *Imperialistas*, outnumbered at least two to one, many on the border speculated it was only a matter of time before Cortina took the city by storm. With the unpredictable and hostile Canales at San Fernando, and Cortina just outside the city, General Berriozábal prepared for the worst.[67] Yet Cortina agreed to call off any attack if Berriozábal would raise $20,000 to pay his four-hundred-man army. When Berriozábal came up with only $2,000, Cortina renewed his threats, this time demanding even more money, as well as one hundred horses and rations for his men.[68]

In late January 1867, after leaving his reliable comrade in arms, Capt. Teodoro Zamora, with sixty men in camp outside Matamoros, Cortina took control of the small customs house at Reynosa where he began collecting duties to pay his men. From Reynosa, Cortina again wrote Juárez asking for recognition as governor. Again he was rebuffed. After leaving a captain and sixty men to hold the town, he led a portion of his small and ragged army on to Camargo, where he was able to purchase badly needed clothing and supplies from merchants in Rio Grande City. After sending an advance guard to Mier, he pushed on upriver himself with a large part of his cavalry, recruiting men and levying *préstamos* as he went. When word reached Mier that Cortina was approaching, several leading merchants and civil officials fled across the river to Roma. Although less than objective, the American press perhaps best summarized the situation: "*Préstamos* follow *préstamos;* seizure follows seizure; confiscation follows confiscation; revolution follows revolution; and perfidy succeeds treachery throughout that infernal region of country, known as the State of Tamaulipas."[69]

As Cortina realized, the long years of incessant violence had ravaged many of the small villages and towns, and fewer and fewer men came forth to join him. Tamaulipas had been bled dry. Moreover, the same number of men Cortina enlisted in the daytime sometimes deserted to Texas after dark.[70] Henry Maltby, fiery editor of the *Ranchero* who hated Cortina with a passion, alleged that Cortina grabbed several men, including a few Tejanos, from a fandango in Texas and "took them across the river and duly converted them into the ranks."[71] But Cortina did increase the size of his army, and he was able to hold the frontier as far upriver as Nuevo Laredo. He also controlled the roads from the river into the interior although Canales clung to the area around San Fernando.

Berriozábal repeatedly asked for reinforcements. When none were forthcoming, he wrote Juárez, asking to be relieved of his command. Far from Mexico City, Tamaulipas was to the besieged commander little more than a land of "thorns." Because of men like Cortina and Canales, the state had "a very sad future." Of all the "bandits" operating in the state, Cortina was the least educated but the most popular, Berriozábal asserted. Waiting to take control of Matamoros, Cortina was content to do little more than "go prowling around the villas of the north ... on a loose horse."[72]

Destiny at Querétaro

On the fertile plains far to the south, events intervened to influence the destinies of Cortina and his small army. With Berriozábal finally raising the money he had been demanding, he rode off with his ragged *Tamaulipecans* to the beckoning of Escobedo at Querétaro. By spring 1867, Napoleon III had recalled his twenty-thousand-man army from Mexico, and Emperor Maximilian took command of a few thousand Mexican Imperial troops at the old colonial city of domes and towers. As the last of the French army embarked for Europe, Cortina and his small army joined Escobedo at Querétaro where a siege had commenced. Although surrounded and outnumbered more than four to one, Maximilian's Imperial army held out for almost a hundred days. Only Gen. Leonardo Márquez and Santiago Vidaurri, with 1,200 cavalry, were able to escape. By the second week of May, however, with the aqueduct carrying the city's water supply cut, food and ammunition scarce, and a leading Imperial officer, Col. Miguel López, allowing the Republican forces to enter the city, the proud Maximilian was left no alternative but to surrender.

Cortina would always take great pride in being with Gen. Ramón Corona on May 15th. On that day, the emperor, ill with dysentery and fever, strode forth from the besieged city to surrender his sword.[73] Despite impassioned pleas for clemency from European monarchs, Secretary of State William Seward, and even Victor Hugo and Giuseppe Garibaldi, Maximilian's fate had been sealed by his infamous decree of October 1865, that had resulted in the death of innumerable Mexicans. Tried and found guilty by a court-martial, Maximilian and Cortina's old enemy Gen. Tomás Mejía and Gen. Miguel Miramón, were led on the sunny morning of June 19 to El Cerro de las Campanas by their executioners. There, on the outskirts of the city, they were lined up against a wall and shot. It is not known if Cortina spoke with Mejía during those final days of the Empire or simply stood by while his old adversary died in a fiery fusillade. Cortina was correct when he observed that the Empire "died in a lake of blood."[74] The long and savage war was over. After fifty-seven years of internal chaos, there was much rejoicing, hopes for peace, and a renewal of life itself.

Three weeks later, on July 8, the once-powerful Santiago Vidaurri, who had served as Maximilian's minister of finance and whom Cortina had once courted and come to hate, was found hiding in a house in Mexico City. Placed in a stagecoach escorted by a squad of cavalry commanded by General Carvajal, he was taken to the plaza of Santo Domingo. There he was thrown into the street, humiliated, beaten, and executed in a reeking dung heap as several hundred citizens cheered as a band played a lively polka.[75] It was a sad ending for a man who had held sway over a large part of northern Mexico.

When the news reached Matamoros of the fall of Querétaro, the city went wild. General Berriozábal ordered the church bells rung and a courier was sent racing across the river to inform the Americans. Rockets lit the sky, cannon boomed, and people rushed into the streets to celebrate, hoping that peace would at last be restored to the troubled land.[76] However, the collapse of the Empire ended neither political intrigue nor violence in Mexico. Although fifty thousand Mexicans lay dead, turbulence and bloodshed continued unabated. Throughout Mexico, Liberals turned on one another with untold acts of calumny and treachery. Betrayal and mistrust, long a way of life in the beleaguered country, became epidemic, and nowhere was it worse than in Tamaulipas.

Battles Fought and Victories Won

From Querétaro, Cortina moved with his small army through the mountains to León. Here on the fertile plains in the state of Guanajuato there was time for rest and recuperation. From León in late July 1867, he wrote a loving letter to his daughter Faustina back in Matamoros. He had always been close to his daughter and painfully anxious about his family. He asked her to pass on his love to Rafaela, sister Carmen, and his mother, Estéfana, who had again taken up residence at Rancho del Carmen. He had been ill, he said, suffering from fever and the shingles, (a viral infection of the skin), but he had recovered and was expecting to move on to San Luis Potosí before again returning to the border.[77]

In the second week of November 1867, while Cortina was with his *Tamaulipecans* in Mexico City, he received heartbreaking news from Matamoros and Rancho del Carmen. His aging mother Estéfana was dead at the age of seventy. Cortina immediately asked for permission to return home to Tamaulipas to take care of "personal matters" and look after his property, much of it having been destroyed in the bloody and prolonged war. Besides, Cortina said, he could better serve the republic on the border. His men were exhausted from months of fighting and endless marches across vast expanses of the battered country, he went on to report, and they too wanted to return home to their families.[78]

Beloved matriarch of the family, Estéfana was respected by everyone who knew her, Texans and Mexicans alike. Few newspapers bothered to note her passing, but one did say she was the mother of the "noted Rio Grande guerrilla chieftain Juan N. Cortina." A "woman of superior ability and great fortitude," the newspaper wrote, she was warmly regarded by the "Americans as a faithful friend," and someone who was "known the length and breath of this extensive border."[79] Ever since the death of his father when he was very young and Estéfana had taken the family to live in Matamoros, Cortina had always been close to his mother. Estéfana did not agree with many of the things her son had done, especially in 1859, but she had never forsaken him, even when Rancho del Carmen was overrun and occupied by alien forces. She had always remained close to the land and steadfast in her love for the family. Despite her illiteracy, there was not a "hamlet from the Nueces to the Sierra Madre in which the name of Doña Estéfana is not a household word," the *Brownsville Daily Ranchero* wrote.[80]

Estéfana's death might have been hastened by the disaster that struck the Lower Rio Grande Valley in early October 1867. On October 6, citizens in Brownsville and Matamoros and at Rancho del Carmen noticed a gentle, northerly breeze, "cool, fresh and bracing, with a momentum of no more than twenty-five or thirty miles per hour."[81] Late in the afternoon, the winds accelerated; by nightfall, rain began to fall in torrents. Soon enough, residents realized they were in the fearful grip of a hurricane. Into the early evening the storm raged, gloomy clouds descending as gust after gust swept over the twin cities, each time with increasing violence and velocity. "Trees began to be dismembered and crushed, buildings began to rock to and fro with every blast, and the rain came in sheets and dashes, like the breaking of furious seas over the brow of a stranded vessel," it was reported.[82]

As the hurricane hissed and roared and the destruction worsened, panic-stricken citizens fled into the streets, hoping to find refuge in secure buildings. Others huddled in prayer. By 10 P.M., the awful storm seemed only to intensify. With a combined population of thirty thousand, both Brownsville and Matamoros "were converted into a howling earthly hell." With the winds increasing to an ever-frightening velocity, even sturdy brick structures collapsed. Lightning flashed about as the shrieking winds muted the thunder. One resident compared the deafening noise overhead to "a thousand trains of cars passing over a thousand bridges at full speed."[83] Timbers were driven through brick walls as if they had been fired from a cannon.

In the Great Storm of 1867, hundreds of homes in Matamoros and Brownsville were seriously damaged or destroyed, and losses were placed at five million dollars.[84] "As we wander amid the crumbling ruins of fallen walls," the *Rio Grande Courier* reported, "and see the crowds of homeless poor, we feel incapable to give the merest conception of that night of terrors." In "the midst of life we are in death," the newspaper continued.[85] Entire blocks in Matamoros were leveled. Even the sturdy Rancho del Carmen was badly damaged.

Caballo-Riding Caudillo

With the French gone and Maximilian dead, many in Brownsville expected Cortina's return to the border. "All we now need is a plain *tortilla*-eating, raw-hide-sleeping and *caballo*-riding governor," the bitter and jingoist *Daily Ranchero* remarked in reference to his possible return. Cortina was just the man for the border, the *Ranchero* joked sarcastically. "He is of the right type, and conveys our ideas better than we could express them with words. A *tortilla* would answer him just as well as a knife-and-fork dinner; a raw hide would answer him to sleep on just as well as a kingly couch."[86] If Cortina did indeed return to the frontier, the *Ranchero* demanded that he stand trial for the "many murders committed on this bank of the Rio Grande." Lest its readers forget Cortina's evil deeds, the newspaper republished his *pronunciamiento* of September 30, 1859.[87]

In early January 1868, rumors had Cortina arriving secretly in Matamoros while other hearsay said he had been executed.[88] But Cortina was still in central Mexico, and in early June newspapers published a proclamation he allegedly cosigned in Mexico City on Cinco de Mayo. With other leading generals, Cortina had announced his support of Jesús González Ortega and his claim to the presidency, or so the proclamation said.[89] In reality, Cortina had not signed the petition but was in the mountains of central Mexico, fighting to maintain the republic.

By March, Cortina's Tamaulipas Brigade returned to the capital. The men were in wretched condition, with many of the soldiers almost naked.[90] Yet Cortina regrouped and returned to the field again. In early June, he decisively routed the forces of Rosalio Flores at Mixquiahuala, an Otomí town on the banks of the Rio Tula in the Valle del Mezquital, northeast of the capital.[91] Throughout the summer, Cortina rode the Sierra de San Miguel in search of dissidents and anyone who dared challenge the republic.[92] On August 16, he wrote Secretary of War Ignacio Mejía from the old colonial town of Chignahuapan, high in the silver mining area on the northeastern slopes of the Sierra de Puebla, saying he was continuing to campaign against the rebels and that he had taken a number of prisoners and was confident of success.[93] He was even using some of his "own private funds" to support his Tamaulipas Brigade and was rendering "good service to the Supreme Government."[94] Cortina has "succeeded where millions of men better educated have failed," one Mexico City newspaper remarked: "Should any one take General Cortina for a fool or a coward he will lose money. He is neither."[95] With the press offering accolades and his deeds receiving praise from government officials, President Juárez again embraced him. Cortina's star was again on the rise.

Yet large areas of Mexico remained in a state of anarchy, and life in the countryside was uncertain and unstable as local or regional caciques competed for power. Roads in the country were unsafe, making travel difficult and dangerous, if not impossible. Largely due to his successes in the state of Puebla, Cortina was called again to Mexico City by Secretary of War Mejía to consult about how to pacify lawless areas of the republic. Cortina "is the man to clean out these scamps," the press reported, referring to the numerous brigands for whom banditry had become a way of life. "He will camp on their trail, night after night and never give them time to rest or to successfully hide from his pursuit."⁹⁶ As to guerrilla warfare, Cortina was the master.

Vargas Revolution

Although large areas of the country did become pacified, Tamaulipas remained in a state of disorder and insurrection. The violence and lawlessness in the state paralyzed commerce, destroyed agriculture, and brought "great distress upon all classes," the American vice consul in Matamoros observed.⁹⁷ On the northeastern fringes of the republic, everyone seemed to pray for peace and tranquility. In this light, Cortina was sent back to the border and his native Tamaulipas, where Braulio Vargas, a former *Juarista* colonel, had pronounced against the central government. Although Vargas had seized a large swath of the southern part of the state, he also claimed parts of the border where it was said one thousand men were under arms and where he was receiving war materials from Texas. On the Rio Grande, Cortina's Rancho El Soldadito was completely gutted by Vargas partisans.⁹⁸

Arriving in Ciudad Victoria with his Tamaulipas Brigade of two hundred men, Cortina was thought too weak to take on Vargas. On November 17, 1868, he wrote President Juárez, saying his first priority was the elimination of the bandits who had infested the state capital. When he apprehended and hanged one of the outlaws, Ramón Velásquez, the anarchy in the city quickly abated. But in rural areas of the state—all the way from Tampico in the south to Matamoros in the northeast and upriver to Nuevo Laredo—Tamaulipas remained unsettled with little if any central authority. The state, he quickly realized, was in worse shape than what had been rumored in Mexico City. Asking for arms and more men, Cortina promised to open a campaign against the various bandit gangs.⁹⁹ Realizing that he was one of the few leaders capable of restoring law and order in Tamaulipas, Escobedo appointed him military commander in the state with full authority to eradicate banditry.

Hearing that robbers and brigands were operating out of the dense thickets near El Guayalejo, south of the capital, Cortina rode out of Ciudad Victoria on December 10 with three hundred men. Two days later, he struck a camp of the brigands, scattered the "rabble" in every direction, captured five men, and immediately executed them.¹⁰⁰ Leaving Ciudad Victoria again in early January 1868, this time in the direction of Croix, Cortina decisively defeated Vargas, killed a number of his followers, and captured his second in command, whom he ordered shot. In retaliation, Vargas was said to have shot Tomás Garza, brother of Gov. Juan José de la Garza and who had been wounded and captured in the fighting. Vargas's men who escaped the fighting fled to the west into the verdant and rugged Huasteca of the Sierra Madre.¹⁰¹

Late in February, Cortina dealt Vargas a second stunning defeat at Sauz, not far from Jiménez, fifty miles northeast of the capital. As Vargas again fled the field, Cortina pursued him into the woods with "great boldness," it was said. When the news reached Matamoros of Cortina's stunning victory, his supporters went into a wild celebration. Bells rang out, rockets were fired into the air, and the local garrison paraded the streets.[102]

Determined to crush the Vargas revolution and with the area around Ciudad Victoria pacified, Cortina moved to Soto la Marina on the river of the same name, not far from the coast, before returning to Jiménez.[103] Shortly thereafter, General Escobedo arrived from San Luis Potosí with one thousand infantry and three hundred cavalry. In the meantime, on May 11, 1869, having assembled a small force of one hundred men in Texas, Servando Canales and his brother, Antonio, crossed the river from Texas, seized Camargo, and pronounced in favor of Vargas and against the "tyrants of unfortunate Mexico."[104] But Cortina responded by moving north and driving Canales out of his home town.[105] Two weeks later, Canales attacked San Fernando, but the government garrison under Col. Juan J. Arrocha threw him back.[106] In June, with the remnants of Vargas's revolutionaries continuing to operate around Linares, in the southeastern part of Nuevo León, Cortina took three hundred cavalry and rode south again to Jiménez. "The bandits have again broken up their forces, thus making their pursuit more difficult, but I pursue them with confidence," Cortina wrote in early June.[107] From Jiménez, he returned again to Soto la Marina, but, when it was rumored Canales was moving on Ciudad Victoria, he headed back to the capital.[108] Throughout October and November, with the bandit war in Tamaulipas winding down, Cortina waited the opportunity to return to the border. Recruiting efforts were already underway in Matamoros.[109]

Republic Imperiled

Despite a particularly violent municipal election in Matamoros in which "knives and pistols were used freely," Tamaulipas had become relatively quiet by early 1870, with most of the military and political leaders working to "sustain the Juárez government."[110] But then rebel generals pronounced against Juárez in San Luis Potosí, and uprisings followed in Zacatecas, Jalisco, and Querétaro. Thousands of angry men took up arms, and again the republic was imperiled. Many leaders in Matamoros and throughout Tamaulipas received invitations to join the insurrection in San Luis Potosí. In neighboring Nuevo León, Gov. Gerónimo Treviño rushed off to San Luis Potosí where the revolutionaries received him with "great demonstration."

It was another trying time for Cortina and Mexico; disorder and chaos threatened to once again engulf the republic. While Cortina rode off to San Luis Potosí with his cavalry, there was serious doubt Juárez could hold onto power. After a long and hard ride through the mountains with his *Tamaulipecans,* Cortina joined other pro-Juárez forces in defeating the rebels near the city in early February. Within weeks he had joined Gen. Sóstenes Rocha in Jalisco, where a large rebel force of five thousand men was defeated at Lo de Ovejo on February 21, 1870. In the bloody fighting, much of it hand to hand, the rebels were overwhelmed, losing eight hundred men killed and wounded, along with twenty-six pieces of artillery. More than one thousand prisoners were also taken.[111] Although the backbone of the insurrection was broken in central Mexico, trouble began anew on the border.

By late May 1870, Gen. Pedro Martínez, a former *Juarista* general and a relative of Mariano Escobedo, pronounced against Juárez in Nuevo León. With one thousand men, armed mostly with antiquated pistols and muskets, Martínez marched on Matamoros, saying he was waging war on the "dictatorship of Don Benito Juárez."[112] At the same time, Martínez sent one hundred men under Col. Emilio Parra to occupy Camargo where the *ayuntamiento* fled across the river to Rio Grande City. John P. Kelsey, commercial agent in Camargo, told Washington the revolutionaries were conducting a "reign of terror," and he asked the commander at Ringgold Barracks to intervene, a request that was promptly denied.[113] Reacting to the continued violence on the frontier, the American consul in Matamoros, Lucius Avery, claimed Martínez was doing little more than spreading "misery and consternation."[114]

Outside Matamoros, Martínez issued a *pronunciamiento* calling on the soldiers inside the city to lay down their arms and join him. Inside the defenses, Gen. Miguel Palacios, with four hundred regulars and eight hundred national guardsmen, declared martial law and braced for an attack. Once again, citizens of the heroic city crowded the ferries to Brownsville. At the height of the crisis, Gen. Pedro Hinojosa, acting mayor of the city, declared himself in favor of Martínez. Just as it seemed the city would fall, word arrived that two thousand well-armed government troops were approaching. Unable to obtain weapons and ammunition from Brownsville, Martínez withdrew his army, only to be decisively defeated at Charco Escondido in Nuevo León. Martínez did, however, continue to hold a few of the towns on the river and even Ciudad Victoria.[115] Meanwhile, Cortina was in Mexico City when he learned that Martínez had risen against the central government and that several of his ranches on the Rio Grande had been burned by the *Pronunciados.* Writing a friend in Mier, Cortina said he would leave the capital as soon as possible, and he asked the "good sons of Tamaulipas" to join him in helping to destroy the revolutionaries under Martínez.[116]

In the election for governor of the state—with Andrés Treviño, Servando Canales, and Cortina as leading candidates—most of the people voted for whoever happened to control their community at the time. When Canales proved victorious, Cortina took the defeat hard, charging that the election was rigged. In Mexico City, Juárez agreed to recognize Canales but only if he reported to the capital for directions.[117] When Canales refused, Cortina hurried north with his cavalry. The never-ending struggle for power in Tamaulipas was entering yet another phase of bloodshed and suffering.

BACK ON THE BORDER

On September 1, 1870, the stagecoach from Monterrey arrived in Matamoros with the news that Cortina was on the march for the border with five hundred cavalry.[118] Arriving on the Rio Grande two weeks later, Cortina was greeted with cheers and good will. Even Henry Maltby of the *Daily Ranchero* welcomed him back to the border, seeing the caudillo as the lesser of two evils. "Perhaps in all the army of Mexico, there is no man more capable than Cortina of ... exterminating the bands of murdering thieves who infest this section," Maltby wrote. The "fighting editor," as Maltby styled himself, was even hoping that Cortina could stop the "depredations of cattle thieves who cross from Mexico into Texas, gather up droves of cattle and re-cross [them] into Mexico." If Cortina could "exterminate the cattle thieves, the pacification of this frontier will follow," Maltby predicted.[119]

As was his custom, the first thing Cortina did after reaching Matamoros was to issue a *pronunciamiento*. In it, he promised to pursue the "bands of highwaymen and kidnappers" without "rest at every hour and in every place."[120] The frontier must and would be pacified. Ten days after arriving on the border, he was already in Reynosa where he was widely cheered. Merchants of the town, Cortina said, should be free to send their goods into the interior without fear of being robbed.[121] His reputation was such that a number of outlaw bands either fled or disbanded in his wake. Two bandit caciques who did not flee, Jesús Hernández and Fabián García, were captured and executed. Continuing upriver to Camargo, Cortina was again cheered as a conquering hero. Less than a month after his arrival on the frontier, the counterinsurgency was over. The violence "heretofore referred to as existing in the State of Tamaulipas has been suppressed," the American consul in Matamoros wrote Secretary of State Hamilton Fish.[122]

With Edmund J. Davis, his compatriot from the Civil War, now governor of Texas, Cortina asked friends to approach Davis and members of the legislature with the idea of a pardon and clemency for him in Texas. Indictments in Cameron, Hidalgo, and Starr counties had always hung over his head. Although he hoped to visit Rancho del Carmen, he might have also been looking for a refuge similar to what he had enjoyed in 1865 and 1866 should future events in Mexico go against him. Cortina was nothing if not a man of contradictions. Although he realized any residency in Texas was out of the question, he remained concerned with the plight of his countrymen in their continuing struggle against deeply rooted racism and a rash of ethnic-inspired acts of violence. Reflecting Cortina's position, in the Lower Rio Grande Valley, forty-one citizens submitted a petition saying the "crimes" Cortina had committed in Texas were "political in their nature." They argued that this, plus Cortina's stellar record in the Mexican military, should warrant a "full and complete pardon." Although a majority of those signing the petition were Mexican Texans from Starr County, three individuals from Cameron County, including the former mayor of Brownsville, Stephen Powers, also signed the document. Powers was quickly emerging as one of the more powerful political voices on the border, and his word carried considerable weight in the state capital. Nevertheless, in April 1871, Davis wrote Powers to say he had no authority to pardon anyone for treason and he had decided to recommend the legislature pass a bill for Cortina's relief.[123]

In Austin, State Senator Albert B. Fountain agreed to sponsor a joint resolution calling on Governor Davis to grant Cortina a full and unconditional pardon.[124] When word reached Brownsville of the idea, however, a political firestorm erupted. Arguing that Cortina was a murderer and a cattle thief, furious citizens vigorously lobbied against the proposition. After the resolution passed a first reading on April 12, 1871, it was postponed indefinitely and then buried in a mountain of bureaucracy.[125] Cortina never returned to Texas.

Chapter Eight

Predator War

Is he not king of the whole frontier?

NEW YORK TIMES

ALTHOUGH CORTINA WOULD NEVER again return to Texas, he never kept his eyes off the state. Realizing the inability of the U.S. Army and local law enforcement officials to secure the vast reaches of the border, he would once again strike at the landholding elite and the forces of oppression. In the process, the reactionary forces of racism, oppression, and fear that had been simmering since 1859 would again come to the forefront of the history of the region. In the process, not only did Cortina come close to instigating a war between the United States and Mexico, but also the victims of the violence he helped to unleash would not be his zealous *Cortinistas* but helpless Tejanos. It was to be a sad and regrettable chapter in the history of Texas.

In 1863, the U.S. Army legitimized stealing livestock when it employed Tejanos to prey on cattle herds in the Nueces Strip. Worse, when General Cortina returned to the frontier in 1871, cattle raids into Texas increased dramatically. Although the affected ranchers greatly exaggerated the effect, the fact remains that the practice reached new heights of intensity and frequency. Clearly orchestrated and directed by Cortina, the raids were carefully planned in the ranchos and small villages on the Mexican side of the river. Most Americans, including Thomas F. Wilson, the American consul in Matamoros, had little doubt that "armed bands of Mexicans" who were involved in the raids were "sheltered and protected" by Cortina.[1] In the years that followed, local, state, and federal authorities in the United States compiled a mountain of evidence implicating Cortina.

Raids fell into a particular pattern. Targeting a given ranch, the raiders, armed with Winchester carbines and six-shooters and numbering anywhere from ten to one hundred, would divide into small parties, cross the river, and rendezvous at a prearranged site in the chaparral. After locating a herd of

Cortinistas gather at a small rancho in northern Tamaulipas prior to a cattle raid into Texas in this 1873 engraving by William de la Montagne Cary. Returning safely to Mexico, the raiders were often cheered as heroes. *Appletons' Journal*, 1873.

cattle, the animals would be pushed south through the night without rest until they reached the river. As associates waited on the south bank, the cattle were herded across the Rio Grande at any one of a number of low-water fords, where there were usually small ranches on both sides of the river. Crossing points included Las Grullas, Sabinito, La Bolsa, Las Rucias, Rancho Nuevo, Prietas, Naranja, and Tulosa. Las Cuevas, though, was the most popular.[2] In Mexico, the stolen cattle were frequently rebranded (usually with Cortina's brand) and sold in Matamoros or in small villages and towns as far away as the Sierra Madre. Some were driven to Bagdad and shipped to Cuba.[3] Collaterally, a lucrative trade in hides sprang up, helping to rejuvenate the economy on the frontier as thousands of hides were shipped to tanneries as far away as New York and Boston.

Popular response to Cortina was, as always, telling. Economic effects and cultural responses derive, of course, from basic needs, and the arrival of a large herd of cattle into the small, impoverished villages of Tamaulipas and Nuevo León was celebrated with joy and festivities.[4] The rustlers were feted as heroes, and so began another chapter in the sometimes-flamboyant, sometimes-desultory, and always-violent life and times of Juan Cortina.

Cattle Raids

Striking back at his old enemies in Texas, Cortina grew rich from the cattle raids, accumulating a fortune that amounted to as much as $800,000. With his newfound wealth, Cortina was able to purchase Rancho Guadalupe from Juan Solís Ballí. Two months later, he acquired several thousand acres of El Rancho Tahuachal from Juan and Donato Longoria. Shortly thereafter, he bought a large adjacent tract of land from the descendants of Leonardo Longoria.[5] At the same time, Cortina purchased a second tract of land on the river from Guadalupe Longoria, widow of Policarpio Farías. In early January 1872, he acquired the hacienda Nuestra Señora Soledad de la Mota from Martina Peña de la Garza and her children.[6] Nine months later, he added the Rancho Maguellitos of Tiburcio Cisneros to his holdings. By late 1873, he had acquired from Francisco Chapa and his son, Antonio Chapa García, yet another large piece of property composed of several thousand acres on the river called La Mesteña. In February 1874, Cortina was able to enlarge El Tahuachal when Manual Garza agreed to sell a large tract of adjacent land. A week later, Fernando Valdéz sold another piece of property on the river, which enlarged El Tahuachal even more.[7] In all, Cortina purchased as many as twenty ranches, large and small, on the frontier.

With the cattle raids intensifying and Cortina's acquiring land and consolidating power, authorities in Texas and Washington feared the situation on the border would spin out of control. Yet many of Cortina's raiders saw their actions as perfectly legitimate. "As far as the people of Mexico are concerned," Lt. Col. Alexander McDowell McCook, commanding the Sub-District of the Rio Grande, recorded, "they believe that the country was wrongfully taken from them, the stock of wild cattle and horses, which have produced the immense herds now grazing there, belonging formerly to their forefathers, they have a right to take them back." Despite the Treaty of Guadalupe Hidalgo, the country "is still a subject of dispute in the hearts of the Tamaulipecos," McCook went on to say.[8]

The numbers correlated with response. The *Brownsville Sentinel* estimated that, in one week alone in Cameron and Hidalgo counties in the summer of 1871, seven thousand cattle worth $210,000 on the Kansas market were crossed into Mexico.[9] Although the count of stolen cattle was undoubtedly exaggerated, newspapers across Texas demanded Washington take action. "The bands of robbers now invading Texas, seem to become more numerous and appear in greater force, well mounted and armed," the *Ranchero* reported.[10] Public officials, too, demanded that something be done about Cortina and his irregular cavalry, Fieles de Cortina and Los Exploradores.

The violence of a *Cortinista* "Cattle Raid on the Texas Border" was dramatically sketched by William de la Montagne Cary for *Harper's Weekly* in 1874. From the time of his 1859 raid on Brownsville, Cortina had loomed large in the American imagination. "Is he not king of the whole frontier?" the *New York Times* asked in 1873. *Harper's Weekly*, January 31, 1874.

To influence public opinion in Texas, the clerk of the 15th Judicial District in Brownsville dusted off old indictments against Cortina and presented them for publication.[11] "It must be remembered that General Cortina was at one time a resident of Texas," the *Ranchero* editorialized, "that he was considered a desperado, that there are now against him [in] the County of Cameron about eighteen criminal indictments, and four in Starr County, and these include many offenses, ranging from murder, robbery, and levying war against the State, down to larceny."[12]

Fluent in Spanish, Lieutenant Colonel McCook had been in Texas before the war and understood the situation on the border as well as anyone. Even he estimated the cattle rustling had increased "ten fold" with Cortina's arrival on the Rio Grande. Not having enough troops to police the river and with the cattle rustling rampant, McCook frankly admitted the situation was out of control and might possibly result in a military confrontation between the United States and Mexico. Ranchers were desperate, the Mexican Texan population was either intimidated or in sympathy with Cortina, and gun battles with the raiders were becoming common. Unless Mexican authorities removed Cortina from the frontier, McCook predicted, "there will be serious trouble less than three months hence."[13]

Agreeing to cooperate with the Americans, Francisco Fuentes Farías, the alcalde of Matamoros, asked authorities on the river to arrest any "evil doers" crossing stolen property into Mexico.[14] At the same time, Thomas Wilson insisted that Gen. Miguel Palacios, commanding the military in Matamoros, confront Cortina. Wilson also wrote editorials for the *Ranchero*, demanding that Cortina be arrested or removed from the frontier. Palacios admitted the "complicity of General Cortina with the robbers," and he promised to take action. In fact, Palacios told Mexico City that it would probably be best if Cortina were ordered away from the border. He also met with McCook at Fort Brown in hopes of maintaining peace and ending Cortina's "evil acts."[15] Palacios went as far as to dispatch several patrols out of Matamoros, one of which caught a band of cattle thieves crossing a stolen heard of cattle upriver from Matamoros. When the rustlers refused to surrender, a fight ensued in which two *Cortinistas* were killed and eight captured.[16] In turn, Cortina countered that Palacios was little more than an American dupe, and he accused him of hiding behind the defenses of Matamoros.

Manuel Treviño, Mexican consul at Brownsville, also flooded Mexico City with complaints about Cortina, but there was little the central government could do. Cortina had simply accumulated too much power. Any attempt to have him arrested would likely result in wide-scale violence, if not a revolution. Still, the Americans kept up the pressure. After consulting with McCook, Wilson warned Washington that "serious complications, if not actual hostilities, will result if General Cortina is not recalled from this frontier by the Mexican Government."[17] Wilson also told the American envoy in Mexico City, Thomas H. Nelson, that Cortina's continued presence on the frontier would likely "lead to serious complications."[18]

Despite the firestorm of complaints coming from South Texas, Cortina remained absorbed by political events in Mexico. In the election of 1871, neither Porfirio Díaz, Sebastián Lerdo de Tejada, nor Juárez received the requisite number of votes, and when Congress proclaimed Juárez president, the country became deeply divided between *Porfiristas, Lerdistas,* and *Juaristas*. Although far from the center of power—independent, and somewhat aloof—Cortina identified with the office holders and military men who supported Juárez.

Gen. Miguel Negrete led a revolt in the Sierra Gordo north of Mexico City in October 1871, but Gen. Sóstenes Rocha, a loyal *Juarista*, soon put it down. A much more serious revolt came on November 8, when Díaz proclaimed himself in revolt against the Juárez regime. His Plan de la Noria, named for his hacienda in Oaxaca, accused the president of being a dictator and having rigged the election. Promising less government and more liberty and a return to the tenets of the Constitution of 1857, the Plan de la Noria also prohibited the indefinite reelection of the chief executive.

Duplicity and Treachery

On October 1, 1871, Cortina watched from Camargo as Gen. Gerónimo Treviño, governor of Nuevo León, announced his support of the Plan de la Noria. Leaving a small force to guard Monterrey, Treviño advanced through the mountains to seize Saltillo. In Matamoros, a small revolt broke out in one of the cavalry regiments, and about twenty men and three officers left to join the revolutionaries. Cortina overtook them a few miles outside the city, however, and the officer who instigated the insurrection was hanged.[19]

By January 1872, Gen. Julián Quiroga advanced against Mier from Monterrey with about one thousand *Porfiristas*, and Cortina was forced to retreat without a fight. With the forces of Gen. Pedro Hinojosa, Quiroga then moved against Camargo, demanding that Cortina give up the town. Without supplies, the ragged *Porfiristas* went into camp on the west bank of the San Juan River in a sleet storm. Bracing for an attack, Cortina rallied six hundred men and rushed to find more recruits from the farms and ranches along the river, appropriating horses and fodder when necessary. In the process, one of his cavalry units, Los Águilas, was accused of pillaging the ranch of Mandinio Peña, a Quiroga supporter who was said to be a man of considerable wealth and influence. When Peña resisted, he was hanged in front of his family by Cortina partisans.[20]

As skirmishes erupted along the San Juan River, Cortina barricaded the town, certain he was to be attacked. Outnumbered and outgunned, he met several times with Quiroga in hopes of negotiating his way out of a difficult situation.[21] Suddenly, on February 2, while the *ayuntamiento* fled across the river to Rio Grande City, Cortina gave up and marched away in the night. In the retreat, more than one hundred of his men went over to Quiroga. "Cortina has been playing a double game by pretending to support the government of President Juárez while acting covertly with the enemy," Wilson wrote from Matamoros.[22] Wilson was certain Cortina "sold Mier to General Quiroga for $7,000 and that he received a large sum to evacuate Camargo." Cortina, Wilson continued, was rapidly gaining a reputation for his "duplicity and treachery."[23]

When Cortina and what remained of his emaciated army reached Reynosa, many feared he would continue downriver to Matamoros, overwhelm Palacios, and then surrender the city to Quiroga and the revolutionaries. Although many in the city supported Cortina, foreigners and the wealthy deeply mistrusted him. Manuel Treviño and the leading merchants in the city, foreign and Mexican, called on Wilson to use his influence with General Palacios to somehow stop Cortina from entering the city. Not only did Wilson meet with Palacios, but he also took Colonel McCook with him. But McCook was not convinced Palacios could stop Cortina, who was "a sort of dictator on the line of the Bravo." Cortina's army, McCook said, had become a "refuge for all the murderers, thieves, and vagabonds on both frontiers." Saying he "fully appreciated the gravity of the situation," Palacios agreed to send a courier to Cortina urging him not to enter Matamoros.[24] Cortina should remain in the field, and if he could not defeat the revolutionists, he could at least harass them. With three hundred regulars and six hundred national guardsmen, Palacios also declared martial law and began reinforcing the city's defenses, including mounting several large siege guns. With Cortina in the chaparral and General Quiroga approaching from upriver, Matamoros was cut off from the interior and isolated. Once again the heroic city was reliant on Brownsville for food and news from the outside world.[25]

Watching and Waiting

While the fighting on the Rio Grande frontier continued unabated, the army Díaz put into the field was defeated in Zacatecas, and the revolt of La Noria collapsed in disarray. Without official orders from Mexico City, Cortina could do little but watch and await events from afar. On April 22, as everyone in Matamoros braced for an attack, Gen. José Ceballos arrived from Veracruz with 550 men and two pieces of artillery. When more reinforcements arrived, generals Treviño and Quiroga, realizing they could not attack the city while Cortina threatened their flanks, drew off and retreated toward Reynosa. The timely arrival of General Ceballos had lifted the siege, and within days he was in pursuit of the revolutionists, incorporating Cortina's cavalry into his army. But Ceballos brought orders relieving Cortina of command and ordering him to Mexico City. Always the elusive fox, Cortina played for time as he had done many times before.[26]

On May 30, 1872, while Cortina waited on the border, Ceballos chased General Treviño out of his stronghold of Monterrey. Other government troops under General Rocha soon reached the city from Saltillo, and Quiroga and Treviño fled north into the desert toward Monclova. Two weeks later, government troops entered Nuevo Laredo, and the revolt in the north crumbled. In Matamoros, the town celebrated the triumph of the government with church bells ringing, bands marching, and soldiers parading. But then, on July 19, the reconnected telegraph to Mexico City carried grievous news: Benito Juárez, the diminutive Zapotec Indian from the mountains of Oaxaca, who had risen from abject poverty to become the greatest man in Mexican history, was dead from a coronary seizure in Mexico City. Sebastián Lerdo de Tejada, chief justice of the Supreme Court, was proclaimed as the acting president.²⁷ As Lerdo took office in Mexico City, American officials renewed their relentless pressure to have Cortina removed from the border. Intelligent, ambitious, but cautions, Lerdo, just as Juárez had done, issued orders for Cortina to report to Mexico City. Again Cortina refused, remaining at his ranch above Matamoros.²⁸

Letters of Blood and Fire

While events transpired south of the border, influential ranchers in Texas loudly complained that *Cortinistas* were continuing to depredate on their stock herds. On March 4, for example, one of Cortina's chief lieutenants, Capt. Sabás García, led a raid deep into the Wild Horse Desert, south of the King Ranch, that drove off 1,600 head of cattle. Arriving back on the south bank with the livestock, the *Cortinistas* were reported to have been welcomed as heroes. The herd was then driven to Matamoros, with Dionisio Cárdenas, the alcalde, purchasing a large number of the animals. After being paid for the livestock, the *Cortinistas* were said to have ridden back to Cortina's Rancho Mogotes for a lively celebration.²⁹

By August 1871, a Cameron County grand jury began "inquiring into the wholesale stealing of cattle which has been, and is constantly, carried on to an alarming extent on this frontier." From interviews with sixty of the more influential ranchers, the jurors concluded that, if the U.S. government did not intervene, there was certain to be a "depopulation and abandonment of all the stock-ranches between the Rio Grande and the Nueces."³⁰ Without mentioning Cortina by name, the jurors accused Mexican authorities of protecting the raiders. The entire lower Valley was "under the control of armed thieves," the grand jury concluded.³¹ While newspapers in Texas riled against Cortina with stories of cattle raids, John Hancock, of Texas, pushed a joint resolution through Congress calling on the government to act immediately and decisively.³² In March 1872, a federal grand jury for the Eastern District of Texas also met in Brownsville. The jury included thirteen men from as far away as Victoria and Galveston, many of them prominent farmers and ranchers. Because of his knowledge of the frontier, John S. Ford was selected as foreman.

After three weeks of seemingly endless testimony, the jurors concluded that Cortina was to blame for all the cattle raids. There was nothing "more galling" to Texans than the "sending of Gen. Juan Nepomuceno Cortina to this frontier," a man who had written his name "in letters of blood and fire," the grand jury agreed.³³ A "reign of terror" had existed for some time "between the Rio Grande and the Nueces." Mercenary marauders, Mexican "officers and soldiers, and Mexican outlaws and bandits"—all guided by Cortina, the "ranking cow and horse thief"—had pushed the United States and Mexico to the brink of war. Moreover, evidence indicated that Cortina had "received a large share of the plunder" from which he had stocked four of his ranches "with cows and horses stolen from Texas." In the Lower Rio Grande Valley alone, five thousand head of stolen cattle were being driven into Mexico monthly. Since Cortina's return to the border, 420,000 livestock valued at $6,300,000 had been lost. Almost in desperation, the jurors asked that Congress establish a commission as soon as possible to investigate the deplorable situation.[34]

Shortly after the grand jury report was released, Texas District Judge William H. Russell impaneled a grand jury at the small courthouse in Edinburg to investigate "Mexican Invasions and Depredations." Hidalgo and adjacent counties had been "held in terror by roving bands of well-armed and organized marauders whose only trade and means of subsistence have been cattle stealing," the jurors concluded.[35] Cattle thieves were brazenly committing their crimes within a few miles of Fort Brown and Ringgold Barracks. The entire judicial system of Hidalgo County was paralyzed because local juries were afraid to convict any *Cortinista* for fear of retaliation. "Each successive acquittal gives new courage and energy" to the rustlers who "prowl over the country and laugh defiance at our laws from their safe retreat across the river." Although not mentioning Cortina, the jurors concluded that "high Mexican officials" were encouraging the raids.[36] At the same time, Judge Russell impaneled yet another grand jury in Cameron County, which reached similar conclusions to those in Edinburg. Beginning in 1865, a systematic invasion of cattle thieves from Mexico had infested the lower Valley. But with Cortina's arrival back on the border, the raids had grown in "boldness and magnitude." The jury, including two Mexican Texans, concluded that "as long as General Cortina remains in an important command on the frontier . . . so long will the depredations on the frontier counties continue."[37]

In the weeks following the release of the grand jury reports, influential stockmen, under the guidance of Mifflin Kenedy, met in Brownsville to form the Stockman's Association of Western Texas for "protection against the marauders."[38] Kenedy and his ranching friends calculated that, since 1865, they had lost in the lower Valley alone four hundred thousand head of cattle worth $6,000,000, along with twenty thousand horses valued at $500,000.[39] From Matamoros, Consul Wilson heightened the rhetoric by vociferously warning Washington that if something was not done about Cortina there was certain to be a war between the United States and Mexico. Mexican officials, both civil and military, were either too corrupt, too weak, or too demoralized by years of incessant warfare to do anything, Wilson said. Besides, the Rio Grande frontier was so remote that it was "impossible for the Government of the Republic to check or control these depredations."[40] The only solution was for the United States to station large numbers of cavalry at various intervals on the Rio Grande and on the Arroyo Colorado.

With leading stock raisers and politicians in South Texas crying for action, the wheels of the federal bureaucracy in Washington began to grind. Hearing the reverberating echoes of discontent, President Ulysses S. Grant realized he must do something to restore order to South Texas, and he asked Secretary of War William Belknap to take action at once. If found in Texas, Cortina was to be arrested immediately, Belknap told Adjutant General E. D. Townsend, who relayed the orders to Gen. Philip Sheridan. Sheridan then wired Gen. Christopher Colon Augur, commanding the Department of Texas, to station as many cavalry units as possible on the border.[41] In response, Augur transferred a company of the 4th Cavalry from San Antonio to Fort Brown, sent a company of the 9th Cavalry to Ringgold Barracks, and authorized Colonel McCook to mount another company of infantry.[42]

As early as August 1871, a cavalry patrol from Fort Brown killed Cypriano Flores, one of Cortina's lieutenants, in a skirmish on the river near La Bolsa. Farther upriver, two other *Cortinistas*, Victor "Coyote" González and Rafael "Cucho" Hinojosa, were captured and turned over to the Mexican military, who promptly hanged them.[43] In December, a detachment out of Ringgold Barracks led by Victor Morel surprised a band of *Cortinistas* led by Julio Hinojosa on the river below the post. Although sixty head of cattle were recovered, the *Cortinistas*, who were said to be "superior bushmen," escaped.[44] The effectiveness of the cavalry on the border was enhanced by Mexican Texan guides who knew the terrain and the chaparral. In April 1872, the Mexican military seized a herd of cattle with Texas brands near Camargo and turned them over to Maj. Thomas McArthur Anderson of the 10th Infantry at Ringgold Barracks.[45] The next month, Gen. José Ceballos, who had replaced Cortina in command of the line of the Rio Bravo, arrested several cattle thieves and returned several herds of cattle to Texas. Well into 1873, the Mexican military returned more and more stolen cattle to Texas.[46]

Encouraged by newspapers in Texas and arguing that the Mexican government was incapable of restraining the border raiders, filibusters again talked of invading northern Mexico, killing Cortina or driving him into the interior, and establishing a boundary line at the Sierra Madre. Despite demands for his capture in Texas and his lack of government legitimacy in Mexico, Cortina became even more daring than before. As such, his raiders did more than just steal cattle. At the same time, many of those committing crimes were only loosely associated with the caudillo. With the Mexican military now cooperating with the Americans, as many as fifty *Cortinistas*, under the leadership of Juan Muñoz and Ignacio Treviño, began operating out of Rancho Lopeño in Zapata County, raiding into Mexico, twice entering Guerrero to force loans on the citizens. Ever since the Cortina War, Cortina had enjoyed wide-scale support in Zapata County, and he continued to be popular among the county's poor. At least forty-six *Cortinistas*, at least

Sombrero-crowned *Cortinistas* cross the Rio Grande with a stolen herd of cattle in this imaginative engraving by William de la Montagne Cary. Although an established illustrator for *Harper's Weekly* and *Frank Leslie's Illustrated Newspaper* and someone who had seen a large part of the American West, there is no evidence that Montagne ever saw the Rio Grande. *Appletons' Journal*, 1873.

half of them residents of the United States, plundered the large mercantile house of O. A. Carolan, in Mier, and carried off goods worth $2,000.[47] The *Cortinistas* also attacked Nuevo Laredo and raided Cerralvo in Nuevo León.[48] Many in Texas were convinced that it was only a matter of time before the raiders seized the customs house at Carrizo.

To authorities in Texas, the presence of an armed force of *Cortinistas* on the soil of the United States was embarrassing and symptomatic of the government's inability to control the border.[49] After he was briefed on the situation, Secretary of State Hamilton Fish complained to Secretary of War Belknap about the "unlawful occupation of the soil of the United States."[50] Acting on President Grant's orders, General Augur was directed to capture or break up the *Cortinistas*.[51] In turn, Augur gave the assignment to Major Anderson at Ringgold Barracks. The only problem was that Anderson's infantry was helpless in such a vast land where the *Cortinistas* were superbly mounted and had "numerous confidantes."⁵² Moreover, many of the smaller Mexican Texan ranchers and farmers on the Texas side of the river not only sympathized with Cortina but also were aiding and abetting his raiders. To complicate matters, a large number of the families in Zapata County were related by blood or marriage to families in Mexico. Proof of the problem was soon made crystal clear. In late March 1872, Capt. Edward Geer Bush and a company of the 10th Infantry left Ringgold Barracks with orders to patrol as far upriver as the Alamo crossing, searching the small ranches in the vicinity as they went. No *Cortinistas* were encountered, but Bush did learn that Muñoz and Treviño with three hundred raiders, mostly Mexican Texans, had left the vicinity of Guerrero with intentions of attacking Nuevo Laredo.⁵³

King of the Whole Frontier

On May 7, 1872, in response to the ever-intensifying situation on the border, a joint resolution of Congress authorized a three-member commission appointed by President Grant to "inquire into depredations on the frontiers of Texas."⁵⁴ Commissioners included Thomas P. Robb, of Georgia, and Richard H. Savage and Fabius J. Mead, of Mississippi. After assembling in New Orleans in early July, the Robb Commission, as it came to be known, proceeded immediately to Brownsville, where county officials heartily embraced them. After hiring a translator, they began work on July 30 but were quickly overwhelmed as hundreds of individuals lined up to testify or present claims. The commissioners worked diligently through the stifling summer heat until early October, when they returned to Washington.⁵⁵ Almost from the beginning it was evident, as might be expected, that the commission was unduly influenced by individuals in Texas who hoped to make a fortune by exaggerating claims against Mexico.

In February 1873, after Thomas O. Osborn replaced Mead, the commission again assembled in New Orleans. Although delayed by storms, the group soon arrived back on the Rio Grande, and after three weeks in Brownsville, the commissioners headed upriver to Rio Grande City. With Mifflin Kenedy and several prominent stockmen on board the *San Juan*, the commissioners were a half-mile above Las Cuevas when they looked up to see a herd of stolen cattle being driven into Mexico.⁵⁶ After hearing testimony at Ringgold Barracks, the commissioners headed through the Brush Country to Corpus Christi before turning back to the King Ranch and San Diego to hear more testimony. After a brief respite in San Antonio, they traveled south to Laredo by stage for more hearings and then upriver to Eagle Pass. From Fort Duncan, they turned east for sessions at Bracketville and Uvalde before returning to San Antonio. In all, the Robb Commission took 1,090 depositions and accepted 423 petitions. Claims by angry Texans amounted to a whopping $48,466,235, of which $44,572,425 was blamed on Mexican raiders. The remaining damages were mostly in the Laredo and Eagle Pass area and were from Indian raids.[57]

At Brownsville, not only did Thomas Wilson, the American consul from across the river, testify, but so did Lt. Col. A. McDowell McCook. Leading stockmen of the area, such as Richard King and John McAllen, also came forth to provide testimony, as did a number of leading Tejano ranchers, such as Carlos Esparza and Pedro Vela. Many of those who testified were men who held deep-rooted grudges against Cortina dating back to 1859. These included Thaddeus M. Rhodes, John S. Ford, William D. Thomas, Adolphus Glavecke, and the Champion brothers, Nicholas, Peter, and Albert. Some of the most damaging testimony came from Mexicans who had once ridden with Cortina and who were familiar with his activities. Most had fallen out with the wily caudillo, and, in most instances, they were less than objective in their testimony. Moreover, some of the depositions were certain to have been enticed and induced by the Anglo ranching elite. Anaclito Padrón, a former *Cortinista*, recalled how, in June 1871, he had been sent by Cortina to protect two hundred cattle that had been stolen in Texas and were being crossed at Cortina's Rancho Tahuachal. Padrón had also helped cross cattle near Matamoros that were driven to the caudillo's Rancho Palito Blanco.[58]

Others followed suit, each giving a slightly different view of Cortina. Another former *Cortinista*, Apolinario Hernández, told the commissioners that, in August 1871, at Rancho Santa Fe near Matamoros, he had watched Cortina brand a number of Texas cattle, altering "the old marks" in the process. A month later, Hernández was at the Rancho Santa Rita, twelve miles upriver from Matamoros, when he saw Capt. Sabás García, one of Cortina's officers, in possession of one hundred stolen cattle. Cortina came in person to divide the stock, the fat steers were sent to market while the cows and yearlings were driven to Cortina's ranches. Hernández went on to relate how the Holguín brothers had crossed five hundred stolen cattle into Mexico at Rancho Rucias. The chief justice of Matamoros arrested and imprisoned the brothers, but, Hernández recalled, Cortina had them released.[59]

Benito García, who lived on the river eighteen miles above Brownsville, said he had known Cortina since childhood. With his profits from stolen Texas cattle, Cortina had purchased Rancho Canela, Rancho Soldadito, and Rancho Palito Blanco, each of which was protected by armed guards. Although once poor, Cortina had grown rich with stolen livestock as he steadily stocked his ranches with vast herds of cattle from Texas. The "cheerful bandit," as García called Cortina, had become one of the wealthiest men in the republic. "Is he not king of the whole frontier?" the *New York Times* editoralized.[60]

Gregorio Villarreal, a resident of Rancho Encantada in Cameron County and a former *Cortinista* sergeant, testified he had seen Cortina receive a large herd of stolen cattle at Camargo. In fact, Villarreal had helped to drive several herds of Texas cattle to Rancho Palito Blanco, where they were sold. Moreover, when Cortina marched his small army to Camargo in 1870, he fed them entirely on Texas beef. When a band of *Cortinistas* was captured in Texas, Villarreal related how Cortina had sent him to Brownsville to purchase their saddles and equipment that were sold at public auction. In Matamoros, Villarreal said, the authorities had once seized 118 head of stolen cattle, but they admitted to receiving only eighteen with Cortina taking the other one hundred.[61]

Victor Morel of Rio Grande City recalled how he had recaptured a herd of thirty to fifty cattle from a band of *Cortinistas* less than three miles from Rio Grande City.[62] William Burke, a lieutenant in the Texas state police, told the commission how he had investigated the theft of numerous herds of cattle. On one occasion, he had given the names of the rustlers to authorities in Matamoros but nothing was done. Burke had personally witnessed Cortina's men driving herds of cattle across the river at Rancho Prietas, three miles above Brownsville. The men had defiantly yelled across the river that they would raid Texas at will and "clean us out," Burke said. He had gone personally to see Cortina and asked him to "clean up the thieves on the Mexican side." Cortina promised he would do so, but nothing happened. Burke was convinced that Cortina was the leader of all the thieves and bandits and, as a result of his leadership had amassed a great fortune.[63]

Cattle inspector Albert Dean testified he had personally seen Cortina meeting with cattle thieves at his headquarters near Matamoros.[64] Another cattle inspector, Thomas C. Sheldon, told the commissioners that one of Cortina's most reliable officers, Capt. Sabás García, had bragged that Cortina gave him permission to raid into Texas.[65] Carlos Esparza, a prominent Cameron County rancher who had lost six hundred cattle and eighty horses in 1871, said Cortina had personally received most of the stolen cattle that had been crossed at Rancho Calabozo. To Esparza, Cortina was a "bad and dangerous man" who was at the head of "all the murderers, robbers and thieves" on both sides of the Rio Grande.[66] Thaddeus M. Rhodes, whose ranch had been burned by the *Cortinistas* in 1859, said there was little doubt that Cortina had stocked his ranches with cattle stolen in Texas. Cortina, Rhodes said, had bragged that he would "take care of the cattle-thieves in Mexico if they would take care of themselves in Texas."[67]

Albert Champion recalled how in September 1871, one of Cortina's officers, Capt. Ildefonso Salinas, stole nine horses from his stage station at La Torrena.[68] William D. Thomas, a rancher now working as a guide and interpreter for the Rangers, said he had confronted one of Cortina's captains, Francisco Milán, who was driving a herd of four hundred stolen cattle into Mexico. Milán told Thomas he was not afraid of the "Gringos." They were "raising cows" for him, and he would kill "them wherever he found them."[69] Pedro Vela remembered how Cortina directed the vaqueros at Rancho Las Cuevas to raid into Texas, but if they stole cattle in Mexico, Cortina told them, he would hang them.[70]

Claiming he had lost thousands of head of cattle in the years from 1869 to 1872, Richard King put in a claim for $2,486,160. King, who was in the process of building a ranching empire in South Texas, had other claims dating back to 1859. There was little doubt, King said, that Cortina was to blame for the cattle rustling and violence.[71] In fact, King himself had almost been killed while on his way from Corpus Christi to his ranch on Santa Gertrudis Creek in the summer of 1872. Near San Fernando Creek, six miles east of the King Ranch, late on the evening of July 31, the ambulance in which King and his driver, Franz Specht, were riding was attacked by eight to ten of Cortina's raiders and riddled with twenty-five to thirty bullets. Although Specht was killed, King managed to escape. From that point on, King would never travel unless he was escorted by at least five to ten heavily armed guards.[72]

Finally, Mifflin Kenedy filed a claim for $670,760 and reminded the commissioners that Cortina had attacked the steamer *Ranchero* in 1860, a result of which he had lost $250,000 in business.[73] Perhaps the most outrageous claims came from the Champion brothers and Adophus Glavecke, who put in claims for lost livestock several times what they had claimed on the tax rolls.[74] Thomas O'Connor, a wealthy stockman from Refugio, claimed he lost thirty thousand livestock. Sterling Neblett Dobie, a great-uncle of J. Frank Dobie, the well-known Texas folklorist of the next century, said that, in 1866, four thousand cattle and 125 horses were stolen from his ranch in Live Oak County.[75]

Prince of Bandits

In early October 1873, after hearing as many as fourteen witness a day, the commission came to realize the "gravity of the present situation of affairs on the frontier," and they returned to Washington, there releasing a preliminary forty-one-page report.[76] Civil authorities in Mexico were powerless to "suppress the lawless bands that have operated from that frontier," they concluded. Reflecting the testimony they had heard, the commission concluded that Cortina was "the protector of the lawless bands" raiding into Texas. A history of General Cortina's career "would be in great part, but a history of the wrong and outrages which have been committed with impunity, for years past, on the residents of our southwestern frontier."[77] Moreover, Mexican authorities had come to possess "a wanton disregard of the authority of this Government and of the rights of its citizens." The situation on the Rio Grande was of such a "serious character" that the United States must take immediate action to "protect its territory from the incursions of hostile expeditions coming from a neighboring power unable to enforce and suppress violence within its own border."[78]

Fascinated with the lawlessness of the Texas-Mexico border, Cortina was again thrust to the forefront of the American imagination. "In the whole calendar of crime along the Rio Grande, there never was a scoundrel who had more power than this adroit and apparently invulnerable cavalier of the plains," the *New York Times* reported.[79] In disdainful courtesy, the "prince of bandits" salutes the American troops "who are too few and too widely scattered to protect the country from his ravages," the newspaper continued.[80]

From the time the Robb Commission first arrived on the Rio Grande, Cortina watched and listened from Matamoros; the more he learned, the more he became incensed. After Lieutenant Colonel McCook's particularly venomous testimony in August 1872, Cortina struck back with one of his lengthy *pronunciamientos*. His question: how could McCook and the other Americans giving testimony not be aware of the theft of cattle by Texans "in all the northern district of Tamaulipas?" Not far from Brownsville, Cortina said, one could see a "constant deposit of animals stolen from Mexico."[81] Moreover, chronic horse stealing by Texans in the vicinity of Matamoros was scandalous. In fact, two herds of more than 150 horses each had been stolen from Mexico and driven into the interior of Texas. Cortina angrily asked, "Where was Gen'l. McCook when the burning of the Chiltipín Ranch and the murder of Mexicans took place all of which was perpetrated by a man who has committed other similar acts against defenseless Mexicans?" How could McCook not be aware of the "inestimable loss of lands sustained by Mexican families ... after the treaty of Guadalupe, and among whom my family is included?" Cortina continued.[82] In fact, McCook should be held responsible for the falsehoods and perjury he was perpetrating. If the commissioners were in search of the truth, they should also quit listening to the Brownsville newspapers. In the "predatory war," Cortina said, the claims of Mexico would easily exceed those of the United States.

Comisión Pesquisidora

Two months after the Robb Commission arrived in Brownsville, President Lerdo de Tejada appointed another commission in far-off Mexico City. This new group would "clear up the facts relating to the injuries complained of by citizens of the United States, as well as those relating to injuries ... to Mexican citizens on the frontier of the North, whether by Indian depredations, robberies of cattle or any other attacks upon persons or property."[83] After traveling to the frontier, listening to witnesses, examining various archives and newspapers, and thoroughly investigating "depredations committed on both sides of the Rio Grande," the Mexican Comisión Pesquisidora was to file "an impartial report of the facts" within six months. Distinguished and educated members of the Comisión Pesquisidora included Agustín Siliceo, Ignacio Galindo, Antonio de Jesús García Carrillo, and Francisco Valdez Gómez, who was to serve as secretary.[84] Unlike its American counterpart, Comisión members were all familiar with the Rio Grande frontier and the history and politics of the region.

By late September 1872, the commission gathered in Monterrey before proceeding on to the border, where they commenced work in Matamoros on November 14. In the months that followed, the Comisión visited all the towns, villages, and ranches on the Mexican side of the great river all the way from Bagdad to beyond Piedras Negras. Compiling a lengthy and thorough history of problems dating back to 1848, the commissioners scoured public archives, including those of Cameron County, examined newspapers from both sides of the border, interviewed over three hundred witnesses, and compiled 17,688 pages of evidence.[85] Unlike the American commission that discouraged citizens of Mexico from testifying, the Comisión invited individuals from both sides of the river to provide testimony. The Comisión was also more discerning than its American counterpart, even inviting individuals to testify in private and rejecting the testimony of a number of border residents who were people of "bad faith" who the Comisión was certain had given "false testimony." But before the Comisión could complete its work, the Texas press—especially the *Brownsville Sentinel*—was criticizing it for its lack of objectivity.[86]

Exaggerations and Distortions

From the beginning, the Comisión was suspicious of much of the testimony heard by the Robb Commission, especially that relating to the number of cattle that had allegedly been driven into Mexico. For example, the Mexican commissioners questioned how ranchers from north of the Nueces in Refugio, San Patricio, Goliad, Lavaca, and Bee counties claimed they had lost so many cattle. Using Texas newspapers to make their point, the Comisión pointed out that thousands of cattle had perished in the Nueces Strip in the severe drought from 1870 to 1873. Weakened by the drought, entire herds had not been stolen but died in the winter of 1872–73. Thousands of starving cattle had also been shot for their hides during the drought. In fact, outlaw "flayers" who had "no respect for the rights of others" had killed hundreds of weakened cattle. Their "shots can be heard at any hour of the night," the Comisión quoted the *Brownsville Sentinel* as saying.[87] One band of thirty "flayers," led by Alberto Garza, operating out of Nueces and Duval counties, was known to have left three hundred carcasses at one location, skinned two hundred cattle in another spot, and taken seventy-five hides from yet another herd they shot.[88]

In addition, thousands of Texas cattle from the Nueces Strip had not been stolen but driven north to Abilene and Dodge City, Kansas, and other railhead towns in Missouri, Kansas, Nebraska, and Wyoming. Other herds of cattle had been shipped to market from ports on the Texas gulf. Although not denying the theft of cattle in Texas, the Comisión pointed out that many of the cattle rustlers were operating from north of the Rio Grande, such as the notorious Pedro and Longinos Lugo, who were using Las Traquilas, in Cameron County, as their headquarters. Another group of cattle thieves was known to operate from Rancho San Pedro on the Texas bank of the river near La Bolsa.[89]

In a lengthy final report, published in both Spanish and English, the Comisión concluded that claims outlined in the Robb report were "absurd" and an "enormous exaggeration." The "complaints of the Texans are groundless," the Mexican report concluded. Based on a mountain of statistical evidence, there was little doubt the Texans were claiming losses of more livestock than they possessed.[90] Just as the Robb report recommended that more American troops be stationed on the border, the Comisión concluded the way to restore peace on the frontier was for the Mexican military to do likewise. Even then, the commission concluded, regular forces were insufficient. Local *Rurales* who knew the land and its people must be recruited and used as auxiliaries.[91]

As expected, a large part of the Comisión's final report was devoted to Cortina, much of it defensive. Although not excusing Cortina's activities on the river prior to the current controversy, the report praised him for his service to the country. Much of the outcry on the border for Cortina's arrest came from a reactionary element in Texas, led by Mifflin Kenedy, that was determined to prevent him from being pardoned. "Never had any direct charge been brought against General Cortina until the question of his pardon" arose, the Comisión concluded. "No crime was committed on the Texas side in which General Cortina's influence was not seen.... Not a cow was stolen in Texas, but General Cortina's hand was not discovered in it."[92] In fact, for years every crime in South Texas had been linked to his name. The Comisión also concluded that several herds of Texas cattle that Cortina was accused of stealing had been legitimately purchased. This did not excuse those that were stolen by men such as Sabás García, but at the time García stole the cattle he was not in the army under Cortina. The Comisión also uncovered one instance where cattle thieves from Texas had crossed into Mexico to recover the body of one of their gang who had been hanged by Cortina.

The Mexican commissioners were particularly critical of several witnesses who testified before the Robb Commission. Such men had distorted the facts or told "palpable falsehoods." Principal among those perjuring themselves was Adolphus Glavecke, who the commission concluded had been at the head of a band of cattle thieves for over a decade and who had used his ranch for the purpose of stealing horses in Mexico. Thaddeus Rhodes was the instigator of another band of cattle rustlers operating in Hidalgo County and had for many years been a "terror in the vicinity of Reynosa." William D. "Red Tom" Thomas was a "horse thief in Mexico and a cattle thief in Texas," the Comisión concluded. One of the individuals who had incriminated Cortina before the Robb Commission, Cecilio Vela, was himself a criminal fugitive from Mexico. Even the *Brownsville Sentinel*, never known for its objectivity, had praised Cortina for his efforts in suppressing cattle rustling, the Comisión pointed out. Moreover, Cortina had organized a special police force for pursuing criminals. This force of *Rurales* had routed the Lugo brothers and their gang at Rancho Albercas on February 2, 1872.[93] Perhaps the Mexico City *Two Republics* put it best when it wrote in August 1873 that "every raid committed upon Texas has been published and reiterated, with the most exaggerated accounts." Claims for stolen cattle "have been inflated until the principle and damages have been aggregated to over 40 million dollars, yet based on 1870 assessed personal property, including livestock, those living in the border counties only had $2,500,000 in such assets."[94]

In the final analysis, both the Mexican and American commissions were less than objective in their conclusions. Mexicans who sympathized or cooperated with Cortina did not testify before the Robb Commission, nor were individuals in Texas willing to give testimony to the Comisión. Both came to the frontier with a preconceived notion of the reasons for the violence and strife and both amassed evidence to substantiate that view. In 1873, as the volatile situation on the frontier reached a breaking point, Foreign Minister José María Lafragua, a courtly scholar and cultivated gentleman, issued far-reaching orders in Mexico City. Cortina was stripped of command of the army on the line of the Rio Grande. It was a telling blow for the forty-nine-year-old caudillo, and it would prove to be his undoing. The curtain was beginning to fall on the final scene of his turbulent military and political career.

Chapter Nine

Caudillo Vanquished

Leaving the rigid bugler there,
Slow swaying 'neath the tree;
A Warning to all Greasers, who
May that way to be.

TEXAS RANGER BALLAD

ALTHOUGH NO LONGER in command of the military on the Rio Grande, Cortina remained a general in the army, and he set his sights on obtaining political power in Matamoros. He had always been popular in the city, and, in November 1873, he began campaigning for the office of president of the *ayuntamiento,* or alcalde. From the beginning, he faced two formidable opponents: Gen. Pedro Hinojosa, who was a native of Tamaulipas and who had fought with the Liberals and served as secretary of war; and Juan Treviño Canales, who enjoyed the support of Servando Canales, governor of the state. In an intensely bitter campaign, General Hinojosa withdrew, leaving Cortina and Canales to hurl "accusations of fraud" at each other.[1] Although the two had been political allies, they now turned on each other with a viciousness rare even for the border. Disorder and chaos became common as heavily armed supporters of both candidates paraded the streets, and both men accused the other of instigating violence.

On election day, December 14, Cortina managed to squeak out a narrow victory. Only hours after the polls closed, however, rumors circulated that the city officials responsible for certifying the election, who were known to be Canales partisans, were refusing to acknowledge Cortina as the victor. As the moment approached to certify the winner, the areas in front of city hall on Plaza Hidalgo and around the nearby streets were full of hundreds of boisterous and heavily armed partisans. While bands played and loyalists waved flags and banners, many in the city feared a general riot. In fact, the American consul predicted yet another "general revolution" in Tamaulipas.

On the streets, there were also rumors that the American military was preparing to intervene.[2]

When the acting president of the *ayuntamiento* tried to leave city hall without declaring a winner, angry *Cortinistas* forced him to return, whereupon he summoned the city police to rescue him. No sooner had the police arrived than a gun battle erupted; two men were killed and thirteen wounded. When it appeared the skirmishing would escalate, Cortina sent his trusted cavalry, Los Águilas, charging into the plaza armed with Winchester repeating rifles. The Eagles were in the process of forcing their way into city hall when several hundred regular soldiers under Col. José Leonides Cristo arrived with two pieces of artillery. After intense negotiations, the *Cortinistas* agreed to withdraw, but only after Cortina was declared alcalde.[3] It would be weeks, however, before the city returned to normalcy.

In power, Cortina used the spoils system to replace all municipal employees, public officials, and police with his loyal supporters. Cortina, one newspaper commented, was known to be "a man of iron will, and his orders are likely to be obeyed and respected." In time, he opened friendly relations with the city council in Brownsville. Cortina also welcomed Cameron County officials to his office and even feted them to an elaborate champagne dinner. "If they had me over there," Cortina joked, "I don't think they would treat me as politely as I have them."[4] Regardless, he looked to establish bridges. When several prisoners from the Cameron County jail escaped into Mexico, he promised he would hunt them down.

Rather than concede the results of the election, Juan Canales and his supporters appealed to the state legislature controlled by the governor, Servando Canales. In a hastily called special session, the legislature declared the results of the election null and void. Always the fighter, Cortina responded by refusing to acknowledge the authority of the legislature. In turn, Governor Canales appealed to the central government. Cortina was consequently informed he must relinquish either his military commission or his position as head of the *ayuntamiento*.[5] As was his custom, he refused to respond and played for time. Out of patience and hearing an endless litany of complaints coming from the border, Lerdo ordered the military to remove him by force.

In Texas, Americans continued to accuse Cortina of complicity in cattle rustling, saying that, in early March 1874, three hundred head of cattle had been crossed at Las Rucias. Such accusations were not surprising given the related assertion that Cortina kept a lawless, desperate group of recognized criminals around him at all times.[6] Although his motivations for continuing the cattle raids in Texas had evolved somewhat from the time he returned to the border in 1871, Cortina never lost his desire to strike back at his old enemies in Texas—nor, for that matter, to grasp monetary reward. As well, the unabated brutalization of Mexican Texans in South Texas that reached a crescendo in the 1870s only fueled Cortina's motivation. Ultimately, though, the old theme that "character is destiny" was confirmed.

Crimes beyond Compare

On November 28, 1873, at least fourteen Mexican sheepherders were attacked at La Chura in Duval County by a party of vigilantes from Dogtown in McMullen County, and seven of the men were hanged.[7] When the Mexican consul in San Antonio asked Gov. Richard Coke to stop the violence in South Texas, the governor replied that, although he regretted the lawlessness, county sheriffs were responsible for enforcing the law in the area. "I will suggest that your herders and stockmen," Coke tensely wrote, "might avoid these inflictions by remaining with their stock on the west side of the Rio Grande."[8] Ignacio Mariscal, the Mexican minister in Washington, bitterly complained to the State Department that "crimes and outrages of all kinds were committed against Mexicans in the State of Texas," for which the perpetrators were not being punished. Texas was "notoriously" hostile to any Mexican living north of the Rio Grande, Mariscal wrote.[9] When Coke finally agreed to send the Rangers into the Nueces Strip, they proved to be as bad as the vigilantes. A Brownsville newspaper accused them of "hanging and shooting people right and left out in Duval and Nueces counties."[10] They were a "terrible scourge to the Mexican population" and were responsible for committing "all manner of outrages, and even murder," Mariscal complained.[11] When and how, the question was asked, would the violence stop?

Alcalde of Matamoros

While serving as alcalde, Cortina did little to improve his public image on the border. In February 1874, Alexander D. Hamilton, the treasurer of Jersey City, New Jersey, absconded with thousands of dollars in negotiable bonds and fled to Matamoros. When the Americans asked for his extradition, Cortina flatly refused. In response, authorities in the United States appealed to Colonel Cristo; he, too, declined to intervene. The Americans then asked the municipal judge in Matamoros to intercede, but the judge was a Cortina partisan and took no action.[12] Escalating the controversy, Consul Wilson publicly accused Cortina of openly offering several Jersey City bonds for sale and implying they had been given to him as a bribe.[13] Moreover, when the Jersey City police arrived in Matamoros, they traced Hamilton to Cortina's house in the city. Finally, the U.S. Department of State appealed directly to Mexico City whereupon Colonel Cristo was ordered to arrest Hamilton and to cooperate with the American authorities.[14]

When Hamilton fled the border, Brownsville City Marshal Cruse Carson hired an interpreter and a guide and with a Mexican cavalry escort provided by Colonel Cristo, he galloped off in pursuit, hoping to collect a $2,500 reward. Reaching San Fernando, Carson learned that Hamilton had gone on to Ciudad Victoria in an ambulance with a priest. Although his cavalry escort returned to the border, Carson followed Hamilton to Ciudad Victoria and on to Tula and Rio Verde, where he discovered that Hamilton had gone to San Luis Potosí and disappeared into the interior of the country.[15] Despite what he told Brownsville officials, Cortina flatly refused to allow anyone accused of committing a crime north of the border to be extradited to Texas.[16]

In the spring of 1875, conditions in South Texas reached new heights of bloodshed and recrimination. The violence escalated in late January when a patrol of Buffalo Soldiers out of Ringgold Barracks killed several *Cortinistas* at Rancho La Grulla, downriver from Rio Grande City. In retaliation a few weeks later, a squad of black soldiers was ambushed near Rancho Solís, two of the soldiers killed, and the bluecoats chased back to the post.[17] In response, Col. Edward Hatch called out the entire garrison of the 9th Cavalry and rode to the ranch, where he arrested nine suspected *Cortinistas* and took them back to Ringgold Barracks as prisoners. Within days, however, all the men were released on bail. Only one man was ever tried—and he was acquitted. To complicate matters, a Starr County grand jury indicted three of the soldiers for killing one of the Mexicans at La Grulla. Colonel Hatch and the army on the border found themselves in a real predicament. If tried before an "all Mexican" jury, army officials in San Antonio warned Washington, the men were likely to be convicted.[18] Ethnic tensions were inflamed when John L. Haynes wrote the *Brownsville Ranchero* criticizing the army for its heavy-handedness in Starr County. But when Hatch protested, the owner and editor of the newspaper, J. S. Mauser, apologized and admitted that Haynes "had always been on the side of the Mexicans."[19]

Nuecestown

By early March, Colonel Hatch watched as seventy-five to one hundred of Cortina's men went into camp on the north bank of the river at La Grulla, Los Diez, and Rancho Solís. With no evidence the men had committed any crimes in Texas, Hatch was reluctant to make any arrests or to use force to drive the men into Mexico, although he suspected they were preparing to launch yet another revolution in Tamaulipas. At the same time, Hatch realized the *Cortinistas* were aided by many of the Mexican Texans living on the Texas bank of the river.[20] Capt. Charles D. Beyer, who commanded a company of Buffalo Soldiers at Roma, had no doubt that men living on both sides of the river as far upriver as Carrizo were engaged in cattle stealing and "hide peeling."[21]

At a subpost at Edinburg, Capt. Francis Moore of the 9th Cavalry became convinced that the men gathering on the north bank were cattle rustlers "aided and abetted by friends and allies" in Texas, and that they were preparing to launch a large raid into the Nueces Strip.[22] Lucius Avery, commercial agent in Camargo, told Washington there was "great excitement among the Mexicans in the neighborhood," and he warned Colonel Hatch to be on guard. After the bloodshed at La Grulla, Avery said, Cortina had sent several letters and messages to his "retainers and friends along the river," directing them to gather horses and arms and prepare for a "secret expedition."[23] In Brownsville, Adolphus Glavecke heard rumors that 150 men were congregating on the south bank of the river, probably to cross into Texas at Las Cuevas.[24]

Splashing across the river in several small groups, the *Cortinistas* reunited at a predetermined rendezvous point in Hidalgo County, some twenty miles north of the border. With intentions of attacking and plundering Corpus Christi, the raiders rode north across the shifting sands of the Wild Horse Desert. Along the way, internal squabbling and missed communication reduced the number of raiders, and the attack on Corpus Christi was called off. Leaving a trail of murder and robbery in their wake, nevertheless, thirty raiders struck the small hamlet of Nuecestown, thirteen miles northwest of Corpus Christi. Here, 150 miles from the border, the raiders brutally killed, looted, humiliated, and whipped several inhabitants.[25] So terrorized were the citizens of Corpus Christi by the news from Nuecestown that hundreds rushed to the town's municipal pier in hopes of fleeing on any boat available.

In Corpus Christi, two posses were quickly organized that rode west to confront the raiders. In a fierce gun battle, one member of a posse was killed, and a Mexican raider who had been wounded at Nuecestown was captured, taken into Corpus Christi, and lynched by a hysterical mob. With much of their stolen booty, the raiders raced for the border, passing through Piedras Pintas, again dividing into small parties as they forded the Rio Grande. One large band did surround and threaten to plunder Roma before crossing the river and heading for Camargo.

As the news of the Nuecestown Raid spread along the Rio Grande, three of the raiders, riding horses with American brands and carrying stolen loot, were arrested in Camargo. Five more were apprehended by Mexican authorities at a ranch below the town.[26] Cortina requested they be sent to Matamoros, but the Mexican government took them to Monterrey and then to Saltillo, instead. When the excitement and anger in Texas abated, they were released.

The brutality and brazenness of the attack on Nuecestown sent shock waves across South Texas. Every Anglo south of the Nueces River appeared vulnerable. It was 1859 all over again, and Cortina was to blame. Once more the cry went out from Austin and Washington demanding the Mexican government remove Cortina from the border. Governor Coke went as far as to telegraph President Grant, saying the cattle raids were threatening to "depopulate" the entire Lower Rio Grande Valley. People were being "ruthlessly murdered" by "foreign desperadoes," the governor said.[27] Commanding the American army in the west, Gen. William T. Sherman was ordered to take action.[28]

Vigilante Retribution

Never before had the political establishment in South Texas been so aroused. What followed was an uncontrolled state of unsurpassed anger, hatred, and violence in which Mexican Texans, the vast majority having no association with Cortina, were indiscriminately killed and brutalized. With a perverted sense of justice and retribution, "minute companies" of vigilantes roamed the countryside, committing untold acts of violence. In several counties, especially Nueces and Duval, Tejanos were driven off their property, their livestock stolen, and their homes burned to the ground. At Rancho La Atravesada in what is today Kenedy County, Anglo vigilantes killed all the adult males. Untold violence was reported at small ranches owned by Mexican Texans such as El Peñascal, Corral de Piedra, and El Mesquite. J. Frank Dobie, who knew as much about the South Texas Brush Country as anyone, estimated the number of Mexican Texans killed in the months following the raid on Nuecestown exceeded the number of Mexicans who died at San Jacinto.[29] So widespread was the savagery that forty-eight Texas Rangers under Capt. Leander H. McNelly, a tough Civil War veteran who had served in the State Police, had to be sent to the area to establish some semblance of law and order. "The acts committed by Americans," McNelly told Texas Adjutant General William Steele, "are horrible to relate; many ranches have been plundered and burned, and the people murdered or driven away; one of these parties confessed to me in Corpus Christi as having killed eleven men on their last raid."[30] But the Rangers, who had been dispatched to help calm the violence and hysteria, were themselves responsible for numerous executions.

Cortina's raiders had taken twenty-five new saddles from the Thomas Noakes store at Nuecestown, and the Rangers gave orders that any Mexican Texan seen riding a new saddle was to be gunned down or hanged on the spot—no questions asked. In the weeks and months following the raid on Nuecestown, the decaying corpses of Tejanos hanging from mesquite trees became a common site along the roads and trails of the region.[31] The situation darkened, and Governor Coke sent Adjutant General William Steele and State Senator Joseph E. Dwyer to investigate. They not only confirmed the wide-scale assassination of Mexican Texans, but Steele and Dwyer also concluded that many of the Texans responsible for the unspeakable violence did not think it a crime to kill a Mexican. Peace would never come to the Nueces Strip, Steele said, until Cortina was "removed entirely from our frontier."[32]

Steele and Dwyer's quantitative view of Cortina's power reflected his larger influence. In control of no fewer than two thousand "armed adherents," Cortina had become "the recognized head and protector of all of the cattle thieves and murderers from Camargo to the mouth of the Rio Grande." With seventy to eighty men around him at all times, he was a terror, the likes of which the border had never seen. "It is a well known fact," Steele wrote, "that not only Cortina himself, but even his mistress, gives orders to judges, as to their decisions in cases, either civil or criminal, and such orders are obeyed." Moreover, Cortina's police force in Matamoros had come to consist of "ruffians, ready at any moment to commit murder, or any other crime, at his bidding."[33] In their investigation, Steele and Dwyer compiled numerous depositions incriminating Cortina in the cattle raids. Replicating their testimony before the Robb Commission, individuals told of having seen stolen Texas cattle at one or more of Cortina's ranches.[34] Brig. Gen. Edward Otho Cresap Ord, commander of the Department of Texas, agreed with Steele that peace could never be restored to the region as long as Cortina remained on the border. Well into the grim fall of 1875, officials in Washington and in South Texas accelerated their efforts to have the Mexican government remove Cortina.

Diabólicos Rinches

After the vigilantes in Nueces County had disbanded, Adjutant General Steele sent Captain McNelly and his high-stepping Rangers to the Rio Grande. On the border, McNelly hired the able and ruthless Jesús Sandoval as a tracker and guide. Sandoval, who owned Rancho Estero Grande (fifteen miles north of Brownsville), hated the *Cortinistas* with a passion. Even before the Rangers arrived in the Valley, he had gained a reputation for hanging cattle thieves. In response, the *Cortinistas* had tried to assassinate him on more than one occasion. Serving as McNelly's grand inquisitor, the Tómas de Torquemada of the border, Sandoval tortured suspects to obtain information not otherwise available.[35]

In Brownsville, the Rangers learned that a cattle buyer from Havana, Cuba, had arrived on the border to purchase several thousand head of Texas beef. Finding the cattle in Texas too expensive, the buyer contracted with Cortina to deliver three thousand head of cattle at $11 a head to be driven to Bagdad, where a steamer waited to take the livestock to Havana. Captain McNelly's first sergeant, George A. Hall, who was fluent in Spanish and who knew the border well, was sent in disguise to Bagdad, where he watched while Cortina and several of his men drove a herd of cattle onto a lighter for the Havana-bound steamer. Able to board the steamer himself, Hall estimated that two-thirds of the cattle bore Texas brands, many from the ranches of King and Kenedy. There was little doubt the livestock had been stolen in Texas.[36] At about the same time, George W. Miller, head of customs at Clarksville, also managed to get on board the schooner *Inez Huston*, which was being used as a lighter, and watch as Cortina, surrounded by a large armed guard, supervised the loading of several hundred cattle.[37] With McNelly's latest dispatches from Brownsville, Governor Coke telegraphed President Grant that there was little doubt the "Mexican bandit" Cortina was shipping stolen Texas cattle to Cuba.[38]

Perhaps even more important than such confirmation of Cortina's activities, Sergeant Hall learned that Cortina needed an additional 250 cattle to complete the contract, and he had dispatched some of his men across the river to steal more cattle. In Brownsville, McNelly prepared to confront the *Cortinistas* when they returned to the border.[39] On June 12, 1875, on the Palo Alto Prairie north of Brownsville—near where Cortina had ambushed the Rangers six years earlier—Captain McNelly spotted Cortina's men driving 265 head of cattle toward the river. Seeing the Rangers, the *Cortinistas* took refuge in the brush and tall grass on a small island in a salt marsh, only to have the Rangers attack wildly. In a running gun battle that lasted for two hours and over six miles, sixteen of the *Cortinistas* were killed. "They fought bravely," McNelly wrote, "every one firing his pistol . . . even when mortally wounded. . . . I have never seen such desperation." Many of the raiders, "after being shot from their horses and severely wounded three or four times, would rise on their elbows and empty their pistols at us with their dying breath," the Ranger captain continued.[40] The only man to escape was José María Holguín, who, although badly wounded, made his way to Matamoros where he found medical help and recovered.

When Cortina learned of the fight on the Palo Alto Prairie, he sent forty men across the river as reinforcements. The American military responded by calling out a company of soldiers from Fort Brown.[41] The soldiers found the stiff and bloody corpses of Cortina's men and brought them into Brownsville, where McNelly had them stacked like cordwood on Market Square as a ghoulish display of Ranger bravado. Hundreds of people from Matamoros, many sullen and withdrawn and cursing the *diabólicos rinches* under every breath, crossed the river to see the dead *Cortinistas*.

L. B. Smith, a seventeen-year-old Ranger who had enlisted along with his father, was the only one of McNelly's men to be killed in the fight. In a long funeral procession, citizens, soldiers, and McNelly's Rangers followed Smith's remains to the Brownsville Cemetery. As the military fired a salute and two bands played a somber dirge, young Smith was laid to rest not far from where the *Cortinistas* were dumped in an unmarked grave.

Perpetual State of Anarchy

From Fort Brown, Colonel Potter telegraphed General Ord in San Antonio that Cortina was arming his followers and threatening to take revenge and launch yet another "border war."[42] Cortina was furious, it was said, and he would seek revenge and invade Texas with an army of no fewer than two thousand men. With telegraph wires alive with news from the Rio Grande, General Ord asked for reinforcements from New Orleans. In Chicago, General Sheridan had doubts that Cortina would cross the Rio Grande, but he, General Sherman, President Grant, and Secretary of the Navy George M. Robeson all agreed that it would be a good idea not only to reinforce Fort Brown with three companies of cavalry and one company of infantry but also to send gunboats to the river.[43] So, with events from the border at the forefront of affairs in Texas again, the legislature authorized yet another investigation into depredations in South Texas. Led by R. B. Hubbard, president of the Senate, the committee concluded that the Lower Rio Grande Valley was in a perpetual state of insecurity and anarchy and that Cortina was to blame.[44] With congressional hearings continuing in Washington, the Texas press screamed for action, some newspapers even demanding the acquisition of large areas of northern Mexico.[45] The venom emanating from north of the Rio Grande seemed to know no bounds. For example, to the *Austin Daily Democratic Statesman*, Cortina was an "ignorant, soulless, selfish scoundrel," a well as a "murderer, an incendiary and a thief."[46]

In Mexico City, John W. Foster, United States minister to Mexico and dean of the diplomatic corps, called at the foreign office on the *zócalo* to query Lafragua about the possibility of the U.S. Army's crossing the border in hot pursuit of cattle rustlers and bandits. At the same time, Foster asked Lafragua to remove Cortina to some remote corner of the Mexican republic. "His removal," Foster said, "would have a very salutatory effect upon the frontier and be accepted as an act of conciliation and peace toward the United States."[47] Simply put, the United States was not willing to extend full diplomatic recognition until the situation on the border was brought under control. When Lafragua replied that Cortina was alcalde of Matamoros, a civil position not subject to the whims of the central government, Foster countered that he still held a commission as general in the army and received a salary from the federal treasury. In response, Lafragua frankly admitted that any intervention on the part of President Lerdo would be viewed unfavorably in Mexico as the government taking sides in the internal affairs of Tamaulipas, specifically in regard to the "personal trouble" Cortina was having with Gov. Servando Canales.[48]

Arrest and Removal

Finally, on May 1, 1875, President Lerdo telegraphed Cortina to appear in the capital to "give a report on certain affairs on the northern frontier."[49] Realizing the seriousness of the situation, Cortina, as he had done before, refused to respond. A second message was consequently sent, again ordering him to Mexico City. Cortina countered by submitting his resignation, thus removing himself from the authority of the central government. At the same time, a petition that Cortina probably initiated was signed by public officials in Matamoros and sent to Mexico City asking that he be allowed to remain on the border. Although it was obvious that Lerdo was determined to remove Cortina, one American newspaper observed that he did "not intend to go."[50] In a game of cat and mouse, Lerdo responded by refusing the resignation and repeating the original order. When Cortina again failed to respond, Lerdo ordered him arrested. At the same time, Lerdo feared touching off yet another revolution in Tamaulipas, so he kept the arrest order secret until Cortina could be apprehended.

The responsibility for the actual arrest fell on the shoulders of Col. Manuel Parrat, who, after having Cortina "shadowed" for several days, decided to apprehend him at his Rancho La Unión, three miles above Matamoros. Before sunup on the morning of July 1, Colonel Parrat rode out of Matamoros with twenty-five men to make the arrest. Not to unduly alarm Cortina and his followers, Parrat let it be known that he was preparing to confront a band of smugglers. He also alerted the American garrison at Fort Brown, and a signal was agreed upon should Cortina manage to escape. Ironically, Cortina spent the night in Matamoros and had ridden out to his ranch with ten of his men before sunup. Shortly after daybreak, Colonel Parrat and his party were within sight of the ranch when they looked up to see Cortina riding toward them with two of his men. As he rode forward, Parrat drew and cocked his pistol, ordering Cortina to dismount. Told he was a prisoner, Cortina hesitated but then responded, "Your prisoner, sir. I believe I rank any officer here." General, Parrat responded, with the arrest warrant in hand, "do you recognize the signature of the president of the republic?" At the same time, he looked around for any means of escape, but Parrat's men had him surrounded. With little alternative, he stepped down from the saddle, flung his gun to the ground, and surrendered.[51] Cortina was placed in a carriage that sped him to Matamoros in a cloud of dust where he was locked up in the artillery barracks.

Cortina's repeated refusal to comply with orders directing him to Mexico was the reason for his arrest, the army announced in Matamoros.[52] General Ord was convinced, however, that it was the decision to send gunboats to the Rio Grande that caused the Mexican government to issue orders for Cortina's arrest.

When word spread that Cortina had been seized, there was near rioting in Matamoros. Some predicted a bloody clash between the Mexican military and angry *Cortinistas* who threatened to rescue their leader at any cost. Anticipating violence, businessmen closed their doors and sent their families to Brownsville. There is "great excitement in Matamoros" and "trouble is expected," one newspaper reported.[53] General Sherman telegraphed Washington that stores and residences were closed in Matamoros and that "panic reigns."[54] In the ranches and farms along the river outside Matamoros, angry men gathered in small groups and threatened to march on the city. Sixteen of Cortina's most loyal supporters, including police officers and the local judiciary, were arrested, and orders were issued prohibiting any hostile group from assembling. Public places such as the city's plazas were declared off limits while soldiers patrolled the streets, day and night. Artillery was pulled into position at key intersections. More telling were rumors the army would shoot Cortina should any attempt be made to rescue him.[55] So serious was the situation that authorities in Brownsville feared rioting on their side of the river.

Despite Colonel Cristo's stated determination to "hold Cortina at all hazards," many on the river thought it only a matter of time before he would be freed. But on the evening of July 5, a guard of fifty cavalry and twenty customs house guards escorted Cortina to Bagdad. Awaiting them was the gunboat *Juárez*, manned with a guard of thirty-six soldiers and a crew of ten. Hustled aboard, Cortina watched helplessly the next morning as the small boat veered south down the choppy waters of the coast past Tampico and Tuxpan to historic Veracruz. Under a tropical sun and a heavy guard, he was hurried on board a special train of the recently completed Ferrocarril Mexicano that clattered west across the *tierra caliente* past Córdoba and Orizaba, through tunnels and past streams and waterfalls, all the time climbing steadily upward. Leaving the verdant banana and coffee groves for the more arid *tierra templada*, Cortina could look out to the north and see the magnificent snow-clad volcanic cone of Pico de Orizaba, the third highest mountain in North America, but his mood was somber and depressed. The train rattled on through the darkness, past green corn fields and small villages to Apizaco, not far from where he had stood so heroically with Comonfort against the French twelve years earlier. On the morning of July 14, 1875, 260 miles from the coast, the Ferrocarril Mexicano entered the great Valley of Mexico. Skirting the shallow brackish waters of Lake Texcoco, the train rolled past ruined Aztec temples, then by the hill where the Virgin Mary was said to have appeared before the young Indian Juan Diego, and finally to the bustling railroad station on Calle de las Estaciones in the heart of the capital. Here, he was greeted by somber-faced soldiers who waited to escort him to prison.[56]

Hearing that Cortina was being brought to the capital, John Foster rushed to the foreign office to assure José María Lafragua that the "removal of Cortina would have a great influence in diminishing our troubles."[57] Furthermore, Foster wrote, "I expressed to him my gratification at the arrest of Cortina, and stated that I had no doubt of its beneficial influence, especially if his removal was to be permanent."[58] Within days, rumors began to circulate that since Cortina had at one time been an American citizen, the United States would ask for his extradition. In Texas, Governor Coke had no such thoughts; he was euphoric, nevertheless. But no one was more delighted by Cortina's arrest than the political and economic elite in South Texas, especially the large stockmen in the Nueces Strip. General Ord, too, was pleased, but he feared that Cortina would somehow find a way to return to the border."[59] Ord told Washington, he was "a bad & dangerous man with both the power and will to embroil the United States of Mexico and the United States of America in serious difficulties."[60]

Specifically, Cortina was charged with smuggling, charging import and export duties without authority, disobeying orders, and acting as an "agent" of the revolution by stealing horses, ammunition, money, and other resources. He was also accused of the murder of Manuel Treviño, brother of former governor Andrés Treviño, along with one of Trevino's servants named Florentino, near Camargo on May 8, 1875.[61]

Prisión Militar de Santiago Tlatelolco

Located on the northwestern outskirts of Mexico City, the sturdy, two-story Prisión Militar de Santiago Tlatelolco had been constructed in the 16th century as a Franciscan college and monastery. Ironically, within blocks of the stone structure, the Aztecs had made their final stand against the army of Hernán Cortés in 1521. Cortina was given one of the thirty large cells that lined an open, inner courtyard. Compared with other prisons in the capital, Santiago Tlatelolco was comfortable and lightly guarded. Visitors were allowed to come and go, and there were few restrictions.

Regardless of his accommodations, a prison is a prison. Cortina had wielded absolute power on the border for years, so his incarceration came as a psychological blow. Still, he was a tough old warrior, and he had been in difficult situations before. After several weeks, as the government gathered information for his court-martial, Cortina was allowed to leave prison and live in the small village of Azcapotzalco, four miles northwest of the capital. But Lerdo's minister of war, Ignacio Mejía, insisted Cortina not leave the environs of Mexico City. Although free from the confines and the humiliation of Santiago Tlateloco, Cortina was nonetheless under house arrest and complained of the "excessive surveillance from the police."[62]

Plan de Tuxtepec

From Azcapotzalco in March 1875, Cortina watched while Lerdo announced plans for reelection. In reaction, Porfirio Díaz, the liberal general and caudillo from Oaxaca who had led the failed revolt of La Noria against Juárez five years earlier, issued his Plan de Tuxtepec charging Lerdo with violating the sovereignty of the states, reducing the right of suffrage to a farce, and squandering public funds. More importantly, the plan called for no reelection of the president or the governors. Throughout the country, Díaz had the reputation of a ruthless but honest soldier, revered for his important role in the victory over the French at Puebla in 1862.

As Díaz struck out for New Orleans and then Brownsville, Cortina provided him with vital information and letters of introduction and support. Cortina's influence on the border, Díaz realized, would have a lot to do with whether he succeeded or failed. Years later, John S. Ford claimed that, while in Brownsville, Díaz was given a large amount of money by some of the leading stockmen and merchants with the understanding that if he took power in Mexico, he would keep Cortina away from the border. On the Rio Grande, Sabás Cavazos, Cortina's half-brother, was said to have loaned Díaz $50,000 in gold.[63]

After forming a government, Díaz, with fewer than forty men and a few officers, crossed the river above Matamoros. Most of those who joined him were "partisans of General Cortina" and border veterans anxious to strike a blow against Lerdo, Thomas Wilson, the American consul, observed.[64] In fact, it was widely acknowledged on the frontier and in Mexico City that "the friends and followers of Cortina are the leading and active spirits of the revolution in Tamaulipas."[65] But the *Cortinistas,* said to number as many as two thousand men, joined the revolution against Lerdo, not because of the Plan de Tuxtepec but because Cortina said they should.[66] With no artillery, at daylight on April 2, 1876, the ninth anniversary of his assault on Puebla in 1867, Díaz's poorly paid and equipped army of four hundred ragged men attacked Matamoros. Although greatly outnumbered by the *Lerdista* army of Gen. Bernabé de la Barra, who declared the city in a state of siege and who rushed across the river to purchase military supplies, Díaz had the advantage of an effective "fifth column" of *Cortinistas* inside the city. As General De la Barra prepared to defend the Casa Mata and the city's defenses, a number of his officers and Gen. Jesús Toledo went over to the *Porfiristas.* Deceived and outmaneuvered, De la Barra and twenty-five of his officers fled to Brownsville, their men turning on them as they went.[67]

Somehow in Mexico, the political winds always seemed to blow from the northeast. "Gen. Díaz owes his success on this frontier to the Cortina party, and he is under their complete control as he could not hold his position a day without their success," Wilson observed.[68] The insurrection of Tuxtepec now had a beachhead on the Rio Grande. After replacing all the municipal officials in Matamoros, Díaz rode south with his rag-tag army, hoping to carry his revolution to Monterrey, through the mountains to Saltillo, spread it south across the central plateau to San Luis Potosí, and drive Lerdo and his government from the capital. Although governors and thousands of recruits flocked to his banner, the *Porfiristas* were dealt a serious setback in the battle of Icamole at Puerto del Indio, in Nuevo León, on May 20, 1876. Shortly thereafter, a 2,500-man *Lerdista* army under Gen. Mariano Escobedo took Mier, Camargo, and Reynosa and chased the *Cortinista* supporters of Díaz out of Matamoros.[69] Giving up on the north, Díaz returned to his native Oaxaca, where he took command of a *Porfirista* army organized by his brother, Félix.

Pronouncing against Lerdo

On May 18, 1876, ten months after being arrested by the "despotic government of Sebastián Lerdo de Tejada" and torn from his home where he "lived quietly" at the side of his family, Cortina declared his support of the Plan de Tuxtepec.[70] Whether Cortina was ideologically attracted to Díaz or simply wanted to use the revolution as an excuse to flee Mexico City remains unclear. From the capital, Foster warned Secretary of State Hamilton Fish that Cortina would probably return to the Rio Grande and again "become a source of annoyance to the Texas border."[71] He was quickly proven correct. From Azcapotzalco on August 20, 1875, Cortina issued a fiery and lengthy *pronunciamiento* professing his devotion to the Constitution of 1857. Angered by the Lerdo government's continuing to gather evidence against him, he was also indignant that the Mexico City *Sufragio* was referring to him as a "bandit, robber and assassin" while praising Andrés Treviño, a political enemy back in Tamaulipas.

As before, Cortina was assisted in writing the *pronunciamiento,* this time by someone well versed in classical literature and familiar with the Irish Catholic statesman, Daniel O'Connell. In the long and rambling document, Cortina recalled his earlier years on the border, even that fateful day in the summer of 1859 when he shot Marshal Shears and his life changed forever. An angry cry for help and redemption, the text hurled barbed spears at Andrés Treviño, the former governor of Tamaulipas, and his brothers, who headed the "Reform Club" in Matamoros that Cortina claimed was corrupt. Like Nero and Machiavelli, Treviño was a ruthless schemer and contriver who assisted the Americans in trying to kill him in 1859. Faust was once again being seduced by Mephistopheles. As one of the most ruthless individuals in Tamaulipas, Treviño had executed countless citizens while he was governor, even dragging some out of a hospital in Matamoros and shooting them in the streets.

Cortina's choleric *pronunciamiento* was first published in the Mexico City *El Monitor Republicano*, reprinted by the English-language *Mexico City Two Republics*, and then by the Matamoros *Eco de Ambas Fronterias*, a newspaper loyal to Cortina.[72] The editors of the *Eco* were certain Cortina would be cleared of all charges and that he would "come once more to live on this frontier among his many friends."[73] After having the document translated at army headquarters in San Antonio, General Ord found it full of "abuse, recrimination, and egotism" and thought it would do little more than appeal to Cortina's "ignorant and unscrupulous adherents." Nevertheless, Ord sent it to army headquarters in Chicago, where it was then forwarded to Secretary of War William W. Belknap, who sent it on to Secretary of State Hamilton Fish.[74]

Shortly after leaving Mexico City, Cortina joined other *Porfirista* generals under Juan N. Méndez in the Sierra del Puebla, but he was turned back at Ahucatlán on the boundary between Hidalgo and Puebla by a much larger *Lerdista* army.[75] Defeated again at San Luis Potosí two weeks later, Cortina struck out for the Rio Grande. When Cortina first appeared back on the border in July 1876, Wilson told Washington, "he was regarded merely as an outlaw." However, when the river communities fell under his control, it became evident he posed a far greater threat to the stability of the Rio Grande frontier and attitudes in Texas hardened once again. Indeed, by early July 1876, Cortina had set up his headquarters at his Rancho Canelo, upriver from Matamoros. Within weeks, he had assembled an army of seven hundred loyal *Tamaulipecos*, seized Bagdad, and began pushing against Matamoros. In August, Nuevo Laredo, Guerrero, and Mier fell to the *Porfiristas*, and, by early September, four hundred revolutionaries under Gen. Baltazar Fuentes were able to enter Camargo, although the town was recaptured by the *Lerdistas*.[76]

Besieging Matamoros

At first, the *Lerdista* commander in Matamoros, Gen. Ignacio Revueltas, was hesitant to recognize Díaz and the Plan de Tuxtepec. Finally acquiescing, he sent an order directing Cortina to Linares, but Cortina promptly refused the order, instead seizing a large mercantile train bound for Monterrey.[77] Partly in retaliation, General Revueltas began arresting anyone in the city suspected of being a *Cortinista*. In the area between Reynosa and Matamoros, the fighting became intense as Cortina's ranches went up in flames and hundreds of families were left homeless. A number of *Cortinistas* were captured and executed. At the same time, Revueltas slapped a three percent tax on the inventory of all merchants in Matamoros. When several businessmen locked their doors instead of paying the tax, he had them arrested and their merchandise sold at public auction.[78]

Almost daily for three months, Cortina sent small parties of men against Matamoros as his artillery pounded away at the city, often into the night. Expecting an assault at any moment, frightened citizens fled to the safety of Brownsville. Fearing yet more turmoil and bloodshed, Wilson telegraphed Washington, asking that the gunboat *Rio Bravo* and the garrison at Fort Brown be readied to intervene.[79] Supported by the Americans and reversing his hard-line stance toward the merchants of the city, General Revueltas promised that "all persons and property shall enjoy all the guarantees that modern civilization can require from any belligerent."[80] With the American military poised to intervene and gunboats on the Rio Grande ready for action, Cortina hesitated in attacking the city. Yet throughout the hot and humid summer of 1876, he and his men clung to the edges of Matamoros as Díaz took power in Mexico City and Lerdo fled into exile.

In December, from his forward camp at Rancho La Unión, Cortina wrote Díaz, saying he was sending a representative to the capital to brief the president on military operations and explain his inability to occupy Matamoros. The main reason, Cortina said, was the military support the United States was giving the *Lerdistas*. At the same time, he professed great friendship for Díaz and said he was determined to take Matamoros.[81] Although he had arrived on the frontier with fewer than one hundred men, with patience, sacrifice, and considerable effort, he had built a formidable fighting force of over one thousand men. In response, Díaz congratulated Cortina, saying he was sure the war on the Rio Grande could not last long. Unbeknownst to Díaz, though, Cortina had opened relations with José María Iglesias, who, as chief justice of the Supreme Court, was asserting his claim to the presidency.[82] Cortina had gone as far as to meet with Gen. Julián Quiroga and allegedly encourage him to recognize Iglesias. However, Quiroga was captured and executed by the *Porfiristas*. Realizing the political winds were with Díaz, Cortina backed away from Iglesias.[83]

On January 3, 1877, Cortina issued a *pronunciamiento* from Rancho la Union signed by eleven officers of the Cortina Brigade and addressed to Minister of War Luis Mier y Terán. Denouncing Lerdo and refusing to recognize Iglesias, Cortina confirmed his allegiance to the Plan de Tuxtepec, as revised at Palo Blanco.[84] One day later, Cortina wrote Díaz from "Constitution Camp" in front of Matamoros, again professing his loyalty while reminding Díaz that many of those who signed on to the reforms at Palo Blanco were officers in his brigade. Although not wanting more "Mexican blood to run," Cortina and his men were willing to sacrifice themselves for the "holy cause" of the republic.[85]

With a *Porfirista* army under Gen. Miguel Blanco on the march for the border, General Revueltas and the *Lerdistas* began serious negotiations with Cortina, and on January 8, they gave up the city. After turning over command to a subordinate, Revueltas caught a steamer for New Orleans and exile. Six days later, after a long march from Mexico City, General Blanco arrived on the outskirts of Matamoros to take command of the Line of the Bravo. Two days after that, Cortina led his men triumphantly into Matamoros "amid the ringing of the church bells and other demonstrations of general rejoicing." On Plaza Hidalgo, Cortina was received by General Blanco "with all the military honors becoming the occasion."[86] Blanco read a *pronunciamiento* thanking Cortina and his men for their heroism, patriotism, loyalty, sacrifice, and service to the nation.[87] Not to be outdone, Cortina issued a *pronunciamiento* of his own, thanking his men for their bravery and perseverance during the lengthy campaign and their "complete triumph" over the "tyrannical and corrupt government" of Lerdo. At the same time, he bid adieu to his men, saying he would soon be going to the capital to see Díaz "to take care of business." As brave sons of the frontier, he asked his men to "ensure order and public tranquility."[88]

Delaying indefinitely his departure for Mexico City, Cortina moved to place partisans in all municipal offices, the customs house, and in all state and federal offices. He also moved to put loyalists in key positions in all the towns and villages along the river.[89] "The partisans of Cortina again occupy all the civil and many of the military offices on the frontier of the Lower Rio Grande," Consul Wilson confirmed, "and Cortina himself is possessed of as much influence and authority as at anytime within the past ten years." Even so, few on either side of the border at the time realized that, with Díaz's ascendancy to power, it was the beginning of the end for Cortina. In the capital, the Americans accelerated diplomatic pressure on Díaz, just as they had on Lerdo, to banish Cortina from the border. In fact, John W. Foster went in person to see Díaz, saying that Cortina should be removed and a well-known and reliable general appointed to pacify the frontier and stop the raids into Texas. Realizing the president was also being unduly influenced by his opponents in Tamaulipas, Cortina wrote the president on February 20, 1877, saying Díaz should not listen to lies coming from the border. Although he did not mention Servando Canales or Andrés Treviño by name, it was obvious to whom Cortina was referring. As he had done before, the canny caudillo hesitated in reporting to Mexico City. Instead, he told Díaz he would send a subordinate to the capital to explain the situation on the frontier.

In the meantime, General Blanco issued orders for Cortina and his men to evacuate Matamoros. In response, Cortina did not directly disobey the orders but replied that his army could not travel because some of the men were almost naked and badly in the need of clothing. Many were without shoes and some were hungry, he said. Blanco was in the process of trying to assist the *Cortinistas* when Servando Canales arrived in the city with a large army and ordered Blanco to arrest Cortina, complaining, among other things, that Cortina had seized and killed a number of cattle on one of his ranches.[90] Knowing any attempt to arrest Cortina would touch off wide-scale violence, Blanco hesitated.

Confronting Díaz

While continuing to assure the president of his loyalty, Cortina promised he would leave for the capital as soon as possible. At the same time, he again reminded Díaz that it was his influence on the border that led to the success of the Plan de Tuxtepec.[91] Díaz responded by repeating the orders for Cortina to appear in Mexico City. When Cortina continued to hesitate, Díaz ordered him arrested. The newly proclaimed president could not afford to have more than one caudillo struggling for power on the Rio Grande while he worked to consolidate power and bring peace to the country. By creating a tough and ruthless force of *Rurales* (usually unmarried and illiterate men from rural areas), Díaz was determined to destroy the brigands who had helped to bring anarchy and disorder to the republic. Moreover, the United States remained reluctant to offer full diplomatic recognition until Díaz resolved the tempestuous situation on the border and put a stop to the cattle raids.

In Cortina's mind, events seemed to accelerate and spin out of control. Late on the evening of February 24, General Blanco arrested him in Matamoros.[92] At the same time, Governor Canales, who now professed to be a loyal *Porfirista*, was appointed as commander of the Mexican army on the Rio Grande. Embarrassed, General Blanco fled to Brownsville. Although Canales urged him to return to Matamoros, Blanco made his way to Mexico City instead. Held under a heavy guard, Canales sent Cortina before a general court-martial.[93] With his army largely disbanded and Canales in military control of the city, there was little Cortina could do. Because of the long-lasting animosity between the two old warriors, there was also no doubt that he would be found guilty. Cortina was not only certain that his cattle and lands would be confiscated but also that Canales would have him executed.[94] Then, while Cortina was held incommunicado in Matamoros, tragic news arrived from Rancho Palito Blanco. Rafaela Cortéz de Cortina was dead at the age of sixty-three. She had stood by her soldier-husband through some of the most arduous and desperate times in the history of the republic, tolerated more than one mistress, and survived a series of devastating wars on the frontier. Seeing her husband locked away in Matamoros and certain to be executed, though, was perhaps too much for her.[95]

In desperation, many old friends and loyal *Cortinistas* wrote Díaz asking that he intervene to save Cortina. When the military court, as expected, found him guilty, Cortina gave notice of appeal, arguing he neither had been allowed to testify nor had he been formally charged with any crime. He also asked Canales for an *indulto*, or pardon.[96] As expected, the verdict and sentence of the court were upheld. Orders followed that Cortina was to be shot by firing squad on the evening of March 8. Cortina again appealed his sentence, but the district judge in the case recused himself on the same day he received the appeal. Cortina appealed again to Canales, but he received only a deaf ear. Despite an angry outcry in the city for mercy, there was little doubt that Canales intended to carry out the execution. Within days, rumors reached Mexico City and New Orleans that Cortina had indeed been executed.[97]

Hearing that his old adversary was to be shot, John Ford rushed across the river to warn Canales that the citizens of Tamaulipas would see the execution as "personal ill feeling." Executing Cortina would be disgraceful, he argued, and such an act would permanently stain Canales's reputation.[98] With Canales unresponsive to all appeals, Cortina's life was now in the hands of the president. From Brownsville, Cortina's loyal nephew, Práxedis Cavazos, a colonel in the *Porfirista* army, joined Cortina's half-brother, Sabás Cavazos, in telegraphing Díaz asking that Cortina's life be spared. By this time, Díaz had already decided to spare Cortina; on March 6, he telegraphed Canales to send the errant caudillo to Mexico City. In fact, Díaz had dispatched a gunboat to take Cortina to Veracruz.[99] Despite Díaz's intervention, Canales came close to executing Cortina anyway. At first, the governor failed to respond to telegrams from Mexico City, and Díaz was forced to send a second, more direct wire with specific orders for Cortina to be sent to the capital.

Under a heavy cavalry guard commanded by Col. Basilio Garza, Cortina was taken from his cell in the midnight darkness of April 8 and escorted to Bagdad, where he was hustled aboard the *Independencia* that embarked for Veracruz.[100] Aboard was a heavy guard along with Colonel Cavazos, who would accompany Cortina to Mexico City.[101] Although tensions ran high in Matamoros, many were tired of the anarchy that had gripped the city for decades and only too glad to see Cortina go. Yet his loyal supporters cursed and wept. Across the river in Brownsville and throughout South Texas, the news that Cortina had again been ordered to Mexico City was received with considerable enthusiasm.

After churning south into the tropics for four days, the *Independencia* arrived at Veracruz on the morning of April 12, where Cortina was hurried aboard the Ferrocarril Mexicano.[102] It was July 1875 all over again. The train took him through the tropical forests and across the savannas of the *tierra caliente* and high onto the central plateau, as had been the case two years earlier. Arriving in the capital late on the evening of April 13, Cortina was allowed to spend the night in the Hotel del Bazár before being taken under guard through the streets to the old prison of Santiago Tlatelolco.[103]

Darkness at Santiago Tlatelolco

Although confined to prison, Cortina was able, at least for a time, to maintain some political influence on the border and even manipulate the elections in Tamaulipas.[104] He also complained to Díaz that he had never been paid for several military accounts, and he needed the money to pay his debts. But most of all, he wanted to return to the border. Much of his property along the Rio Grande had been seized by Canales, he said, and one ranch was being used as a military barracks.[105] Díaz politely responded that he could not leave the capital, that conditions on the border were still unsettled, and that it would be dangerous for him to travel.[106] The real reason, Cortina thought, was that Díaz wanted diplomatic recognition from the United States. In prison and increasingly desperate, he turned to an old liberal friend and loyal *Porfirista*, Secretary of War Manuel González, whom he hoped would intercede with the president. He also asked González to remind Díaz of the support he had given the Plan de Tuxtepec on the frontier. Moreover, when Díaz's revolution spread to other parts of Mexico, he had supported it with all his energy.

After three months at Santiago Tlatelolco, Cortina did not even know the charges against him. Práxedis Cavazos worked hard to have him exonerated, even publishing a decree in the Mexico City *La Patria* asserting his uncle's integrity and innocence, but there was little he could do.[107] After weeks of legal maneuvering, Cortina was able to get his case before a military tribunal, which decided that, because his alleged crimes had been committed on the border, he should be tried by authorities in Tamaulipas. González went as far as to order an escort to take him back to Matamoros, but, knowing his fate would again be in the hands of Governor Canales, Cortina appealed the decision. On the evening he was to depart for the border, a district judge in the capital overruled the decree, and Cortina remained at Santiago Tlatelolco.[108]

From his prison cell on June 3, 1877, Cortina wrote a letter to the editors of the *El Monitor Republicano*, one of the capital's larger newspapers, complaining of having been "locked up in a dungeon" and not allowed to communicate with anyone. He had been insulted by "cowardly and infamous people" who called him a "bandit and a liar." Such men were acting like "Masons" and spreading lies that if he were released from prison, he would flee the capital. His only hope for justice was a fair and impartial court-martial.[109]

At Santiago Tlatelolco, Cortina was sick a large part of the time and one of his arms became partly paralyzed. He was fearful he would spend the rest of his "sad and final days in this horrible prison," he told Díaz. "I don't want to belong to any government anymore," he despondently continued.[110] Every few weeks from his cell at Santiago Tlatelolco, Cortina wrote Díaz pleading to be released. In October 1877, he reminded the president, yet again, that he had helped to "destroy an evil government," and if Díaz would quit listening to his political enemies back in Tamaulipas, he would be exonerated. With his health continuing to deteriorate, he wanted to go "back to a private life." Díaz responded, saying he recognized Cortina's "important services to the national cause," but his fate was in the hands of a judge.[111] Instead, his guard was doubled, and he was watched day and night as if he were a "big criminal."[112]

In November 1877, Cortina wrote the president that Canales had taken several head of cattle and almost one hundred horses from one of his ranches, and he was continuing to use another ranch as a barracks. On the Texas side of the river, he was unable to collect the rent from Rancho del Carmen.[113] Díaz responded by saying he had ordered Canales to acknowledge the number of livestock he had seized.[114] Two months later, and eight months after being confined at Santiago Tlatelolco, Cortina had still not been formally charged, and he told the president he had been "completely abandoned." Cortina also wrote the minister of war, but he was told only that his case had yet to be assigned to a specific judge. Cortina had contacted the district judge in the capital, but was told the judge knew nothing of the case, much less why Cortina was being held in prison.[115] Hearing that Canales and his political enemies were spreading lies that he was fomenting revolt and trying to escape, Cortina again professed his loyalty to the new government.[116] Growing impatient with Cortina's persistence, Díaz would only say that he had heard no such rumors.[117] Even after President Rutherford B. Hayes formally recognized the Mexican government on April 10, 1878, it appeared as if Díaz was holding Cortina only to please the Americans.[118] On the frontier, Canales continued to consolidate power and seize his land and livestock.

Despite the fact that cattle raids by *Cortinistas* into Texas had virtually ground to a halt with Cortina's imprisonment, Congress remained concerned about the situation on the Rio Grande. In the House of Representatives, German-born, Cuero-resident Gustav Schleicher, who represented South Texas and happened to be chair of the Committee on Foreign Affairs, conducted lengthy hearings, recalling events as far back as 1859 that widely condemned Cortina. Those who came to Washington to appear before Schleicher's committee included Thomas F. Wilson, John L. Haynes, Leander McNelly, and a host of army officers and prominent ranchers. The general consensus was that if Cortina were allowed to return to the border, the cattle raids and violence would resume.[119]

With the continued rancor toward him in Texas, Cortina continued to spark the interest of the eastern press. To many in the United States, he remained larger than life. In January 1878, some eight months after he was imprisoned by Díaz, a reporter for the *New York Herald* made his way to Santiago Tlatelolco to interview the old warrior. "So you want to shake hands with old Cortina!" the officer in charge of the prison asked, saying he could grant an interview only by special permission. After he was told the people in the United States, especially those living in Texas, were anxious to hear from "their old friend Cortina," the officer finally relented. Escorted down a long and dimly lit corridor guarded by motionless soldiers with fixed bayonets, the correspondent found Cortina "in a large apartment" standing near a barren window surrounded by old friends. "The general received me cordially [and] felt flattered at being an object of the *Herald*'s attention," the reporter wrote. His subsequent description spoke volumes:

> He did not look at all ferocious. Dressed in neat broadcloth and with a new black slouched hat on his head, he looked like a lately prosperous merchant now under a cloud. He appeared to suffer from his confinement, although his room was large, airy and furnished with more comforts than one expects to see in a prison. A man of medium height and slender build, he appears to the casual observer like a responsible old gentleman. Catching, now and then, a glance from those small, sharp, snappy, restless eyes, one is apt to feel less comfortable in his presence. His curved upper lip, too, though covered with a closely cut mustache and overshadowed by a long, flat, nose is indicative of anything but mildness and fair dealing. His dark face is set off by a lengthy beard, in which the gray predominates over the black.[120]

The years were indeed telling: the reporter judged that Cortina was sixty years old although he was only fifty-four.

Before departing, the reporter thanked the old general "for the pleasure of seeing a man who had been, no doubt, so badly slandered." "Yes, slander is the word," Cortina snapped, a sparkle in his eyes. He was accused of all sorts of crimes and "bad men had, under his name, committed crimes which were laid at his door." It was absurd, he argued, to bring up what happened so long ago. He was comfortable in prison, he said, but wanted to "walk about the streets." Although he expected to be free in two or three weeks, he was not interested in returning to Texas, where a $10,000 reward hung over his head. Defiantly snapping his fingers, Cortina said he was not worried about his many enemies in Texas. They had always lied about him, and, besides, he still had a few friends there.[121]

Only hours after questioning Cortina, the *Herald* correspondent was granted an interview with President Díaz. He asked about Cortina, saying that the "quite interesting old gentleman" wanted to be free. With a smile, Díaz replied, "It is just possible—indeed. It is very probably that Mr. Cortina may be too sanguine in his hopes of liberty. Of course I cannot tell how near or how far that hoped for event may be. The machinery of justice is very slow, and I think it is better for all concerned that he should remain where he is. He may seem a mild, interesting old gentleman when you contemplate him in his present quarters, but I fear his old nature would return if he were permitted to go back to his former haunts on the frontier."[122] In Texas, the press agreed, continuing in its principle to inflame public opinion against Cortina. The *Galveston News*, for instance, editorialized that Cortina in prison was "like an old rat caught in a trap." No matter where he was, Cortina was a "very dangerous man" who should be "watched closely for like an unloaded gun, there is no telling when he is going to go off and hurt someone."[123]

Far from Matamoros

In Tamaulipas, Canales, too, remained concerned the courts would release Cortina and he would return to the border. In time, President Díaz agreed that Cortina could leave prison but not Mexico City. Unable to leave the area, Cortina went back to the elegant *colonia* of Azcapotzalco in the northwestern outskirts of the capital and the village's baroque colonial structures and churches—the same place where he had lived when President Lerdo de Tejada first released him from prison in July 1875. Although closely watched by the police, he moved into a new house at 21 Real de Comonfort, built at government expense, in a neighborhood of some of the republic's wealthiest citizens, far from the shacks, tenements, and unpaved, sewerless streets of Mexico City.[124] Never one to waste a moment of life, Cortina married María de Jesús López, who was several decades younger and who, family lore holds, was a plain servant girl hired to wash Cortina's clothes and help clean his cell at Santiago Tlatelolco.

Frantic to return to Matamoros, Cortina solicited letters from some of his old Liberal friends. José Justo Álvarez attested to his gallantry at San Luis Potosí in 1860. Miguel Negrete said he had served honorably against the French and remembered how Cortina had remitted large amounts of gold to the struggling republic from Matamoros in 1864. Cortina has always carried out orders with "valor and patriotism," Negrete continued. Sostenes Rocha confirmed that Cortina had fought bravely during the final days of the Empire, as well as at Lo de Ovejo in 1870.[125] Yet President Díaz remained steely and uncompromising.

Although plagued by rheumatism, Cortina took daily walks to the cypress-shaded *plaza principal*. There, the gray-bearded old general, only a shell of his former self, often sat for hours beneath the weathered limestone and elegantly carved facade of the seventeenth-century church of the Dominican monastery of St. James and St. Philip. A short walk away from the main plaza, past colorful flower gardens, was the Parque de Ahuehuetes, where horse races and family picnics were common. From the main plaza, a street

An aging and gray-bearded Cortina poses with his third wife, María de Jesús López, at their home on Calle de Comonfort in Azcapotzalco, outside Mexico City, only a few years before his death in 1894. *Benson Latin American Collection, University of Texas at Austin.*

railway carried passengers past orchards and maguey fields to the bustling *zócalo* in Mexico City. The great plaza was the heart of the city and the soul of a nation. Here were history and power, an intersection where ragged Indians and poor mestizos rubbed shoulders with international diplomats and wealthy Mexicans from all over the republic. Looming over the plaza from the north were the impressive basalt and gray sandstone buttresses and twin towers of the National Cathedral, the largest in the republic.[126] The setting, in short, was lovely.

Despite the natural beauty of the great central Valley of Mexico, Cortina yearned to return home to the steeples and towers of Matamoros and the sun-baked grim savannas and mesquite thickets of Tamaulipas. Finally, in the spring of 1891, after more than a decade of imprisonment and house arrest, Díaz granted permission for a short visit to Matamoros. Escorted by his young wife, the rheumatic and silver-bearded Cortina gleefully caught the train for the border. Arriving in Matamoros, an aging Práxedis Cavazos was said to have arranged an elaborate banquet for the old general. Among cheering and toasting, Cortina asked about his old enemies in Texas, many of whom were dead. Adolphus Glavecke crossed the river to attend the banquet, and it was said the two old men talked, broke bread, and forgave.[127] At the same time, the State Department and public officials in Texas kept the pressure on Díaz to keep Cortina away from the border. "This old rascal, gray and aged in crime," the *New York Times* announced, "is a born bandit and murderer." No "red-handed Apache or any other savage or Indian has ever caused to our countrymen one-tenth of the sorrow and misery that this villain has."[128]

Back at Azcapotzalco, Cortina devoted considerable effort to obtaining documentation from the department of war and marine to substantiate his long service to the republic. The aging and infirm old soldier was at his home in October 1891, when another gray-haired old warrior arrived on the streetcar from the capital. Angered by what he perceived as falsehoods in Hubert Howe Bancroft's recently published *History of the North Mexican States and Texas,* John Ford had traveled south by train through the night to see Cortina. Bancroft had somehow confused the Cortina War with Cortina's activities during the Civil War. In particular, Bancroft concluded that Cortina had burned Roma in 1859 and captured Brownsville in 1864. He had also concluded that Ford had driven cattle into Mexico to help feed the French army and had joined the Imperialists against Cortina.[129] Ford, ever a stickler for detail and adamant in his version of history, was hoping Cortina would help set the record straight. Although the two old veterans had been on the opposing sides of history for much of their stormy lives, Ford insisted they had "been personal friends for years." Indeed, after pleasantries and stories of tumultuous times on the Rio Grande, Cortina gave Ford a letter saying

Cortina posed in his military uniform either in Matamoros or Mexico City shortly before his death in 1894. *Author's collection.*

that Bancroft's account of the burning of Roma was "without foundation." He had not seized Brownsville in 1864, nor had Ford joined the French. "Mr. Bancroft must have been imposed upon by some man who was in the habit of stating falsehoods," Cortina wrote. He "could have learned this had he applied to me for the facts."[130] Back in Texas, Ford fondly remembered Cortina's "courtesy and hospitality." His young wife María, Ford said, was "good looking," although the only known photograph of her defies this observation.[131]

Hearing that a prolonged drought had devastated large parts of Tamaulipas and his cattle and horses were dying by the hundreds, Cortina pleaded with Díaz in August 1892 to allow him to return to Matamoros for three months to employ some vaqueros to round up his horses and drive them to the capital to be sold.[132] Polite as usual, Díaz responded that it would not be "prudent" for Cortina to leave Mexico City.[133] Cortina desperately yearned to return to Matamoros, but Díaz was relentless in refusing his request. Nonetheless, in 1892 and again in 1893, it was widely reported in Texas that Cortina had not only returned to the border but had also instigated a revolution and had been captured and imprisoned at the old colonial fortress of San Juan de Ulloa in Veracruz harbor.[134] American reporters rushed to Matamoros for details, only to learn that such stories were only rumors. "Those who best know him say that the general has too much sense, and at the same time is too old to join or sanction any revolutionary movement at this time of his life," the *Corpus Christi Weekly Caller* concluded.[135]

In the twilight of his life, Cortina was said to have remarked that at last he had made peace with the "Texas people" and that he wanted to leave the world without enemies. At 5:40 in the evening of October 30, 1894, the old general died painlessly at his residence in Azcapotzalco of pneumonia and heart failure. It was said his mind was clear to the end. Given the many adventures composing his life and times, his death was almost anticlimactic. The high-riding border caudillo, or *el jefe de fronterizo* as the Mexico City press labeled him, was seventy years old.[136] He had served forty-five years, three months, and twenty-four days in the Mexican military, rising from a common soldier in the lowly Matamoros militia to a powerful general in the army of Benito Juárez and military governor of Tamaulipas.[137] At 9:00 on the morning of November 1, after mourners assembled at his home on Calle de Comonfort, Cortina's body was carried with full military honors in an impressive funeral cortege four miles through the village of Tacuba to the hill and green trees of the Panteón de Dolores, near the fortress of Chapultepec where he was laid to rest. There were no eulogies, anywhere, north or south of the Rio Grande.

Response to Cortina's death varied from dismissive to sublime. Although more than once he had brought the United States and Mexico to the brink

Far from his native Tamaulipas, Cortina died peacefully at his home in Azcapotzalco on October 30, 1894, and was buried with little notice in the Panteón de Dolores. *Photo by author.*

of war, only a few newspapers bothered to note his passing.[138] The *Brownsville Daily Herald* dismissed him in six lines. A few elderly citizens did recall some thirty-four years earlier how the "outlaw leader" had captured the city and became a "menace to civilization."[139] One Mexico City obituary mentioned only that he was a "native of Matamoros ... advanced in age" and that he had always possessed a "bellicose attitude towards the inhabitants beyond the Rio Grande."[140] In San Antonio, an aging John S. Ford consented to write his recollections of Cortina for a local newspaper.[141] Whatever the written response, on All Souls and Saints Day, November 2, hundreds of Mexico residents made their way to the hillside at Chapultepec, to the graves of their loved ones to lay wreaths and light candles and enjoy a meal of *pan de muerto*, dead man's bread. A few were certain to have noticed a freshly covered grave and the final resting place of the old warrior, Juan Nepomuceno Cortina. It was all part of the cycle of life and death in a very turbulent time in a very violent land. But nature itself seemed to have the last comment: three days after Cortina's death, one of the most violent earthquakes in Mexican history shook the capital.

Conclusion

He was a man, take him all in all,
I shall not look upon his like again.

WILLIAM SHAKESPEARE, *HAMLET*

EVERY SUNDAY, FOR YEARS, María de Jesús López would make her way to the Panteón de Dolores to place fresh flowers on the grave of her husband. But in the decades that followed, many of the realities and events that had shaped and molded Cortina's incredible life were already fading to memory. Despite his grave being only a stone's throw from the immaculate Rotonda de los Hombres Ilustres (where some of the great men of the republic rest), weeds would eventually grow around his burial site and someone would vandalize his tombstone. In Mexico, he would largely be forgotten. But far from the bustling capital, in the small cantinas and across the mesquite-infested ranchos on the Texas-Mexico border, lively *corridos* recalling his daring deeds could be heard for decades:

> The famed General Cortina is quite sovereign and free,
>   the honor due him is greater, for he saved a Mexican's life.
> Long live General Cortina, who had come out of his prison:
>   he came to visit his friends that he had left in Tamaulipas.
> The Americans made merry, they got drunk in the saloons,
>   out of joy over the death of the famed General Cortina.[1]

On the ragged edge of a Rio Grande frontier rife with rebellion, where boundaries were often shifting and insecure, the entire history of the Texas-Mexico border could have been radically different had not the political undercurrents that accompanied American expansionism and the sweep of empire been so ubiquitous and the Brownsville legal establishment so conniving and perfidious. In the years after 1848, Cortina seemed content with dual national allegiances. At the time, the border was only a line on a map where people were free to come and go and national identities were not particularly pertinent. Although always a Mexican at heart, Cortina could just have easily become part of a new legal and political system and even accepted the idea of the Rio Grande as the international boundary, perhaps even prospering in the expanding American market economy, as did his half-brother, Sabás Cavazos, and other Tejanos such as Santos Benavides at Laredo. Although psychologically scarred by the Mexican War and the Treaty of Guadalupe Hidalgo, open confrontation and a fervent challenge to American sovereignty were not necessarily inevitable. But in a region with a long history of revolution, where institutional controls were lax, he was torn between two nations and two national visions.[2]

Caught in the vortex of American expansionism and nation building, Cortina became an audacious revolutionary. Angered by the land grant litigation of corrupt Brownsville attorneys and judges, he grew to despise the American legal system, and in the process he became politically marginalized and then branded a criminal. Had Cortina remained subservient to the deep-rooted corruption and racism in South Texas, there would not have been a Cortina War, and the events that followed might have been far less violent.

Friend or foe, on the border Cortina's legacy would endure. He survived some of the most tumultuous and difficult times in the history of Texas and Mexico. He fought the Texas Rangers and blatantly defied authorities in Texas for two decades. He battled the U.S. Army, harassed the Confederate Army, ambushed foreign and Mexican Imperialists, attacked Juárez's beleaguered Liberals, hanged countless unnamed bandits, and fought anyone else who dared get in his way. Caught in the chronic instability of nineteenth-century Mexico, he defied one president, revolted against a second, and fell victim to the political power and intrigues of a third. He claimed to be a Mexican patriot, yet deserted his nation during its greatest crisis. He fought the U.S. Army at La Ebonal and at Rio Grande City, but formed an alliance with the Union Army only three years later. Although practically illiterate and lacking the ideological sophistication of many of his contemporaries, he rose to political and military heights of which the more literate could only dream.

The portrait of Cortina that finally did emerge was shaped by his adversaries in Texas who possessed the pen and access to the press but little objectivity. To many he was little more than a cold-blooded killer. Yet well into the twentieth century the scattered scraps of his amazing life remained shrouded under a cloud of misconceptions, half-truths, and deeply embedded prejudices. Consequently, traditional histories of the borderlands are replete with a one-dimensional Cortina, a ruthless desperado who raided Brownsville in

Conclusion

1859 and instigated a bloody border war. Such histories not only paint him as just another ignorant, sombrero-crowned border bandit, but also ignore his pivotal place in the dangerous and often deadly world of nineteenth-century Mexican politics and military history.

In reality, Cortina was a man of immense nuances, contradictions, paradoxical views, and incredible survival instincts. An enigma in many ways, his labyrinthine historical record is fraught with examples of his fearless and enterprising spirit, yet he was often excessively violent, erratic, pompous, callous, and plagued by an ego that knew no bounds. Although seen by many as ruthless and cruel, he was also known to treat friends and enemies with respect and compassion.

Undeniably a "social bandit" in his early struggle for equality and justice in Texas, he emerged in Mexico as a respected and courageous defender of the republic. Always coveting power and glory, he became a rugged, fearless, and, at times, ruthless frontier caudillo, an authoritarian warlord with shifting and complex allegiances. Caught in the endemic sectional disputes typical of northeastern Mexico, he rose above local partisan politics to become military governor of Tamaulipas and a general in the army of the floundering liberal republic. Had he not briefly gone over to the Empire, his star might have risen even higher.

Sadly, north of the Rio Grande at the same time, the wounds opened by American expansion and hegemony, which Cortina had vigorously opposed, prevailed well into the next century. Yet in one sense, Cortina's life helps to exemplify the transnationalism of a region of the United States that did not give up the peso as the medium of exchange until the latter part of the nineteenth century. In fact, his actions helped shape the history of Texas and Mexico for decades.

Facing innumerable dilemmas and caught in the raging tide of history, Cortina struggled for much of his life, as he said in 1875, to defend the Mexican name in Texas. Always marching to a different drummer and believing himself indomitable, his life remains not only an integral part of the rich and vivid history of the borderlands but also a powerful symbol in the long and difficult struggle for equality and justice.

More than one hundred years after his death, Cortina's greatest influence may indeed be on the history of Texas rather than that of his native Mexico. Decades before Mexican American civil rights leaders such as José Tomás Canales struggled to end Texas Ranger and vigilante oppression of Mexican Texans in South Texas and Nicasio Idar established La Gran Liga Mexicanista to protest lynching and discrimination, or Héctor P. García launched the American G.I. Forum, there was Juan Nepomuceno Cortina. Yet Cortina was different from Canales, Idar, or García. Whereas these leaders tried to engender change by working within the existing social and political system,

Cortina resorted to armed defiance and rebellion at the end of a pistol. Like Nathaniel Bacon, Robert Jenkins, Thomas Dorr, and Daniel Shays, Cortina became one of the few individuals in the history of the Western world to have a war named after him.

Today his life and struggle remains enshrined in Mexican American popular culture as symbolic of resistance to oppression and intolerance. Through all the sound and fury that was the violent history of Texas and Mexico, this remarkable man established his niche in the grand sweep of time.

Notes

INTRODUCTION

1. Dobie, *A Vaquero of the Brush Country*, 50. In Live Oak County, Dobie's uncle, Sterling Neblett Dobie, had once lost a herd of cattle to the *Cortinistas*.
2. Ibid., xii, 50.
3. Webb, *The Texas Rangers: A Century of Frontier Defense*, 176.
4. Ibid., 176–77.
5. Woodman, *Cortina: The Rogue of the Rio Grande*, 2, 8.
6. Ibid., 9.
7. C. Goldfinch, *Juan N. Cortina, 1824–1892: A Re-Appraisal*, 10–11, 15.
8. Ibid., 44.
9. Rippy, "Border Troubles along the Rio Grande, 1848–1860," 93.
10. C. Goldfinch, *Cortina, A Re-Appraisal*, 59.
11. Ibid., 67. Also, McWilliams, *North from Mexico: The Spanish Speaking People of the Untied States*, 106–108, 126.
12. C. Goldfinch, *Cortina, A Re-Appraisal*, 67.
13. Castillo and Camarillo, *Furia y Muerte: Los Bandidos Chicanos*, 85–112.
14. Hobsbawm, *Primitive Rebels: Studies in Archaic Forms of Social Movements in the 19th and 20th Centuries*, 13–27.
15. De León, *They Called Them Greasers: Anglo Attitudes Toward Mexicans in Texas, 1821–1900*, 53–55, 83–85; Montejano, *Anglos and Mexicans in the Making of Texas, 1836–1986*.
16. Rosebaum, *Mexicano Resistance in the Southwest: The Sacred Right of Self-Preservation*, 42.
17. Carlos Larralde, "Beyond Banditry: The Cortinista Movement of 1848–1876," 4, 11, unpublished article courtesy of the author. Also, Larralde and Jacobo, *Juan N. Cortina and the Struggle for Justice in Texas*. Unfortunately, the image used for the cover of this book and in Jerry Thompson's *Juan Cortina and the Texas-Mexico Frontier, 1859–1877*, 70, and in the first edition of the *New Handbook of Texas History*, 2:344, is not Cortina. See also Larralde: *Mexican American Movements and Leaders*.
18. Webster, "Texan Manifest Destiny and the Mexican Border Conflict, 1865–1880."
19. Douglas, "Juan Cortina: El Caudillo de la Frontera."
20. Ibid., 130.
21. Ibid., 131.
22. Ibid.
23. Callahan, "Mexican Border Troubles: Social War, Settler Colonialism, and the Production of Frontier Discourses, 1848–1880," 167–68. Like other previous scholars, however, Callahan fails to utilize a host of Mexican documents available on the subject.

24. Johnson, *Revolution in Texas: How a Forgotten Rebellion and Its Bloody Suppression Turned Mexicans into Americans*, 23.

25. Ibid.

26. Young, *Catarino Garza's Revolution on the Texas-Mexico Border*, 8, 19.

27. A portion of Cortina's November 23, 1859, *pronunciamiento* has even been reproduced in a popular textbook on the history of the United States. See D. Goldfinch et al., *The American Journey: A History of the United States*, 391.

28. McMurtry, *Lonesome Dove*, 111. Also, Larry McMurtry to Mr. Freling, April 15, 1989, in "Archie P. McDonald: Personal Reflections," *Re Arts & Letters* 17 (Spring 1991), 41–46.

29. McMurtry, *Lonesome Dove*, 118.

30. Michener, *Texas*, 561–62.

CHAPTER ONE

1. Juan N. Cortina to the Public, September 8, 1875, "Texas Frontier Troubles," 44th Cong., 1st sess., 117–18. This collection of records will hereafter be referred to as *TFT.* Three cases are listed in the records of the Cameron County District Court prior to Cortina's September 1859 raid on Brownsville. See Cause no. 156, *State of Texas vs. Nepomeceno* [sic] *Cortina and José Cisneros;* Cause no. 478, *A. J. Mason vs. Napomuceno Cortines* [sic]; and Cause no. 670, *Robert Shears vs. Juan N. Cortina*, which resulted from the shooting of the marshal. Minutebook B, 12th Judicial District, District Clerk's Office, Brownsville, Texas, 232, 255, 265, 277, 416. For Cortina's pinto horse, see J. T. Hunter, "Captain J. T. Hunter Tells of the Cortina War," 5. At the time he wrote his article on Cortina in 1911, Hunter claims that he was the last survivor of Tobin's company of Texas Rangers.

2. *Matamoros Daily Ranchero*, September 24, 1870. Early family records use the name Cortinas. By 1859, the name Cortina, especially in the English-language press, had become common and has become standard for most scholarship. Cortina, too, came to use "Cortina" instead of "Cortinas." He is certain to have been named after the fourteenth-century Czech priest, Juan Nepomuceno, who became vicar-general of Prague and confessor of the queen of Bohemia, beatified by Pope Innocent XII in 1721, and whose feast day is May 16.

3. Ibid. Much of the Goseascochea and Cortina genealogy can be seen at: http://www.somosprimos.com/inclan/goseascochea.htm. By 1838, his mother, Estéfana, had indeed moved the family to Matamoros. Matamoros Census (1838), Archivo Municipal de Matamoros (AMM). Estéfana is listed as thirty-eight, his brother, José María, as fourteen, and Nepomuceno as twelve. His sister, María del Carmen, is not enumerated. Courtesy of Armando Alonzo.

4. Ford, *Rip Ford's Texas*, ed. Oates, 262; *San Antonio Express*, November 3, 1894.

5. Ford, *Rip Ford's Texas*, 262.

6. *New York Daily Herald*, July 29, 1865; *Houston Tri-Weekly Telegraph*, July 21, 1865; *New Orleans Daily Crescent*, May 18, 1866. The story appears to have originated with the *Matamoros Daily Ranchero*.

7. Jeremiah Galván Affidavit, Samuel P. Heintzelman Papers, Library of Congress (LC), Washington, D.C.

8. Ford, *Rip Ford's Texas*, 261.

9. Ibid.

10. Stephen Powers to D. R. Porter and Duff Green, February 2, 1860, enclosed with Duff Green to Lewis Cass, February 4, 1860, General Records of the Department of State, Dispatches from Special Agents, Record Group (RG) 59, National Archives (NA), Washington, D.C.

11. Stephen Powers to [Richard] Taylor and [Ángel] Navarro, January 14, 1860, Sam Houston Papers, Texas State Archives (TSA).

12. Ibid.

13. Ibid.

14. Kearney and Knopp, *The Historical Cycles of Matamoros and Brownsville*, 108. Largely based on what Ford wrote of Cortina, a number of writers and historians falsely concluded that Cortina had red hair and a red beard.

15. Ford, *Rip Ford's Texas*, 261. Trinidad Cortina's first wife was María Concepción Treviño. Estéfana Goseascochea, born in Camargo in 1797, had previously married Vicente Cavazos in 1815. Camargo Baptismal Records, 1764–1879 (Corpus Christi: Spanish American Genealogical Association, 1989); *Camargo Marriage Records, 1764–1879* (Corpus Christi: Spanish American Genealogical Association, 1989); Bello, ed., "The Descendants of Feliciana Goseascochea and Juan José Tijerina as Declared by María Hilaria Guerra de Cavazos," 1–4; Ruth T. Bello to Author, May 14, 20; September 15, 1991. Various records list Cortina's mother as Gozcascochea, Gaeceascoechea, Goceascochea, and Goseascaechea.

16. Camargo Baptism Records, May 7, 1809 (José Eusebio de Jesús Cortinas) and December 26, 1811 (José Esteban Cortinas).

17. C. García, *Captain Blas María de la Garza Falcón: Colonizer of South Texas*, 34; Don Hingo, "Texas" First Aristocracy: Robber or Robin Hood," *Houston Genealogical Journal* 17, no. 2 (1989): 62–65.

18. Cruz, *Let There Be Towns: Spanish Municipal Origins in the American Southwest, 1610–1810*, 87–88.

19. Lea, *King Ranch*, 1:159, 441.

20. C. Goldfinch, *Cortina, A Re-Appraisal*, 33. José de Goseascochea was the son of José Manuel Goseascochea and Catarina Malas de Echevarría. Cortina's grandmother, Francisca Xaviera de la Garza, died in Camargo on August 20, 1833.

21. *New York Times*, May 11, 1890.

22. Vigness, "Indian Raids on the Lower Rio Grande, 1836–1837," 19–21.

23. *El Mercurio* (Matamoros), October 20, 1837.

24. Stanley C. Green, "Popular Religion on the Texas-Tamaulipas Border: Revilla/Guerrero, 1750–1861," *Catholic Southwest: A Journal of History and Culture* 15 (2004): 77.

25. Gatschet, "The Karankawa Indians," in *Papers, Peabody Museum of American Archaeology and Ethnology*, 1:50–51; *Reports of the Committee of Investigation Sent in 1873 by the Mexican Government to the Frontier of Texas*, 407. Six years earlier on May 10, 1852, a raiding party of forty Karankawas and Tampacuas robbed and killed five men near Lake Campacuas in Hidalgo County. This "brutal outrage" was said to have generated considerable excitement in the area. *Brownsville American Flag*, May 18, 1852; Testimony of Thaddeus M. Rhodes and Antonio Tijerina, *Richard King vs. United Mexican States, Before the General Claims Commission, United States and Mexico*, 99–100, 112–13; Salinas, *Indians of the Rio Grande Delta: Their Role in the History of Southern Texas and Northeastern Mexico*, 63, 94.

26. Juan N. Cortina to the Public, September 8, 1875, *TFT*, 117–18.

27. Nance, *After San Jacinto: The Texas Mexican Frontier, 1836–1841*, 148–49.

28. Haynes, *Soldiers of Misfortune: The Somervell and Mier Expeditions*, 98.

29. Cortina, Compiled Military Service Record, Archivo de Secretaría de Defensa, Mexico City.

30. Baptismal Records, Immaculate Concepción Cathedral, March 20, 1855, 1:179. Courtesy of Ruth T. Bello.

31. Marriage Register, Dolores Tijerina and Juan Nepomuceno Cortina, July 1, 1845, Matamoros Parish Archives. Courtesy of Ruth T. Bello and Cathleen Shoemaker. Also, Shoemaker to Thompson, March 9, 1992.

32. Dolores "Grande" was said to have died "nine or ten years before her mother." Since Feliciana Goseascochea died at the age of fifty-seven on November 11, 1855, this would place Dolores's death a short time after her marriage to Cortina. "Plats, Affidavits, etc.," Cameron County Clerk's Office, 235. Copy courtesy of Cathleen Shoemaker. Rafaela Cortéz was born on April 13, 1813, in Camargo. Shoemaker to Thompson, March 9, 1992. Two daughters with the name Dolores were born to María Feliciana Goseascochea and Juan Tijerina and are identified as "Grande" and "Chica." Cortina was married to the older Dolores, or "Grande." For resolving the confusion between the two Doloreses, see Ruth T. Bello, "The Descendants of Feliciana Goceascochea and Juan José Tijerina: The Problem of the Two Sisters Named Dolores," *Los Tejanos: Journal of Hispanic Genealogy and History* (1991). Also, Seventh Census (1850), Cameron County, Texas,

NA; Jesús Ramírez Zamora and Ventura Ramírez, Affidavit, July 11, 1907, Frank Cushman Pierce Collection, Brownsville Historical Association, Brownsville, Texas.

33. Baptism Register, March 13, 1846, Matamoros. Courtesy of Cathleen Shoemaker.

34. Marriage Register, Juan N. Cortina and Rafaela Cortéz, January 20, 1850, Immaculate Concepción Cathedral, 1:4, Catholic Archives of Texas, Austin. Earlier the same day, Juan had been a witness himself at the marriage of a friend, Carlos Esparza, who wed Francisca García.

35. Seventh Census (1850), Cameron County, Texas, NA. If the census is correct, Felícitas was born sometime in 1844, one year before Cortina's marriage to María Dolores Tijerina. Cortina is listed on the 1850 census as thirty-five; in reality he was twenty-six. Based on a baptismal in Camargo dated April 1, 1813, Rafaela would have been thirty-seven at the time. The 1870 Cameron County census lists her as fifty, which would indicate she was thirty at the time. Rafaela died at Rancho Palito Blanco in Tamaulipas in March 1877 (see chapter 9, p. 236), Mexico City, *El Siglo Diez y Nueve*, March 31, 1877. Faustina is listed on the 1870 census as twenty-one. Ninth Census (1870), Cameron County, Texas. On early maps, Rancho del Carmen is frequently referred to as "Rancho de Doña Estéfana."

36. A. Werbiskie Affidavit, January 10, 1860, "Difficulties on [the] Southwestern Frontier," 36th Cong., 1st sess. (April 1860), 65. These records will hereafter be referred to as *DSF*. Also, C. Goldfinch, *Cortina, A Re-Appraisal*, 33. Cortina's San José Ranch is frequently misplaced off the Espíritu Santo grant far to the northwest of Rancho del Carmen. Los Fresnos, a ranch on the river, should not be confused with modern-day Los Fresnos. Ford, *Rip Ford's Texas*, 269. For the exact location, see *Corpus Christi Ranchero*, October 22 1859, quoting the *Brownsville Flag*, October 15, 1859, and "Map of Cortina's Entrenchments," Samuel P. Heintzelman Papers, LC. Also, Charles Stillman to Ángel Navarro and R. H. Taylor, January 18, 1860, Sam Houston Papers, TSA. Somers Kinney said San José was "a few miles out" from Rancho del Carmen. *Brownsville Flag*, quoted in *New Orleans Daily Picayune*, October 24, 1859.

37. After 1858, Cortina is not listed on the tax rolls in Cameron County until 1865 when he paid taxes in person on 465 horses valued at $6,950 and 203 cattle worth $1,200. Tax Rolls, 1848–66, Cameron County Tax Assessor-Collector's Office, Brownsville, Texas. Absent in Mexico in 1866, his taxes were paid for him by A. Cortéz. The Agricultural Census for 1860 has him owning twenty horses, one hundred cattle, and fifty acres of unimproved land. 1860 Agricultural Census, Cameron County, Texas, NA.

38. *Matamoros Daily Ranchero*, September 24, 1870.

39. Ibid.

40. Richardson, ed., *A Compilation of the Messages and Papers of the Presidents*, 6:2292.

41. Bauer, *Mexican War, 1846–1848*, 52–57.

42. *Matamoros Daily Ranchero*, September 24, 1870.

43. Bauer, *Mexican War*, 52–57.

44. Ibid., 59–63.

45. Cortina, Compiled Military Service Record, Archivo de Secretaría de Defensa, Mexico City.

46. *Matamoros Daily Ranchero*, September 24, 1870.

47. Ibid.

48. Ibid.

49. *Brownsville Daily Ranchero*, August 1, 1871.

50. *Matamoros Daily Ranchero*, September 24, 1870.

51. C. Goldfinch, *Cortina, A Re-Appraisal*, 31–32. Also, *The Handbook of Texas Online*, s.v. "John James Dix, Jr.," http://www.tsha.utexas.edu/handbook/online/articles.

52. Ford, *Rip Ford's Texas*, 363.

53. Ibid.

54. Ibid., 364.

55. Adolphus Glarvke [sic] Affidavit, January 16, 1860, *DSF*, 65. The original of the affidavit can be found in the Sam Houston Papers at the TSA. Charles Goldfinch speculates at length as

to the year of the alleged murder. The earliest case in the Brownsville District Court involving Cortina is styled *State vs. Nepomocino Cortines* [sic] *and José Cisneros*, Cause No. 156, July 16, 1856. Unfortunately, the documents in the case have been lost and the specifics cannot be determined with certainty. A civil case, *A. J. Mason vs. Nepemocino Cortines* [sic], (Cause no. 478), which was dismissed at the "cost of the plaintiff," was filed in late 1854 or early 1855. C. Goldfinch, *Cortina, A Re-Appraisal*, 21–22. Minutebook A, District Clerk's Office, 144, 226, 255, 289, and 347.

56. *San Antonio Express*, November 3, 1894; Ford, *Rip Ford's Texas*, 261.
57. Graf, "The Economic History of the Lower Rio Grande Valley, 1820–1975," 374.
58. Ford, *Rip Ford's Texas*, 363.
59. Francis W. Latham to Howell Cobb, March 10, 1859, Letters Received, Secretary of the Treasury, Collector of Customs at the Port of Point Isabel, RG 56, NA.
60. *The Handbook of Texas Online*, s.v. "Mexican-American Land Grand Adjudication," http://www.tsha.utexas.edu/handbook/online/articles.
61. *Texas State Gazette* (Austin), March 23, 1850, quoting the *Brownsville American Flag*, February 6, 1850; *Memorial of Enrique Sánchez and Others, Citizens and Residents of the Territory and Valley of the Rio Grande*, 31st Cong., 1st sess., 1–3; House Executive Documents, 34th Cong., 3rd sess., 705–707; *Nueces Valley* (Corpus Christi), October 12, 1872.
62. *Texas State Gazette* (Austin), March 23, 1850.
63. Ibid.
64. *Austin Southern Intelligencer*, n.d., John L. Haynes Papers, Center for the Study of American History, University of Texas at Austin (CAH).
65. Ibid.
66. Ibid.
67. Dugan, "The 1850 Affair of the Brownsville Separatists," 270–87.
68. Greaser and De la Teja, "Quieting Title to Spanish and Mexican Land Grants in the Trans-Nueces: The Bourland and Miller Commission, 1850–1852," 455.
69. Ibid., 462.
70. Shearer, "The Carvajal Disturbances," 208–12; Quintellen McMillen, "Surveyor General: The Life and Times of José María Jesús Carvajal," 124–29, 171. Copy courtesy of the author. Chance, *José María de Jesús Carvajal: The Life and Times of a Mexican Revolutionary*, 18–54.
71. Kearney and Knopp, *Boom and Bust*, 73.
72. Cortina, Compiled Military Service Record, Archivo de Secretaría de Defensa, Mexico City.
73. Bell and Smallwood, *The Zona Libre, 1858–1905: A Problem in American Diplomacy*, 1–5.
74. Ibid.
75. Minutebook I (1850–59), 1–69, Brownsville City Council, City Secretary's Office, Brownsville.
76. Ibid.
77. Stillman, *Charles Stillman, 1810–1875*, 9–11.
78. Kearney and Knopp, *Boom and Bust*, 73. Also, *The Handbook of Texas Online*, s.v. "Stephen Powers," http://www.tsha.utexas.edu/handbook/online/articles.
79. *The Handbook of Texas Online*, s.v., "William Neale," http://www.tsha.utexas.edu/handbook/online/articles.
80. Kearney and Knopp, *Boom and Bust*, 71–72.
81. Lea, *King Ranch*, 1:71–89.
82. Domenech, *Missionary Adventures in Texas and Mexico: A Personal Narrative of Six Years Sojourn in These Regions*, 228.
83. Seventh Census (1850), Eighth Census (1860), and Ninth Census (1870), Cameron County, NA. There is a discrepancy in the various censuses for the age of Peter Champion.
84. Kearney and Knopp, *Boom and Bust*, 76.
85. Robert Mario Salmon, "Don José Ramón as Brownsville Capitalist, 1822–1879," Paper Delivered at the Texas State Historical Association (1986), 1; Salmon, "Don José San Román

as Brownsville Capitalist, 1822–1879," 54–68. Also, *The Handbook of Texas Online*, s.v. "José San Román," http://www.tsha.utexas.edu/handbook/online/articles.

86. Seventh Census (1850), Cameron County. The family name is given in most antebellum records as Glaevecke. Sometime after the Civil War the first "e" was dropped and the name was given as Glavecke. Tombstone of María Concepción Glavecke and Refugia Glavecke, Brownsville City Cemetery.

87. Commissioners Court Minutes (1848–62), Cameron County Clerk's Office, Brownsville; Minutebook I (1850–59), 123, 346–47, City Secretary's Office, Brownsville; and List of Candidates Qualifying, September 14, 1854, Cameron County, RG 307, TSA, Austin. Younger brother Gaspar was elected constable in 1848 at the age of twenty-one. He married Juanita Gonzales Garza in November 1853, in Brownsville. Marriage Book A, Parish Archives, Immaculate Concepción Cathedral, 256. In 1848, Adolphus Glavecke was also placed in charge of "Highway District No. 6." The Adolphus Glavecke family is not listed on the 1860 Cameron County census. For Glavecke's indictment, see *State of Texas vs. Adolphus Glaevecke*, Cause no. 385, Minutebook B, District Clerk's Office. A number of civil cases involving the controversial Glavecke can be found in the minutes of the district court, especially after 1865. For example, see Cause nos. 899, 900, 988, 994, 995, and 1,197. For Glavecke's land, see 1850 Agricultural Census, Cameron County, NA. Also, Ruth T. Bello to Jerry Thompson, May 14, 20; September 15; and October 3, 15, 1991, author's files. Also, *The Handbook of Texas Online*, s.v. "Adolphus Glaevecke," http://www/tsha/utexas.edu/handbook/online/articles. In 1875, District Attorney Angel Navarro charged Glavecke, who was clerk of the district court at the time, of flatulently listing "a large number of names as registered and qualified voters" of Cameron County. *State of Texas vs. Adolphus Glaevecke*, August 21, 1875, James B. Wells Papers, CAH.

88. *Antonio Tijerina vs. Adolphus Glavecke*, Minutebook B, 398–99, 577–79, District Clerk's Office.

89. Real Estate Records, Cameron County, Texas, Volume F (1853–57), 5–7. Copy courtesy of Ruth T. Bello and Cathleen Shoemaker, author's files. Also, María Josefa Cavazos, Feliciana Goseascochea de Tijerina, and Estéfana Goseascochea de Cortina, Agreement of Division of Espiritu Santo, November 20, 1853, No. 1115, Filed May 7, 1875, James B. Wells Papers, CAH.

90. *Estéfana Goseascochea de Cortina vs. Antonio Cantú et al.*, Cause no. 525, July 24, 1856, Minutebook A, 315, Cameron County District Clerk's Office, Brownsville, Texas.

91. Adolphus Glarvke [sic] Affidavit, January 16, 1860, *DSF*, 65.

92. *State vs. Adolph Glavecke*, Cause No. 385, Minutebook B, 51, Cameron County District Clerk's Office. Also, W. W. Nelson, Grand Jury Report (Spring 1859), 12th Judicial District, January 18, 1860, Sam Houston Papers, TSA. Also, *Rafael García Cavazos et al. vs. Charles Stillman et al.*, in "Impeachment of Judge Watrous," 2 (1856–57), 34th Cong., 3rd sess.

93. W. W. Nelson, Grand Jury Report (Spring 1859), 12th Judicial District, Sam Houston Papers, TSA; Cause nos. 388, 389, and 390, Minutebook B, 12th Judicial District. Also, *State of Texas vs. Nepomesino [sic] Cortina*, Cause nos. 388, 389, and 391, Minutebook B, 51, Cameron County District Clerk's Office.

94. Proclamation! Juan Nepomuceno Cortinas to the Inhabitants of the State of Texas, and especially those of the city of Brownsville, September 30, 1859, *DSF*, 70–71. An original can be found in Mexican Border Papers, Letters Received (LR), Adjutant General's Office (AGO), RG 94, NA. Although Cortina blamed Glavecke for the death Col. Trueman Cross, assistant quartermaster general, who was ambushed and murdered a few miles west of Fort Brown. Many on the Rio Grande frontier, then and later, blamed Cortina for the murder. Who killed Colonel Cross as well as the circumstances of his death will probably never be known. *New York Times*, May 11, 1890.

95. Seventh Census (1850), Cameron County, Texas, NA.

96. *Brownsville American Flag*, August 20, 1856.

97. W. P. Reyburn to F. A. Hatch, November 21, 1859, *DSF*, 65. Many of the documents relating to Cortina's 1859 Brownsville Raid can also be found in "Hostilities on the Rio Grande," 36th Cong., 1st sess. (March 1860). This set of records will hereafter be referred to as *HRG*.

98. Kearney and Knopp, *Boom and Bust*, 81–82.
99. Minutebook B, District Clerk's Office, 122, 206–207, Brownsville, Texas.
100. C. Yard to Wm. Tennison, January 4, 1860, Sam Houston Papers, TSA.
101. Minutebook I (1850–59), Brownsville City Secretary's Office, 76, 83.
102. Numerous depositions were taken during this particular dispute. For an outline of the charges, see E. B. Barton to Edwin B. Scarborough, August 1, 1853, and Scarborough to Barton, May 4, 1853, both in RG 307, Cameron County, TSA.
103. Minutebook B, District Clerk's Office, 206–207, Brownsville, Texas.
104. Navarro and Taylor to Houston, February 4, 1860, Sam Houston Papers, TSA.
105. *Brownsville American Flag*, August 20, 1856.
106. Ford, *Rip Ford's Texas*, 364. For Cortina being a deputy sheriff, see A. M. McCook to Acting Assistant Adjutant General, April 4, 1872, LR, AGO, RG 94, NA.
107. W. W. Nelson, Indictments by the Spring 1859 District Court, Sam Houston Papers, TSA.
108. Kearney and Knopp, *Boom and Bust*, 82; Cameron County Commissioners Court Minutes, 1848–62, 282, County Clerk's Office, Brownsville.
109. Navarro and Taylor to Houston, February 4, 1860, Sam Houston Papers, TSA.
110. W. P. Reyburn to F. A. Hatch, November 21, 1859, *DSF*, 65; List of Candidates Qualifying, August 4, 1856, Cameron County, RG 307, TSA; Commissioners Court Minutes, 1848–62, 290, County Clerk's Office, Brownsville.
111. [Gilbert Kingsbury] to Sis[ter] María, August 16, 1858, Gilbert Kingsbury Papers, CAH. Kingsbury used the pen name of F. F. Fenn. Also, Theo. C. Yard to Wm. Tennison, January 4, 1860, Sam Houston Papers, TSA.
112. "Impeachment of Judge Watrous," 2:1856–1857, no. 913 (Washington, D.C.: Cornelius Wendell, 1857), 34th Cong., 3rd sess., no. 175, 1–6; James Thompson, "Nineteenth Century History of Cameron County," 36; Ruby A. Woolridge, "Espíritu Santo Grant," in *Studies in Brownsville History*, ed. Kearney, 114–19.
113. Cortina Proclamation, September 30, 1859, LR, AGO, RG 94, NA. Among the various court cases, see *Charles J. Cana & Wife y Jacob Mussina vs. María J. Cavazos et al.*, *Manuel Treviño Cavazos vs. Charles Stillman*, and *María Josefa Cavazos vs. Miguel Parades et al.* All are in the James B. Wells Papers, CAH.
114. Wm. A. Tennison to Dear General, January 3, 1860, Sam Houston Papers, TSA.
115. *Austin Southern Intelligencer*, n.d., John L. Haynes Papers, CAH.
116. Kearney and Knopp, *Boom and Bust*, 77.
117. Rankin, *Twenty Years among the Mexicans: A Narrative of Missionary Labor*, 81.

CHAPTER TWO

1. Kearney and Knopp, *Boom and Bust*, 99–100.
2. *Austin Southern Intelligencer*, n.d., John L. Haynes Papers, CAH.
3. De León, *They Called Them Greasers*, 53. Also, De León, *Mexican Americans in Texas: A Brief History*, 38–39.
4. Quoted in De León, *They Called Them Greasers*, 82. On the Cart War, see Ellen Schneider and Paul H. Carlson, "Gunnysacks, Carreteros, and Teamsters: The South Texas Cart War of 1857," *Journal of South Texas* 1 (Spring 1988): 1–9; Callahan, "Mexican Border Troubles," 156–62.
5. *State Gazette Appendix Containing Debates in the House of Representatives*, 62–63. For Dougherty, see *The Handbook of Texas Online*, s.v. "Edward Dougherty," http://www.tsha.utexas.edu/handbook/online/articles.
6. *State Gazette Appendix Containing Debates in the House of Representatives*, 63.
7. Ibid., 63–64.
8. Charles Stillman Affidavit, January 18, 1860, *HRG*, 15–16. The original affidavit is in the Sam Houston Papers at the TSA.
9. Ibid.
10. Kearney and Knopp, *Boom and Bust*, 100, 106–107.

11. D. E. Twiggs to L. Thomas, January 11, 1859, and General Order No. 1, February 5, 1859, *DSF,* 8.

12. F. W. Latham et al. to John B. Floyd, March 9, 1859, *DSF,* 12–14. The original of the five-page petition can be found in LR, AGO, RG 94, NA. Besides Latham, those signing the petition included José San Román, Francisco Yturria, Jeremiah Galván, Simón Celaya, Somers Kinney, Israel B. Bigelow, and Forbes Britton of Corpus Christi.

13. Twiggs to S. Cooper, March 28, 1859, *DSF,* 14–15.

14. Gilbert Kingsbury, Untitled Account of the Cortina War, n.d., Gilbert Kingsbury Papers, CAH.

15. Eighth Census (1860), Cameron County, Texas, NA.

16. Rayburn and Rayburn, eds., *Century of Conflict, 1821–1913: Incidents in the Lives of William Neale and William A. Neale, Early Settlers in South Texas,* 64–65. These recollections, written many years after the fact, should be read with caution. Many of Neale's errors relative to Cortina, however, have been corrected by the editors. Gabriel Catsel (Catcel) died on June 20, 1863. Cameron County Index to Probate Records. Vol. 1 (1848–1924), Rio Grande Collection, University of Texas–Pan American, Edinburg, Texas.

17. Juan N. Cortina to the Public, September 9, 1875, *TFT,* 118. Also, Affidavit, Robert Shears, January 14, 1860, Sam Houston Papers, TSA. Another version of the incident has Cortina standing in the door of a saloon smoking a cigar when he observed the incident in Market Square. *New York Times,* May 11, 1890.

18. Robert Shears Affidavit, January 14, 1860, *HRG,* 17. J. T. Canales, who hoped someday to write a biography of Cortina, said the shooting was at the corner of Washington and 12th streets. Canales, *Bandit or Patriot: An Address by J. T. Canales before the Lower Rio Grande Valley Historical Society at San Benito, Texas, October 15, 1951,* 10.

19. Juan N. Cortina to the Public, September 8, 1875, *TFT,* 118.

20. Kingsbury, Untitled Account of the Cortina War, Gilbert Kingsbury Papers, CAH; "Report of the Grand Jury on the Disturbances of the Country," in *New Orleans Daily True Delta,* December 31, 1859.

21. Affidavit, [Jeremiah Galván?], n.d., Samuel P. Heintzelman Papers, LC.

22. Paredes, *Texas-Mexican Cancionero,* 139–40.

23. Kingsbury, "Texas. The Rio Grande Valley. Cortina." Gilbert Kingsbury Papers, CAH.

24. Shears Affidavit, January 14, 1860, *HRG,* 17. Shears brought a civil case against Cortina, saying that on July 13, 1860 [1859], Cortina had "grievously wounded" him in the left shoulder and had prevented "others from going to [his] assistance." In the Confederate District Court on May 8, 1862, with Adolphus Glavecke as foreman of a grand jury, Cortina "being three times solemnly called came not but made default," and was ordered to pay $5,000. *Robert Shiers* [sic] *vs. Juan N. Cortina,* Cause No. 670, Minutebook B, District Clerk's Office, 232–33. After the Civil War, Shears again became marshal. *Matamoros Daily Ranchero,* February 24, 1866.

25. *State vs. Juan Nepomocino* [sic] *Cortina et al.,* Cause no. 394, 395, and 396. Minutebook B, District Clerk's Office, 78, 92.

26. Glavecke Affidavit, January 17, 1860, *HRG,* 13.

27. Ibid.

28. Ibid.

29. Ibid.

30. "Report of the United States Commissioners to Texas," 42d Cong., 3d sess., no. 39:29. If Glavecke was telling the truth, it remains somewhat of a mystery why he did not bother to warn the authorities in Brownsville

31. Stephen Powers et al. to Hardin R. Runnels, October 2, 1859, *DSF,* 21.

32. Grand Jury Report, n.d., *DSF,* 93. Some sources, including the Committee of Public Safety, place the beginning of the raid as early as 3 A.M. while others have it much later, some shortly before daybreak. Maj. Samuel P. Heintzelman, who arrived in Brownsville with the army in the wake of the raid and who conducted an extensive investigation of the causes of the violence, gave

4 A.M. as the time. Heintzelman's data on the Cortina War, gathered from a number of written and first-hand accounts, is generally reliable as is Heintzelman's private journal. Thompson, ed., *Fifty Miles and a Fight: Major Samuel Peter Heintzelman's Journal of Texas and the Cortina War*. Many of the raiders can be identified from the numerous Cameron County indictments. For the men assembling in Matamoros on the night of the raid, see testimony of W. D. Thomas in *Richard King vs. United Mexican States*, 80–86. Also, Rankin, *Twenty Years among the Mexicans*, 83; and Thompson, *Juan Cortina*, 101–102.

33. S. P. Heintzelman to Robert E. Lee, March 1, 1860, *TFT*, 3; and Grand Jury Report, January 8, 1860, Washington Daniel Miller Papers, TSA.

34. Fitzpatrick to Cass, January 4, 1860, Matamoros Dispatches, Records of the Department of State, RG 59, NA.

35. Parisot, *The Reminiscences of a Texas Missionary*, 97.

36. Unsigned Letter, *New Orleans Daily Picayune*, October 10, 1859, quoted in *DSF*, 39–40.

37. W. P. Reyburn to F. A. Hatch, November 21, 1859, *DSF*, 65. Also, Memorandum for the Information of the Secretary of War, in relation to the troubles on the Rio Grande frontier, n.d., LR, AGO, RG 94, NA.

38. Francis W. Latham to David E. Twiggs, September 28, 1859, *DSF*, 32; *San Antonio Daily Herald*, October 6, 1859; Report of the Grand Jury on the Disturbances of the Country, A. B. Bacon, District Attorney, in LR, AGO, RG 94, NA.

39. Rayburn and Rayburn, eds., *Century of Conflict*, 66–67. Also, *New Orleans Daily Picayune*, October 11, 1859; *New Orleans Daily True Delta*, October 11, 1859.

40. Francis W. Latham to Howell Cobb, October 6, 1859, LR, Secretary of the Treasury, RG 56, NA; *Brownsville American Flag Extra*, October 1, October 29, 1859; *Galveston Weekly News*, October 8, 1859; *San Antonio Daily Herald*, October 6, 11, November 8, 1859; *New Orleans Daily Picayune*, October 11, 1859. A number of the men responsible for killing Morris were individuals who had been released from the jail. Before his death, it was said Morris was forced to remove the shackles of at least one individual. *New York Times*, May 11, 1890.

41. Shears Affidavit, January 14, 1860, *HRG*, 17.

42. R. Fitzpatrick to Lewis Cass, October 1, 1859, Dispatches from United States Consuls in Matamoros, 1826–1906, Records of the Department of State, RG 59, NA. Also, S. P. Heintzelman to Robert E. Lee, March 1, 1860, *TFT*, 3–4; *State of Texas vs. Juan Nepomuceno Cortina et al.*, January 18, 1860. The Committee of Public Safety, however, in a petition to Governor Runnels, said Johnson was "killed almost immediately." *DSF*, 21; and *San Antonio Daily Herald*, October 11, 1859. Indictments resulting from the raid and the Cortina War that followed include: Cause nos. 391, 394–98, and 418. In Cause no. 395, Cortina and four hundred others were charged with the murder of Jesús Montes. In Cause no. 397, Cortina and the same four hundred were indicted for the murder of John Fox (*State of Texas vs. Juan Nepomuceno Cortina and Four Hundred Others*). In the death of Viviano García, see *State of Texas vs. Juan Nepomuceno Cortina, Juan Vela & Others*. In yet another indictment (Cause no. 418), Cortina was charged with treason. See Minutebook B, District Clerk's Office. Specifics are taken from copies of the indictments in the Sam Houston and Washington Daniel Miller Papers, TSA. Alejo Vela had previously been indicted for horse stealing but had been released when, ironically, Adolphus Glavecke posted his bail. *State vs. Alejo Vela*, Cause no. 312, Minutebook A. 434, 438, and 472, District Clerk's Office.

43. Thompson and Jones, *Civil War and Revolution on the Rio Grande Frontier: A Narrative and Pictorial History*, 115–17. See chapter 6, p. 172–74.

44. Grand Jury Report, November 9, 1859, Sam Houston Papers, TSA. This report was reprinted in the *New Orleans Daily True Delta*, December 31, 1859. There is some confusion as to where Glavecke found refuge. Galván's affidavit in the Heintzelman Papers does not mention him being at his store. W. P. Reyburn clearly states that Glavecke took refuge in the store of Samuel A. Belden. Glavecke, in his account of the raid in Chatfield's *Twin Cities of the Border*, written in the early 1890s, not long before his death on February 4, 1900, confirms that he had hidden in Galván's store. W. P. Reyburn to F. A. Hatch, November 21, 1859, *TFT*, 66; Glavecke,

"The Story of Old Times," in *Twin Cities of the Border*, ed. Chatfield, 23; "Brownsville City Cemetery," available with permission at http://www.usgennet.org/usa/tx/topic/cemeteries/Etx/Cameron.

45. Glavecke, "The Story of Old Times," in *Twin Cities of the Border*, ed. Chatfield, 23.
46. *San Antonio Daily Herald*, November 8, 1859.
47. S. P. Heintzelman to Robert E. Lee, March 1, 1860, *TFT*, 3–4.
48. Charles Goldfinch interview of A. W. Champion, grandson of Alexander Werbiskie, quoted in C. Goldfinch, *Cortina, A Re-Appraisal*, 44.
49. Francisco Yturria Affidavit, January 19, 1860, Sam Houston Papers, TSA.
50. A. Werbiskie Affidavit, January 10, 1860, *HRG*, 12; *American Star Extra* (Brownsville), October 29, 1859; and *New Orleans Daily Picayune*, October 11, 1859.
51. Cortina Proclamation, September 30, 1859, *DSF*, 71.
52. Ibid.
53. Ibid., 70.
54. Heintzelman to Lee, March 1, 1860, *TFT*, 3–4; and 1860 Census, Cameron County, NA.
55. *El Prismo* (Tampico), October 13, 1859.
56. Edmund J. Davis et al. to Hardin R. Runnels, November 30, 1859, Hardin R. Runnels Papers, TSA; and Grand Jury Report, November 10, 1859, Sam Houston Papers, TSA.
57. "Difficulties between the People of Texas and Mexico," 36th Cong., 1st sess., House, 3. Scott's comment in March 1860, was in reference to not only the September 1859 raid on Brownsville but also the Cortina War that followed.
58. *Brownsville American Flag*, October 8, 1859.
59. Grand Jury Report, January 18, 1860, Washington Daniel Miller Papers, TSA.
60. *State of Texas vs. Juan Nepomuceno Cortina et al.*, November 19, 1859; *State of Texas vs. Juan Nepomuceno Cortina, Juan Vela, & Others*, November 7, 1859; *State of Texas vs. Juan Nepomuceno Cortina and Four Hundred Others*, January 8, 1860; all in Washington Daniel Miller Papers, TSA. A. F. Watson, Jas. Martin, Marcos Guerra, Francis Campbell, W. D. Thomas, Norberto Gonzales, Juan Antonio Longoria, Peter Champion, Adolphus Glavecke, Alex Werbiski, and Peter Champion all served as witnesses in the death of John Fox. In the death of Vivian García, J. B. Bigelow, José M. Otero, William D. Thomas, J. D. Fernández, William W. Nelson, Yturria, Werbiskie, and Glavecke testified.
61. *Robert Shears vs. Juan N. Cortina*, Case no. 670, Minutebook B, 232, District Clerk's Office, Brownsville, Texas.
62. Latham to Cobb, October 6, 1859, LR, Secretary of the Treasury, RG 56, NA; *Brownsville American Flag Extra*, October 1, 1859. Also, Heintzelman notes from the *Brownsville American Flag*, n.d., Samuel P. Heintzelman Papers, LC.
63. Latham to Cobb, October 6, 1859, Letters Received, Secretary of the Treasury, RG 56, NA; and Latham to David E. Twiggs, September 28, 1859, *DSF*, 32.
64. *New Orleans Daily Picayune*, January 22, 1860.
65. Ibid., October 19, 1859.
66. O. A. Carolan Affidavit, January 13, 1860, Sam Houston Papers, TSA.
67. Cortina Proclamation, September 30, 1859, LR, AGO, RG 94. The only known copy in Spanish is at the Beineke Library, Yale University, New Haven, Connecticut. A handwritten copy can be found with R. Fitzpatrick to Lewis Cass, October 1, 1859, Matamoros Dispatches, RG. 59, NA. See also, *El Jaque* (Matamoros), quoted in *Reports of the Committee of Investigation Sent in 1873*, 136; and Walraven, "Ambivalent Americans: Selected Spanish-Language Newspapers' Response to Anglo Domination in Texas, 1830–1910."
68. For Peña as the likely author, see R. Fitzpatrick to Lewis Cass, January 4, 1860, Matamoros Dispatches, RG 59, NA. In a speech in Ciudad Victoria in late January 1860, José María de Jesús Carvajal called Peña a "wolf in sheep's clothing." Peña later served as editor of *Monitor de la Frontera* and other Matamoros newspapers. *Corpus Christi Ranchero*, February 11, 1860; and *Daily Ranchero* (Brownsville), July 8, 1868. For no other reason than the fact that he was well educated, others speculated that José María may have been the author.

Notes to Pages 47–52

69. Cortina Proclamation, September 30, 1859, LR, AGO, RG 94. To help incite public opinion against Cortina, the proclamation was also published in the Brownsville *Daily Ranchero,* May 18, 1867.
70. Cortina Proclamation, September 30, 1859, LR, AGO, RG 94.
71. Kingsbury, Untitled Account of the Cortina War, Gilbert Kingsbury Papers, CAH.
72. Ibid.
73. Henry Webb et al. to Hardin R. Runnels, October 2, 1859, *DSF,* 21–22.
74. *New Orleans Daily Picayune,* November 8, 1859.
75. A. Werbiski Affidavit, January 10, 1860, Sam Houston Papers, TSA.
76. *New Orleans Daily Picayune,* October 11, 1859.
77. [Kingsbury] to Chief Clerk Post Office Department, October 3, 1859, Gilbert Kingsbury Papers, CAH. Also, *Galveston Daily News,* November 10, 1859; *New Orleans Daily True Delta,* November 8, 1859; Rankin, *Twenty Years among the Mexicans,* 83.
78. Rankin, *Twenty Years among the Mexicans,* 83; McMillen, "Carvajal," 173.
79. [Kingsbury] to Chief Clerk Post Office Department, October 3, 1859, Gilbert Kingsbury Papers, CAH.
80. *New Orleans Daily True Delta,* December 11, 1859.
81. Latham to Twiggs, September 28, 1859, *DSF,* 32.
82. *New Orleans Daily Picayune,* November 20, 1859.
83. E. R. Hord to [Runnels], September 29, 1859; and Edmund J. Davis to Runnels, October 7, 1859; both in Hardin R. Runnels Papers, TSA.
84. Davis to Runnels, October 7, 1859, Hardin R. Runnels Papers, TSA.
85. Henry Webb et al. to Runnels, October 2, 1859, *DSF,* 21–22.
86. Ibid.
87. *Brownsville American Flag Extra,* October 19, 1859; *Corpus Christi Ranchero,* November 19, 1859.
88. *Brownsville American Flag Extra,* October 19, 1859.
89. Ibid.
90. *New Orleans Daily Picayune,* January 22, 1860.
91. John Hemphill to James Buchanan, October 8, 1859, *DSF,* 33.
92. *Journal of the House of Representatives, Eighth Legislature, State of Texas,* 18, 52, 117.
93. Franklin Chase to Henry R. LaReintrie, October 22, 1859, Dispatches from Mexico, Records of the Department of State, RG 59, NA, enclosing copies of the *Brownsville American Flag Extra,* October 1, 1859. Also, *El Prisma* (Tampico), October 13, 1859.
94. Robert M. McLane to Lewis Cass, December 7, 1859, Dispatches from Mexico, RG 59, NA.
95. Ibid.
96. D. E. Twiggs to S. Cooper, October 7, 1859, *DSF,* 31.
97. Ibid.
98. Galván Affidavit, n.d., Samuel P. Heintzelman Papers, LC.
99. Report of the Grand Jury upon the Disturbances of the Country, December 9, 1859, Washington Daniel Miller Papers, TSA.
100. Kingsbury, Untitled Account of the Cortina War, Gilbert Kingsbury Papers, CAH.
101. Ibid.
102. Latham to Cobb, December 21, 1859, Letters Received, Secretary of the Treasury, RG 56, NA.
103. Unsigned letter addressed to Frank F. Fenn, December 16, 1859, Sam Houston Papers, TSA. It is speculated the letter was unsigned for fear that it would fall into the hands of Cortina.
104. Stephen Powers to James Buchanan, October 18, 1859, *DSF,* 35.
105. W. P. Reyburn to F. A. Hatch, November 21, 1859, *DSF,* 67.
106. "Cortina, the Leader, and his Character," October 10, 1859, in *New Orleans Daily Picayune,* n.d., *DSF,* 39–40; *New Orleans Daily Picayune,* October 19, 1859.

107. Seventh Census (1850), Cameron County, NA. Also, *Indianola Courier,* October 22, 1859; Stephen Powers to H. R. Runnels, October 23, 1859, Hardin R. Runnels Papers, TSA.
108. S. P. Heintzelman to John Withers, March 1, 1860, *TFT,* 4; *New Orleans Daily Picayune,* October 24, 1859.
109. Israel B. Bigelow, letter, October 23, 1859, in *Galveston News,* quoted in *DSF,* 47–48; and W. P. Reyburn to F. A. Hatch, November 21, 1859, *DSF,* 68–69.
110. Bigelow letter, October 23, 1859, in *Galveston News,* quoted in *DSF,* 47–48.
111. W. B. Thompson to Stephen Powers and J. G. Brown[e], October 25, 1859, *DSF,* 69; *Brownsville American Flag Extra,* October 25, 1859, in *DSF,* 68–69. A copy of the extra of the *Brownsville American Flag* can also be found in the records of the Adjutant General's Office at the NA and at the Beineke Library at Yale University, New Haven, Connecticut.
112. *Brownsville American Flag Extra,* October 25, 1859.
113. *New Orleans Daily Picayune,* November 8, 1859; *San Antonio Daily Herald,* November 5, 1859.
114. *Brownsville American Flag Extra,* October 25, 1859, in *DSF,* 44–45.
115. Israel B. Bigelow, letter, November 1, 1859, in *Galveston News,* n.d., quoted in *DSF,* 48–49.
116. *Brownsville American Flag Extra,* October 25, 1858, in *DSF,* 44–45.
117. *Galveston Daily News,* November 8, 1859; *Corpus Christi Ranchero,* November 11, 1859.
118. Ibid.
119. W. B. Thompson to Stephen Powers and J. G. Brown[e], October 25, 1859, *DSF,* 69. The *Corpus Christi Ranchero* in an article titled. "A Fight With Cortina," also utilizes this same quote. *Corpus Christi Ranchero,* November 11, 1859.
120. Brownsville *Evening Ranchero,* July 5, 1876, in *Twin Cities of the Border,* ed. Chatfield, 15.
121. W. B. Thompson to Stephen Powers and J. G. Brown[e], October 25, 1859, *DSF,* 69; S. P. Heintzelman to John Withers, March 1, 1860, *TFT.* Thompson listed Cortina's dead at eight.
122. Juan Nepomuceno Cortina, letter, October 26, 1859, *DSF,* 69–70. The letter was published in the *Brownsville American Flag Extra,* October 29, 1859.
123. *Brownsville American Flag Extra,* October 29, 1859, in LR, AGO, RG 94, NA; Francis Campbell to S. Powers, n.d., Samuel P. Heintzelman Papers, LC.
124. *Brownsville American Flag Extra;* October 29, 1859; *New Orleans Daily Picayune,* November 8, 1859. Also, Kingsbury, Untitled Account of the Cortina War, Gilbert Kingsbury Papers, CAH.
125. *Brownsville American Flag Extra,* October 25, 1859, *DSF,* 44–45; Edmund J. Davis et al. to [Runnels], November 30, 1859, Hardin R. Runnels Papers, TSA. Cadena is the same man who joined the Union Army at Brownsville in late 1863 and who became a second lieutenant in the 2nd Texas Cavalry only to desert in June 1864. Thompson, *Mexican Texans in the Union Army,* 17–19, 48.
126. Heintzelman notes from the *Brownsville American Flag Extra,* October 25, 1859, Samuel P. Heintzelman Papers, LC.
127. *State of Texas vs. Juan Nepomuceno Cortina and Four Hundred Others,* January 8, 1860, Washington Daniel Miller Papers, TSA. In the indictment, the natives are identified only as Carlos, Cano, Francisco, Juan Ojos, Chiquitos, Fernando, Andrés, Faustino, Rafael, and Manuel. Also, Heintzelman notes from the *Brownsville American Flag,* October 15, 1859.
128. *New Orleans Daily True Delta,* November 16, 1859.
129. "Cortina Raids," *Texas Siftings* 3 (August 4, 1883).
130. Stephen Powers to D. R. Porter and Duff Green, February 2, 1860, enclosed with Green to Cass, February 4, 1860, RG 59, NA. Also, "Report of the Grand Jury on the Disturbances of the Country," in *New Orleans Daily True Delta,* December 31, 1859.
131. Ford to [Runnels], November 22, 1859, Hardin R. Runnels Papers, TSA.
132. *El Jaque* (Matamoros), n.d., quoted in *Corpus Christi Ranchero,* December 17, 1859.
133. William Neale to Sam Houston, January 16, 1860, Sam Houston Papers, TSA. William Neale did erect, however, a large grave marker over his son's grave in the Brownsville Cemetery.

134. Ibid.
135. Ibid. Before being elected state senator, Scarborough was publisher of the *Brownsville American Flag.*
136. Ibid.
137. Ibid.
138. Ibid.
139. Ibid. Also, List of Property, burnt, stolen, or destroyed by Juan Nepomusina [sic] Cortinas, January 23, 1860, *TFT,* 48–49.
140. Ibid.
141. *Corpus Christi Ranchero,* November 26, 1859; *New Orleans Daily Picayune,* November 26, 1859; *New Orleans Daily True Delta,* November 8, 1859.
142. *New Orleans Daily Picayune,* November 26, 1859.
143. Cortina to Estevan Powers, October 31, 1859, Samuel P. Heintzelman Papers, LC.
144. W. P. Reyburn to F. A. Hatch, November 21, 1859, *DSF,* 66.
145. Heintzelman notes from the *Brownsville American Flag,* December 2, 1859.
146. F. M. Campbell to S. Powers, November 21, 1859, Samuel P. Heintzelman Papers, LC; *Indianola Courier,* n.d., quoted in *New Orleans Daily Picayune,* November 26, 1859.
147. Campbell claim for Damages, in *Depredations on the Frontiers of Texas,* hereafter referred to as *DFT,* (1872), 53.
148. *New Orleans Daily Picayune,* October 10, 11, 1859; *New Orleans Daily True Delta,* October 11, 1859. Much of the news that appeared in the New Orleans newspapers was taken verbatim from the extras of the *Brownsville American Flag.*
149. Stephen Powers to James Buchanan, October 18, 1859; J. C. Harris et al. to James Buchanan, October 25, 1859; Harris to the Secretary of War, October 24, 1859; all in *DSF,* 34–37. Also, *New Orleans Daily Picayune,* October 25, 1859.
150. John Slidell to the President, October 25, 1859, *DSF,* 37.
151. *Corpus Christi Ranchero,* November 12, 1859; *New Orleans Daily Picayune,* November 13, 1859; *New Orleans Daily True Delta,* November 15, 1859; *Indianola Courier Extra,* November 10, 1859.
152. *San Antonio Herald,* extra, n.d.; *Corpus Christi Ranchero,* November 12, 26, 1859; *Galveston Daily Civilian,* November 11, 1859; *Indianola Commercial Bulletin,* November 12, 1859; all in LR, AGO, RG 94, NA.
153. *New Orleans Daily True Delta,* November 22, 1859.
154. *San Antonio Daily Herald,* November 22, 1859. Cortina had become so well known that in distant Presidio del Norte, George S. Macmanus complained to Secretary of State Lewis Cass that the state of Chihuahua was "overrun by a band of desperate outlaws ... worse in their bloody deeds and daring character than the dreaded Cortinas." Macmanus to Cass, Chihuahua Consular Dispatches, RG 59, NA.
155 *Corpus Christi Ranchero,* November 5, 1859.
156. Ibid., November 12, 1859.
157. Charles Lovenskiold to Runnels, November 26, 1859, Hardin R. Runnels Papers, TSA. Individuals who would play a large role in the history of the region, such as William H. Maltby and Mat Nolan, enlisted as privates. John L. Haynes agreed to serve as quartermaster.
158. *Corpus Christi Ranchero,* November 19, 1859.
159. Ibid. Also, *Brownsville American Flag,* October 29, 1859, in LR, AGO, RG 94, NA; *Corpus Christi Ranchero,* November 15, 1859.
160. Diary, Thomas John Noakes, November 7, 1859, in DeGarmo, *Pathfinders of Texas, 1836–1846,* 266.
161. Diary, Thomas John Noakes, November 9, 1859. The Cameron County Grand Jury that met in early November in Brownsville also concluded that Cortina had a thousand men. Report of the Grand Jury on the Disturbances of the Country, A. B. Bacon, District Attorney, Copy in LR, AGO, NA.

162. Ibid.

163. Ibid.

164. *Indianola Courier,* November 13, 1859, quoted in *New Orleans Daily True Delta,* November 18, 1859. Also, *San Antonio Daily Herald,* November 16, 1859.

165. *Goliad Messenger Extra,* November 11, 1859, quoted in *New Orleans Daily Picayune,* November 18, 1859. Also, *New Orleans Daily Picayune,* November 26, 1859.

166. *San Antonio Ledger and Texan Extra,* December 4, 1859.

167. *New Orleans Daily True Delta,* December 10, 1859.

168. *Indianola Courier,* November 12, 1859, in LR, AGO, RG 94, NA.

169. *New Orleans Daily Picayune,* November 13, 1859.

170. *San Antonio Herald Extra,* n.d., in LR, AGO, RG 94, NA.

171. Ibid.

172. *Victoria Advocate,* n.d., quoted in *New Orleans Daily Picayune,* November 18, 1859.

173. *Austin Southern Intelligencer,* n.d., John L. Haynes Papers, CAH. In New Orleans and in San Antonio, Lockridge had previously promoted a filibustering expedition to Arizona, probably to invade Sonora. After serving as a volunteer in the Cortina War, Lockridge became a major in the Confederate Army of New Mexico and was killed at the Battle of Valverde on February 21, 1862. Baylor, *Into the Far, Wild Country: True Tales of the Old Southwest,* ed. Thompson, 77, 82; Earl W. Fornell, "Texans and Filibusters in the 1850s," *Southwestern Historical Quarterly* 59 (April 1956): 417–27; M. Hall, *Sibley's New Mexico Campaign,* 99–101; *San Antonio Daily Herald,* May 6, 1859, quoting the *New Orleans Bee,* n.d.; and *New Orleans Daily Picayune,* January 7, 1860.

174. *San Antonio Alamo Express,* August 25, 1860, quoting the *San Antonio Daily Herald,* n.d.

175. *New Orleans Daily Picayune,* November 20, 1859, quoted in *San Antonio Daily Herald,* October 29.

176. *San Antonio Daily Herald Extra,* n.d., in LR, AGO, RG 94, NA.

177. *Austin Southern Intelligencer,* n.d., John L. Haynes Papers, CAH.

178. *San Antonio Alamo Express,* October 1, 1860, quoting the *San Antonio Daily Herald,* n.d., in LR, AGO, RG 94, NA.

179. Twiggs to Secretary of War, November 16, 1859, LR, AGO, RG 94, NA. Reprinted in *DSF,* 58. Cortina was said to be paying his men a dollar a day.

180. [Twiggs] to [John Floyd], November 12, 1859; Twiggs to Secretary of War, November 16, 1859; both in LR, AGO, RG 94, NA. Reprinted in *DSF,* 55.

181. Abstract of Ordnance and Ordnance Stores on hand at Brazos Santiago, September 30, 1859, LR, AGO, RG 94, NA. Also, *San Antonio Daily Herald,* November 16, 1859.

182. Twiggs to Secretary of War, November 17, 1861, LR, AGO, RG 94, NA.

183. Twiggs to Secretary of War, November 21, 1859, LR, AGO, RG 94, NA.

184. Runnels to Wm. G. Tobin, October 13, 1859, Hardin R. Runnels Papers, TSA. Also, *San Antonio Daily Herald,* October 18, 1859.

185. Wm. G. Tobin to [Hardin Runnels], November 16, 1859, Hardin R. Runnels Papers, TSA.

186. Affidavit, [Jeremiah Galván?], Samuel P. Heintzelman Papers, LC.

187. *New Orleans Daily Picayune,* November 26, 1859; *New Orleans Daily True Delta,* December 3, 1859; and J. T. Hunter, "Cortina War," 1:3–4.

188. *Corpus Christi Ranchero,* November 26, 1859.

189. Ibid.

190. Ibid.

191. W. P. Reyburn to F. A. Hatch, November 21, 1859, *DSF,* 67.

192. J. T. Hunter, "Cortina War," 3–4. Also, *New Orleans Daily True Delta,* December 3, 1859.

193. John S. Ford to W. D. Thomas, February 22, 1860, Samuel P. Heintzelman Papers, LC; Thompson, ed., *Fifty Miles and a Fight: Major Samuel Peter Heintzelman's Journal of Texas and the Cortina War,* 32; Utley, *Lone Star Justice: The First Century of the Texas Rangers,* 111.

194. *Corpus Christi Ranchero,* November 26, 1859; *New Orleans Daily True Delta,* December 3,

1859. Some newspaper accounts placed the number of Americans hanged by Cortina as high as six. *Corpus Christi Ranchero Extra,* n.d., in LR, AGO, RG 94, NA.

195. Wm. G. Tobin to H. B. Runnels, November 27, 1859, Sam Houston Papers, TSA; *Corpus Christi Ranchero,* November 26, 1859; *San Antonio Ledger and Texan Extra,* December 4, 1859; *San Antonio Daily Herald,* December 6, 1859; *Corpus Christi Ranchero Extra,* n.d., in LR, AGO, RG 94, NA; *San Antonio Herald Extra,* n.d., in LR, AGO, RG 94, NA; J. T. Hunter, "Cortina War," 5. The Rangers killed were William McKay, Thomas Grier, and Nicholas R. Millett.

196. Claim of Julius Verbaum, January 26, 1860, *TFT,* 54–55.

197. Tobin to Runnels, November 27, 1859, Sam Houston Papers, TSA; Powers to Runnels, October 23, 1859, Hardin R. Runnels Papers, TSA. Twenty-nine-year-old Lt. Loomis Lyman Langdon of the 1st Artillery was on his way downriver from Fort Duncan to Fort Brown with his family when he was informed of the outbreak of violence in the lower Valley. Crossing the river at Edinburg, he was escorted to Matamoros by Simon García, one of the leading citizens of New Monterrey. Langdon was later given $1,720 for all his baggage and personal items, including the "wardrobe of three ladies," that was left at Ringgold Barracks and lost to Cortina. "Report of the Committee on Claims," 36th Cong., 2d sess., (February 1861), 1; *Galveston Weekly News,* October 8, 1859; *New Orleans Daily True Delta,* October 11, 1859; Thompson, ed., *Fifty Miles and a Fight,* 137.

198. *Corpus Christi Ranchero,* December 3, 1859.

199. Ibid. Also, *Austin Tri-Weekly Intelligencer,* n.d., quoted in *San Antonio Daily Herald,* November 16, 1859.

200. Tobin to Runnels, November 27, 1859, Sam Houston Papers, TSA.

201. *San Antonio Daily Herald,* December 31, 1859.

202. Affidavit [Jeremiah Galván?], Samuel P. Heintzelman Papers, LC.

203. Wm. G. Tobin to H .B. Runnels, November 27, 1859, Sam Houston Papers, TSA. Also, Heintzelman notes, mostly from the *Brownsville American Flag,* Samuel P. Heintzelman Papers, LC.

204. Heintzelman to John Withers, March 1, 1860, *TFT,* 6.

CHAPTER THREE

1. Broadside, November 26, 1859, LR, AGO, RG 94, NA. Also, Cortina Proclamation, November 23, 1859, *DSF,* 79. The style and syntax in the *pronunciamiento* is similar to that of the September 30 *pronunciamiento,* indicating that once again Cortina probably sought the composition and editorial skills of Miguel Peña.

2. Broadside, November 26, 1859, LR, AGO, RG 94, NA.

3. Ibid.

4. *Brownsville American Flag,* November 26, 1859; *Corpus Christi Ranchero,* December 3, 1859.

5. Kingsbury, Untitled Account of the Cortina War, Gilbert Kingsbury Papers, CAH.

6. *San Antonio Herald Extra,* n.d., copy in LR, AGO, RG 94, NA.

7. John Graham, Claim for Damages, January 23, 1860, *TFT,* 35.

8. Robert Shears, Claim for Damages, January 24, 1860, *TFT,* 51–52.

9. Adolphus Glavewecke [*sic*], Claim for Damages, January 23, 1860, *TFT,* 34.

10. E. Basse, Claim for Damages, January 23, 1860, *TFT,* 15.

11. James G. Brown, Claim for Damages, n.d., *TFT,* 17.

12. Gabriel Catsell [*sic*], Claim for Damages, January 24, 1860, *TFT,* 20.

13. Israel B. Bigilow [*sic*], Claim for Damages, January 28, 1860, *TFT,* 15.

14. J. M. Ward, Claim for Damages, January 28, 1860, *TFT,* 55.

15. James Johnson and R. West, Claim for Damages, January 28, 1860, *TFT,* 56.

16. Hugh O'Connor, Claim for Damages, January 28, 1860, *TFT,* 60.

17. James Martin and A.G. Milstead, Claim for Damages, January 25, 1860, *TFT,* 47.

18. Nathaniel White, Claim for Damages, n.d., *TFT,* 57–58.

19. Francis M. Campbell, Claim for Damages, *DFT* (1872), 43.

20. William Johnson, Claim for Damages, January 26, 1860, *TFT,* 36.
21. James Mallett [*sic*], Claim for Damages, January 27, 1860, *TFT,* 44–45.
22. Jacob Miller, Claim for Damages, January 28, 1860, *TFT,* 46–47.
23. James Maxwell, Claim for Damages, January 27, 1860, *TFT,* 45–46.
24. Josiah Turner, Claim for Damages, *DFT* (1872), 44.
25. Affidavit, Peter Champion, January 13, 1860, Sam Houston Papers, TSA.
26. *Galveston Daily News,* November 8, 1859.
27. Affidavit, Peter Champion, January 13, 1860, Sam Houston Papers, TSA.
28. Peter Champion, Claim for Damages, January 25, 1860, *TFT,* 21–22. Also, *DFT* (1872), 44th Cong., 1st sess., 43.
29. Peter Champion, Claim for Damages, January 24, 1860, *TFT,* 21–22.
30. *Corpus Christi Ranchero,* November 19, 1859.
31. Charles Stillman Claim for Damages, January 24, 1860, *TFT,* 61.
32. Edmund J. Davis et al. to [Runnels], December 12, 1859, Sam Houston Papers, TSA.
33. William Neale and Nestor Maxan, Claim for Damages, January 23, 1860, *TFT,* 48–49.
34. Neale, "Centennial Oration by the Honorable William Neale," in *Twin Cities of the Border,* ed. Chatfield, 13.
35. Affidavit, Thaddeus M. Rhodes, January 13, 1860, Sam Houston Papers, TSA; Thaddeus M. Rhodes, Claim for Damages, January 26, 1860, *TFT,* 50–51; Rhodes Testimony, *Richard King vs. United Mexican States,* 98–103. A heavyset man with blue eyes and a full beard, Rhodes had married Rafaela Hernández four years earlier and had become deputy collector and inspector of customs at Rancho Rosario.
36. Salomé Young, Claim for Damages, January 25, 1860, *TFT,* 58. The *San Antonio Daily Herald,* February 10, 1860, quoting the *Brownsville American Flag,* n.d., reported that Young had lost 1,600 head of cattle. Also, Amberson, McAllen, and McAllen, *I Would Rather Sleep in Texas,* 170–71.
37. Mifflin Kenedy, Claim for Damages, January 28, 1860, *TFT,* 59–60; and Kenedy, Claim for Damages, *DFT* (1872), 44.
38. *Corpus Christi Ranchero,* November 5, 1859.
39. Affidavit of William D. Thomas and Nathaniel White, November 6, 1859, *DSF,* 49–50. Originally published in the *Corpus Christi Ranchero,* November 12, 1859, and the *Galveston News,* November 10, 1859, both in LR, AGO, RG 94, NA. Also, list of property taken or destroyed by Juan Nepomucino [*sic*] Cortinas ... January 24, 1860, *TFT,* 53; *DFT* (1872), 44; and *New Orleans Daily Picayune,* November 13, 1859. An analysis of the July 1860 Cameron County census indicates that upriver from Rancho Bastón, 197 of 320 dwellings (62 percent) were found "unoccupied" or destroyed. Eighth Census, Cameron County, Texas, NA.
40. Various Claims, January 25–29, *TFT,* 24, 33, 48–48.
41. Miguel Gonzalos [*sic*], Claim for Damages, n.d., *TFT,* 34.
42. Dimas Barreda [*sic*], Claim for Damages, January 26, 1860, *TFT,* 15.
43. *DFT* (1872), 15–62. A month after the Battle of Rio Grande City, for example, Kelsey, the largest merchant in Rio Grande City, wrote José San Román: "Cortina took from me and damaged otherwise near five thousand worth of Mds." Kelsey promised to "make a claim on Uncle Sam for a pile ... whether I get it or not." True to his word, he submitted claims amounting to $31,757. John Kelsey to José San Román, January 26, 1860, San Román Papers, CAH; and John P. Kelsey to Commanding Officer at Ringgold Barracks, *TFT,* 38.
44. Cecilio Solís, Affidavit, January 12, 1860, Sam Houston Papers, TSA.
45. Thompson, ed., *Fifty Miles and a Fight,* 119.
46. Ibid., 120–21.
47. Ibid., 126. Also, *San Antonio Daily Herald,* December 29, 1859.
48. S. P. Heintzelman to Robert E. Lee, March 1, 1860, *TFT,* 2; Thompson, ed., *Fifty Miles and a Fight,* 131–32; *New Orleans Daily True Delta,* December 28, 1859. Capt. James Brewster Rickett's company of the 1st Artillery had arrived a week earlier.

49. Thompson, ed., *Fifty Miles and a Fight*, 132–33; Heintzelman to Lee, March 1, 1860, *TFT*, 7.
50. Thompson, ed., *Fifty Miles and a Fight*, 132–34.
51. Ibid., 136–37.
52. Ibid., 136.
53. Heintzelman to Lee, March 1, 1860, *TFT*, 2; Thompson, ed., *Fifty Miles and a Fight*, 138.
54. [Heintzelman], List of persons killed by Cortinas on the Rio Grande, *TFT*, 75. Featherston was the only regular army soldier killed during the Cortina War. *New Orleans Daily Picayune*, December 30, 1859.
55. Heintzelman to Lee, March 1, 1859, *TFT*, 7.
56. *Dallas Herald*, January 4, 1860.
57. Ibid.
58. Ibid. Also, Heintzelman Pocket Diary, December 14, 15, 1859, Samuel P. Heintzelman Papers, LC; Heintzelman to Washington, December 16, 1859, Cortina War Letters Sent Book, Samuel P. Heintzelman Papers, LC. Hereafter referred to as CWLSB.
59. Heintzelman to S. Cooper, December 18, 1859, CWLSB, Samuel P. Heintzelman Papers, LC.
60. Samuel P. Heintzelman Journals, LC, December 16, 1859.
61. *Report of the Committee of Investigation Sent in 1873*, 195.
62. Tobin to Runnels, December 16, 1859, Hardin R. Runnels Papers, TSA.
63. Hidalgo County Commissioners Court Minutes, vol. A (1853–86), 69–70, Edinburg, Texas.
64. See *State of Texas vs. Teodoro Zamora* (horse stealing), *State vs. Luis López* (larceny), *State vs. José María Martínez* (larceny), *State vs. Trinidad de los Santos* (larceny), *State vs. Juan Nep. Cortina* (horse stealing), *State vs. Anselmo Rosales* (horse stealing), *State vs. Manuel Tapia* (horse stealing), *State vs. José Ma. Martínez* (mule stealing), *State vs. Juan Manl. Zamora* (horse stealing), and *State vs. Melciades de Luna* (horse stealing), all of which are indictments in the fall 1859 term of the district court. With Thadeus M. Rhodes as foreman, the grand jury had a majority of Tejanos. Many of these cases were continued and then dropped in April 1872. Minutes of the District and County Clerk, Hidalgo County, Texas, vol. A (1853–1886), Edinburg, Texas.
65. Heintzelman Pocket Diary, December 21, 1859, Samuel P. Heintzelman Papers, LC.
66. Heintzelman to Lee, March 1, 1860, in *TTF*, 13.
67. Thompson, ed., *Fifty Miles and a Fight*, 145; *Corpus Christi Ranchero*, December 17, 1859; Kingsbury to Mr. Editor, December 29, 1859, Gilbert Kingsbury Papers, CAH. Davis, who had established Rancho Davis just below what became Rio Grande City shortly after the Mexican War, was said to have formed a close "association with the Mexicans," from whom he had acquired a "peculiar style of manner, a mixture of Western frankness and the stateliness of the Spaniard; a low-toned voice, and a deference mixed with assurance." Eighth Census (1860), Starr County, Texas; Viele, *Following the Drum: A Glimpse of Frontier Life*, 145–46.
68. See indictments 194 to 207 against Polinar Sárate, Frylan [Froilán] Cavazos, Desiderio Vela, Palmario Sárate, Victor Morán, Gregorio Aguilar, Bacilio Vela, Ramón Benavides, Fermín Guzmán, Secundo Garza, Lucino Hernández, Dionicio Molla, and Rafael Peña, all in Index to Judgements and Orders, Starr County, Texas, vol. 1 (1858–65), Rio Grande City, Texas. Cortina and "20 other Mexicans" were indicted three times for murder. Also, District Court Records, vol. 3-A (1848–61), Starr County, Rio Grande City, Texas. Like the cases in Hidalgo County, these cases were later dismissed or dropped from the trial docket. Also similar to Hidalgo County, the indictments were handed down by a grand jury composed largely of Tejanos.
69. *DFT* (1872), 32, 36.
70. Ford to Houston, December 29, 1859, enclosed with Green to Cass, January 10, 1859 [1860], General Records of the Department of State, Dispatches from Special Agents, RG 59, NA.
71. *Corpus Christi Ranchero*, January 27, 1860; *New Orleans Daily Picayune*, January 22, 1860. Davis and María Hilaria de la Garza Martínez were the parents of twelve children. Greene, *When Rio Grande City Was Young*, 5.

72. *San Antonio Express,* November 3, 1894.
73. Ford, *Rip Ford's Texas,* 272; *New Orleans Daily True Delta,* January 7, 14, 1860.
74. *New Orleans Daily Picayune,* January 22, 1860; J. T. Hunter, "Cortina War," 7–8.
75. *Corpus Christi Ranchero,* January 7, 1860. Also, *New Orleans Daily True Delta,* January 14, 1860. Another account is in Heintzelman to Washington, December 27, 1859, CWLSB, Samuel P. Heintzelman Papers, LC.
76. Rufus [Abercrombie Byler] to Dearest One [Martha C. Russelman], December 29, 1859, Dobie-Byler Papers, CAH.
77. Ibid.
78. J. T. Hunter, "Historical Reminiscences," *San Antonio Daily Express,* n.d. Clipping in "Cortina File," Library of the Daughters of the Republic of Texas at the Alamo, San Antonio; Heintzelman to Lee, March 1, 1860, *TTF,* 9. An outline of the different engagements of the Cortina War can be found in General Orders no. 11, November 23, 1860, Samuel P. Heintzelman Papers, LC. Also, *Galveston Tri-Weekly News,* January 3, 1860; *San Antonio Daily Herald,* January 6, 1859; R. Fitzpatrick to Cass, January 6, 1860, Matamoros Dispatches, RG 59, NA.
79. *Corpus Christi Ranchero,* January 7, 1860; *New Orleans Daily True Delta,* January 14, 1860.
80. These valuable records were sent to Gov. Hardin R. Runnels but are not in the Hardin R. Runnels or Sam Houston Papers or elsewhere at the Texas State Archives and are presumed to have been lost or destroyed. Report of the Grand Jury on the Disturbances of the County, A. B. Bacon, District Attorney, November 1859, Hardin R. Runnels Papers, TSA. Also, *Texas State Gazette* (Austin), January 14, 1860; *San Antonio Alamo Express,* October 1, 1860, quoting *Brownsville American Flag,* n.d.
81. The *Austin Southern Intelligencer Extra* on the morning of January 7 was typical: "Glorious News. Cortina & Men Badly Whipped. 60 Outlaws Killed." *Austin Southern Intelligencer Extra,* January 7, 1860, enclosed with Duff Green to Lewis Cass, Dispatches from Special Agents, Records of the Department of State, RG 59, NA.
82. Tobin to Houston, January 2, 1860, Sam Houston Papers, TSA.
83. Ford to [Houston], December 29, 1859, Sam Houston Papers, TSA.
84. Fitzpatrick to Cass, January 6, 1861, Matamoros Dispatches, RG 59, NA.
85. Ford to Houston, December 29, 1859, enclosed with Green to Cass, January 10, 1860, Records of the Department of State, RG 59, NA.
86. *Corpus Christi Ranchero,* January 14, 1860.
87. Ibid.
88. *Corpus Christi Ranchero,* January 27, 1860.
89. Eighth Census (1860), Starr County, Texas.
90. Noah Cox to Heintzelman, December 27, 1859, Samuel P. Heintzelman Papers, LC; Heintzelman to Cooper, December 27, 1859, CWLSB, Samuel P. Heintzelman Papers, LC. Also, Thompson, ed., *Fifty Miles and a Fight,* 157.
91. Heintzelman to Wm. G. Tobin, January 2, 1860, CWLSB, Samuel P. Heintzelman Papers, LC.
92. Affidavit, Santiago Solís, January 12, 1860, Sam Houston Papers, TSA.
93. Affidavit, O. H. Carolan, January 13, 1860, Sam Houston Papers. TSA.
94. Thompson, ed., *Fifty Miles and a Fight,* 161.
95. Ford, *Rip Ford's Texas,* 276.
96. *El Jaque* (Matamoros), January 14, 1860.
97. Samuel P. Heintzelman Journals, LC, January 31, 1860.
98. Fitzpatrick to Cass, April 1, 1860, Matamoros Dispatches, RG 59, NA.
99. J. Thompson to John B. Floyd, June 23, 1860, LR, AGO, RG 94, NA.
100. Samuel P. Heintzelman Journals, LC, February 10, 1860.
101. Heintzelman to Withers, February 10, 1860, CWLSB, Samuel P. Heintzelman Papers, LC. Also, Orders no. 10, February 8, 1860; and Orders no. 11, January 28, 1860; both in Cortina War Orders Book, Samuel P. Heintzelman Papers, LC.

102. *Corpus Christi Ranchero*, April 7, 1860; Tobin to Houston, February 6, 1860, Sam Houston Papers, TSA.

103. Ford, *Rip Ford's Texas*, 285–86. If Ford is correct, it is possible he gained his information while visiting Cortina at Azacapotzalco outside Mexico City in October 1891.

104. *Report of the Committee of Investigation Sent in 1873*, 195.

105. Heintzelman to Lee, March 1, 1860, *TTF*, 10; *Brownsville American Flag*, February 9, 1860; *New Orleans Daily Picayune*, February 12, 1860; *New Orleans Daily True Delta*, February 12, 1860; *San Antonio Daily Herald*, February 14, 1860. At the time, there was considerable confusion over exactly what happened at La Bolsa. The best initial accounts are Ford to Heintzelman, February 8, 1860; and Loomis Langdon to Heintzelman, April 28, 1860; both in Samuel P. Heintzelman Papers, LC. See also, Heintzelman to Withers, April 29, 1860, CWLSB, Samuel P. Heintzelman Papers, LC.

106. Heintzelman to Withers, April 29, 1860, CWLSB, Samuel P. Heintzelman Papers, LC.

107. Endorsement on Stoneman to Withers, June 1, 1860, LR, AGO, RG 94, NA.

108. *Report of the Committee of Investigation Sent in 1873*, 195.

109. *New Orleans Daily Picayune*, February 12, 1860.

110. Heintzelman to Lee, March 1, 1860, in *TTF*, 11.

111. Ibid.

112. Heintzelman to Ford, February 4, 1860, Samuel P. Heintzelman Papers, LC. Also, Heintzelman to Ford, February 5, 1860; Heintzelman to A. T. Lee, February 4, 1860; and Heintzelman to Stoneman, February 4, 1860; all in Samuel P. Heintzelman Papers, LC. Also, Heintzelman to Joaquín Arguilles, February 11, 1860, CWLSB, Samuel P. Heintzelman Papers, LC; and Langdon to Heintzelman, February 4, 1860, LR, AGO, RG 94, NA. For specifics on the incident, see Thompson, ed., *Fifty Miles and a Fight*, 188–91.

113. Samuel P. Heintzelman Journals, LC, February 8, 1860.

114. *Corpus Christi Ranchero*, February 15, 1860.

115. Samuel P. Heintzelman Journals, LC, February 15, 1860. Also, Heintzelman to John Withers, February 29, 1860, *Difficulties between the People of Texas and Mexico*, 5. The original of this letter is in LR, AGO, RG 94, NA, and is copied in CWLSB, Samuel P. Heintzelman Papers, LC.

116. Ford, *Rip Ford's Texas*, 295; George Stoneman and John S. Ford to C. W. Thomas, March 18, 1860, in *TTF*, 80–81. Also, Stoneman to Heintzelman, March 18, 1860; Stoneman to Heintzelman, March 19, 1860; Heintzelman to Stoneman, March 18, 1860; and Ford to Heintzelman, March 18, 1860; all in Samuel P. Heintzelman Papers, LC; Heintzelman to Withers, March 18, 1860, LR, AGO, RG 94, NA; and *Corpus Christi Ranchero*, March 24, 1860.

117. Heintzelman to Withers, March 8, 1860, LR, AGO, RG 94, NA.

118. García to General of Brigade, March 11, 1860; Heintzelman to García, March 11, 1860; Heintzelman to Stoneman, March 12, 1860; all in Samuel P. Heintzelman Papers, LC. Also, Arnold, *Jeff Davis's Own: Cavalry, Comanches, and the Battle for the Texas Frontier*, 276–77.

119. Heintzelman to Withers, February 29, 1860, LR, AGO, RG 94, NA.

120. Samuel P. Heintzelman Journals, LC, April 6, 1860. For details, see Thompson, ed., *Fifty Miles and a Fight*, 125–26 and Ford, *Rip Ford's Texas*, 296–97.

121. R. E. Lee to Andrés Treviño, April 2, 1860, in Jenkins, ed., *Robert E. Lee on the Rio Grande: The Correspondence of Robert E. Lee on the Texas Border, 1860*, 12–13. Most of the letters in this collection are from *TTF*. Also, Heintzelman to Manuel Treviño, April 3, 1860, CWLSB, Samuel P. Heintzelman Papers, LC.

122. Lee to the Civil and Military Authorities of the City of Reynosa, Mexico, April 7, 1860, Jenkins, ed., *Robert E. Lee on the Rio Grande*, 13–14.

123. Lee to G. García, April 12, 1860, Jenkins, ed., *Robert E. Lee on the Rio Grande*, 20–21.

124. Andrés Treviño to Lee, April 15, 1860, LR, AGO, RG 94, NA.

125. Samuel P. Heintzelman Journals, LC, April 9, 1860.

126. Francisco Zepeda to Lee, April 8, 1860, *TTF*, 86–87. Translated copy in LR, AGO, RG 94, NA.

127. Heintzelman to Lee, March 1, 1860, *TTF,* 13.
128. Sam Houston Inaugural Address, Executive Record Book (December 27, 1859–November 1, 1862), TSA.
129. Haley, *Sam Houston,* 366.
130. *New Orleans Daily True Delta,* January 1, 1860.
131. Houston to Ford, December 30, 1859, Sam Houston Papers, TSA. A copy of Houston's personal letter to Cortina could not be located although its general content can be ascertained by Houston's comments to Ford.
132. Ibid.
133. Ford to Houston, February 8, 1860, Sam Houston Papers, TSA.
134. Sam Houston, Proclamation by the Governor of the State of Texas, December 28, 1859, Sam Houston Papers, TSA.
135. Houston to All Texians, January 7, 1860, Sam Houston Papers, TSA.
136. Samuel P. Heintzelman Journals, LC, January 16, 1859; Withers to Heintzelman, January 4, 1860, Samuel P. Heintzelman Papers, LC; Orders to Ángel Navarro and Richard Taylor, January 2, 1860, in A. Williams and Barker, eds., *The Writings of Sam Houston, 1813–1863,* 7:395–96. Houston's letter to Navarro and Taylor was reprinted in the *San Antonio Daily Herald,* January 20, 1859. Also, *San Antonio Daily Herald,* January 5, 6, 1860; Heintzelman to Tobin, January 16, 1860, CWLSB, Samuel P. Heintzelman Papers, LC; and Houston to Navarro and Taylor, January 2, 1860, miscellaneous newspaper clipping, n.d., Sam Houston Papers, TSA.
137. *Austin Southern Intelligencer,* n.d., John L. Haynes Papers, CAH.
138. *Brownsville American Flag,* n.d., quoted in *San Antonio Daily Herald,* January 24, 1860. From the time the two men arrived on the border, they were somewhat at odds with each other. Navarro was miffed that Taylor took upon "himself the whole responsibility of the commission" and that he was constantly "putting on airs." Navarro was "young and inexperienced" and valued only as an interpreter, or so Taylor thought. Navarro to Houston, February 15, 1860 (first quotation); Navarro to Houston, February 18, 1860 (second quotation); both in Sam Houston Papers, TSA.
139. Ángel Navarro to Houston, January 4, 1860, Sam Houston Papers, TSA.
140. José Antonio Navarro to Juan Nepomuceno Cortina, January 4, 1860, Sam Houston Papers, TSA. The younger Navarro also carried a letter of introduction from Jas. Walworth to José San Ramón, one of the most influential men on the border. See Jas. Walworth to José San Ramón, January 2, 1860, San Ramón Papers, CAH.
141. Navarro and Taylor to Houston, February 4, 1860, Sam Houston Papers, TSA.
142. E. B. Scarborough to Peter Champion, January 2, 1860, Sam Houston Papers, TSA. Somehow, Houston must have obtained a copy of Scarborough's letter.
143. *Corpus Christi Ranchero,* February 11, 1860.
144. Quoted in the *Austin Southern Intelligencer,* n.d., John L. Haynes Papers, CAH.
145. *Austin Southern Intelligencer,* n.d., John L. Haynes Papers, CAH.
146. Taylor to Houston, January 16, 1860, Sam Houston Papers, TSA.
147. Navarro and Taylor to Houston, February 4, 1860; Heintzelman to Navarro and Taylor, February 2, 1860; both in Sam Houston Papers, TSA.
148. Roy Sylvan Dunn, "The KGC in Texas, 1860–1861," *Southwestern Historical Quarterly* 70 (April 1967): 543–69; C. A. Bridges, "The Knights of the Golden Circle: A Filibustering Fantasy," *Southwestern Historical Quarterly* 44 (January 1941): 287–302; Ollinger Crenshaw, "The Knights of the Golden Circle: The Career of George Bickley," *American Historical Review* 47 (October 1941): 23–50; *Galveston Weekly News,* February 16, 1861. Also, May, *Manifest Destiny's Underworld,* 43–44.
149. Samuel P. Heintzelman Journals, LC, April 12, 1860. As many as one hundred of the filibusters were led by the notorious William Robertson "Big Bill" Henry, the grandson of Patrick Henry. Henry, who had been shot in the leg in the skirmish with Cortina at La Bolsa, was later killed in a gun battle in San Antonio's Main Plaza in 1862. May, *Manifest Destiny's Underworld,* 43; Thompson, ed., *Fifty Miles and a Fight,* 126–27.

150. Navarro and Taylor to Houston, February 4, 1860, Sam Houston Papers, TSA; Thompson, ed., *Fifty Miles and a Fight,* 230.

151. Stephen Powers to Taylor and Navarro, January 14, 1860, Sam Houston Papers, TSA.

152. Navarro and Taylor to Houston, February 4, 1860, Sam Houston Papers, TSA.

153. Navarro to Houston, January 26, 1860, Sam Houston Papers, TSA.

154. Navarro and Taylor to Houston, February 4, 1860, Sam Houston Papers, TSA.

155. Navarro to Houston, February 15, 1860, Sam Houston Papers, TSA.

156. Navarro to Houston, January 31, 1860, Sam Houston Papers, TSA.

157. Navarro and Taylor to Houston, February 4, 1860, Sam Houston Papers, TSA.

158. *New Orleans Daily True Delta,* n.d., in Sam Houston Papers, TSA.

159. Houston to John B. Floyd, February 13, 1860, Sam Houston Papers, TSA. This letter was published in the *San Antonio Daily Herald,* March 9, 1860.

160. Houston to McCulloch, February 13, 1860, Sam Houston Papers, TSA.

161. F. Britton to Houston, March 3, 1860, Sam Houston Papers, TSA. Within a year, Britton was dead. *Corpus Christi Ranchero,* April 6, 1861.

162. Ibid.

163. Ibid.

164. Houston to John B. Floyd, March 8, 1860, in "Difficulties between the People of Texas and Mexico," 6–7.

165. Houston to Jno. B. Floyd, March 8, 1860, Sam Houston Papers, TSA.

166. L. D. Evans to Houston, March 19, 1860, Sam Houston Papers, TSA.

167. W. R. Drinkard to Houston, March 14, 1860, in "Difficulties between the People of Texas and Mexico," 7.

168. Houston to Tobin, March 3, 1860, Sam Houston Papers, TSA. If Tobin responded to Houston's request, the reply has been lost to history.

169. Houston Proclamation, March 21, 1860, Sam Houston Papers, TSA.

170. Duff Green to Lewis Cass, December 3, 1859, Dispatches from Special Agents, RG 59, NA. Also, Richard E. Ellis, "Duff Green," in Roller and Twyman, eds., *Encyclopedia of Southern History,* 558; Fletcher M. Green, "Duff Green: Industrial Promoter," *Journal of Southern History* 2 (February 1936): 28–42; Fletcher M. Green, "Duff Green, Militant Journalist of the Old School," *American Historical Review* 52 (January 1947): 2437–68. The papers of Duff Green and his son, Ben E. Green, are in the Southern Historical Collection at the University of North Carolina, Chapel Hill.

171. Green to Cass, December 10, 1859, Dispatches from Special Agents, RG 59, NA.

172. Green to Cass, December 24, 1859, Dispatches from Special Agents, RG 59, NA.

173. Ibid.

174. Green to Cass, January 7, 1859 [1860], Dispatches from Special Agents, RG 59, NA.

175. Green to Cass, January 9, 1859 [1860], Dispatches from Special Agents, RG 59, NA.

176. Green to Cass, [February] 10, 1860, Dispatches from Special Agents, RG 59, NA. Green enclosed a newspaper clipping in which Houston outlines the state's budget for the Texas Senate. "The Executive is looking anxiously toward a settlement of our difficulties upon the Rio Grande; but he may yet be compelled by the force of circumstances to call into the field the entire force at his command." Houston to Gentlemen of the Senate, newspaper clipping, n.d., enclosed with ibid.

177. Jeremiah Galván to Heintzelman, June 24, 1860, Samuel P. Heintzelman Papers, LC.

178. Lee, Special Orders, April 30, 1860, LR, AGO, RG 94, NA.

179. Lee to S. Cooper, April 26, 1860, LR, AGO, RG 94, NA.

180. Lee to Cooper, May 2, 1860; Lee to Stoneman, May 1, 1860; Lee to Brackett, May 1, 1860; all in LR, AGO, RG 94, NA.

181. Lee to Cooper, May 7, 1860, LR, AGO, RG 94, NA.

182. Lee to Cooper, May 8, 1860, LR, AGO, RG 94, NA.

183. *Corpus Christi Ranchero,* May 26, 1860.

184. Stoneman to Withers, June 1, 1860; Henry J. Hunt to Asst. Adjt. Gen'l., Dept. of Texas, June 1, 1860; Lee to Cooper, June 13, 1860; all in LR, AGO, RG 94, NA.

185. *Texas State Gazette* (Austin), April 27, 1861. In Austin, it was rumored Cortina had crossed the river and killed eighteen Americans in Roma.
186. Stoneman to Heintzelman, July 8, 1860, Samuel P. Heintzelman Papers, LC.
187. Ibid.
188. Stoneman to Withers, June 1, 1860, LR, AGO, RG 94, NA.
189. Cortina, Compiled Military Service Record, Archivo de Secretaría de Defensa, Mexico City.

CHAPTER FOUR

1. *Corpus Christi Ranchero*, March 30, 1861.
2. John S. Ford to Edward Clark, April 16, 1861, McAllen Ranch Archives, Linn, Texas.
3. Lott and Martínez, *The Kingdom of Zapata*, 42–43.
4. Gardner W. Pierce to [John Z. Leyendecker], June 1, 1861, John Z. Leyendecker Papers, CAH; Baum, *The Shattering of Texas Unionism: Politics in the Lone Star State During the Civil War Era*, 75–76.
5. *Corpus Christi Ranchero*, April 20, 1861.
6. Gardner W. Pierce to [John Z. Leyendecker], June 1, 1861, John Z. Leyendecker Papers, CAH.
7. *Corpus Christi Ranchero*, April 20, 1861; *Alamo Express* (San Antonio), April 20, 1861.
8. Henry Redmond to John S. Ford, April 12, 1861, Edward Clark Papers, TSA. Also, John D. Mussett to Captain Brown, October 18, 1861, Letters Received, Confederate District of Texas, New Mexico, and Arizona, RG 109, NA.
9. Mussett to Stephen Powers, April 12, 1861, Edward Clark Papers, TSA. This same letter is in Letters Received, Confederate Adjutant General's Office, RG 401, NA.
10. Eighth Census (1860), Zapata County, Texas, NA.
11. *Corpus Christi Ranchero*, May 18, 1861.
12. Ford to Nolan, April 17, 1861, Edward Clark Papers, TSA; *Corpus Christi Ranchero*, April 27, 1861. As a result of his service during the Mexican War, Nolan had become known in South Texas as the "Boy Bugler of the Battle of Cerro Gordo." For his election as sheriff, see *Corpus Christi Ranchero*, August 11, 1860. In the years after the Mexican War, Nolan joined Capt. John S. Ford's company of Rangers in the Nueces Strip as a bugler. Later he was elected sheriff of Nueces County. Nolan was murdered in Corpus Christi on December 22, 1864. B. Walraven, *Corpus Christi: The History of a Texas Seaport*, 53.
13. Pierce to [Leyendecker], June 1, 1861, John Z. Leyendecker Papers, CAH.
14. *Corpus Christi Ranchero*, April 27, 1861. Santiago Vela, fifty-seven, a victim of "*una armada de aquel estado*," was buried in Guerrero at 10 A.M. on the same day, April 15, 1861. Registro Civil de Guerrero, *Libro de Defunciones, 1860–1861*, 26–27, Nuevo Guerrero Archives, Nuevo Guerrero, Tamaulipas. Ford would write that Nolan "killed eleven of the '*pronunciadores*' at eleven shots," perhaps further indicating that it was a massacre. "Memoirs of John S. Ford," CAH, 921.
15. *Committee of Investigation Sent in 1873*, 66; and *Galveston Tri-Weekly News*, May 7, 1861. For a more detailed study of the turmoil in Zapata County, see Thompson, *Vaqueros in Blue and Gray*, 15–23; and Thompson, *Mexican Texans in the Union Army*, 1–7.
16. Redmond to Ford, May 14, 1861, John S. Ford Papers, Haley Memorial Library and History Center, Midland, Texas.
17. *Texas State Gazette* (Austin), June 8, 1861; Ysidro Vela to Ford, May 14, 1861, John S. Ford Papers, Haley Memorial Library and History Center.
18. *Texas State Gazette* (Austin), June 8, 1861.
19. M. Sanders to Ford, May 27, 1861, Edward Clark Papers, TSA.
20. H. Clay Davis to Nolan, May 5, 1861, Edward Clark Papers, TSA.
21. *Corpus Christi Ranchero*, June 8, 1861; [Juan G. Garza] to Jefe Político del Distrito del Norte, May 19, 1861, Correspondencia del Alcalde de Guerrero, Nuevo Guerrero Archives.
22. [Garza] to Santos Benavides, May 18, 1861, Correspondencia del Alcalde de Guerrero; *Texas State Gazette* (Austin), June 15, 1861.

23. Gardner W. Pierce to [John Z. Leyendecker], June 1, 1861, John Z. Leyendecker Papers, CAH.

24. *Corpus Christi Ranchero*, May 18, 1861; Redmond to Ford, May 23, 1861, Broadside File, TSA.

25. Benavides to Ford, May 23, 1861, John S. Ford Papers, Haley Memorial Library and History Center. Ford copies Benavides's letter verbatim in his memoirs. John S. Ford Memoirs, CAH, 3:923–24. Gen. E. Kirby Smith was so excited that he authorized Benavides to raise a regiment of "Partisan Rangers" on the border. Also, Benavides to Ford, May 14, 1861, John S. Ford Papers, Haley Memorial Library and History Center and *Corpus Christi Ranchero* June 1, 8, 1861. Benavides told José María Hinojosa that ten of Cortina's "men were left dead on the field and that the others were dispersed in all directions." [Juan G. Garza] to Jefe Político del Distrito del Norte, May 22, 1861, Correspondencia del Alcalde de Guerrero. Yet in a letter to his friend Santiago Vidaurri, Benavides said seven *Cortinistas* were killed. Benavides to Vidaurri, June 10, 1861, Correspondencia de Santiago Vidaurri, Archivo Gen. del Estado de Nuevo León, Monterrey, Mexico.

26. Pierce to [Leyendecker], June 1, 1861, John Z. Leyendecker Papers, CAH. Also, *Texas State Gazette* (Austin), June 15, 1861.

27. Vidaurri to Secretary of State, July 1, 1861, *Benito Juárez: Documentos, Discursos y Correspondencia*, 4:619–21. Hereafter referred to as *Correspondencia de Juárez* and by volume.

28. [Juan G. Garza] to Santos Benavides and Cristobal Benavides, May 31, 1861, Correspondencia del Alcalde de Guerrero, Archivo de Nuevo Guerrero. Copy courtesy of Stanley Green.

29. Ford to Benavides, May 29, 1861, and June 2, 1861, both in John S. Ford Papers, Haley Memorial Library and History Center; and John S. Ford Memoirs, CAH, 3:926–27; Mat[ias] Longoria to President de Guerrero Ayuntamiento, May 29, 1861, Nuevo Guerrero Archives.

30. John Littleton to Ford, June 12, 1861, enclosed with Ford to Clark, June 14, 1861, Edward Clark Papers, TSA.

31. Ford to Clark, June 14, 1861, Edward Clark Papers, TSA; and John S. Ford Memoirs, CAH, 6:921.

32. Ford to Clark, July 14, 1861, Edward Clark Papers, TSA. Five years later, on December 8, 1866, Davis accidentally shot and killed himself with a shotgun near Rio Grande City while riding in a carriage on a hunting expedition with several officers from Ringgold Barracks. *New Orleans Daily Crescent*, December 22, 1866; *Corpus Christi Ranchero*, May 18, 1861; *Brownsville Daily Ranchero*, December 12, 1866.

33. Ford to Clark, June 14, 1861, Edward Clark Papers, TSA.

34. Ford to Clark, June 30, 1861, Edward Clark Papers, TSA; M. Capistrán to [Ford], October 19, 1861, Letters Received, Dist. of Texas, N.M., and Arizona, RG 109, NA.

35. *Two Republics* (Mexico City). September 1, 1875; Thompson, *Juan Cortina*, 81.

36. Ridley, *Maximilian and Juárez*, 126–27.

37. Ibid.

38. J. W. Hunter, "The Fall of Brownsville," 4–5, CAH; Leonard Pierce to William Seward, March 1, 1862, *Official Records of the Union and Confederate Navies in the War of the Rebellion* (hereafter referred to as *OR*), I, 9, 674. Also, Tyler, "Cotton on the Border, 1861–1865," 456. Some of the larger firms operating on the Rio Grande included: Droege, Oetling and Company; Brown, Fleming and Company; Harding, Pullin and Company of London; Lloyd's of London; Treviño Brothers; Oliver Brothers of Monterrey; Attrill and Lacosta; and Marks and Company. See Daddysman, *Matamoros Trade*, 31. For an excellent account of Matamoros during the war, see Delaney, "Matamoros: Port for Texas during the Civil War," 473–87; Ed. J. Allen to John Price, January 12, 1866, LR, AGO, RG 94, NA; Wooster, *Texas and Texans in the Civil War*, 120; Rippy, *The United States and Mexico*, 238.

39. Daddysman, *Matamoros Trade*, 33; Rayburn and Rayburn, eds., *Century of Conflict*, 83; Theodorus Bailey to Gideon Welles, *OR* I, 17, 403. Also, *Brownsville Daily Ranchero*, December 16, 1866; and Tyler, *Santiago Vidaurri and the Southern Confederacy*, 106–108.

40. *Matamoros Daily Ranchero*, January 18, 1866; *New York Herald*, July 2, 29, 1865; *Brownsville Weekly Ranchero*, June 15, 1867.

41. *Houston Tri-Weekly Telegraph*, December 8, 1864; Parisot, *Reminiscences of a Texas Missionary*, 56.

42. Hinojosa, *A Borderlands Town in Transition: Laredo, 1755–1870*, 83; J. A. Quintero to J. P. Benjamin, December 1, 1862, John T. Pickett Papers, LC.

43. *Brownsville Bandera Americana*, January 2, 1863, quoted in the *Monterrey Boletín Oficial*, n.d., copy in John T. Pickett Papers, LC. Also, Quintero to Benjamin, January 30, 1863, John T. Pickett Papers, LC; Journal of James Hampton Kuykendall, December 27, 28, 1863, CAH.

44. *Brownsville Fort Brown Flag*, February 2, 1863, quoted in the *Corpus Christi Ranchero*, January 22, 1863; *Brownsville Bandera Americana*, February 2, 1863, quoted in the *Monterrey Boletín Oficial*, n.d., copy in John T. Pickett Papers, LC.

45. Quintero to Benjamin, January 30, 1863, John T. Pickett Papers, LC.

46. *Reports of the Committee of Investigation Sent in 1873*, 69; H. P. Bee to Albino López, April 22, 1863, *OR*, I, 15, 1051–53.

47. *Corpus Christi Ranchero*, January 15, 23, February 5, 1863; *Houston Tri-Weekly Telegraph*, February 2, 1863; *Confederate Veteran* (1922), 473; Quintero to Benjamin, January 30, 1863, John T. Pickett Papers, LC.

48. H. P. Bee to Albino López, March 19, 1863; Albino López to [H. P. Bee], March 20, 1863, *OR*, I, 15, pt. 1, 133; Octaviano Zapata to Antonio Pérez, July 24, 1863, Correspondencia de Santiago Vidaurri, Archivo Gen. del Estado de Nuevo León. At this time, Leonard Pierce Jr., the American consul in Matamoros, reported that he had three hundred muskets in his possession. It is probable these arms were intended for Zapata's guerrillas. L. Pierce Jr., to W. H. Seward, April 10, 1863, Matamoros Consular Dispatches, RG 59, NA.

49. Benavides to William O. Yager, September 3, 1863, *OR*, I, 14, 285; *Reports of the Committee of Investigation Sent in 1873*, 200–203; *Corpus Christi Ranchero*, September 17, 1863.

50. Smart, *Viva Juárez! A Biography*, 58, 81, 100, 151, 155, 164, 170, 291; Ruiz, *Triumph and Tragedy: A History of the Mexican People*, 235; *Houston Tri-Weekly Telegraph*, August 28, 1863.

51. Hamilton P. Bee to Manuel Ruiz, September 12, 1863, *OR*, I, 26, pt. 2, 222; Bee to Ruiz, September 12, 1863, *OR*, 1, 26, pt. 2, 222.

52. Nathaniel P. Banks to Abraham Lincoln, November 3, 1863, *OR*, I, 26, pt. 1, 396. Also, Banks to H. W. Halleck, November 4, 1863, *OR*, I, 25, pt. 1, 397–98; and Banks to Halleck, November 6, 1863, *OR*, I, 26, pt. 1, 399–400.

53. Townsend, *A Yankee Invasion of Texas*, 18–19.

54. Thompson, *Mexican Texans in the Union Army*, 10–15; A. Lincoln to Edwin M. Stanton, August 4, 1862, in *The Collected Works of Abraham Lincoln*, 5:357; Cortina to John L. Haynes, September 12, 1863, letter in private collection.

55. *Houston Tri-Weekly Telegraph*, November 12, 1863, quoting the *Brownsville Fort Brown Flag*, October 30, 1863.

56. James Duff to E. R. Tarver, November 11, 1863, *OR*, I, 26, pt. 1, 439–43; Bee to Edmund P. Turner, October 28, 1863, *OR*, I, 26, pt. 1, 448–49; Adrián J. Vidal, C.S.R., (Union), RG 54, NA; Thompson, *Vaqueros in Blue and Gray*, 71–74. Also, *Houston Tri-Weekly Telegraph*, November 12, 1863, quoting the *Brownsville Fort Brown Flag*, October 30, 1863.

57. Duff to Tarver, November 11, 1863, *OR*, I, 26, pt. 1, 439–44. Also, Williams, *With the Border Ruffians*, 201. Dashiell, son of the Texas adjutant general, was buried in the old Brownsville Cemetery, not far from where William Neale, one of Cortina's victims from his September 28, 1859, raid, lay buried.

58. Duff to Tarver, November 11, 1863, *OR*, 1, 26, pt. 1, 439–43.

59. Several of Vidal's men were later arrested for murders committed in Mexico and were executed by firing squad in Matamoros in January 1867. *Brownsville Daily Ranchero*, January 18, 1867; *Galveston Weekly News*, November 18, 1863. Also, Tarver to Commanding Officer at Ringgold Barracks, October 18, 1863, Bee Letterbook, United States Military Academy, West Point (USMA). One of those killed in the violence was Thomas Jefferson Barthelow whose wife and three children survived when they were secluded by a Mexican boy. E-mail, Ernestine Grace to author, June 30, 2002. Author's files.

60. Bee to Ruiz, October 28, 1863, both in *OR*, I, 26, pt. 1, 450; and Bee to Ruiz, November 8, 1863, *OR*, I, 26, pt. 1, 434–35; Ruiz to Bee, October 28, 1863, *OR*, I, 26, pt. 1, 450; *Houston Tri-Weekly Telegraph*, November 12, 1863, quoting the *Brownsville Fort Brown Flag*, October 30, 1863.

61. *Houston Tri-Weekly Telegraph*, November 12, 1863, quoting the *Brownsville Fort Brown Flag*, October 30, 1863. Also, Ruiz to Juárez, November 4, 1863, in Sánchez Gómez, ed., *Catálogo de fuentes de la historia de Tamaulipas: Segunda parte, Biblioteca Nacional de Mexico, Departamento de Manuscritos*, 48.

62. Charles Stillman to Dear Eliz[abeth], December 1, 1863, Charles Stillman Papers, Harvard University Library.

63. Bee to Turner, November 5, 1863, *OR*, I, 26, pt. 1, 435–35.

64. N. P. Banks to H. W. Halleck November 6, 1863, *OR*, I, 26, pt. 1, 399–400. Banks referred to Cobos as a "desperate man." Thompson, *Juan Cortina*, 30. Also, Bee to A. G. Dickinson, March 3, 1863, Letters Received, Dist. of Texas, N.M., and Arizona, RG 109, NA.

65. Unsigned letter to Juárez, November 7, 1863, *Correspondencia de Juárez*, 8:314–16; *Houston Tri-Weekly Telegraph*, November 27, 1863; Kearney and Knopp, *Boom and Bust*, 127–28; José María Cobos to his Companions in Arms, November 6, 1863, *OR*, I, 26, pt. 1, 401.

66. Pierce to [Seward], January 16, 1864, Matamoros Consular Dispatches, RG 59, NA; *Houston Tri-Weekly Telegraph*, February 5, 1864; Tilley, ed., *Federals on the Frontier: The Diary of Benjamin F. McIntyre, 1862–1864*, 288–89; Bee to Edmund P. Turner, November 15, 1863, *OR*, 1, 26, pt. 2, 415; Juan Nepomuceno [Cortina] to the Public, November 8, 1863, *OR*, I, 26, pt. 1, 406–407; Banks to Halleck, November 6, 1863, *OR*, I, 26, pt. 1, 399–400; Santiago Vidaurri to Benito Juárez, November 7, 1863, *Correspondencia de Juárez*, 8:315; and Eufemio Rojas to Juárez, December 12, 1863, in Sánchez Gómez, ed., *Catálogo de fuentes de la historia de Tamaulipas*, 32. Bee was under the impression that Cobos had been executed on the main plaza in Matamoros. Turner to Bee, November 15, 1863, *OR*, I, 26, pt. 2, 415.

67. Banks to Halleck, November 7, 1863, *OR*, I, 26, pt. 1, 403; Banks to Pierce, November 7, 1863, *OR*, I, 26, pt. 1, 405.

68. Manuel Ruiz to the Garrison of Matamoros, November 7, 1863; Ruiz to the Citizens of Matamoros, November 7, 1863; both in *OR*, I, 26, pt. 1, 404; Banks to Halleck, November 6, 1863, *OR*, I, 26, pt. 1, 399–400; Thompson, *Juan Cortina*, 31; Ruiz to Juárez, November 8, 1863, in Sánchez Gómez, ed., *Catálogo de fuentes de la historia de Tamaulipas*, 24.

69. Herron to Charles P. Stone, January 16, 1864, *OR*, I, 34, pt. 2, 92–93; Tilley, ed., *Federals on the Frontier*, 290; Ruiz to Juárez, December 21, 1863, *Correspondencia de Juárez*, 8:452–54.

70. N. J. T. Dana to Stone, December 2, 1863, *OR*, I, 26, pt. 1, 840. Also, Muster Roll of Vidal's Partisan Rangers, Adjutant Gen.'s Records, TSA. Muster rolls of the 1st and 2nd Texas Cavalry were reprinted in *Adjutant General's Report, 1873* (Austin, 1875), 111–12.

71. A. J. Vidal to H. Clamp [sic], May 30, 1864, Vidal, Compiled Service Record, RG 94, NA; Thompson, *Mexican Texans in the Union Army*, 27.

72. Banks to Halleck November 9, 1863, *OR*, I, 26, pt. 2, 405.

73. Tilley, ed., *Federals on the Frontier*, 293; Banks to Halleck, November 6, 1863, *OR*, I, 26, pt. 1, 400.

74. Quintero to Benjamin, November 26, 1863, *OR*, I, 26, pt. 2, 890.

75. John A. McClernand to Cortina, April 6, 1864, *OR*, I, 34, pt. 3, 60; McClernand to Cortina, April 7, 1864, *OR*, I, 34, pt. 3, 73.

76. Cortina to McClernand, April 7, 1864, *OR*, I, 34, pt. 3, 73–74.

77. C. S. West to J. B. Magruder, December 2, 1863, *OR*, 26, pt. 2, 468; Turner to Bee, December 5, 1863, *OR*, I, 26, pt. 2, 483.

78. Cortina to Vidaurri, November 30, 1863, Correspondencia de Santiago Vidaurri, Archivo Gen. del Estado de Nuevo León.

79. Vidaurri to Juárez, December 6, 1863, *Correspondencia de Juárez*, 8:451–52; Juárez to Vidaurri, December 13, 1863, *Correspondencia de Juárez*, 8:459.

80. Jesús Terán to Juárez, December 21, 1863, *Correspondencia de Juárez*, 8:455.

81. Vidaurri to Juárez, December 27, 1863, *Correspondencia de Juárez,* 8:475–76; Vidaurri to Cortina, December 4, 1863, Correspondencia de Vidaurri, Archivo Gen. del Estado de Nuevo León.

82. Cortina to Vidaurri, December 28, 1863, Correspondencia de Santiago Vidaurri, Archivo Gen. del Estado de Nuevo León. Vidaurri had previously sent a small number of men to assist Cortina while asking for armaments, especially rifles, which Cortina was unable to deliver.

83. Dana to Stone, December 11, 1863, *OR,* I, 26, pt. 1, 843–44. Also, Abbott, "Business Travel Out of Texas during the Civil War: The Travel Diary of S. B. Brush, Pioneer Austin Merchant," 263.

84. Dana to Stone, December 18, 1863, *OR,* I, 26, pt. 1, 864–65.

85. Tilley, ed., *Federals on the Frontier,* 290; Agreement to Establish Peace and Order in Tamaulipas, January 1, 1864, *Correspondencia de Juárez,* 8:527; Herron to Stone, January 16, 1864, *OR,* 1, 34, pt. 2, 92; Herron to Banks, January 10, 1864, *Correspondencia de Juárez,* January 10, 1864, 8:532. Also, Daddysman, *Matamoros Trade,* 96.

86. Tilley, ed., *Federals on the Frontier,* 290; *Houston Tri-Weekly Telegraph,* January 16, 1864; Ruiz to Herron, January 15, 1864, *Correspondencia de Juárez,* 8:540–41.

87. Ruiz to Juárez, January 12, 1864, *Correspondencia de Juárez,* 8:533–34.

88. Herron to Banks, January 10, 1864, *Correspondencia de Juárez,* 8:532.

89. Ruiz to Herron, January 15, 1864, *Correspondencia de Juárez,* 8:542.

90. Tilley, ed., *Federals on the Frontier,* 290.

91. Ruiz to Juárez, January 5, 1864, *Correspondencia de Juárez,* 8:529.

92. Ruiz to Juárez, January 8, 1864, *Correspondencia de Juárez,* 8:531. Also, Herron to Stone, January 16, 1864, *OR,* 1, 34, pt. 2, 92; Pierce to Seward, January 16, 1864, Matamoros Consular Dispatches, RG 59, NA. This letter was printed in "Conditions of Affairs in the Republic of Mexico," no. 1262, 301–302. See also, Tilley, ed., *Federals on the Frontier,* 291.

93. Pierce to [William H. Seward], January 16, 1864, Matamoros Dispatches, RG 59, NA; Ruiz to Herron, January 15, 1864, *Correspondencia de Juárez,* 8:543. Also, *Galveston Weekly News,* January 26, 1864.

94. *Frank Leslie's Illustrated Newspaper,* February 20, 1864; Herron to Stone, January 15, 1864, *OR,* I, 34 pt. 1, 84; *Houston Tri-Weekly Telegraph,* February 1, 5, 1864.

95. Tilley, ed., *Federals on the Frontier,* 291.

96. Pierce to Herron, January 12, 1864, *OR,* I, 34, pt. 1, 81

97. Cortina to Vidaurri, January 12, 1864, Correspondencia de Vidaurri, Archivo Gen. del Estado de Nuevo León.

98. Vidaurri to Cortina, January 16, 1864, Correspondencia de Vidaurri, Archivo Gen. de Estado de Nuevo León. Cortina responded, hoping Vidaurri would intercede to release Treviño, one of his "most loyal followers." Cortina to Vidaurri, January 20, 1864, Correspondencia de Vidaurri, Archivo Gen. de Estado de Nuevo León.

99. Ruiz to Herron, January 15, 1864, *Correspondencia de Juárez,* 8:535. This same letter is in *OR,* I, 34, pt. 1, 82. Also, *Harpers Weekly,* February 6, 1864.

100. Herron to Charles P. Stone, January 16, 1864, *OR,* I, 34, pt. 2, 93; Herron to Stone, January 15, 1864, *OR,* I, 34, pt. 2, 82. Regiments included the 19th Iowa, 20th Wisconsin, and 94th Illinois. Tilley, ed., *Federals on the Frontier,* 291.

101. Herron to Ruiz, January 12, 1864, *OR,* I, 34, pt. 1, 83. This same letter is reprinted in *Correspondencia de Juárez,* 8:535–36.

102. H. Bertram to Herron, January 12 [13], 1864, *OR,* I, 34, pt. 1, 83.

103. Tilley, ed., *Federals on the Frontier,* 292. Also, *Houston Tri-Weekly Telegraph,* February 1, 1864.

104. Ruiz to Juárez, January 14, 1864, *Correspondencia de Juárez,* 8:536–37. Also, Herron to Stone, January 15, 1864, *OR,* I, 34, pt. 1, 84; *Houston Tri-Weekly Telegraph,* February 5, 1864.

105. Ruiz to Herron, January 15, 1864, *Correspondencia de Juárez,* 8:542–43.

106. Cortina to the Inhabitants [of Matamoros], January 14, 1865, *Correspondencia de Juárez,* 8:538–39.

Chapter Five

1. M. M. Kimmey to Seward, May 21, 1864, *OR*, I, 1, 34, pt. 4, 166–67; Memorandum of Godfrey in Seward to Stanton, August 29, 1864, *OR*, III, 4, 647.
2. Cortina to Vidaurri, January 27, 1864, Correspondence de Vidaurri, Archivo Gen. del Estado de Nuevo León.
3. Cortina to Vidaurri, January 18, 1864, Correspondencia de Vidaurri, Archivo Gen. del Estado de Nuevo León.
4. Cortina to Juárez, January 21, 1864, *Correspondencia de Juárez*, 8:549.
5. Ruiz to Juárez, January 14, 1864, *Correspondencia de Juárez*, 8:536–37; Ruiz to Juárez, January 20, 1864, *Correspondencia de Juárez*, 8:547–48.
6. Cortina to Juárez, February 5, 1864, *Correspondencia de Juárez*, 8:555–56. Also, Juárez to Matias Romero, February 1, 1864, *Correspondencia de Juárez*, 8:555; and Andrés Treviño to Juárez, February 2, 1864, *Correspondencia de Juárez*, 8:551; Cortina to Juárez, February 25, 1864, *Correspondencia de Juárez*, 8:557.
7. Cortina to Juárez, February 6, 1864, *Correspondencia de Juárez*, 8:556–57.
8. Cortina to Vidaurri, February 20, 1864, Correspondencia de Vidaurri, Archivo Gen. del Estado de Nuevo León.
9. *New York Herald*, October 9, 1865.
10. J. A. Quintero to J. P. Benjamin, January 25, 1864, John T. Pickett Papers, LC; Tyler, *Santiago Vidaurri and the Southern Confederacy*, 137.
11. Tyler, *Santiago Vidaurri and the Southern Confederacy*, 138; Quintero to Benjamin, February 28, 1864, John T. Pickett Papers, LC.
12. Cortina to the Troops of this Garrison, February 27, 1864, *Correspondencia de Juárez*, 8:662.
13. "Presented in of honor of the intrepid Cavalry Colonel J. N. Cortina by the friends of Justice on the frontier." Several years later, Cortina gave the sword to a nephew, Col. Práxedis Cavazos. Cavazos's widow, Sarah Sada de Cavazos, gave the sword to José T. Canales who presented it to the Brownsville Historical Society in 1952.
14. Cortina to Juárez, March 27, 1864, *Correspondencia de Juárez*, 8:704; Cortina to Juárez, March 29, 1864, *Correspondencia de Juárez*, 8:705.
15. Quintero to Benjamin, April 3, 1864, John T. Pickett Papers, LC.
16. Smart, *Viva Juárez!*, 311.
17. Herron to Stone, January 16, 1864, *OR*, I, 34, pt. 2, 93; and Herron to Stone, January 26, 1864, *OR*, I, 34, pt. 2, 218.
18. "Foreign Question," n.d., in "Conditions of Affairs in the Republic of Mexico," 51.
19. Cortina to Herron, April 8, 1864, Francis J. Herron Papers, Manuscript Department, New York Historical Society (NYHS), New York, New York; Cortina to Herron, February 10, 1864, Francis J. Herron Papers, NYHS.
20. Cortina to Herron, February 3, 1864, Herron Papers; Cortina to Herron, April 21, 1864, Francis J. Herron Papers, NYHS.
21. Cortina to [Herron], April 18, 1864, Francis J. Herron Papers, NYHS.
22. Cortina to Herron, April 7, 1864, Francis J. Herron Papers, NYHS.
23. Cortina to Herron, April 18, 1864, Francis J. Herron Papers, NYHS.
24. Cortina to Colonel McDye, May 13, 1864, Francis J. Herron Papers, NYHS.
25. *Matamoros Daily Ranchero*, February 1, 1866; H. M. Hubbard, Special Orders No. [no number], May [7], 1865, Lew Wallace Papers, Indiana Historical Society (IHS), Indianapolis, Indiana. Also, Quintero to Benjamin, January 25, 1864; and Quintero to Benjamin, April 7, 1864; both in John T. Pickett Papers, LC; and *Brownsville Daily Ranchero*, July 25, 1867. Also, "Foreign Question," n.d., in "Conditions of Affairs in the Republic of Mexico," 51. In May 1866, a Cameron County grand jury indicted Herron for kidnapping. *New Orleans Daily Crescent*, May 23, 1866. Henry Maltby, the fiery editor of the *Brownsville Daily Ranchero* would never forgive General Herron. See *Brownsville Daily Ranchero*, March 17, 1868; September 21, 1869.

26. Quintero to Benjamin, April 7, 1864, John T. Pickett Papers, LC. Quintero enclosed a memorandum of his meeting with Juárez.

27. John A. McClernand to Cortina, April 7, 1864, *OR*, I, 34, pt. 3, 73.

28. McClernand to Cortina, April 8, 1864, *OR*, I, 34, pt. 3, 87.

29. J. B. Magruder to John Slidell, April 27, 1864, *OR*, I, 34, pt. 3, 796.

30. L. de Geofroy to Seward, n.d., "Conditions of Affairs in the Republic of Mexico," 309.

31. De Geofroy to Seward, April 26, 1864; Seward to De Geofroy, April 30, 1864; Seward to De Geofroy, May 28, 1864, Seward to De Geofroy, June 22, 1864 (quote); all in "Conditions of Affairs in the Republic of Mexico," 308–11.

32. Cortina to Benavides, May 23, 1864, Letters Received, District of New Mexico, Arizona, and Texas, RG 109, NA. A note by Silva at the bottom of the letter dated May 24 indicates that it was intended for Col. John S. Ford.

33. Magruder to Cortina, May 22, 1864, *OR*, I, 34, pt. 3, 835.

34. Dabbs, *The French Army in Mexico, 1861–1867: A Study in Military Government*, 84; Kératry, *La contre-guérilla francaise au Mexique*, 105. Abandoning one of their ships in the Rio Panuco with a large amount of arms, the French had evacuated Tampico on January 13, 1863. Frederick Jonson to Earl Russell, January 27, 1863; Jonson to Russell, August 29, 1863, Dispatches from the British Consul in Tampico, Mexico, Foreign Office, British National Archives, Kaw, Great Britain.

35. Franklin Chase to Seward, April 28, 1864, Tampico Consular Dispatches, RG 59, NA; Dabbs, *French Army in Mexico*, 99; Chance, *José María de Jesús Carvajal*, 181–82. The feared and ruthless Du Pin was a painter, intellectual, photographer, writer, specialist in topography, and someone addicted to gambling. Besides French, Du Pin spoke English, Spanish, Arabic, and some Chinese. Physically broken, he died in poverty at Montpellier, France, on August 27, 1868. Mignard, *Charles Louis du Pin (1814–1868): 'Un intellectuel baroudeur' né à Lasgraïsses*, 4–11. Gérard Mignard to author, January 25, 2006; Mignard to author (e-mails), February 10, 12, 14; March 22, 28, 29, April 6, 23, 26, May 1, 2, 4, 11, 2006.

36. Cortina to Foreign Minister, May 5, 1864, in Toral, ed., *Historia documental militar de la intervención francesa en México y el denominado segundo imperio*, 269.

37. Ford to J. E. Slaughter, June 5, 1864, Letters Received, Dist. of Texas, N.M., and Arizona, RG 109, NA. Also, Ford to Slaughter, June 20, 1864, *OR*, I, 34, pt. 4, 684–85.

38. Ford, *Rip Ford's Texas*, 369.

39. Cortina to the Public, August 20, 1876, *TFT*, 116.

40. Cortina to Herron, June 18, 1864, Francis J. Herron Papers, NYHS.

41. Ford to Slaughter, June 20, 1864, *OR*, I, 34, pt. 4, 685.

42. Pierce to [Seward], September 1, 1864, Matamoros Consular Dispatches, RG 59, NA; *Weekly State Gazette* (Austin), September 21, 1864; Dabbs, *French Army in Mexico*, 99; José María Cortina to the Inhabitants of the Heroic City of Matamoros, August 22, 1864, "Conditions of Affairs in the Republic of Mexico," 197. Also, Charles du Pin Memoirs, Ministère de Guerre, Paris, France, Paris, 318. Courtesy of Gérard Mignard.

43. Dabbs, *French Army in Mexico*, 135.

44. Ford to the Officer in Command of the French Forces on the Rio Grande near Boca del Río, August 24, 1864, *OR*, I, 42, pt. 2, 1089.

45. A. Veron to the Colonel Commanding Confederate Forces, [August 25, 1864], *OR*, I, 42, pt. 2, 1089–90.

46. Charles du Pin Memoirs, Ministère de Guerre, Paris, 319–20.

47. Quintero to Benjamin, September 5, 1864, John T. Pickett Papers, LC; *Brownsville Daily Ranchero*, September 29, 1870; Thompson, *Juan Cortina*, 58.

48. *Weekly State Gazette* (Austin), September 21, 1864, quoting the *San Antonio Herald*, n.d.

49. Ford, *Rip Ford's Texas*, 375.

50. Ford to J. E. Dwyer, September 3, 1864. *OR*, I, 41, pt. 3, 909; Ford, *Rip Ford's Texas*, 375.

51. John S. Ford Memoirs, CAH, 6:1124.

52. Cortina to Ford, August 31, 1864, John S. Ford Papers, Haley Memorial Library and History Center.

53. Ford, *Rip Ford's Texas*, 370. Also, Cortina to Ford, August 31, 1864, John S. Ford Papers, Haley Memorial Library and History Center; Ford to Cortina, August 31, 1864, John S. Ford Papers, Haley Library.

54. Ford, *Rip Ford's Texas*, 372.

55. Cortina to Ford, September 8, 1864, John S. Ford Papers, Haley Memorial Library and History Center.

56. Ford, *Rip Ford's Texas*, 373.

57. Servando Canales, Julián Cerda, Mariano G. Hidalgo, and José A. Puente, Account of Cortina's Actions, October 1, 1864, John S. Ford Papers, Haley Memorial Library and History Center.

58. Ibid.

59. Pierce to Herron, September 8, 1864, *OR*, I, 41, pt. 3, 101; Pierce to [Seward], September 1, 1864, Matamoros Consular Dispatches, RG 59, NA. Also, Townsend, *Yankee Invasion of Texas*, 110–11.

60. Ford, *Rip Ford's Texas*, 373.

61. H. M. Day to Cortina, September 8, 1864, "Conditions of Affairs in the Republic of Mexico," 402.

62. Day to George B. Drake, September 14, 1864, *OR*, I, 41, pt. 3, 184. Also, *Matamoros Daily Ranchero*, August 12, 1865; Denis Donohoe to Frederick Bruce, May 29, 1865, enclosed with Frederick Bruce to Lord Russell, June 10, 1865, in Barnes and Barnes, eds., *The American Civil War through British Eyes: Dispatches from British Diplomats, Vol. 3, February 1863–December 1865*, 322–23.

63. G. H. Giddings to Ford, September 17, 1864, John S. Ford Papers, Haley Memorial Library and History Center; Giddings to Ford, September 9 (three dispatches), 10, and 16, John S. Ford Papers, Haley Memorial Library and History Center; *Weekly State Gazette*, (Austin), September 28, 1864; John S. Ford Memoirs, CAH, 6:1127–30.

64. Day to George B. Drake, September 14, 1864, *OR*, 41, pt. 3, 184.

65. Ibid.

66. Ford, *Rip Ford's Texas*, 375.

67. A. Veron to [Day], September 7, 1964, *OR*, I, 41, pt. 3, 100.

68. Ibid.

69. J. G. Walker to Slaughter, October 1, 1864, *OR*, I, 41, pt. 3, 972.

70. Ford to Commanding Officer, U.S. Forces, September 12, 1864, *OR*, I, 41, pt. 3, 947.

71. Day to Ford, September 13, 1864, *OR*, I, 41, pt. 3, 947. Lt. Col. H. S. Smith of the 91st Illinois allowed Ford's couriers to proceed to the Union headquarters on the north end of the island without being blindfolded, thus enabling the Rebels "to see the exact number and position of our guns and to form a fair estimate of the number of our troops." As a result Day ordered Smith arrested and preferred charges against him.

72. Day to George B. Drake, October 9, 1864, *OR*, I, 41, pt. 3, 721.

73. De Geofroy to Seward, September 23, 1864, "Conditions of Affairs in the Republic of Mexico," 316. Also, Seward to William L. Dayton, October 3, 1864; Canby to Banks, September 15, 1864; Seward to Canby, September 30, 1864, Wm. L Dayton to Seward, October 7, 1864; and Seward to Dayton, October 10; all in "Conditions of Affairs in the Republic of Mexico," 398–400.

74. Seward to De Geofroy, September 30, 1864; Ed. R. S. Canby to Banks, September 15, 1864; Day to Drake, October 9, 1864; all in "Conditions of Affairs in the Republic of Mexico," 317–19.

75. Thos. F. Drayton to J. G. Walker, September 26, 1864, enclosing statements of Juan N. Cortina (September 23, 1864), Thomas F. Drayton (September 22, 1864), Thos. F. Drayton to Juan N. Cortina (September 23, 1864), and agreement of Juan N. Cortina, J. S. Espiundola [sic], and Thos. F. Drayton (September 23, 1864), *OR*, I, 41, pt. 3, 958–59; Walker to Slaughter, Octo-

ber 1, 1864, *OR*, I, 41, pt. 3, 972. A copy of the September 23, 1864, agreement can also be found in the John S. Ford Papers, Haley Memorial Library and History Center.

76. Ford, *Rip Ford's Texas*, 376.

77. Day to George B. Drake, October 9, 1864, *OR*, I, 41, pt. 3, 721.

78. *Brownsville Daily Ranchero*, September 24, 1870; Thompson, *Juan Cortina*, 48, 59; Geo. F. Emmons to Seward, March 8, 1865, Matamoros Consular Dispatches, RG 59, NA.

79. Ford, *Rip Ford's Texas*, 376; Drayton to Thomas [sic] Mejía, September 28, 1864, *OR*, I, 41, pt. 3, 973; Charles du Pin Memoirs, Ministère de Guerre, Paris, 323.

80. Ford, *Rip Ford's Texas*, 383.

81. Pitner, *Maximilian's Lieutenant*, 119.

82. Rivière, *La marina francesa en México*, 94. For the original French copy, see Rivière, *La marine francaise au Mexique*. All references will hereafter be to the Spanish translation.

83. *Brownsville Daily Ranchero*, May 26, 1870.

84 *Houston Tri-Weekly Telegraph*, December 8, 1864; Slaughter to Mejía, November 18, 1864, in *New York Herald*, July 2, 1864.

85. Rivière, *La marina francesa en México*, 94–95.

86. M. Dolan to Hurlbut, March 2, 1865, *OR*, I, 48, pt. 1, 1,058.

Chapter Six

1. Cortina to Miguel Negrete, April 24, 1864 [1865], "Conditions of Affairs in the Republic of Mexico," 323–24; M. Dolan to S. A. Hurlbut, April 16, 1865, *OR*, 3, 4, 106; Franklin Chase to Frederick Seward, April 18, 1865, Tampico Consular Dispatches, RG 59, NA; and Romero to William H. Seward, July 10, 1865, "Conditions of Affairs in the Republic of Mexico." 320–21.

2. Cortina to Negrete, April 24, 1864 [1865], "Conditions of Affairs in the Republic of Mexico." 323.

3. Lerdo de Tejada to Negrete, May 12, 1865, "Conditions of Affairs in the Republic of Mexico." 324.

4. Kearney and Knopp, *Boom and Bust*, 143.

5. J. M. Cortina to Comisario de Guerrero, April 7, 1865, quoting Juan N. Cortina's edict of April 5, 1865, Nuevo Guerrero Archives.

6. *Houston Tri-Weekly Telegraph*, April 21, 1865.

7. Dolan to Hurlbut, April 16, 1865, *OR*, 3, 4, 106.

8. E. B. Brown to J. S. Crosby, May 26, 1865, LR, AGO, RG 94, NA.

9. *New York Herald*, July 26, 1865.

10. Juárez to Pedro Santacilia, July 13, 1865, *Correspondencia de Juárez*, 10:104.

11. Juárez to Santacilia, July 27, 1865, *Correspondencia de Juárez*, 10:129.

12. *New York Herald*, July 2, 1865.

13. Brown to J. N. Cortina, July 7, 1865; Brown to F. Steele, July 7, 1865, J. B. Rush to N. Headington, July 7, 1865; Charles Black to Steele, July 8, 1865, Brown to Steele, July 8, 1865; all in LR, AGO, RG 94, NA.

14. Steele to Tomás Mejía, August 3, 1865, LR, AGO, RG 94, NA.

15. Rankin, *Twenty Years among the Mexicans*, 128.

16. *Brownsville Daily Ranchero*, July 28, 1865, September 13, 1867, December 11, 1867; *San Antonio Tri-Weekly Herald*, September 16, 1865; Owen and Owen, *Generals at Rest: The Grave Sites of the 425 Official Confederate Generals*, 335; Ben Z. Grant, "A Texas Governor Buried in Mexico," *Marshall News Messenger*, January 3, 1999; Ben Z. Grant, "Finding Governor Murrah," *Marshall News Messenger*, March 14, 1999.

17. Terrell, *From Texas to Mexico and the Court of Maximilian in 1865*, 10–18; Rolle, *The Lost Cause: The Confederate Exodus to Mexico*, 84–85.

18. Rivière, *La marina francesa en México*, 155. Also, Marquis de Montholon to Seward, October 19, 1865, *OR*, 3, 4, 1241. This same letter is in "Conditions of Affairs in the Republic of Mexico," 338–39.

19. *Matamoros Daily Ranchero,* October 14, 1865. Also, Dabbs, *French Army in Mexico,* 143–44.
20. Rivière, *La marina francesa en México,* 148; M. Webster, "Texan Manifest Destiny," 44.
21. Cortina to Brown, June 17,1865, photocopy courtesy of Carlos Larralde.
22. *Matamoros Daily Ranchero,* July 4, 5, 1865.
23. *New York Daily Tribune,* July 25, 1865, from the *Matamoros Daily Ranchero,* July 4, 1865.
24. *New York Herald,* September 6, 1865. Cortina was forty-one years old at the time.
25. *New York Herald,* July 15, 1865; *Matamoros Daily Ranchero,* June 27, 29, 1865; *New York Daily Tribune,* July 14, 1865; Steele to F. C. Newhall, July 1, 1865, LR, AGO, RG 94, NA. On his way downriver from Ringgold Barracks, General Steele took possession of the *Señorita* and brought it to Brownsville.
26. Sheridan to J. A. Rawlins, July 6, 1865, *OR,* 3, 4, 1053.
27. *Matamoros Daily Ranchero,* July 16, 1865; Schoonover, ed., *Mexican Lobby: Matías Romero in Washington, 1861–1867,* 78.
28. Steele to Newhall, July 1, 1865, LR, AGO, RG 94, NA.
29. Grant to Stanton, November 6, 1865, *OR,* 3, 4, 1254.
30. Brown to Mejía, May 31, 1865, LR, AGO, RG 94, NA.
31. G. García, ed., *Documentos inéditos o muy raros para la historia de México,* 30, 46–47; M. Webster, "Texan Manifest Destiny," 44.
32. Richter, *The Army in Texas during Reconstruction,* 24.
33. While reviewing Charles du Pin's lengthy unpublished memoirs, Gérard Mignard found the names of several former Confederates who served with the contra-guerrillas. These include William Moore, William Wilson, Robert Russell, Albert Elwin, and Joseph Wollen, all of whom Du Pin singled out for having courageously scouted behind enemy lines. Gérard Mignard to Thompson, e-mail, June 11, 2006.
34. Sheridan to Grant, August 1, 1865, *OR,* 3, 4, 1148.
35. Sheridan to Grant, August 18, 1865, 3, 4, 1192.
36. *Matamoros Daily Ranchero,* June 18, 1865.
37. Sheridan to Steele, July 7, 1865, LR, AGO, RG 94, NA.
38. Juárez to Santacilia, July 27, 1865, *Correspondencia de Juárez,* 10:129.
39. Tomás Mejía to E. B. Brown, July 6, 1865, LR, AGO, RG 94, NA.
40. Sheridan to Steele, July 13, August 7, 1865, LR, AGO, RG 94, NA. Also, L[ucius] Avery to [Seward], August 19, October 9, December 20, 1865, Matamoros Consular Dispatches, RG 59, NA.
41. *New York Herald,* July 17, 29, 1865.
42. *New York Daily Tribune,* May 10,1865.
43. *Matamoros Daily Ranchero,* November 26, 1865.
44. *Galveston Weekly News,* May 10, 1865. Also, *Weekly State Gazette* (Austin), May 10, 1865.
45. *Galveston Weekly News,* May 17, 1865.
46. *New York Daily Tribune,* May 12, 1865.
47. *Houston Tri-Weekly Telegraph,* June 16, 28, 1865; *Galveston Weekly News,* June 21, 1865; Thompson, "Adrián J. Vidal: Soldier of Three Republics," 74–84; Thompson, "Mutiny and Desertion on the Rio Grande: The Strange Saga of Captain Adrián J. Vidal," 160–69.
48. M. Kenedy to John Wilson, June 10, 1865, Kenedy Letterbook, King Ranch Archives, Kingsville, Texas. A few years later, Vidal's remains were moved to the Kenedy family plot in a dark corner of the old Brownsville Cemetery. Vidal had married Ana Chavero late in the Civil War and from this union Ana Adriana was born on August 17, 1865. She married Louis R. Cowen in Brownsville on April 14, 1887 and died in the city on February 24, 1954. Saul Vela to author, August 5, 1996. Letter in author's files.
49. *Matamoros Daily Ranchero,* June 11, 1865.
50. *Matamoros El Orden,* February 16, 1865.
51. Frederick Steele Diary, August 7, 1865, Frederick Steele Papers, Special Collections, Stanford University Library, Palo Alto, California. According to Matías Romero, both Grant and

Sheridan were "disgusted" with Steele's friendship with Mejía and the *Imperialistas*. Schoonover, ed., *Mexican Lobby*, 96.

52. Frederick Steele Diary, August 11, 1865, Steele Papers, Special Collections, Stanford University.

53. *New York Herald*, September 20, 1865; *Matamoros Daily Ranchero*, September 26, 1865. Mejía was born at Tierra Blanca, Guanajuato, on September 17, 1820, the son of María Martina and Cristóbal Mejía.

54. Pitner, *Maximilian's Lieutenant*, 102.

55. *New York Herald*, July 21, 26, 1865. Also, Brown to Steele, July 7, 1865, LR, AGO, RG 94, NA; *Matamoros Daily Ranchero*, July 23, 1865.

56. *Matamoros Daily Ranchero*, September 19, 1865.

57 Rankin, *Twenty Years among the Mexicans*, 122.

58. Ibid., 125.

59. Ibid., 127.

60. Droeg, Oetting, et al. to Steele, August 14, 1865, Frederick Steele Papers, Stanford University.

61. *New York Daily Herald*, August 17, 1865.

62. *New York Daily Tribune*, September 22, 1865.

63. Cortina to Steele, August 17, 1865, Frederick Steele Papers, Stanford University.

64. Cortina to Steele, September 24, 1865; Cortina to Steele, October 4, 1865; Frederick Steele Papers, Stanford University.

65. Kératry, *The Rise and Fall of the Emperor Maximilian, A Narrative of the Mexican Empire, 1861–67 from Authentic Documents with the Imperial Correspondence*, 70; Dabbs, *French Army in Mexico*, 85.

66. Dabbs, *French Army in Mexico*, 85. Also, Franklin Chase to Frederick W. Seward, June 9, 1864, March 27, 1865, Tampico Consular Dispatches, RG 59, NA.

67. Pedro Martínez to the Citizens of Galeana, Yturbide, and Rio Blanco, May 22, 1866, "Conditions of Affairs in the Republic of Mexico," 222–23.

68. A. Gonzales to Mariano Escobedo, May 30, 1866, "Conditions of Affairs in the Republic of Mexico," 223–24. Also, Franklin Chase to Frederick W. Seward, March 27, 1866, Tampico Consular Dispatches, RG 59, NA.

69. Wallace, "Notes to be taken into account," n.d., Lew Wallace Papers, IHS. Wallace's was certain to have gained his knowledge of the area from Carvajal, who was in the United States at the time.

70. *New York Herald*, October 20, 1865. Also, *New York Daily Tribune*, July 1, 1865.

71. Frederick Steele Diary, August 11, 1865, Steele Papers, Stanford University.

72. F. de León to Federico Steele, August 13, 1865, Steele Papers, Stanford University.

73. M. Webster, "Texan Manifest Destiny," 46; Chance, *José María de Jesús Carvajal*, 184–90.

74. Escobedo to the Inhabitants of the State of Tamaulipas, October 19, 1865; Escobedo to his Subordinates, October 19, 1865; both in *New York Herald*, November 23, 1865. Also, Dabbs, *French Army in Mexico*, 148–49.

75. Escobedo to Mejía, October 23, 1865; Mejía to Escobedo, [October 23, 1865], both in "Conditions of Affairs in the Republic of Mexico," no. 1261, 338–39.

76. *New York Herald*, November 28, 1865.

77. Avery to [Seward], October 26, 1865, Matamoros Consular Dispatches, RG 59, NA.

78. *New York Herald*, November 10, 16, 18, 20, 1865; *Matamoros Daily Ranchero*, October 25, 1865; Weitzel to Steele, October 25, 1865, LR, AGO, RG 94, NA.

79. D. de la Bedolliero to Weitzel, November 8, 1865, LR, AGO, RG 94, NA.

80. G. Clouse to [Weitzel], November 9, 1865, LR, AGO, RG 94, NA. Also, Mejía to [Weitzel], November 9, 1865; both in LR, AGO, RG 94, NA; and *New York Herald*, December 4, 1865.

81. Weitzel to Clouse, November 10, 1865, LR, AGO, RG 94, NA.

82. Clouse to [Weitzel], November 6, 1865, LR, AGO, RG 94, NA.

83. *New York Herald,* October 27, 1865.
84. Escobedo to the Minister of War and Marine [Mejía], November 14, 1866, "Conditions of Affairs in the Republic of Mexico," 357–60.
85. *Matamoros Daily Ranchero,* November 9, 1865.
86. Avery to [Seward], January 15, 1866, Matamoros Consular Dispatches, RG 59, NA.
87. *Matamoros Daily Ranchero,* October 25, 1865.
88. Ibid., October 28, 1865.
89. Ibid., November 10, 1865.
90. Ibid., November 17, 1865.
91. *New York Herald,* October 20, 1865.
92. Weitzel to Mejía, January 2, 1866; Mejía to Weitzel, January 2, 1866; both in *Houston Tri-Weekly Telegraph,* January 19, 1866, and "Conditions of Affairs in the Republic of Mexico," 504–505.
93. Escobedo to Juárez, December 1, 1865, *Correspondencia de Juárez,* 10 474–75.
94. Escobedo to Juárez, December 19, 1866, *Correspondencia de Juárez,* 11:647–48.
95. Manuel Gómez to Juárez, December 2, 1865, *Correspondencia de Juárez,* 10:474–75.
96. *Matamoros Monitor of the Frontier,* December 16, 1865.
97. *New York Herald,* July 2, 1865.
98. Statement of Wm. D. St. Clair, November 7, 1865, LR, AGO, RG 94, NA.
99. Wm. D. St. Clair to Edmund De Buck, November 6, 1865, LR, AGO, RG 94, NA. Also, Franz Benter to De Buck, November 5, 1865; De Buck to D. D. Wheeler; R. Rico to [De Buck], November 5, 1865; Statement of Henry Edmonds (watchman on the *Rio Grande*), November 14, 1865; Weitzel to H. G. Wright, November 5, 1865; Wright to Weitzel, November 9, 1865, all in LR, AGO, RG 94, NA.
100. Sheridan to [U. S. Grant], January 28, 1866; G. S. Dodge to R. Clay Crawford, January 12, (two letters), 1866, LR, AGO, RG 94, NA; Lew Wallace to Crawford, November 22, 1865, Lew Wallace Papers, IHS; Lew Wallace, *An Autobiography,* 2:865–66; R. Miller, *Arms across the Border: United States Aid to Juárez During the French Intervention in Mexico,* 44–45; Morsberger and Morsberger, *Lew Wallace: Militant Romantic,* 199–200. Dodge had encouraged Crawford by telling him that three hundred filibusters could be recruited in Galveston and that arms could be procured in New Orleans. "All you have to do, my dear general, is to adhere to your instructions ... I have not the slightest doubt of your zeal and discretion," Wallace wrote Crawford. "Rest assured that you shall have all the honor of success." Later, learning of the "unhappy affair at Bagdad," Wallace told Carvajal he would go "straight to Washington and have [Crawford] effectively disposed of." Wallace to Carvajal, January 24, 1866, Lew Wallace Papers, IHS. Unfortunately, many of the letters in the Adjutant Gen.'s Records at the National Archives relevant to the raid on Bagdad have faded to the point of being illegible.
101. E. D. Townsend endorsement, January 18, 1866, quoting Court-Martial Order No. 43, Department of the Cumberland, June 14, 1865, on J. Hubley Ashton to Hamilton Fish, January 18, 1866, LR, AGO, RG 94, NA. Other leaders implicated in the raid on Bagdad included Wm. D. St. Clair, Thomas D. Sears, Theodore Lamberton, Benjamin Shaw, Alexander McDonald, and Edgar McDonald.
102. Testimony of Frank J. White, A. C. Decker, and Albert A. M. McGaffie, "Military Commission Appointed to Investigate and Report upon the Facts Relative to the Capture of the Town of Bagdad on the Mexican Side of the Rio Grande on January 5, 1866," AGO, RG 393, NA. Hereafter referred to as Bagdad Commission Investigation. A. F. Reed to Crawford, December 18, 1865, LR, AGO, RG 94, NA. This letter, along with a number of others, was found in Crawford's baggage when he was arrested in New Orleans. Reed to Crawford, January 3, 1866, LR, AGO, RG, 94, NA.
103. Crawford to Geo. P. Edgar, December 18, 1865, LR, AGO, RG 94, NA.
104. Enrique A. Mejía to Romero, January 17, 1877, *Correspondencia de Juárez,* 10:546–47.
105. *Galveston Tri-Weekly News,* January 24, 1866. Also, *New Orleans Daily Crescent,* January 17, 1866.

106. Pitner, *Maximilian's Lieutenant*, 106.

107. *Matamoros Daily Ranchero*, January 6, 1866; J. D. Davis to R. M. Hall, January 5, 1866, LR, AGO, RG 94, NA; Testimony of Frank Benter, Bagdad Commission Investigation, AGO, RG 393, NA.

108. *Matamoros Daily Ranchero*, January 7, 1866. Lucius Avery, U.S. commercial agent in Matamoros, concluded that many of the outrages that were reported in the Matamoros newspapers were greatly exaggerated. Lucius Avery to [Seward], January 13, 1866, Matamoros Consular Dispatches, RG 59, NA. Much of the plundering, Avery asserted a few days later, was by residents of Bagdad. Avery to Seward, January 24, 1866, Matamoros Consular Dispatches, RG 59, NA; *New Orleans Daily Crescent*, January 17, 1866.

109. *Matamoros Daily Ranchero*, January 27, 1866.

110. Escobedo to Weitzel, January 5, 1866, LR, AGO, RG 94, NA.

111. Enrique A. Mejía to Romero, January 17, 1866, *Correspondencia de Juárez*, 10:546–47.

112. Francisco de León to J. D. Davis, January 5, 1866, Exhibit A, Bagdad Commission Investigation, AGO, RG 393, NA. A copy of this letter is in LR, AGO, RG 94, NA. Also, *New Orleans Daily Crescent*, January 17, 1866.

113. Escobedo to Juárez, March 17, 1866, *Correspondencia de Juárez*, 10:762. Also, *Houston Tri-Weekly Telegraph*, January 24, 1866.

114. Mejía to Romero, January 17, 1866, *Correspondencia de Juárez*, 10:546–47.

115. Frank J. White to W. D. Morrison, January 22, 1866, LR, AGO, RG 94, NA; White to Morrison, Exhibit E, Bagdad Commission Investigation, AGO, RG 393, NA. Also, White to Morrison, January 22, 1866, LR, AGO, RG 94, NA.

116. *New Orleans Daily Crescent*, February 9, 1866; *Galveston Tri-Weekly News*, February 2, 1866.

117. Pitner, *Maximilian's Lieutenant*, 110, 114.

118. Wright to W. T. Clark, January 27, 1866; Wright to Geo. L. Hartsuff, January 27, 1866; both in LR, AGO, RG 94, NA.

119. Sheridan to Stanton, May 9, 1866, LR, AGO, RG 94, NA.

120. Enrique A. Mejía to Matías Romero, March 6, 1866, LR, AGO, RG 94, NA.

121. Romero to [Seward], March 30, 1866, LR, AGO, RG 94, NA.

122. Weitzel to C. H. Whittlesey, January 27, 1866, LR, AGO, RG 94, NA.

123. *Galveston Tri-Weekly News*, February 2, 1866; *New Orleans Daily Crescent*, February 9, 1866; and *Matamoros Daily Ranchero*, January 23, 25, 1866.

124. *Matamoros Daily Ranchero*, January 24, 1866.

125. *Galveston Tri-Weekly News*, February 2, 1866. Also, *Matamoros El Ranchero Diario*, January 24, 1866; Avery to [Seward], January 24, 1866, Matamoros Consular Dispatches, RG 59, NA; Franklin Chase to Seward, February 16, 1866, Tampico Consular Dispatches, RG 59, NA, enclosing copy of *Tampico El Iris* [February 10, 1866]. One hundred twenty-three angry Matamoros merchants also sent a protest to the British vice consul, Charles Bagwell, as well as General Mejia, General Weitzel, and newspapers throughout the United States and Mexico. What happened at Bagdad was an "act of vandalism without parallel in modern history" and a "disgrace to the national and military honor of the United States," the merchants asserted. Moreover, American officials on the frontier were condoning daily offenses "against the professed neutrality of the United States." The arbitrary interference by the Americans might lead to the "entire ruin and destruction [of] the whole population of this frontier, and upon the commercial community of Matamoros," the merchants went on to say. Dimas de Torres Velásquez, the Spanish consul, C. V. Frossard, the French representative, Luis Schuhmacher the Prussian consul, and Charles Bagwell, the British vice consul, attested to the facts of the protest. *Pronunciamiento*, January 16, 1866, enclosed with Charles Bagwell to Earl Clarendon, January 25, 1866, Dispatches from the British Vice Consul at Matamoros, Mexico, Foreign Office, British National Archives, Kaw, Great Britain.

126. Sheridan to Grant, January 17 (two letters), 1866; and Sheridan to H. G. Wright, January 17, 1866; all in LR, AGO, RG 94, NA.

127. *New Orleans Daily Crescent,* January 27, 1866; *Matamoros Daily Ranchero,* February 9, 1866; *Galveston Tri-Weekly News,* January 26, 1866. In New Orleans, Crawford was arrested by the military and confined at Fort Jackson at Savannah, Georgia, where he later escaped.

128. Grant endorsement on Commission Report, March 1, 1866, LR, AGO, RG 94, NA.

129. Escobedo to Juárez, January 29, 1866, *Correspondencia de Juárez,* 10:602–603.

130. Escobedo to Juárez, March 17, 1866, *Correspondencia de Juárez,* 10:762.

131. Juan A. Zambrano to Juárez, January 25, 1866, *Correspondencia de Juárez,* 10:571; *Brownsville Daily Ranchero,* December 20, 1866; *Flake's Daily Galveston Bulletin,* January 12, 1867.

132. Miguel Negrete to Cortina, January, n.d., 1866, *Correspondencia de Juárez,* 10:559.

133. *Brownsville Daily Rio Grande Courier,* November 8, 1866. Schoonover, *Mexican Lobby,* 147.

134. *Brownsville Daily Ranchero,* September 25, 1867; January 15, 1868; *New Orleans Daily Picayune,* January 6, 1867. González Ortega was later released, given a pension by Juárez, and died in 1881. For González Ortega's patriotism during the early struggle against the French, see Chávez Orozco, *Jesús González Ortega: Defensor de la Patria.*

135. Joseph Smith [Carvajal] to Wallace, May 18, 1865, Lew Wallace Papers, IHS; Chance, *José María de Jesús Carvajal,* 189.

136. Escobedo to Juárez *Correspondencia de Juárez,* 10:762.

137. *Matamoros Daily Ranchero,* March 13, 21, 23, 1866; *New Orleans Daily Crescent,* April 2, 16, 1866.

138. Cortina to Pierce, March 13, 1866, quoted in *Matamoros Daily Ranchero,* March 21, 27, 1866.

139. Parisot, *Reminiscences of a Texas Missionary,* 102–103, 107; Kearney and Knopp, *Boom and Bust,* 162; Thompson, *Juan Cortina,* 101; *Matamoros Daily Ranchero,* May 16, 22, 1866. For a general study of the hanging of Mexican Americans, see Carrigan and Webb, "The Lynching of Persons of Mexican Origin or Descent in the United States, 1848 to 1928."

140. *New Orleans Daily Crescent,* July 10, 1866.

141. Parisot, *Reminiscences of a Texas Missionary,* 99–100.

142. *New Orleans Daily Crescent,* July 10, 1866.

143. Ibid.

CHAPTER SEVEN

1. Pitner, *Maximilian's Lieutenant,* 116; *New Orleans Daily Crescent,* August 2, 1866.

2. *Matamoros Daily Ranchero,* February 4, 1866.

3. *Galveston Daily News,* May 22, 1866, quoting *New Orleans Daily Crescent,* n.d.

4. *New Orleans Daily Crescent,* February 26, April 16, 1866; *Matamoros Daily Ranchero,* February 13, 1866.

5. *New Orleans Daily Crescent,* May 15, 1866.

6. Ibid. Also, *Galveston Daily News,* May 11, 1866; *Houston Tri-Weekly Telegraph,* May 16, 1866; Rafael Olvera to General, April 27, 1866, in *San Antonio Daily Herald,* May 13, 1866; D. M. Frosard to Mariscal, Bazaine Archives, April 30, 1866, García Collection, Benson Latin American Library, University of Texas at Austin; Dabbs, *French Army in Mexico,* 167–68.

7. *Galveston Daily News,* May 11, 1866, quoting the *Matamoros Daily Ranchero,* n.d.; Frosard to Mariscal, April 30, 1866, Bazaine Archives, containing Olvera's official report of April 30, 1866.

8. *Matamoros Daily Ranchero,* May 4, 1866. Also, *New Orleans Daily Crescent,* May 15, 1866; *Galveston Daily News,* May 11, 1866.

9. Cortina to Juárez, August 26, 1866, *Correspondencia de Juárez,* 11:349–50

10. Escobedo to Juárez, October 9, 1866; Escobedo to Juárez, December 19, 1866; Juárez to [Pedro Santacilia], November 26, 1866, all in *Correspondencia de Juárez,* 11:537–38, 624, 647–48.

11. *Matamoros Daily Ranchero,* June 14, 15, 1866; *New Orleans Daily Crescent,* June 21, 1866.

12. Pitner, *Maximilian's Lieutenant,* 129; *Brownsville Daily Ranchero,* September 26, 1866; Avery to Seward, June 18, 1866, Matamoros Consular Dispatches, RG 59, NA.

13. Pitner, *Maximilian's Lieutenant*, 130.

14. Escobedo to Minister of War and Marine, June 19, 1866; Escobedo to Minister of War and Marine, June 20, 1866, both in "Conditions of Affairs in the Republic of Mexico," 226–29. Most of these letters and dispatches are also in Toral, ed., *Historia documental militar de la intervención francesa en México & el denominado segundo imperio*, 516–35. Also, Zorrilla, *Gobernadores, obispos y rectores*, 22–23.

15. Pitner, *Maximilian's Lieutenant*, 130.

16. Ibid., 131.

17. Ibid., 132–33.

18. Escobedo to Minister of War, June 19, 1866, "Conditions of Affairs in the Republic of Mexico," 228–29.

19. Escobedo to General of the Republic, June 16, 1866, "Conditions of Affairs in the Republic of Mexico," 227–28. Of the two hundred wagonloads of goods that were seized, twenty-seven were given to Canales as compensation for his part in the defeat of the Imperialists. What remained were returned to the owners, upon their paying an export duty. *New Orleans Daily Crescent*, July 30, 1866; Dabbs, *French Army in Mexico*, 172–73.

20. Sostenes Rocha, List of killed, wounded, and prisoners at the battle of Santa Gertrudis, on 16th of June 1866, "Conditions of Affairs in the Republic of Mexico," 229–33.

21. Lucius Avery to William H. Seward, June 18, 1866, Matamoros Consular Dispatches, RG 59, NA.

22. *Brownsville Daily Ranchero*, September 26, 1866. Also, *San Antonio Daily Herald*, July 6, 1866; *New Orleans Daily Crescent*, June 21, 1866, quoting the *Brownsville Rio Grande Courier*, June 18, 1866.

23. M. Escobedo to General of the Republic, June 16, 1866, "Conditions of Affairs in the Republic of Mexico," no. 1294, 227.

24. Tomás Mejía, José María J. Carvajal, et al., Agreement for the surrender of Matamoros, agreed to on June 22 and signed on June 23, "Conditions of Affairs in the Republic of Mexico," 233; *Brownsville Daily Ranchero*, September 26, 1866; Chance, *José María de Jesús Carvajal*, 192–96. "Sporting a huge moustache and huger whiskers," Carvajal had just arrived on the border from New York. For his attempts to raise money and recruits in the United States, see Morsberger and Morsberger, *Lew Wallace*, 196–97, 204–205; Chance, *José María de Jesús Carvajal*, 183–88; and Miller, *Arms across the Border*, 48–51.

25. *Galveston Tri-Weekly News*, July 11, 1866, quoting the *New Orleans Times*, n.d. Also, *Galveston Tri-Weekly News*, July 28, 1866; *San Antonio Daily Herald*, July 6, 1866; Avery to [Seward], June 29, 1866, Matamoros Consular Dispatched, RG 59, NA. The American consul in Tampico, Franklin Chase, reported the steamer *Colonel Holcomb* arrived in Tampico on June 29, with part of General Mejía's "distressed looking passengers." With "feelings of hatred," the *Imperialistas* in Tampico blamed "American Gold and American Rifles," for Mejía's defeat. So intense were feelings in the coastal city that Chase was not allowed to fly the American flag over the consulate. Chase to Frederick Seward, July 2, 1866, Tampico Consular Dispatches, RG 59, NA.

26. *Galveston Weekly News*, July 11, 1866, quoting the *New Orleans Times*, n.d.

27. *Tampico Boletín de Noticias*, August 8, 1866. Also, Chase to William H. Seward, August 8, 1866; Chase to Frederick W. Seward, August 15, 1866; both in Tampico Consular Dispatches, RG 59, NA. Backed by French gunboats, the Imperial defenders consisted of 150 demoralized and disloyal American artillerymen, besides the 350 Mexicans, all of whom had been with Mejía at Matamoros.

28. Avery to [Seward], August 9, 1866, Matamoros Consular Dispatches, RG 59, NA. During Carvajal's siege of the city from November 20, 1861 to February 24, 1862, nearly one-half of the buildings in the city were either burned or destroyed, including the American consulate, Avery later asserted. Avery to J. C. B. Davis, January 29, 1870, Matamoros Consular Dispatches, RG 59, NA.

29. Avery to [Seward], August 9, 1866, Matamoros Consular Dispatches, RG 59, NA.

30. [E. A.] Mejía to [Mariano] Escobedo, August 4, 1866, "Conditions of Affairs in the Republic of Mexico," 240.

31. *Galveston Tri-Weekly News,* September 10, 1866.

32. Avery to Seward, August 13, 1866, Matamoros Consular Dispatches, RG 59, NA. *Galveston Daily News,* August 17, 1866.

33. Wallace to My Dear Sue, August 16, 1866, Lew Wallace Papers, IHS; Morsberger and Morsberger, *Lew Wallace,* 204.

34. Wallace to My Dear Sue, August 7, 1866, Lew Wallace Papers, IHS. Allegedly carrying breadstuffs but with five thousand muskets and one thousand sabers carefully concealed beneath deck, the *Everman* left New York City on August 26 and arrived at Brazos Santiago on August 6 where the arms were transferred to the steamer *Tamaulipas* for transportation to Matamoros. After the arms were unloaded and the revolution erupted, Wallace had the arms transferred to the north bank where they were later taken to Roma and sold to Escobedo. The *Everman* was to be followed by the *Suwanee,* which was also loaded with weapons, as well as the *General Sherman,* which was be turned over to the Republican authorities. The *Suwanee,* however, was wrecked and went down off the Florida Keys. Wallace wrote that the "disgraceful" yet "bloodless revolution" in Matamoros was the "funniest affair I ever beheld." In "the town not a shot was fired, not a person hurt, yet the revolution was complete." The revolt against Carvajal was conceived and executed "by the thieves, bandits, and outlaws who have congregated by hundreds in Matamoros, which, as respects the rest of Mexico, has always been what the Five Points are to New York," Wallace continued. Wallace, *Autobiography,* 2:871, 875–86; Morsberger and Morsberger, *Lew Wallace,* 203–205; Wallace to Lerdo de Tejada, October 24, 1866, Lew Wallace Papers, IHS.

35. *Pronunciamiento,* Servando Canales, August 13, 1866, "Conditions of Affairs in the Republic of Mexico," 242. Some thought Canales to be under the influence of Gonzales Ortega. Also, Lucius Avery to William H. Seward, August 13, 1866, Matamoros Consular Dispatches, RG 59, NA. With Canales's approval, the arms, which had yet to be paid for, were hastily transferred to Brownsville.

36. Sebastián Lerdo de Tejada to Santiago Tapia, September 12, 1862, "Conditions of Affairs in the Republic of Mexico," 242–43. Also, Avery to Seward, September 18, 1866, Matamoros Consular Dispatches, RG 59, NA.

37. Avery to Seward, September 18, 1866, Matamoros Consular Dispatches, RG 59, NA.

38. Avery to Seward, August 23, 1866, Matamoros Consular Dispatches, RG 59, NA.

39. *Brownsville Daily Ranchero,* October 12, 1866.

40. Avery to Seward, September 28, 1866, Matamoros Consular Dispatches, RG 59, NA.

41. *Brownsville Daily Ranchero,* October 24, 1866.

42. Avery to Seward, September 3, 1866, Matamoros Consular Dispatches, RG 59, NA.

43. *New Orleans Daily Picayune,* November 28, 1866.

44. *Brownsville Daily Ranchero,* November 15, 1866.

45. Post Returns, Fort Brown, December 1866, AGO, RG 393, NA.

46. *New Orleans Daily Crescent,* December 9, 1866; *New Orleans Daily Picayune,* November 29, December 6, 7, 8, 1866.

47. *Brownsville Daily Ranchero,* November 27, 1866.

48. P. H. Sheridan to J. A. Rawlings, December 11, 1866, "Conditions of Affairs in the Republic of Mexico," 487.

49. *Brownsville Daily Ranchero,* November 28, 1866.

50. Ibid. Also, M. B. Marshall to Seward, December 1, 1866, Matamoros Consular Dispatches, RG 59, NA.

51. *Brownsville Daily Ranchero,* November 19, 1866; *New Orleans Daily Picayune,* December 6, 1866; *San Antonio Daily Herald,* December 9, 1866.

52 *New Orleans Daily Picayune,* December 7, 1866; *Brownsville Daily Ranchero,* November 29, 1866.

53. *Brownsville Daily Ranchero*, November 28, 1866.

54. Ibid. Also, *Brownsville Daily Ranchero*, November 28, 1866; *New York World*, December 6, 1866; *San Antonio Daily Herald*, December 9, 1866.

55. For exchange of notes between Canales, Escobedo, and Sedgwick, see *New Orleans Daily Crescent*, December 8, 1866. See also, *Brownsville Daily Ranchero*, January 23, 31, 1867.

56. *Galveston Tri-Weekly News*, December 5, 1866; *Brownsville Daily Ranchero*, November 28, 1866.

57. Sheridan to Grant, December 10, 1866, "Conditions of Affairs in the Republic of Mexico," 545.

58. Sheridan to Grant, November 27, 1866, "Conditions of Affairs in the Republic of Mexico," 544.

59. *Brownsville Rio Grande Courier*, December 7, 1866, quoted in "Conditions of Affairs in the Republic of Mexico," no. 1294, 488.

60. *New Orleans Daily Picayune*, December 11, 1866.

61. *Brownsville Daily Ranchero*, December 1, 1866.

62. Ibid., December 2, 1866.

63. *Brownsville Daily Ranchero; New Orleans Daily Picayune*, December 8, 1866.

64. *New Orleans Daily Picayune*, February 8, 1867; Post Returns, January 1867, Ringgold Barracks, AGO, RG 94, NA.

65. *Brownsville Daily Ranchero*, January 25, 29; February 2, 1867; *Galveston Daily News*, January 25, 29, 1867.

66. Manuel A. Gómez to Juárez, March 18, 1866, *Correspondencia de Juárez*, 10:767–68.

67. *Galveston Daily News*, July 16, 1866; *Galveston Daily News*, January 8, 1867.

68. *Flake's Daily Galveston Bulletin*, January 18, 1867.

69. *Galveston Daily News*, February 8, 1867. Also, *Houston Tri-Weekly Telegraph*, April 1, 1867; *Flake's Daily Galveston Bulletin*, February 8, 1867.

70. *Galveston Daily News*, February 1, 1867.

71. *Galveston Daily News*, February 18, 1867, quoting the *Brownsville Daily Ranchero*, February 15, 1867.

72. Berriozábal to Juárez, February 28, 1867, *Correspondencia de Juárez*, 11:1010.

73. Thompson, *Juan Cortina*, 82; *Two Republics* (Mexico City), September 1, 1875.

74. *Brownsville Daily Ranchero*, September 24, 1870. With the news from Querétaro and Mexico City, vicious rumors of Cortina's role in the final days of the Empire were circulated on the frontier. One correspondent in Brownsville said Cortina had been given command of the guard over Maximilian and his conservative generals and that he had "escaped" with them out of the country. See *Galveston Daily News*, June 25, 1867.

75. For details of the execution, see *Brownsville Daily Ranchero*, September 27, 1867. Also, Hyde, *Mexican Empire: The History of Maximilian and Carlota of Mexico*, 311; Roel, *Nuevo León: Apuntes históricos*, 199–200. Also, J. J. Gallegos, "Santiago Vidaurri: Regional Power, Trade and Capital Formation in Northern Mexico." Copy courtesy of the author.

76. *Brownsville Daily Ranchero*, May 28, 1867; *Flake's Daily Galveston Bulletin*, May 28, July 1, 1867.

77. Cortina to Faustina Cortina, July 30, 1867, St. Augustine Parish Archives, Laredo, Texas. It is speculated that Fr. Florencio Andrés, who loved Laredo and regional history and who compiled considerable genealogical data on prominent families of the area, acquired this letter somewhere, possibly in Mexico, and placed it in the church archives. Only small portions of the letter are legible.

78. Cortina to Minister of War, November 24, 1867, Compiled Military Service Record, Archivo de Secretaría de Defensa, Mexico City.

79. *Dallas Herald*, December 7, 1867.

80. *Brownsville Daily Ranchero*, November 13, 1867. Copy courtesy of Práxedis G. Cavazos. Doña Estéfana was buried in the Cavazos Family Cemetery not far from Rancho del Carmen and the banks of the Rio Grande. A century later the cemetery was bulldozed and plowed under

by a local farmer. P. G. Cavazos found portions of tombstones in a nearby irrigation canal. Interviews with P. G. Cavazos, including a tour of the site where Rancho del Carmen once stood, October 19, 20, 1999.

81. *Brownsville Daily Ranchero,* November 15, 1867.
82. Ibid.
83. Ibid.
84. M. B. Marshall to William H. Seward, October 12, 1867, Matamoros Consular Dispatches, RG 59, NA. Also, *New Orleans Crescent,* October 29, 1869; *Two Republics* (Mexico City), October 26, November 2, 6, 9, 1867.
85. *Rio Grande Courier,* n.d., quoted in the *New Orleans Daily Crescent,* October 29, 1867. Also, *Houston Tri-Weekly Telegraph,* October 30, 1867; *Galveston Daily News,* October 19, 1867.
86. *Brownsville Daily Ranchero,* April 13, 1867. This same quote, although shortened, was repeated in the June 13, 1867, issue of the *Daily Ranchero.* With the collapse of the Empire, Maltby had taken the *Ranchero* back to Brownsville.
87. *Brownsville Daily Ranchero,* May 18, 1867.
88. Ibid., January 23, 1867.
89. *Two Republics* (Mexico City), June 27, 1868, quoting the *Brownsville Courier,* n.d.; *Brownsville Daily Ranchero,* June 2, 3, 1868.
90. *Brownsville Daily Ranchero,* March 17, June 4, 1868.
91. *Two Republics* (Mexico City), June 3, 1868, quoting *La Opinión Nacional,* n.d.; *Brownsville Daily Ranchero,* June 11, 1868 quoting *El Siglo Diez y Nueve* (Mexico City), n.d.
92. *Brownsville Daily Ranchero,* August 28, September 5, 1868
93. Cortina to Ignacio Mejía, August 16, 1868, quoted in *Brownsville Daily Ranchero,* September 12, 1868.
94. *Brownsville Daily Ranchero,* September 26, 1868, quoting *El Monitor Republicano* (Mexico City), n.d.
95. *Two Republics* (Mexico City), June 27, 1868.
96. *Brownsville Daily Ranchero,* October 6, 1868.
97. Avery to [Seward], May 19, 1869, Matamoros Consular Dispatches, RG 59, NA.
98. *Brownsville Daily Ranchero,* November 8, 1868.
99. Cortina to Juárez, November 17, 20, 1868, *Correspondencia de Juárez,* 11:695.
100. Cortina to Juárez, December 14, 1868, *Correspondencia de Juárez,* 11:703. Also, *Brownsville Daily Ranchero,* January 3, 1869.
101. *Two Republics* (Mexico City), January 27, 1869.
102. *Brownsville Daily Ranchero,* March 4, 6, 9, 1869.
103. *Two Republics* (Mexico City), July 17, 1869.
104. Ibid., June 12, 1869; *Brownsville Daily Ranchero,* May 18, 1869.
105. Avery to [Seward], May 19, 1969, Matamoros Consular Dispatches, RG 59, NA; *Brownsville Daily Ranchero,* May 27, 1869
106. Juan J. Arrocha to Miguel Palacios, May 26, 1869, in *Brownsville Daily Ranchero,* May 29, 1869.
107. Cortina to Juan José de la Garza, June 5, 1869, quoted in *Brownsville Daily Ranchero,* July 15, 1869.
108. *Brownsville Daily Ranchero,* June 26, July 13, 1869.
109. Avery to Seward, May 19, 1869, Matamoros Consular Dispatches, RG 59, NA.
110. *Two Republics* (Mexico City), January 8, 1870 (first quote); Avery to J. C. B. Davis, January 28, 1870 (second quote). Also, *San Luis Potosí Boletín Oficial,* January 19, 1870.
111. Cortina, Military Service Records, Defensa; Bancroft, *History of Mexico,* vol. 6, 1861–1887, 373–74.
112. Avery to Davis, May 27, 1870, Matamoros Consular Dispatches, RG 59, NA; *Two Republics* (Mexico City), June 25, 1870; *Brownsville Daily Ranchero,* May 28, 31, 1870.
113. John P. Kelsey to Secretary of State, May 24, 30, 1870, Camargo Consular Dispatches, RG 59, NA.

114. Avery to Davis, May 27, 1870, Matamoros Consular Dispatches, RG 59, NA.; *Brownsville Sentinel,* May 27, 1870

115. *Brownsville Daily Ranchero,* June 21, July 2, 1870. Avery to Hamilton Fish, August 17, 1870, Matamoros Consular Dispatches, RG 59, NA.

116. Cortina to Francisco Flores, June 13, 1870, quoted in *Brownsville Daily Ranchero,* July 14, 1870.

117. Thomas F. Wilson to Hamilton Fish, n.d., Matamoros Consular Dispatches, RG 59, NA.

118. Wilson to Fish, September 2, 1870, Matamoros Consular Dispatches, RG 59, NA.

119. *Brownsville Daily Ranchero,* September 22, 1870.

120. Cortina *Pronunciamiento,* September 19, 1870, quoted in *Brownsville Daily Ranchero,* September 22, 1870. Thomas F. Wilson, consul in Matamoros, clipped a copy of the *pronunciamiento* from the *Daily Ranchero* and included it with his September 30, 1870, letter to Secretary of State Hamilton Fish. Also, Thompson, *Juan Cortina,* 69.

121. Cortina to Aspe, September 29, 1870, quoted in *Brownsville Daily Ranchero,* October 6, 1870.

122. Wilson to Fish, September 30, 1870, Matamoros Consular Dispatches, RG 59, NA.

123. Edmund J. Davis to S. Powers, April 8, 1871, James B. Wells Papers, CAH.

124. *Nueces Valley* (Corpus Christi), October 12, 1872. The resolution and a copy of the petition are reproduced in C. Goldfinch, *Cortina, A Re-Appraisal,* 53–57.

125. C. Goldfinch, *Cortina: A Re-Appraisal,* 58.

Chapter Eight

1. Wilson to William Hunter, August 1, 1871, Matamoros Consular Dispatches, RG 59, NA.

2. M. Kenedy to A. McD. McCook, April 6, 1872, LR, AGO, RG 94, NA. Also, "Depredations on the Rio Grande," 434.

3. *Two Republics* (Mexico City), January 28, 1870 [1871].

4. "Depredations on the Rio Grande," 434.

5. *Relación de las escrituras públicas otorgadas en esta Ciudad de 1833 a 1929,* Archivo Municipal de Matamoros (AMM), hojas 6, 7. Courtesy of Oscar Rivera Saldaña. By this time, he had already acquired Rancho de la Bolsa.

6. *Relación de las escrituras públicas,* hojas 7, 18, AMM.

7. Ibid., hojas 18–19, AMM.

8. McCook to Actg. Asst. Adjutant General, April 4, 1872, LR, AGO, RG 94, NA.

9. *Brownsville Sentinel,* July 14, 1871, contained in ibid. Cortina's old enemy, John S. Ford, was the editor of the *Sentinel* while James Daugherty served as publisher. A few of the Tejano ranchers such as Sabás Cavazos and Carlos Esparza, were able to recover some of their stolen cattle.

10. *Brownsville Daily Ranchero,* August 1, 1871, contained in Wilson to Hunter, August 1, 1871, Matamoros Consular Dispatches, RG 59, NA.

11. Robert B. Foster, Certification and List of Indictments, August 19, 1871, in Matamoros Consular Dispatches, RG 59, NA.

12. Ibid. Also, *Two Republics* (Mexico City), August 26, 1871.

13. McCook to Wilson, August 2, 1871, Matamoros Consular Dispatches, RG 59, NA.

14. Francisco Fuentes Farías to the Justices of the Peace and Chiefs of the Rural Police, July 18, 1871, published in *Brownsville Sentinel,* July 21, 1871.

15. Wilson to McCook, August 3, 1871 (first quote); and Palacios to Wilson, August 17, 1871 (second quote); both in Matamoros Consular Dispatches, RG 59, NA.

16. *Two Republics* (Mexico City), April 13, 1872.

17. Wilson to Hunter, August 9, 1871, Matamoros Consular Dispatches, RG 59, NA.

18. Wilson to Thos. H. Nelson, August 3, 1871, Matamoros Consular Dispatches, RG 59, NA.

19. Wilson to Hunter, November 13, 1871, Matamoros Consular Dispatches, RG 59, NA.

20. Avery to Wilson, January 31, 1872, Matamoros Consular Dispatches, RG 59, NA; *Nueces Valley* (Corpus Christi), February 10, 17, 1872.

21. Lucius Avery to Hunter, February 6, 1872, Camargo Consular Dispatches, RG 59, NA.
22. Wilson to Hunter, February 10, 1872, Matamoros Consular Dispatches, RG 59, NA.
23. Ibid. For more criticism of Cortina, see *Two Republics* (Mexico City), January 24, 1872.
24. Statement of McCook, n.d., enclosed with Belknap to Secretary of State, May 14, 1872, LR, AGO, RG 94, NA.
25. Wilson to Hunter, April 7, 1872; Miguel Palacios, El C. General Miguel Palacios, Comandante Militar de la Plaza de Matamoros, á sus Habitantes, April 8, 1872; and English translation of same; Gerónimo Treviño, General en Jefe del Ejercito Constitucional del Norte á los Matamorenses, April de 1872; all in Matamoros Consular Dispatches, RG 59, NA.
26. Wilson to Hunter, May 9, 1872, Matamoros Consular Dispatches, RG 59, NA; and Anderson to Act. Asst. Adjt. General, May 28, 1872, LR, AGO, RG 94, NA.
27. *Matamoros Boletín Oficial,* July 25, 1872.
28. *Two Republics* (Mexico City), October 5, 1872.
29. *Nueces Valley* (Corpus Christi), March 23, 1872.
30. Report of the Grand Jury of Cameron County, Texas, August 28, 1871, "Report of the Committee on Foreign Relations," 45th Cong., 2d sess., 89. Hereafter referred to as *RCFR.*
31. Ibid., 90.
32. For example see, *Nueces Valley* (Corpus Christi), September 17, 1871; March 23, 1872.
33. *Brownsville Daily Ranchero,* March 26, 1872; *Nueces Valley* (Corpus Christi), April 6, 1872; and *RCFR,* 91–93. Of the twenty-one men on the grand jury, Ford was the only individual from the border. A copy of the grand jury report is also enclosed with H. P. Kellogg (U.S. Senator from Louisiana) to Charles A. Whitney, April 1, 1872, LR, AGO, RG 94, NA.
34. Ibid.
35. Report of the Grand Jury of Hidalgo County, at the Spring Term of 1872, in regard to Mexican Invasions and Depredations, April 5, 1872, in LR, AGO, RG 94, NA.
36. Ibid.
37. *Brownsville Daily Ranchero and Republican,* April 24, 1872; and *Nueces Valley* (Corpus Christi), April 6, 1872.
38. Wilson to Hunter, March 27, 1872, Matamoros Consular Dispatches, RG 59, NA.
39. Kenedy to McCook, April 6, 1872, LR, AGO, RG 94, NA.
40. Ibid.
41. Endorsements on C. A. Whitney to C. B. Darrell, April 1, 9, 11, 1872, LR, AGO, RG 94, NA.
42. Augur to Townsend, April 12, 1872; Augur, Circular Letter, n.d., 1872; and Augur endorsement on McCook to Actg. Asst. Adjutant General, April 4, 1872; all in LR, AGO, RG 94, NA.
43. O. W. Budd to Augur, August 22, 1872, LR, AGO, RG 94, NA.
44. Andrew Sheridan to Acting Assistant Adjutant General, December 10, 1872; and Sheridan to Ayuntamiento of Camargo, December 9, 1972; both in LR, AGO, RG 94, NA.
45. T. M. Anderson to Acting Asst. Adjt. Gen'l., April 17, 1872, LR, AGO, RG 94, NA.
46. Anderson to Act'g. Ass't. Adjt. General, May 28, 1972, LR, AGO, RG 94, NA; Fish to Belknap, May 15, 1873; Thomas H. Nelson to Fish, April 25, 1873; J. M. Lafragua to Nelson, April 12, 1873; [Ignacio] Mejía to Citizen Minister of Foreign Affairs, April 9, 1873; all in LR, AGO, RG 94, NA.
47. E. G. Bush to Post Adjutant, March 31, 1872, LR, AGO, RG 94, NA. Also, List of those who entered Mier, Mexico, n.d., enclosed with ibid.
48. Charles Wilson to William Hunter, March 17, 1872, Guerrero Consular Dispatches, RG 59, NA; and *Nueces Valley* (Corpus Christi), March 30, 1872.
49. *Matamoros El Fronterizo,* March 27, 1872; Charles Winslow to Wilson, March 14, 1872; and Wilson to Hunter, March 29, 1872; both in Matamoros Consular Dispatches, RG 59, NA.
50. Hamilton Fish to W. W. Belknap, April 7, 1872; and Winslow to Hunter, March 17, 1872; both in LR, AGO, RG 94, NA.
51. E. D. T. to Augur (telegram), April 1, 1872; and Fish to Belknap, April 17, 1872; both in LR, AGO, RG 94, NA.

52. Bush to Post Adjutant, March 31, 1872, LR, AGO, RG 94, NA.
53. Ibid. Also, T. M. Anderson to Act. Asst. Adjutant General, April 2, 1872, LR, AGO, RG 94, NA.
54. *DFT* (1872), 1.
55. *DFT* (1874), 2.
56. Ibid., 19.
57. Ibid., 3.
58. Anaclito Padrón Testimony, *DFT* (1872), 12–13.
59. Apolinario Hernández Testimony, *DFT* (1872), 13, 21, 32. Much of Hernández's testimony can be found in Lea, *King Ranch*, 1:274–75,
60. *New York Times*, January 14, 1873. See also, Benito García Testimony, *Richard King vs. United Mexican States*, 103–104.
61. Gregorio Villarreal Testimony, *DFT* (1872), 15, 17, 27, 32; Villarreal Testimony, *Richard King vs. United Mexican States*, 123–29.
62. Victor Morel Testimony, *DFT* (1872), 15.
63. William Burke Testimony, *DFT* (1872), 15–16, 31. Burke's testimony can also be found in *Richard King vs. United Mexican States*, 71–75,
64. Albert Dean Testimony, *DFT* (1872), 31.
65. Thomas C. Sheldon Testimony, *DFT* (1872), 31.
66. Carlos Esparza Testimony, *DFT* (1872), 31; Esparza Testimony in *Richard King vs. United Mexican States*, 92–98.
67. Thaddeus M. Rhodes Testimony, *DFT* (1872), 31.
68. Albert Champion Testimony, *DFT* (1872), 33.
69. W. D. Thomas Testimony, *DFT* (1872), 16; and Thomas Testimony in *Richard King vs. United Mexican States*, 85–86. While working as a guide for the army and the Rangers in pursuit of *Cortinistas* in 1875, Thomas accidentally shot and killed himself. *New York World*, June 19, 1875.
70. Pedro Vela Testimony, *DFT* (1872), 33.
71. Claims of Richard King, *DFT* (1872), 46, 54, 57; and *Richard King vs. United Mexican States*, 64–66.
72. Lea, *King Ranch*, 1:273–74.
73. *DFT* (1872), 44, 54, 56–59.
74. Ibid., 44, 47, 54, 59.
75. Ibid., 49, 51. "Outline of the Dobie Family of Virginia and Texas," typescript courtesy of Dudley Dobie.
76. *DFT* (1872), 2.
77. Ibid., 23.
78. Ibid., 39–40.
79. *New York Times*, October 14, 1874.
80. Ibid. Also, *Austin Daily Democratic Statesman*, April 21, May 23, 1874.
81. "Gen. Juan N. Cortina to the Frontiersmen on both banks of the River Bravo," August 27, 1872, Christopher C. Augur Papers, Newberry Library, Chicago, Illinois. Copy courtesy of Robert Wooster. This *pronunciamiento* is not in Thompson, *Juan Cortina*.
82. Ibid.
83. *Two Republics* (Mexico City), October 12, 1872.
84. *Reports of the Committee of Investigation Sent in 1873*, iii (first quote); *Two Republics* (Mexico City), October 26, 1872 (second quote). First published in Mexico City in 1873 as *Informe General de la Comisión Pesquisidora de la Frontera del Norte*, the 443-page report was translated into English and published in New York in 1875.
85. *Reports of the Committee of Investigation Sent in 1873*, iv, 35.
86. See criticisms of the *Brownsville Sentinel* in George W. Clarke's *Two Republics* (Mexico City), March 1, 1873. See also *El Monitor Republicano* (Mexico City), June 22, 1877.
87. *Report of the Committee of Investigation Sent in 1873*, 45, 55, quoting the *Brownsville Sentinel*,

February 14, 1873. For documenting the drought, the Mexican Comisión used the *Brownsville Daily Ranchero*, June 13, 1872; *Brownsville Sentinel*, January 14, 1873; *San Antonio Express*, February 27, March 27, 1873; and the *San Antonio Weekly Herald*, March 18, 1873.

88. *Report of the Committee of Investigation Sent in 1873*, 56, quoting *Brownsville Daily Ranchero*, March 1, 1873.

89. *Report of the Committee of Investigation Sent in 1873*, 84–85, 88–89.

90. Ibid., iii–iv. José T. Canales would later write that when printed copies of the Mexican Comisión Report appeared in Brownsville and Matamoros, Francisco Yturria bought all the copies and had them destroyed. Canales, *Bandit or Patriot*, 16.

91. Canales, *Bandit or Patriot*, 214.

92. Ibid., 153–54.

93. Ibid., 157, 160–62, quoting the *Brownsville Sentinel*, January 27, 1871. For a summation of the finding of the Mexican Border Commission, see *San Antonio Express*, January 3, 1873.

94. *Two Republics* (Mexico City), August 23, 1873.

CHAPTER NINE

1. Wilson to Hunter, December 22, 1873, Matamoros Consular Dispatches, RG 59, NA.
2. Ibid.
3. Ibid.
4. *Two Republics* (Mexico City), February 8, 1874, quoting *Brownsville Daily Ranchero*, n.d.
5. Wilson to Hunter, April 18, 1874, Matamoros Consular Dispatches, RG 59, NA.
6. Wilson to Hunter, March 8, 1874, Matamoros Consular Dispatches, RG 59, NA.
7. James O. Luby, Inquest Proceedings, December 8, 1873, Dispatches from the Mexican Consulate in the United States, RG 94, NA.
8. Richard Coke to M. Morales, May 8, 1874, in *Two Republics* (Mexico City), September 6, 1874.
9. Ign. Mariscal to Mr. Secretary, January 30, 1875, Mexican Consulate Dispatches, RG 59, NA.
10. *Two Republics* (Mexico City), September 6, 1874, quoting *Brownsville Daily Ranchero*, n.d.; *San Antonio Herald*, May 12, 1875, quoting *Galveston Daily News*, May 5, 1875.
11. Mariscal to Mr. Secretary, January 30, 1875, Mexican Consulate Dispatches, RG 59, NA.
12. Wilson to Hunter, March 10, 21, 1874, Matamoros Consular Dispatches, RG 59, NA.
13. Wilson to Hunter, July 5, 1876, Matamoros Consular Dispatches, RG 59, NA.
14. Wilson to Hunter, April 22, 23; May 7, 1874, Matamoros Consular Dispatches, RG 59, NA.
15. Jno. Jay Smith, Statement of Expenses, May 31, 1874; Wilson to Hunter, May 31, 1874; both in Matamoros Consular Dispatches, RG 59, NA. Hamilton later returned voluntarily to the United States.
16. Wilson to Hunter, April 18, 1875; Wilson to Julius A. Skelton, April 18, 1875; both in Matamoros Consular Dispatches, RG 59, NA. One such case was that of Juan Flores who was accused of murder in Refugio County.
17. *New York World*, May 23, 1875; *San Antonio Express*, February 15, 17, 24, 1875; Leiker, *Racial Borders: Black Soldiers along the Rio Grande*, 54–55.
18. J. F. Wade to Assistant Adjutant General, May 12, 1875, LR, AGO, RG 94, NA.
19. J. S. Mauser to J. H. Tachau, February 17, 1875, LR, AGO, RG 94, NA. Also, Theodore A. Davis to Editor of the *Brownsville Ranchero*, February 11, 1875, LR, AGO, RG 94, NA.
20. Edward Hatch to Assistant Adjutant General, March 10, 1875, LR, AGO, RG 94, NA.
21. C. D. Beyer to Post Adjutant at Ringgold Barracks, March 4, 1875, LR, AGO, RG 94, NA.
22. Francis Moore to Post Adjutant, Ringgold Barracks, March 8, 1875, LR, AGO, RG 94, NA.
23. Lucius Avery to Hunter, April 24, 1875, Camargo Consular Dispatches, RG 59, NA.

24. A. Glavecke to John E. Mix, March 8, 1875, LR, AGO, RG 94, NA.

25. Hager, "The Nuecestown Raid of 1875: A Border Incident," 258–70. Also, Dodson, "The Noakes Raid"; Morris, "The Mexican Raid of 1875 on Corpus Christi," 175, also at http://www.tsha.utexas.edu/publications/journals/shq/online/v004/. Later, the sons of Thomas Noakes sought claims of $50,000 against the Mexican government for which they were paid $7,125 in 1945. *The Handbook of Texas Online*, s.v. "Nuecestown Raid of 1875," http://www.tsha.utexas.edu/handbook/online/articles.

26. Avery to Hunter, April 24, 1875, Camargo Consular Dispatches, RG 59, NA. Also, *Corpus Christi Weekly Gazette*, June 5, 1875; Avery to Wilson, April 6, 1875; John Vale to Collector of Customs at Brownsville; both in *Adjutant General's Report* (1875), 39, 41.

27. Coke to Grant, March 30, 1875, LR, AGO, RG 94, NA.

28. E. D. T. to Sherman, March 31, 1875, LR, AGO, RG 94, NA.

29. Dobie, *Vaquero of the Brush Country*, 62.

30. L. H. McNelly to William Steele, April 29, 1875, as quoted in Dobie, *Vaquero of the Brush Country*, 238–39.

31. Hager, "The Nuecestown Raid of 1875," 267–68.

32. *Adjutant General's Report* (1875, 8).

33. Ibid., 10.

34. For example, see the testimony of Jesús Sandoval in *Adjutant General's Report* (1875), 17–20.

35. Durham, *Taming the Nueces Strip: The Story of McNelly's Rangers*, 54. Also, Parsons and Little, *Captain L. H. McNelly, Texas Ranger: The Life and Times of a Fighting Man*, 192; Utley, *Lone Star Justice*, 162.

36. Geo. A. Hall Affidavit, June 11, 1875, in *Adjutant General's Report* (1875), 32–33; *TFT*, 129. Also, Joseph E. Dwyer to Ord, July 5, 1875, enclosed with Ord to Assistant Adjutant General, September 10, 1875, in LR, AGO, RG 94, NA; *New York World*, June 13, 1875.

37. Affidavit of John L. Haynes, June 21, 1875, in *Adjutant General's Report* (1875), 47–48.

38. Coke to Pres. of the U.S., June 6, 1875, LR, AGO, RG 94, NA.

39. McNelly Congressional Testimony, January 29, 1876, *TFT*, 14–15.

40. Quoted in Durham, *Taming the Nueces Strip*, 59–62. For details, see Parsons and Little, *L. H. McNelly*, 198–201. Also, Utley, *Lone Star Justice*, 163; *San Antonio Express*, June 14, 19, 1875. Just as the legacy of the *Cortinistas* would survive through lively *corridos*, the Texas Rangers had their demeaning and racist ballads:

> From mortal fear and loss of blood,
> The Bugler's limbs, they quiver.
> But knowing well he ne'er again
> Would see his Rio Grande river,
> He braced himself, and gazed around
> Like tiger cat at bay:
> Then yelled, "Viva el Cortina!"
> Which was his final say.
>
> Then hastily we pack our traps,
> And take our morning meal.
> Fall into line, answer the roll,
> And southward silently steal,
> Leaving the rigid bugler there,
> Slow swaying 'neath the tree;
> A warning to all Greasers, who
> May that way to be.

Dallas Weekly Herald, May 1, 1875. Courtesy of Chuck Parsons.

41. Townsend to Belknap, June 14, 1875; Belknap to O. E. Babcock, June 15, 1975; both in LR, AGO, RG 94, NA. Arrested later, Holguín was extradited and served time in Huntsville. Parsons and Little, *Captain L. H. McNelly*, 339, n.24; *New York World*, June 13, 1875.
42. Ord to Belknap, June 17, 1875, LR, AGO, RG 94, NA.
43. Wm. D. Whipple to Adjutant General, June 14, 1875; Sherman to W. D. Whipple, June 15, 1875; Sheridan to H. Crosby, June 16, 1875; Sheridan to Townsend, June 16, 1875; Sheridan to Sherman, June 16, 1875; Grant to Sec'y of War, June 17, 1875; all in LR, AGO, RG 94, NA.
44. *Austin Daily Democratic Statesman*, January 8, March 1875; May 23, June 10, 16, 27, 1877.
45. *Two Republics* (Mexico City), March 22, 1876; *San Antonio Express*, December 1, 1875.
46. *Austin Daily Democratic Statesman*, July 17, 1875.
47. John W. Foster to Fish, May 4, 1875, *TFT*, 152.
48. Ibid. At least one newspaper in Mexico City denied that American diplomatic pressure had anything to do with Cortina's arrest. *El Siglo Diez y Nueve* (Mexico City), July 30, 1875.
49. Foster to Fish, July 12, 1875, *TFT*, 160; *New York World*, May 21, 1875.
50. *New York World*, June 6, 13, 1875. Also, *Austin Tri-Weekly Statesman*, July 17, August 20, 26, 1875.
51. *New York Times*, July 2, 3, 1875; *Two Republics* (Mexico City), July 28, 1875; *New York World*, June 6, August 16, 1875; *Austin Daily Democratic Statesman*, July 4, 17; August 20, 26, 1875; Foster to Fish, July 12, 1875, *TFT*, 160.
52. Proclamation by José L. Christo [sic], July 1, 1875, in *New York Times*, July 11, 1875. Three individuals who provided information that helped facilitate Cortina's arrest were later assassinated.
53. *New York World*, July 12, 1875.
54. Wm. D. Whipple to Adj. Gen'l., July 2, 1875, LR, AGO, RG 95, NA. Also, *Austin Daily Democratic Statesman*, July 17, August 20, 26, 1875.
55. *New York Times*, July 2, 3, 9, 1875.
56. Foster to Fish, July 12, 1875, *TFT*, 160; *Two Republics* (Mexico City), July 28, 1875.
57. Foster to Fish, July 7, 1875, *TFT*, 160–61.
58. Ibid.
59. *Matamoros Alcancel Num. 66 del Eco de Ambas Fronteras*, October 8, 1875, contained with Ord Endorsement, October 4, 1875; Belknap to Secretary of War, October 28, 1875, LR, AGO, 1875, NA, and published in *TFT*, 115–19.
60. Ord to Adjutant General, October 4, 1875, LR, AGO, RG 94, NA.
61. Cortina, Compiled Military Service Record, Archivo de Secretaría de Defensa, Mexico City.
62. *Two Republics* (Mexico City), May 31, 1876.
63. Ford, *Rip Ford's Texas*, 413–14. Allegedly, the loan was never repaid.
64. Cortina to Díaz, August 17, 1877, *Archivo del General Porfirio Díaz, Memorias y Documentos*, 18:273. In February 1878, Cavazos traveled to Mexico City in an attempt to collect the debt. At a stately banquet in the capital, he was said to have drunk two glasses of liquor after which he fell ill and died. Cavazos's family has always held that Díaz was responsible for having him poisoned. After an elaborate funeral, which Díaz staged in the capital, Col. Práxedis Cavazos took the remains by train to Veracruz and then on the *Independencia* (the same vessel that had carried Cortina to prison in 1876) to Bagdad and then to Brownsville where he was buried at San Pedro near the Cavazos Ranch. Cavazos, "Cavazos Family History," 1–2; Cavazos, "Dedication and Unveiling Ceremony of a State Historical Marker for the Sabás Cavazos Cemetery," October 26, 1996. Copy courtesy of P. G. Cavazos. Also, P. G. Cavazos interview with author, October 19, 20, 1999.
65. *Two Republics* (Mexico City), April 5, 1876.
66. Ibid., April 19, 1876.
67. McCormack, "Porfirio Díaz en las Fronteras Texana, 1875–1877," 402; Perry, *Juárez and Díaz: Machine Politics in Mexico*, 415–28; Wilson to Hunter, January 8, March 23, April 1, 3, 1876, Matamoros Consular Dispatches, RG 59, NA; *Galveston News*, April 4, 1876.

68. Wilson to Fish, April 12, 1876, Matamoros Consular Dispatches, RG 59, NA.

69. Perry, *Juárez and Díaz*, 233–34; Wilson to Fish, April 16, 24, May 18, 20, 1876, Matamoros Consular Dispatches, RG 59, NA.

70. Juan N. Cortina to the Nation, May 18, 1876, in "Report and Accompanying Documents of the Committee on Foreign Affairs on the Relations of the United States with Mexico," 45th Cong., 2d sess., no. 701:198. Also, *Two Republics* (Mexico City), May 31, 1876; Foster to Fish, May 26, 1876, enclosing Cortina *pronunciamiento* from *El Monitor Republicano* (Mexico City), May 26, 1876. Also, *San Antonio Express*, September 2, 1876.

71. Foster to Fish, May 26, 1876, *Committee on Foreign Affairs* (1878), 198.

72. Ord Endorsement, October 4, 1875, *TFT*, 120. The *pronunciamiento* was translated at department headquarters in San Antonio by Lt. Alfred Maurice Raphall. *Mexico City Two Eagles*, September 1, 1875; Citizen General Juan N. Cortina and his Accusers Before the Nation, August 20, 1875, *TFT*, 115–19. Also, Thompson, *Juan Cortina*, 74–85.

73. *Matamoros Eco de Ambas Fronteras*, October 8, 1875; *TFT*, 120.

74. Ord Endorsement, October 4, 1875, enclosing copy of *Matamoros Eco de Ambas Fronteras*, September 8, 1875; Belknap to Secretary of War, 28, 1875, LR, AGO, RG 94, NA

75. Ballard, *Juárez and Díaz*, 245; *Two Republics* (Mexico City), June 7, 1876.

76. Avery to Hunter, September 19, 1876, Camargo Consular Dispatches, RG 59, NA; John F. Valls to Secretary of State, September 9, 1876, Matamoros Consular Dispatches, RG 59, NA; *El Siglo Diez y Nueve* (Mexico City), July 22, August 26, September 2, 5, October 9, 1876.

77. *El Monitor Republicano*, (Mexico City), March 16, 1877.

78. *Brownsville El Progreso*, quoted in *El Siglo Diez y Nueve* (Mexico City), August 8, 1876; January 23, 1877; Wilson to Hunter, December 26, 1876; January 3, 1877, Matamoros Consular Dispatches, RG 59, NA. Revueltas also threatened to execute several of the businessmen including Francisco Yturria.

79. Wilson to Fish, July 6, 7, 1876, Matamoros Consular Dispatches, RG 59, NA.

80. Cortina to Wilson, December 2, 1876; Wilson to Hunter, December 5, 1876; both in Matamoros Consular Dispatches, RG 59, NA.

81. Cortina to Díaz, December 12, 1876, *Archivo del General Porfirio Díaz, Memorias y Documentos*, 14:278. The Cortina Brigade consisted of two battalions of the National Guard and units he entitled Los Fieles de Camargo, Los Rifleros de Bagdad, Los Guias de Tamaulipas, Los Carabineros de Tamaulipas, Los Exploradores de la Frontera, and Los Fieles de Bagdad. *El Monitor Republicano*, (Mexico City), March 2, 1877.

82. *El Siglo Diez y Nueve* (Mexico City), January 6, 1877; Wilson to Hunter, December 5, 1876, Matamoros Consular Dispatches, RG 59, NA.

83. *El Siglo Diez y Nueve* (Mexico City), January 24, 1877

84. *El Monitor Republicano* (Mexico City), March 2, 1877.

85. Cortina to Díaz, January 10, 1877, *Archivo del General Porfirio Díaz, Memorias y Documentos*, 16:37.

86. Wilson to Hunter, January 8, 1877, Matamoros Consular Dispatches, RG 59, NA.

87. Miguel Blanco to Cortina, February 17, 1877, contained with Wilson to Hunter, February 17, 1877, Matamoros Consular Dispatches, RG 59, NA. Also, *Two Republics* (Mexico City), March 10, 1877; *El Monitor Republicano* (Mexico City), March 8, 1877.

88. Gen. Juan N. Cortina to [the] Brigade of National Guard Under his Command, February 16, 1877, contained with Wilson to Hunter, February 17, 1877, Matamoros Consular Dispatches, RG 59, NA.

89. *El Siglo Diez y Nueve* (Mexico City), January 27, 1877.

90. *El Monitor Republicano* (Mexico City), March 27, May 29, 1877.

91. Cortina to Díaz, February 20, 1877, *Archivo del General Porfirio Díaz, Memorias y Documentos*, 18:137.

92. *El Monitor Republicano* (Mexico City), March 7, 1877.

93. Wilson to Hunter, February 24, 1877, Matamoros Consular Dispatches, RG 59, NA; *San Antonio Express,* April 24, 1877.
94. Wilson to Hunter February 28, 1877, Matamoros Consular Dispatches, RG 59, NA.
95. *El Siglo Diez y Nueve* (Mexico City), March 13, 1877.
96. Ibid., March 30, 1877.
97. *El Monitor Republicano* (Mexico City), March 25, 1877.
98. Ford, *Rip Ford's Texas,* 413–14.
99. Práxedis Cavazos and Sabás Cavazos to Díaz, March 9, 1877, *Archivo del General Porfirio Díaz, Memorias y Documentos,* 19:203; Canales to Minister of War, March 28, 1877, in *El Monitor Republicano* (Mexico City), May 2, 1877.
100. Canales to Díaz, April 9, 1877, *Archivo del General Porfirio Díaz, Memorias y Documentos,* 19:216. Also, *El Monitor Republicano* (Mexico City), April 3, 11, 1877.
101. Canales to Díaz, April 9, 1877, *Archivo del General Porfirio Díaz, Memorias y Documentos,* 21:96; and Plácido Vega to Díaz, April 26, 1877, in Flaquer, ed., *Catálogo de documentos—Carta de la colección Porfirio Díaz, Tamaulipas, Marzo 1876–Noviembre 1885,* 2:21.
102. Luis Mier y Terán to Díaz, April 12, 1877, *Archivo del General Porfirio Díaz, Memorias y Documentos,* 19:136; *El Monitor Republicano* (Mexico City), April 15, 18, 1877; *El Siglo Diez y Nueve* (Mexico City), April 3, 1877.
103. *El Monitor Republicano* (Mexico City), May 19, 1877.
104. *Two Republics* (Mexico City), December 2, 1877.
105. Cortina to Díaz, May 24, 1877, *Archivo del General Porfirio Díaz, Memorias y Documentos,* 22:182.
106. Díaz to Cortina, May 24, 1877, *Archivo del General Porfirio Díaz, Memorias y Documentos,* 22:182.
107. *El Siglo Diez y Nueve* (Mexico City), June 16, 1877.
108. Ibid., June 9, 1877.
109. *El Monitor Republicano* (Mexico City), June 6, 1877.
110. Cortina to Manuel Gonzáles, August 17, 1877, *Archivo del General Porfirio Díaz, Memorias y Documentos,* 26:273–74.
111. Díaz to Cortina, October 3, 1877, *Archivo del General Porfirio Díaz, Memorias y Documentos,* 27:186. Also, *San Antonio Daily Express,* May 24, 1908.
112. Cortina to Díaz, October 2, 1877, *Archivo del General Porfirio Díaz, Memorias y Documentos,* 27:185–86.
113. Cortina to Díaz, November 9, 1877, *Archivo del General Porfirio Díaz, Memorias y Documentos,* 28:20–21.
114. Díaz to Cortina, November 12, 1977, *Archivo del General Porfirio Díaz, Memorias y Documentos,* 28:21.
115. Cortina to Díaz, January 18, 1878, *Archivo del General Porfirio Díaz, Memorias y Documentos,* 28:147–48.
116. Cortina to Díaz, January 26, 1878, *Archivo del General Porfirio Díaz, Memorias y Documentos,* 28:157.
117. Díaz to Cortina, January 28, 1878, *Archivo del General Porfirio Díaz, Memorias y Documentos,* 28:157.
118. Villegas, *United States Versus Porfirio Díaz,* 156.
119. Report of the Special Committee on the Mexican Border Troubles, February 29, 1876, in "Report and Accompanying Documents of the Committee on Foreign Affairs on the Relations of the United States with Mexico," 150–66.
120. *New York Herald,* January 14, 1878; *Galveston Daily News,* January 23, 1878.
121. *Galveston Daily News,* January 23, 1878.
122. *New York Herald,* January 14, 1878.
123. *Galveston Weekly News,* January 20, 1878.

124. *San Antonio Daily Express,* May 24, 1908.

125. Statements by José Justo Alvarez, March 15, 1881, Miguel Negrete, n.d., and Sostenes Rocha, November 16, 1881, all in Cortina, Compiled Military Service Record, Archivo de Secretaría de Defensa, Mexico City.

126. Johns, *The City of Mexico in the Age of Díaz,* 4–5.

127. Although there is scant documentary proof of Cortina's visit to the border, Charles W. Goldfinch, while writing his thesis at the University of Chicago, interviewed Albino Canales of Premont, Texas, who was eleven years old at the time of Cortina's visit, and who remembered the banquet. Being the son-in-law of José T. Canales, Goldfinch was also privy to a great deal of oral history. C. Goldfinch, *Cortina, A Re-Appraisal,* 63. One of the *corridos* Américo Paredes was able to recover in the 1950s recalled Cortina's last visit to the border. From the tone of Díaz's letters to Cortina, however, it seems unlikely that he would have permitted Cortina to return to Matamoros. Cortina did visit Matamoros, as confirmed by his military service record, however.

128. *New York Times,* May 11, 1890.

129. Bancroft, *History of the North Mexican States and Texas,* 2:448, 468.

130. Cortina to Ford, October 17, 1891; Ford Statement, January 21, 1897; both in John S. Ford Papers, Haley Memorial Library and History Center. A draft of Ford's article that appeared in the *San Antonio Express,* November 2, 1890, can also be found in the John S. Ford Papers at the Haley Memorial Library and History Center. A clipping of the same letter from the *Dallas Times Herald,* n.d., can be found in the Bancroft Papers, Newspapers Clippings, Bancroft Library. Courtesy of Carlos Larralde. In his *History of the North Mexican States and Texas,* Bancroft does have the basic facts of the Cortina War essentially correct.

131. Ford, Cortina Observations, n.d., John S. Ford Papers, Haley Memorial Library and History Center.

132. Cortina to Díaz, August 23, 1892, Díaz Papers, Universidad Iberoamericana.

133. Díaz to Cortina, August 17, 1892, Díaz Papers, Universidad Iberoamericana.

134. *El Correo de Laredo,* September 23, 1891; *Corpus Christi Weekly Caller,* September 26, October 3, 1891; December 1, 1893; *San Antonio Express,* November 15, 1893.

135. *Corpus Christi Weekly Caller,* December 1, 1893. Also, *San Antonio Daily Express,* November 15, 1893.

136. Espuela, Gen. Juan N. Cortina. Courtesy of P. G. Cavazos.

137. Calculated from Cortina's Compiled Military Service Record, Archivo de Secretaría de Defensa, Mexico City.

138. *Mexico City La Patria,* November 1, 1894; *San Antonio Daily Express,* November 2, 3, 1894; *Brownsville Daily Herald,* November 5, 1894.

139. *Brownsville Daily Herald,* November 5, 1894. At the time of his death, Cortina would have found it interesting that the Reds and Blues, with torchlight parades, *pachangas,* and fiery *gritos,* were struggling for political control of Brownsville and Cameron County.

140. *Two Republics* (Mexico City), November 2, 1894.

141. *San Antonio Daily Express,* November 3, 1894.

Conclusion

1. Paredes, *A Texas-Mexican Cancionero: Folksongs of the Lower Border,* 23, 47–48; Paredes, *"With His Pistol in His Hand": A Border Ballad and Its Hero,* 138–40. "El General Cortina" took three stanzas from different *corridos.* The first refers to the shooting of Marshal Shears in Brownsville in 1859; the second makes reference to Cortina's visit to the border in 1891; and the last refers to his death. Both Paredes and C. Goldfinch mistakenly place Cortina's death in 1892.

2. Reséndez, *Changing National Identities at the Frontier: Texas and New Mexico, 1800–1850,* 265–71.

Bibliography

MANUSCRIPTS AND ARCHIVAL COLLECTIONS

Archivo General del Estado de Nuevo León, Monterrey, Nuevo León. Correspondencia de Santiago Vidaurri.
Archivo General del Estado de Tamaulipas, Ciudad Victoria, Tamaulipas.
Archivo Histórico Municipal de Matamoros, Matamoros, Tamaulipas.
Archivo de Secretaría de Defensa, Mexico City. Cortina, Juan, Compiled Military Service Record.
Benson Latin American Collection, University of Texas at Austin. Bazaine, Achille Francois, Papers. García, Genaro, Papers. Mexico and the United States General Claims Commission, Papers. Romero, Matís, Papers (microfilm).
British National Archives, Kaw, Great Britain. Consular Dispatches, Tampico, Mexico, Records of the Foreign Office. Vice Consular Dispatches, Matamoros, Mexico. Records of the Foreign Office.
Brownsville Historical Society, Brownsville, Texas. Champion, A. A., Papers. Egly, Victor, "Memorandom [sic] Book From tim[es] I comenced [sic] to Steamboadings [sic]" (photocopy).
Center for the Study of American History, University of Texas at Austin. Bee, Hamilton P., Papers. Ford, John S., Memoirs (seven volumes). Haynes, John L., Papers. Kingsbury, Gilbert D., Papers. Kuykendall, James Hampton, Journal. Leyendecker, John Z., Papers. Powers, Stephen, Papers. Robertson, George Lee, Papers. Wells, James B., Papers.
Harvard University Library. Stillman, Charles, Papers.
Hayley Memorial Library, Midland, Texas. Ford, John S., Papers.
King Ranch Archives, Kingsville, Texas. Kenedy, Mifflin, Letterbook. King, Richard, Letters.
Library of Congress, Washington, D.C. Heintzelman, Samuel Peter, Papers and Journals. Pickett, John T., Papers, Domestic Correspondence of the Confederacy, Office of the Secretary of State, Manuscript Division. Sheridan, Philip, Papers.
Ministère de Guerre, Paris, France. Du Pin, Charles, Memoirs.
National Archives, Washington, D.C. Applications from Former Confederates for Presidential Pardons (Amnesty Papers), Record Group 94. Consular Dispatches, Camargo, Mexico, Records of the United States Department of State, Record Group 59. Consular

Dispatches, Chihuahua, Mexico, Records of the United States Department of State, Record Group 59. Consular Dispatches, Matamoros, Mexico, Records of the United States Department of State, Record Group 59. Consular Dispatches, Monterrey, Mexico, Records of the United States Department of State, Record Group 59. Consular Dispatches, Tampico, Mexico, Records of the United States Department of State, Record Group 59. Cotton Bureau Records, Confederate Department of the Treasury, Record Group 395. Eighth Census (1860), Zapata County, Texas, Cameron County, Texas, and Hidalgo County, Texas. Letters Received, Confederate Adjutant General's Office, Records of the Confederate War Department, Record Group 401. Letters Received, Confederate Trans-Mississippi Department, Records of the Confederate War Department, Record Group 109. Letters Received, Confederate District of Texas, New Mexico, and Arizona, Records of the Confederate War Department, Record Group 109. Letters Received, Department of Texas, Records of the Adjutant General's Office, Record Group 393. Military Commission Appointed to Investigate and Report upon the Facts Relative to the Capture of the Town of Bagdad on the Mexican Side of the Rio Grande on January 5, 1866, Records of the Adjutant General's Office, Record Group 393. Post Returns, Brazos Santiago, Records of the Adjutant General's Office, Record Group 393. Post Returns, Fort Brown, Records of the Adjutant General's Office, Record Group 393. Post Returns, Ringgold Barracks, Records of the Adjutant General's Office, Record Group 393. Records of the United States and Mexican Claims Commissions (1872–73), Record Group 76. Vidal, Adrián J., Compiled Service Record, United States Department of War, Record Group 94.

Newberry Library, Chicago, Illinois. Augur, Christopher, Papers.

New York Historical Society, New York, New York. Brown, Egbert B., Papers. Herron, Francis J., Papers.

Nuevo Guerrero Archives, Nuevo Guerrero, Tamaulipas. Correspondencia del Alcalde de Guerrero. Registro Civil de Guerrero.

Special Collections, Library, United States Military Academy, West Point, New York. Bee, Hamilton P., Letterbook.

Texas State Archives, Austin, Texas. Broadside File. Clark, Edward, Papers. Davis, Edmund J., Papers. Hamilton, Andrew J., Papers. Houston, Sam, Papers. McCluskey, John B., Papers. Menn, Alfred E., "Cortina–Scourge of the Rio Grande" (typescript). Miller, Washington Daniel, Papers. Muster Roll, Vidal's Partisan Rangers, Adjutant General's Records. Record Book of the Second Texas Cavalry, 1863–64, Adjutant General's Office. Runnels, Hardin R., Papers.

Universidad Iberoamericana, Mexico City, Mexico. Díaz, Porfirio, Papers.

NEWSPAPERS

Austin

Daily Democratic Statesman, April 1874–June 1877. *Southern Intelligencer,* February 1859–December 1859. *Tri-Weekly Intelligencer,* November 1859. *Tri-Weekly Statesman,* August 1875. *Texas State Gazette,* March 1850–September 1864. *Weekly State Gazette,* September 1864–May 1865.

Brownsville

American Flag, May 1855–April 1860. *Bandera Americana,* January 1863. *Boletín Extraor-*

dinario, November–December 1865. *Cosmopolitan*, April 1890. *Daily Herald*, November 1894. *Daily Ranchero*, September 1866–August 1871. *Daily Ranchero and Republican*, April 1872. *El Correo del Rio Grande*, January 1867. *Evening Ranchero*, July 1876. *Fort Brown Flag*, April 1862–October 1863. *La Bandera*, July 1862–September 1863. *Lower Rio Grande*, October 1894. *Rio Grande Courier*, July 1866–December 1866. *Rio Grande Sentinel*, June 1871–January 1873. *Texas Sentinel*, April 1878–November 1881. *Loyal National Union Journal*, March 1864–July 1864.

Corpus Christi
Advertiser, August 1867. *Nueces Valley*, October 1857–October 1872. *Ranchero*, October 1859–July 1861, January 1863–September 1863. *Weekly Caller*, September 1891–December 1893. *Weekly Gazette*, June 1875.

Dallas Herald, November 1867–May 1875.

El Correo de Laredo, September 1891.

Flake's Daily Galveston Bulletin, January 1867–July 1867.

Frank Leslie's Illustrated Newspaper, February 1864.

Galveston
Daily Civilian, November 1859. *Daily News*, May 1866–January 1878. *Tri-Weekly News*, January 1860–January 1866. *Weekly News*, October 1859, January 1864–January 1878.

Harpers Weekly, February 1864.

Houston Tri-Weekly Telegraph, July 1865–October 1867.

Indianola
Commercial Bulletin, November 1859. *Courier*, October–November 1859.

Matamoros
Boletín Oficial, July 1872. *Daily Ranchero*, May 1865–September 1870. *Eco de Ambas Fronterizo*, October 1875. *El Fronterízo*, March 1872. *El Jaque*, January 1860. *El Mercurio*, October 1837. *El Orden*, February 1865. *Ranchero*, May 1865–September 1870. *El Ranchero Diario*, January 1866.

Mexico City
El Foro, July 1873–August 1877. *El Monitor Republicano*, September 1868–June 1877. *El Siglo Diez y Nueve*, June 1868–June 1877. *El Voz de Mexico*, October 1894. *La Opinion*, January 1868–February 1884. *La Patria*, November 1894. *Two Republics*, June 1867–November 1894.

Monterrey Boletín Oficial, January 1863.

New Orleans
Bee, January 1864–December 1867. *Daily Crescent*, May 1866–October 1869. *Daily True Delta*, December 1859. *Daily Picayune*, October 1859–January 1867. *Tägliche Deutsche Zeitung*, January 1866–June 1867. *Times Picayune*, November 1859–January 1860.

New York
Herald, July 1865–January 1878. *Daily Tribune*, July 1865. *Times*, January 1873–May 1890. *World*, May 1875–June 1875.

Paris
L'Illustration, Journal Universel, January 1863–February 1866. *Le Monde Illustré*, January 1863–March 1866.

San Antonio
Alamo Express, August 1860–May 1861. *Daily Herald*, October 1859–July 1866. *Daily Ledger*

and Texan, December 1859. *Express*, January 1873–November 1894. *Ledger*, June 1851–February 1867. *Weekly Alamo Express*, October 1860–April 1861. *Weekly Herald*, April 1855–March 1873.

San Luis Potosí Boletín Oficial, January 1870.

Santa Margarita Ranchero, December 1863.

Tampico

Boletín de Noticias, August 1866. *El Iris*, February 1866. *El Prisma*, October 1859.

BOOKS

Adjutant General's Report, 1873. Austin, 1875.

Amberson, Mary Margaret McAllen, James A. McAllen, and Margaret H. McAllen, *I Would Rather Sleep in Texas.* Austin: Texas State Historical Association, 2003.

Anderson, Gary Clayton. *The Conquest of Texas: Ethnic Cleansing in the Promised Land, 1820–1875.* Norman: University of Oklahoma Press, 2005.

Archivo del General Porfirio Díaz, Memorias y Documentos. 32 vols. Mexico City: Editorial Elede, 1959.

Arnold, James R. *Jeff Davis's Own: Cavalry, Comanches, and the Battle for the Texas Frontier.* New York: John Wiley and Sons, 2000.

Bancroft, Hubert Howe. *History of Mexico.* Vol. 6, *1861–1887*. San Francisco: History Company, 1888.

———. *History of the North Mexican States and Texas.* 2 vols. San Francisco: History Company, 1886.

Barnes, James J., and Patience P. Barnes, eds. *The American Civil War through British Eyes: Dispatches from British Diplomats, Volume 3, February 1863–December 1865.* Kent, Ohio: Kent State University Press, 2005.

Bauer, Jack. *Mexican War, 1846–1848.* New York: Macmillan, 1974.

Baum, Dale. *The Shattering of Texas Unionism: Politics in the Lone Star State during the Civil War Era.* Baton Rouge: Louisiana State University Press, 1998.

Bay, Betty. *Historical Brownsville: Original Townsite Guide.* Brownsville, Tex.: Brownsville Historical Association, 1980.

Baylor, George Wythe. *Into the Far, Wild Country: True Tales of the Old Southwest*, ed. Jerry Thompson. El Paso: Texas Western Press, 1996.

Bell, Samuel E., and James M. Smallwood. *The Zona Libre, 1858–1905: A Problem in American Diplomacy.* El Paso: Texas Western Press, 1982.

Benito Juárez: Documentos, Discursos y Correspondencia. 15 vols. Mexico City: Secretaría del Patrimonio Nacional, 1964–69.

Blanchot, Colonel Ch., *Memoires L'intervention francaise au Mexique.* 3 vols. Paris: Libraire Emile Nourry, 1911.

Camargo Baptism Records, 1764–1864. Corpus Christi, Tex.: Spanish American Genealogical Association, 1989.

Camargo Marriage Records, 1764–1879. Corpus Christi, Tex.: Spanish American Genealogical Association, 1989.

Canales, J. T. *Bandit or Patriot: An Address by J. T. Canales before the Lower Rio Grande Valley Historical Society at San Benito, Texas, October 15, 1951.* San Antonio, Tex.: Arts Graficas, 1951.

Canseco, José Raúl. *Historia de Matamoros.* N.p., N.d.
Carreño, Alberto María, ed. *Archivo del General Porfirio Díaz: Memorias y documentos.* Mexico City: Editorial "Elede," 1949.
Castillo, Pedro, and Alberto Camarillo. *Furia y muerte: Los bandidos chicanos.* Los Angeles: Aztlán Publications, 1973.
Chance, Joseph E., *José María de Jesús Carvajal: The Life and Times of a Mexican Revolutionary.* San Antonio, Tex.: Trinity University Press, 2006.
Chatfield, W. H. *Twin Cities of the Border and the Country of the Lower Rio Grande.* New Orleans: L E. P. Brandao, 1893.
Chávez Orozco, Luis, *Jesús González Ortega: Defensor de la patria.* Saltillo: Colegio Coahuilense de Investigaciones Históricas, 1981.
Coker, Caleb, ed. *The News from Brownsville: Helen Chapman's Letters from the Texas Military Frontier, 1848–1852.* Austin: Texas State Historical Association, 1992.
The Collected Works of Abraham Lincoln. New Brunswick, N.J.: Rutgers University Press, 1953.
A Compendium of the War of the Rebellion, Compiled and Arranged from Official Records of the Federal and Confederate Armies Reports of the Adjutant Generals of the Several States, The Army Registers and Other Reliable Documents and Sources. Dayton, Ohio: Morningside Bookshop, 1978.
Cosío Villegas, Daniel. *The United States versus Porfirio Díaz.* Lincoln: University of Nebraska Press, 1963.
Cruz, Gilbert R. *Let There Be Towns: Spanish Municipal Origins in the American Southwest, 1610–1810.* College Station: Texas A&M University Press, 1988.
Dabbs, Jack A. *The French Army in Mexico, 1861–1867: A Study in Military Government.* The Hague, The Netherlands: Mouton, 1963.
Daddysman, James W. *The Matamoros Trade: Confederate Commerce, Diplomacy, and Intrigue.* Newark: University of Delaware Press, 1984.
Davis, Edwin Adams. *Fallen Guidon: The Story of Confederate General Jo Shelby's March to Mexico.* College Station: Texas A&M University Press, 1995.
Debroise, Oliver. *Mexican Suite: A History of Photography in Mexico.* Austin: University of Texas Press, 1994.
DeGarmo, Mrs. Frank. *Pathfinders of Texas, 1836–1846: Being the Stories of Pioneer Families That Builded Well for Nueces County and Corpus Christi.* Austin: Von Boeckmann-Jones, 1951.
De León, Arnoldo. *Apuntes Tejanos.* 2 vols. Ann Arbor, Mich.: University Microfilms, 1978.
———. *Mexican Americans in Texas: A Brief History.* Arlington Heights, Ill.: Harlan Davidson, 1992.
———. *The Tejano Community.* Albuquerque: University of New Mexico Press, 1982.
———. *They Called Them Greasers: Anglo Attitudes toward Mexicans in Texas, 1821–1900.* Austin: University of Texas Press, 1983.
De Palo, William A., Jr. *The Mexican National Army, 1822–1852.* College Station: Texas A&M University Press, 1997.
Dobie, J. Frank. *A Vaquero of the Brush Country.* Austin: University of Texas Press, [1929] 1998.
Domenech, Emmanuel H. D. *Missionary Adventures in Texas and Mexico: A Personal Narra-*

tive of Six Years' Sojourn in Those Regions. London: Longman, Brown, Green, Longmans, and Roberts, 1858.

Durham, George. *Taming the Nueces Strip: The Story of McNelly's Rangers*. Austin: University of Texas Press, 1962.

Elton, J. F., *With the French in Mexico*. London: Chapman and Hall, 1867.

Flaquer, Mirabel Miró, ed. *Catálogo de documentos—Carta de la colección Porfirio Díaz, Tamaulipas, Marzo 1876–Noviembre 1885*. 2 vols. Ciudad Victoria: Universidad Autónomo de Tamaulipas, 1985.

Ford, John S. *Rip Ford's Texas*. Edited by Stephen B. Oates. Austin: University of Texas Press, 1963.

Foster, John W., *Diplomatic Memoirs*. 2 vols. Boston: Houghton Mifflin, 1909.

Fremantle, James Arthur Lyon. *The Fremantle Diary: Being the Journal of Lieutenant Colonel James Arthur Lyon Fremantle, Coldstream Guards, on His Three Months in the Southern States*. Edited by Walter Lord. London: Andre Deutsch, 1856.

Gallaway, B. P., ed. *Dark Corner of the Confederacy*. Dubuque, Iowa: Kendall-Hunt, 1972.

Gálvez Medrano, Arturo. *Santiago Vidaurri: Exaltación del regionalismo nuevoleonés*. Monterrey: Archivo General del Estado de Nuevo León, 2000.

García, Cleotilde P. *Captain Blas María de la Garza Falcón: Colonizer of South Texas*. Austin, Tex.: San Felipe Press, 1984.

García, Genaro, ed. *Documentos inéditos o muy raros para la historia de México*. Mexico City, 1910.

García, Paul, and José María Sánchez. *Tamaulipas en la guerra contra la intervención francesa*. Mexico City: Sociedad Mexicana de Geografía y Estadística, 1962.

Garza, Israel Cavazos. *Diccionario biográfico de Nuevo León*. 2 vols. Monterrey, 1984.

Goldfinch, Charles W. *Juan N. Cortina, 1824–1892: A Re-Appraisal*. Chicago, 1950.

———, and José T. Canales. *Juan N. Cortina: Two Interpretations*. New York: Arno Press, 1974.

Goldfinch, David, et al. *The American Journey: A History of the United States*. Upper Saddle River, N.J.: Pearson, 2006.

González Ramos, Manuel Humberto. *Historia del Puerto de Bagdad, Tamaulipas, Mexico*. Matamoros: N.p., 2005.

Greene, Shirley Brooks. *When Rio Grande City Was Young*. Edinburg, Tex.: Pan American University, 1987.

Gregg, Robert D. *The Influence of Border Troubles on Relations between the United States and Mexico, 1876–1910*. New York: Da Capo Press, [1937] 1970.

Grimm, Agnes G. *Llanos mesteñas, Mustang Plains*. Waco: Texian Press, 1985.

Haley, James L. *Sam Houston*. Norman: University of Oklahoma Press, 2002.

———. *Texas: An Album of History*. Garden City, N.Y.: Doubleday, 1985.

Hall, Frederic. *Life of Maximilian I, Late Emperor of Mexico, With a Sketch of the Empress Carlota*. New York: James Miller, 1868.

Hall, Martin H. *Sibley's New Mexico Campaign*. Austin: University of Texas Press, 1960.

Hanna, Alfred Jackson, and Kathryn Abbey Hanna. *Napoleon III and Mexico: American Triumph over Monarchy*. Chapel Hill: University of North Carolina Press, 1971.

Hart, John Mason. *Anarchism and the Mexican Working Class, 1860–1931*. Austin: University of Texas Press, 1987.

———. *Empire and Revolution: The Americans in Mexico since the Civil War.* Berkeley: University of California Press, 2000.
Haynes, Sam W. *Soldiers of Misfortune: The Somervell and Mier Expeditions.* Austin: University of Texas Press, 1990.
Herrera, Octavio. *Breve historia de Tamaulipas.* Mexico City: El Colegio de Mexico, 1999.
———. *Visión histórica de Reynosa.* Reynosa: Ayuntamiento de Reynosa, 2005.
Hinojosa, Gilberto Miguel. *A Borderlands Town in Transition: Laredo, 1755–1870.* College Station: Texas A&M University Press, 1983.
Hobsbawm, Eric J. *Primitive Rebels: Studies in Archaic Forms of Social Movements in the 19th and 20th Centuries.* New York: Fredrick A. Praeger, 1959.
Hughes, W. J. *Rebellious Ranger: Rip Ford and the Old Southwest.* Norman: University of Oklahoma Press, 1964.
Hunt, Jeffrey William. *The Last Battle of the Civil War: Palmetto Ranch.* Austin: University of Texas Press, 2002.
Hunter, John Warren. *Heel-Fly Time in Texas.* Bandera, Tex.: Frontier Times, 1931.
Hutton, Paul Andrew. *Phil Sheridan and His Army.* Lincoln: University of Nebraska Press, 1985.
Hyde, H. Montgomery. *Mexican Empire: The History of Maximilian and Carlota of Mexico.* London: Macmillan, 1946.
Iglesias, José María. *Autobiografía del Sr. Lic. D. José M. Iglesias.* Mexico City: Antigua Imprenta de E. Murguía, 1893.
———. *Revistas históricas sobre la intervención francesa en Mexico.* 3 vols. Mexico City: Imprenta de Gobierno en Palacio, 1867–69.
La intervención francesa en México según el archivo del Mariscal Bazaine. Mexico City: Librería de la Vda. De Ch Bouret, 1910.
Irby, James. *Backdoor to Bagdad.* El Paso: Texas Western Press, 1977.
Jenkins, John H., ed. *Robert E. Lee on the Rio Grande: The Correspondence of Robert E. Lee on the Texas Border, 1860.* Austin: Jenkins Publishing, 1988.
Johns, Michael. *The City of Mexico in the Age of Díaz.* Austin: University of Texas Press, 1997.
Johnson, Benjamin Heber. *Revolution in Texas: How a Forgotten Rebellion and Its Bloody Suppression Turned Mexicans into Americans.* New Haven, Conn.: Yale University Press, 2003.
Journal of the House of Representatives, Eighth Legislature, State of Texas. Austin: John Marshall, 1860.
Kearney, Milo, and Anthony Knopp. *Boom and Bust: The Historical Cycles of Matamoros and Brownsville.* Austin, Tex.: Eakin Press, 1991.
Kearney, Milo, ed. *More Studies in Brownsville History.* Brownsville, Tex.: Pan American University at Brownsville, 1989.
———. *Still More Studies in Brownsville History.* Brownsville, Tex.: University of Texas at Brownsville, 1991.
———. *Studies in Brownsville History.* Brownsville, Tex.: Pan American University at Brownsville, 1986.
Kelly, Pat. *River of Lost Dreams: Navigation on the Rio Grande.* Lincoln: University of Nebraska Press, 1986.

Kératry, Émile de. *La contre-guérilla francaise au Mexique.* Paris: Librairie Internationale, 1868.

———. *The Rise and Fall of the Emperor Maximilian, A Narrative of the Mexican Empire, 1861–67, from Authentic Documents with the Imperial Correspondence.* London: Sampson Low, Son, and Marston, 1868.

Kerby, Robert L. *Kirby Smith's Confederacy: The Trans-Mississippi South, 1863–1865.* New York: Columbia University Press, 1972.

Knapp, Frank A., Jr., *The Life of Sebastián Lerdo de Tejada: A Study of Influence and Obscurity.* Austin: University of Texas Press, 1951.

Larralde, Carlos. *Carlos Esparza: A Chicano Chronicle.* San Francisco: R & E Research Associates, 1977.

———. *Mexican American Movements and Leaders.* Los Alamitos, Calif.: Hwong Publishing Co., 1976.

———, and José Rodolfo Jacobo. *Juan N. Cortina and the Struggle for Justice in Texas.* Dubuque, Iowa: Kendall/Hunt Publishing, 2000.

Lea, Tom. *The King Ranch.* 2 vols. Boston: Little, Brown, 1957.

Leiker, James N. *Racial Borders: Black Soldiers along the Rio Grande.* College Station: Texas A&M University Press, 2002.

Lonn, Ella. *Foreigners in the Confederacy.* Gloucester, Mass.: P. Smith, 1965.

———. *Foreigners in the Union Army and Navy.* Baton Rouge: Louisiana State University Press, 1952.

Lott, Virgil N., and Mercurio Martínez. *The Kingdom of Zapata.* Austin: Eakin Press, 1983.

Mahoney, Harry Thayer, and Marjorie Locke. *Mexico and the Confederacy, 1860–1867.* San Francisco: Austin and Winfield, 1998.

May, Robert E. *Manifest Destiny's Underworld: Filibustering in Antebellum America.* Chapel Hill: University of North Carolina Press, 2002.

McMurtry, Larry. *Lonesome Dove.* New York: Simon and Schuster, 1985.

McWilliams, Carey. *North from Mexico: The Spanish Speaking People of the United States.* New York: Greenwood Press, 1968.

Medrano, Arturo Gálvez. *Regionalismo y gobierno general: El caso de Nuevo León y Coahuila, 1855–1864.* Monterrey: Gobierno del Estado de Nuevo León, 1993.

Metz, Leon Claire. *Border: The U.S.-Mexico Line.* El Paso, Tex.: Mangan Books, 1989.

Michener, James A. *Texas.* New York: Random House, 1985.

Mignard, Gerard. *Charles-Louis du Pin (1814–1868): "Un intellectuel baroudeur" né ◼ Lasgraïsses.* Toulouse, France: N.p., 1996.

Miller, Robert Ryal. *Arms across the Border: United States Aid to Juárez during the French Intervention in Mexico.* Philadelphia: American Philosophical Society, 1973.

Montejano, David. *Anglos and Mexicans in the Making of Texas, 1936–1986.* Austin: University of Texas Press, 1987.

Moreno, Daniel, ed. *El sitio de Querétaro: Según protagonistas y testigos.* Mexico City: Editorial Porrúa, 1972.

Morsberger, Robert E., and Catharine M. Morsberger. *Lew Wallace: Militant Romantic.* New York: McGraw-Hill, 1980.

Nance, John Milton. *After San Jacinto: The Texas-Mexican Frontier, 1836–1841.* Austin: University of Texas Press, 1963.

———. *Attack and Counterattack: The Texas-Mexico Frontier, 1842*. Austin: University of Texas Press, 1964.
Navarro, José Antonio. *Defending Mexican Valor in Texas: José Antonio Navarro's Historical Writings, 1853–1857*. Ed. David R. McDonald and Timothy Matovina. Austin: State House Press, 1995.
Niox, Gustave Léon. *Expédition du Mexique 1861–1867*. Paris: Librairie Militaire de J. Dumoine, 1874.
Oates, Stephen B. *Confederate Cavalry West of the River*. Austin: University of Texas Press, 1961.
Owen, Richard, and James Owen. *Generals at Rest: The Grave Sites of 425 Official Confederate Generals*. Shippensburg, Pa.: White Mane, 1997.
Owsley, Frank Lawrence. *King Cotton Diplomacy: Foreign Relations of the Confederate States of America*. Chicago: University of Chicago Press, 1959.
Paredes, Américo. *A Texas-Mexican Cancionero: Folksongs of the Lower Border*. Urbana: University of Illinois Press, 1976.
———. *"With His Pistol in His Hand": A Border Ballad and Its Hero*. Austin: University of Texas Press, 1958.
Parisot, P. R. *Reminiscences of a Texas Missionary*. San Antonio, Tex.: Johnson Brothers Printing, 1899.
Parks, Joseph H. *General Edmund Kirby Smith, C.S.A.* Baton Rouge: Louisiana State University Press, 1992.
Parsons, Chuck, and Marianne E. Hall Little. *Captain L. H. McNelly, Texas Ranger: The Life and Times of a Fighting Man*. Austin, Tex.: State House Press, 2001.
Pérez, Octavio Herrera. *El norte de Tamaulipas y la conformación de la frontera México–Estados Unidos, 1835–1855*. Ciudad Victoria: El Colegio de Tamaulipas, 2003.
Perry, Laurens Ballard. *Juárez and Díaz: Machine Politics in Mexico*. DeKalb: Northern Illinois University Press, 1978.
Pierce, Frank F. *A Brief History of the Lower Rio Grande Valley*. Menasha, Wisc., 1917.
Pitner, Ernst. *Maximilian's Lieutenant: A Personal History of the Mexican Campaign, 1864–1867*. Edited by Gordon Etherington-Smith. Albuquerque: University of New Mexico Press, 1993.
Rankin, Melinda. *Twenty Years among the Mexicans: A Narrative of Missionary Life*. Cincinnati, Ohio: Chase and Hall, 1875.
Rawson Edward K., Charles W. Steward, and William H. Moody, eds. *Official Records of the Union and Confederate Navies in the War of the Rebellion*. 30 vols. Washington, D.C.: GPO, 1894–1927.
Rayburn, John C., and Virginia Kemp Rayburn. *Century of Conflict, 1821–1913: Incidents in the Lives of William Neale and William A. Neale, Early Settlers in South Texas*. Waco: Texian Press, 1966.
Reports of the Committee of Investigation Sent in 1873 by the Mexican Government to the Frontier of Texas. New York: Baker and Godwin Publishers, 1875.
Reséndez, Andrés. *Changing National Identities at the Frontier: Texas and New Mexico, 1800–1850*. Cambridge: Cambridge University Press, 2005.
Richard King vs. United Mexican States, Before the General Claims Commission, United States and Mexico. Washington, D.C.: Press of Byron S. Adams, 1923.

Richardson, James D., ed. *A Compilation of the Messages and Papers of the Confederacy.* 2 vols. Nashville: United States Publishing Company, 1906.

———. *A Compilation of the Messages and Papers of the Presidents, 1789–1897.* 10 vols. Washington, D.C.: GPO, 1897.

Richer, Juan E. *Reseña histórica de Nuevo Laredo.* Ciudad Victoria: Oficina Tipográfica del Gobierno, 1901.

Richter, William L. *The Army in Texas during Reconstruction, 1865–1870.* College Station: Texas A&M University Press, 1987.

Ridley, Jasper. *Maximilian and Juárez.* New York: Ticknor and Fields, 1992.

Ripley, Eliza More McHatton. *From Flag to Flag: A Woman's Adventures and Experiences in the South during the War, in Mexico, and in Cuba.* New York: D. Appleton, 1889.

Rippy, Fred J. *The United States and Mexico.* New York: Alfred A. Knopf, 1926.

Rivière, Henri Laurent. *La marina francesa en México.* Edited by Leonardo Pasquel and translated by Renato Gutiérrez Zamora. Veracruz, 1967.

———. *La marine francaise au Mexique.* Paris: Challamel, aîné, 1881.

Robertson, Brian. *Wild Horse Desert: The Heritage of South Texas.* Edinburg, Tex.: New Santander Press, 1985.

Roeder, Ralph. *Juárez and His Mexico.* New York: Viking, 1947.

Roel, Santiago. *Correspondencia particular de D. Santiago Vidaurri, gobernador de Nuevo León (1855–1864), Tomo primero, Juárez-Vidaurri.* Monterrey: Impresora Monterrey, 1946.

———. *Nuevo León: Apuntes históricos.* Monterrey: Ediciones Castillo, 1985.

Rolle, Andrew F. *The Last Cause: The Confederate Exodus to Mexico.* Norman: University of Oklahoma Press, 1965.

Roller, David C., and Robert W. Twyman, eds. *Encyclopedia of Southern History.* Baton Rouge: Louisiana State University Press, 1979.

Rosenbaum, Robert J. *Mexicano Resistance in the Southwest: The Sacred Right of Self-Preservation.* Austin: University of Texas Press, 1981.

Ruiz, Ramón Eduardo. *Triumph and Tragedy: A History of the Mexican People.* New York: W. W. Norton, 1992.

Salas, Carlos González. *Diccionario biografico de Tamaulipas.* Ciudad Victoria, 1984.

Salinas, Martín. *Indians of the Rio Grande Delta: Their Role in the History of Southern Texas and Northeastern Mexico.* Austin: University of Texas Press, 1990.

Samora, Julián, Joe Bernal, and Albert Peña. *Gunpowder Justice: A Reassessment of the Texas Rangers.* South Bend, Ind.: University of Notre Dame Press, 1979.

Sánchez Gómez, María del Pilar, ed. *Catálogo de fuentes de la historia de Tamaulipas: Segunda parte, Biblioteca Nacional de Mexico, Departamento de Manuscritos.* Ciudad Victoria: Universidad Autónoma de Tamaulipas Instituto de Investigaciones Histórias de Tamaulipas.

Scholes, Walter V. *Mexican Politics during the Juárez Regime, 1855–1872.* Columbia: University of Missouri Press, 1957.

Schoonover, Thomas, ed. *Mexican Lobby: Matías Romero in Washington, 1861–1867.* Lexington: University Press of Kentucky, 1986.

———. *A Mexican View of America in the 1860s: A Foreign Diplomat Describes the Civil War and Reconstruction.* Rutherford, N.J.: Fairleigh Dickinson University Press, 1991.

Schuler, Louis J. *The Last Battle in the War between the States, May 13, 1865.* Brownsville, Tex.: Springman-King, 1960.

Sierra, Rosario, and Graciela Verdín, eds. *Correspondencia Juárez-Vidaurri, 1855–1864, Vol. III* (Monterrey: Archivo General del Estado de Nuevo León, 2005).
Simpson, Brooks D. *Let Us Have Peace: Ulysses S. Grant and the Politics of War and Reconstruction, 1861–1868*. Chapel Hill: University of North Carolina Press, 1991.
Sinkin, Richard N. *The Mexican Reform, 1855–1876: A Study in Liberal Nation-Building*. Austin, Tex.: Institute of Latin American Studies, 1979.
Smart, Charles Allen. *Viva Juárez: A Biography*. Philadelphia: J. B. Lippincott, 1963.
State Gazette Appendix, Containing Debates in the House of Representatives of the Eighth Legislature, of the State of Texas. Austin, Tex.: John Marshall and Co., 1860.
Steele, William. *Report of the Adjutant General of the State of Texas for the Year 1875*. Houston: A. C. Gray, 1875.
Stevenson, Sara Yoke. *Maximilian in Mexico: A Woman's Reminiscences of the French Intervention, 1862 to 1867*. Whitefish, Mont.: Kessinger Publishing, n.d.
Stillman, Chauncey Devereux. *Charles Stillman, 1810–1875*. New York: N.p., 1956.
Stout, Joseph A., Jr. *Schemers and Dreamers: Filibustering in Mexico, 1848–1921*. Fort Worth: Texas Christian University Press, 2002.
Tamayo, Jorge L. *Ignacio Zaragoza: Correspondencia y documentos*. Mexico City: Editorial Libros, 1979.
Terrell, Alexander Watkins. *From Texas to Mexico and the Court of Maximilian in 1865*. Dallas: Book Club of Texas, 1933.
Texas Frontier Troubles. 44th Cong., 1st sess., no. 343.
Thompson, Jerry. *Juan Cortina and the Texas-Mexico Frontier, 1859–1877*. El Paso: Texas Western Press, 1994.
———. *Mexican Texans in the Union Army*. El Paso: Texas Western Press, 1986.
———. *Vaqueros in Blue and Gray*. Austin: State House Press, 2000.
———. *A Wild and Vivid Land: An Illustrated History of the South Texas Border*. Austin: Texas State Historical Association, 1997.
———, ed. *Fifty Miles and a Fight: Major Samuel Peter Heintzelman's Journal of Texas and the Cortina War*. Austin: Texas State Historical Association, 1998.
———, ed. *Texas and New Mexico on the Eve of the Civil War: The Mansfield and Johnston Inspections, 1859–1861*. Albuquerque: University of New Mexico Press, 2001.
———, with Lawrence Jones III. *Civil War and Revolution on the Rio Grande Frontier: A Narrative and Photographic History*. Austin: Texas State Historical Association, 2004.
Tijerina, Andrés. *Tejanos and Texas under the Mexican Flag, 1823–1836*. College Station: Texas A&M University Press, 1994.
———. *Tejano Empire: Life on the South Texas Ranchos*. College Station: Texas A&M University Press, 1998.
Tilley, Nannie M., ed. *Federals on the Frontier: The Diary of Benjamin F. McIntyre, 1862–1864*. Austin: University of Texas Press, 1963.
Toral, Jesús de León, ed. *Historia documental militar de la intervención francesa en México & el denominado segundo imperio*. Mexico City: Secretaría de la Defensa Nacional, 1967.
Townsend, Stephen A. *Yankee Invasion of Texas*. College Station: Texas A&M University Press, 2006.
Trudeau, Noah Andre. *Out of the Storm: The End of the Civil War, April–June 1865*. Baton Rouge: Louisiana State University Press, 1994.

Tucker, Phillip Thomas. *The Final Fury: Palmito Ranch, The Last Battle of the Civil War.* Mechanicsburg, Pa.: Stackpole Books, 2001.

Tyler, Ronnie C. *Santiago Vidaurri and the Southern Confederacy.* Austin: Texas State Historical Association, 1973.

U.S. War Department. *The War of the Rebellion: A Compilation of the Official Records of the Union and Confederate Armies.* 128 vols. Washington, D.C.: GPO, 1880–1901.

Utley, Robert M. *Lone Star Justice: The First Century of the Texas Rangers.* New York: Oxford University Press, 2002.

Vanderwood, Paul J. *Disorder and Progress: Bandits, Police, and Mexican Development.* Lincoln: University of Nebraska Press, 1981.

Viele, Teresa Griffin. *Following the Drum: A Glimpse of Frontier Life.* Lincoln: University of Nebraska Press, 1984.

Villegas, Daniel Cosío. *Historia moderna de México.* Vol. 6. Mexico City: Editorial Hermes, 1970.

———. *The United States Versus Porfirio Díaz.* Lincoln: University of Nebraska Press, 1963.

Wallace, Lew. *An Autobiography.* Vol. 2. New York: Harper and Brothers, 1906.

Waller, John L. *Colossal Hamilton of Texas: A Biography of Andrew Jackson Hamilton, Militant Unionist and Reconstruction Governor.* El Paso: Texas Western Press, 1968.

Walraven, Bill. *Corpus Christi: The History of a Texas Seaport.* Woodland Hills, Calif.: Windsor Publications, 1982.

Warner, Ezra E. *Generals in Blue: Lives of the Union Commanders.* Baton Rouge: Louisiana State University Press, 1972.

———. *Generals in Gray: Lives of the Confederate Commanders.* Baton Rouge: Louisiana State University Press, 1970.

Watson, William. *Adventures of a Blockade Runner.* London, 1892.

Webb, Walter Prescott. *The Texas Rangers: A Century of Frontier Defense.* Austin: University of Texas Press, [1935] 1965.

Weckmann, Luis, ed. *Las relaciones Franco-Mexicanas.* Vol. 2 (1839–67). Mexico City: Secretaría de Relaciones Exteriores, 1962.

Wilkins, Frederick. *The Law Comes to Texas: The Texas Rangers, 1870–1901.* Austin, Tex.: State House Press, 1999.

Williams, Amelia W., and Eugene C. Barker, eds. *The Writings of Sam Houston, 1813–1863.* 8 vols. Austin: Jenkins Publishing, 1970.

Williams, R. H. *With the Border Ruffians, Memories of the Far West, 1852–1868.* Edited by E. W. Williams. Lincoln: University of Nebraska Press, 1982.

Woodman, Lyman L. *Cortina: Rogue of the Rio Grande.* San Antonio, Tex.: Naylor, 1950.

Wooldridge, Ruby A., and Robert B. Vezzetti. *Brownsville: A Pictorial History.* Norfolk, VA: Donning, 1982.

Wooster, Ralph A. *Lone Star Generals in Gray.* Austin, Tex.: Eakin Press, 2000.

———. *Texas and Texans in the Civil War.* Austin, Tex.: Eakin Press, 1995.

Wright, Marcus J., comp. *Texas in the War, 1861–1865.* Edited by Harold B. Simpson. Hillsboro, Tex.: Hill College Press, 1965.

Young, Elliott. *Catarino Garza's Revolution on the Texas-Mexico Border.* Durham, N.C.: Duke University Press, 2004.

Zorrilla, Juan Fidel. *Gobernadores, obispos y rectores.* Ciudad Victoria: Universidad Autónoma de Tamaulipas, 1979.

ARTICLES AND OTHER PUBLISHED MATERIALS

Abbott, Peyton O. "Business Travel Out of Texas during the Civil War: The Travel Diary of S. B. Brush, Pioneer Austin Merchant." *Southwestern Historical Quarterly* 96 (October 1992).
Adams, David B. "Embattled Borderland: Northern Nuevo León and the Indios Bárbaros, 1686–1870." *Southwestern Historical Quarterly* 95 (July 1991).
Ashcraft, Allan C. "Fort Brown, Texas, in 1861." *Texas Military History* 3 (Spring 1963).
———. "The Union Occupation of the Lower Rio Grande Valley in the Civil War." *Texas Military History* 8 (1970).
Baldridge, Lillian Weems. "Cattle Bandit Extraordinary." *Cattlemen* 34 (June 1947).
———. "Cortina: Man of Destiny." *Valley Morning Star* (Harlingen, Tex.), January 5, 1957.
Bello, Ruth T., ed. "The Descendants of Feliciana Goceascochea and Juan José Tijerina as Declared by María Hilaria Guerra de Cavazos." *Journal of Hispanic Genealogy and History* (1990).
Broussard, Ray F. "Vidaurri, Juárez, Comonfort's Return from Exile." *Hispanic American Historical Review* 69 (May 1969).
Carrigan, William D., and Clive Webb. "The Lynching of Persons of Mexican Origin or Descent in the United States, 1848–1928." *Journal of Social History* 37, no. 2 (2003).
Cavazos, P. G. "Cavazos Family History." *Newsletter of the Brownsville Historical Association* 17 (March–April 2000).
Champion, A. A. "The Miller Hotel in the Antebellum Period." In *More Studies in Brownsville History*. Edited by Milo Kearny. Brownsville, Tex.: Pan American University at Brownsville, 1989.
Cheeseman, Bruce S. "'Let Us Have 500 Good Determined Texans': Richard King's Account of the Union Invasion of South Texas, November 12, 1863, to January 20, 1864." *Southwestern Historical Quarterly* 101 (July 1997).
Clendenen, Clarence C. "Mexican Unionists: A Forgotten Incident of the War between the States." *New Mexico Historical Review* 39 (1964).
Cohen, Barry M. "The Texas-Mexico Border, 1858–1867." *Texana* 6 (Summer 1968).
Comtois, Pierre. "War's Last Battle." *America's Civil War* 5 (July 1992).
"Cortina Raids." *Texas Siftings* 3 (August 4, 1883).
Crimmins, M. L. "The Cortina Trouble in 1859 and 1860." *Frontier Times* 17 (December 1939).
Davenport, Herbert. "General José María Jesús Carbajal." *Southwestern Historical Quarterly* 55 (April 1952).
Delaney, Robert W. "Matamoros: Port for Texas during the Civil War." *Southwestern Historical Quarterly* 58 (April 1955).
"Depredations on the Rio Grande: A Tale of Two Cities." *Appletons' Journal* 9 (March 29, 1873).
Dodson, Ruth. "The Noakes Raid." *Frontier Times* (July 1946).
Dugan, Frank H. "The 1850 Affair of the Brownsville Separatists." *Southwestern Historical Quarterly* 61 (October 1957).
Ellis, L. Tuffy. "Maritime Commerce on the Far Western Gulf, 1861–1865." *Southwestern Historical Quarterly* 77 (October 1973).
Gatschet, Albert S. "The Karankawa Indians." In *Papers of the Peabody Museum of American Archaeology and Ethnology*. Cambridge, Mass.: Harvard University, 1888–1904.

Glavecke, Adolphus. "The Story of Old Times." In W. H. Chatfield, *Twin Cities of the Border and the Country of the Lower Rio Grande*. New Orleans: E. P. Brandao, 1893.

Greaser, Galen D., and Jesús de la Teja. "Quieting Title to Spanish and Mexican Land Grants in the Trans-Nueces: The Bourland and Miller Commission, 1850–1852." *Southwestern Historical Quarterly* 61 (April 1992).

Hager, William M. "The Nuecestown Raid of 1875: A Border Incident." *Arizona and the West* 1 (Autumn 1959).

Hanna, Kathryn Abbey. "The Roles of the South in the French Intervention in Mexico." *Journal of Southern History* 20 (1954).

Hingo, Don. "Texas' First Aristocracy: Robber of Robin Hood." *Houston Genealogical Journal* 7 (1989).

Hobratsch, Ben M. "Yorktown on the Rio Grande: Texas Hopes for French Intervention during the Civil War." *Journal of South Texas* 18 (Fall 2005).

Hunter, J. T. "Captain J. T. Hunter Tells of the Cortina War." *Hunter's Magazine* 2 (November 1911).

"Juan Cortina: Chicano Nightmare of the Texas Rangers." *Magazin* 1 (November 1971).

Kiel, Frank Wilson, ed., "'Wir Waren unser 20 Mann gegen 150' ('We were 20 men against 150') The Battle of Las Rucias: A Civil War Letter from a German-Texan Soldier in the 1864 Union Invasion of the Lower Rio Grande Valley." *Southwestern Historical Quarterly* 105 (January 2002).

Knapp, Frank A., Jr. "A Note on General Escobedo in Texas." *Southwestern Historical Quarterly* 55 (January 1952).

Larios, Ávila. "Brownsville-Matamoros Lifeline." *Mid-America* 60 (April 1958).

Larralde, Carlos. "J. T. Canales and the Texas Rangers." *Journal of South Texas* 10 (Spring 1997).

———. "Juan Cortina's Spy: Elena Villarreal de Ferrer." *Journal of South Texas* 11 (Spring 1998).

Marshall, Bruce. "Santos Benavides: 'The Confederacy on the Rio Grande.'" *Civil War* 3 (May–June 1990).

Marten, James. "True to the Union: Texans in the U.S. Army." *North and South: The Magazine of the Civil War Conflict* 3 (November 1999).

McCormack, Richard Blaine. "Porfirio Díaz en las Fronteras Texana, 1875–1877." *Historia Mexicana* 5 (January–March 1956).

McDaniel, Ruel. "Cortina!" *Texas Parade* 21 (June 1960).

———. "Juan Cortina—Hero or Bandit." In *The Best of True West*. New York: Julian Messner, 1964.

Meiners, Fredericka. "The Texas Border Cotton Trade, 1862–1863." *Civil War History* 23 (December 1977).

Miller, Robert Ryal. "Matías Romero: Mexican Minister to the United States during the Juárez-Maximilian Era." *Hispanic American Historical Review* 45 (May 1965).

Morris, Leopold. "The Mexican Raid of 1875 on Corpus Christi." *Quarterly of the Texas State Historical Association* 4 (1900–1901).

Neale, William. "Centennial Oration by the Honorable William Neale." In W. H. Chatfield, *Twin Cities of the Border and the Country of the Lower Rio Grande*. New Orleans: E. P. Brandao, 1893.

Oates, Stephen B. "John S. 'Rip' Ford: Prudent Cavalryman, C.S.A." *Southwestern Historical Quarterly* 64 (January 1961).
Rippy, J. Fred. "Border Troubles along the Rio Grande, 1848–1860." *Southwestern Historical Quarterly* 23 (October 1919).
Robinson, Robert L. "The U.S. Navy vs. Cattle Rustlers: The *U.S.S. Rio Bravo* on the Rio Grande, 1875–1879." *Military History of Texas and the Southwest* 15, no. 2 (1979).
Sayers, William Edward. "Bandit or Robin Hood: He Played Tag with Texas." In *Off the Beaten Path*. Fort Worth: F. L. Motheral, 1973.
Schneider, Ellen, and Paul H. Carlson, "Gunnysackers, *Carreteros*, and Teamsters: The South Texas Cart War of 1857." *Journal of South Texas* 1 (Spring 1988).
Schoonover, Thomas. "Confederate Diplomacy and the Texas-Mexican Border, 1861–1865." *East Texas Historical Journal* 11 (Spring 1973).
Shearer, Ernest C. "The Carvajal Disturbances." *Southwestern Historical Quarterly* 55 (October 1951).
Sibley, Marilyn McAdams. "Charles Stillman: A Case Study of Entrepreneurship on the Rio Grande, 1861–1865." *Southwestern Historical Quarterly* 77 (October 1973).
Smith, Mitchell. "The 'Neutral' Matamoros Trade, 1861–1865." *Southwest Review* 36 (Autumn 1952).
Smyrl, Frank H. "Texans in the Union Army, 1861–1865." *Southwestern Historical Quarterly* 65 (October 1961).
"Story of Chicano Folk Hero Juan Cortinas Who Captured Brownsville." *Chicano Times Newspaper*, December 5–19, 1975.
Stuart, Ben C. "Rio Grande Raiders: How the Noted Cortina Attacked, Captured, and Terrorized Brownsville." *Texas Magazine* 11 (March 1910).
Thompson, Jerry. "Adrián J. Vidal: Soldier of Three Republics." *Hispanic Genealogical Journal* 14 (1996).
———. "Mutiny and Desertion on the Rio Grande: The Strange Saga of Captain Adrián J. Vidal." *Military History of Texas and the Southwest* 11 (1975).
———. "A Stand along the Border: Santos Benavides and the Battle for Laredo." *Civil War Times Illustrated* 26 (August 1980).
Townsend, Stephen A. "A Peace Deferred: Major General Lew Wallace, Peacemaker on the Lower Rio Grande." *Journal of South Texas* 8 (Spring 1995).
Trudeau, Noah Andre. "The Story of the War's Final Days." *Civil War Times Illustrated* 29 (July–August 1990).
Tyler, Ronnie C. "Cotton on the Border, 1861–1865." *Southwestern Historical Quarterly* 73 (April 1970).
———. "Santiago Vidaurri and the Confederacy." *The Americas* 26 (July 1969).
Tyson, Carl Newton. "Texas: Men for War; Cotton for Economy." *Journal of the West* 14 (January 1975).
U.S. Congress. House. "Claims for Spoliations Committed by Indians and Mexicans." 36th Cong., 1st sess., no. 1070.
———. "Committee on Military Affairs in Relation to the Texas Border Troubles." 45th Cong., 2d sess.
———. "Conditions of Affairs in the Republic of Mexico." 39th Cong., 2d sess., Parts 1, 2, and 3, no. 1261, 1262.

———. "Correspondence with Ministers to Mexico." 40th Cong., 1st sess.
———. "Depredations on the Frontiers of Texas." 44th Cong., 1st sess.
———. "Depredations on the Texas Frontiers." 42nd Cong., 3d sess.
———. "Difficulties between the People of Texas and Mexico." 36th Cong., 1st sess., no. 1064.
———. "Difficulties on Southwestern Frontier." 36th Cong., 1st sess., no. 1050.
———. "Messages of the President of the United States and Accompanying Documents." 40th Cong., 2d sess., Parts 1 and 2.
———. "Republic of Mexico." 39th Cong., 1st sess.
———. "Report Accompanying Documents of the Committee on Foreign Affairs on the Relations of the United States with Mexico." 45th Cong., 2d sess.
———. "Report of the United States Commissioners to Texas." 42d Cong., 3d sess.
———. "Texas Frontier Troubles." 44th Cong., 1st sess.
———. "Troubles on Texas Frontier." 36th Cong., 1st sess., no. 1056.
U.S. Congress. Senate. "Committee on Claims, to Whom Was Referred the Memorial of Lieutenant Loomis L. Langdon, of the United States Army." 36th Cong., 1st sess.
———. "Hostilities on the Rio Grande." 36th Cong., 1st sess., no. 1031.
———. "Impeachment of Judge Watrous." 34th Cong., 3d sess.
———. "Memorial of Duff Green, President of the Sabine and Rio Grande Railroad Company." 36th Cong., 1st sess., no 1038.
———. "Message from the President of the United States Communicating . . . Papers Relative to Mexican Affairs." 38th Cong., 1st sess., no. 1029.
———. "Message of the President Communicating . . . Information Respecting the Occupation by French Troops of the Republic of Mexico." 39th Cong., 1st sess., no. 1237.
Vigness, David M. "Indian Raids on the Lower Rio Grande, 1836–1837." *Southwestern Historical Quarterly* 59 (July 1955).
Villegas, Daniel Cosio. "Border Troubles in Mexican–United States Relations." *Southwestern Historical Quarterly* 72 (July 1968).
Wallace, Lew, "A Buffalo Hunt in Northern Mexico." *Scribners Monthly* 17 (March 1879).
Webster, Michael G. "Intrigue on the Rio Grande: The *Rio Bravo* Affair, 1875." *Southwestern Historical Quarterly* 74 (October 1970).
Weinert, Richard P. "Confederate Border Troubles with Mexico." *Civil War Times Illustrated* 3 (October 1964).
Wilson, D. M. "The Last Battle of the War." *Confederate Veteran* 18 (1910).
Wooster, Ralph A. "The Texas Gulf Coast in the Civil War." *Texas Gulf Historical and Biographical Record* 1 (November, 1965).

Papers, Theses, and Dissertations

Ash, Bette Gay Hunter. "The Mexican-Texans in the Civil War." Master's thesis, East Texas State University, 1972.
Callahan, Manuel. "Mexican Border Troubles: Social War, Settler Colonialism, and the Production of Frontier Discourses, 1848–1880." Ph.D. diss., University of Texas, 2003.
Case, Robert P. "The Path to Personal Power: The First Administration of Porfirio Díaz, 1876–1880." Ph.D. diss., Northern Illinois University, 1973.
Cervantes, Alfonso. "'Border Raiding, Internal Conflict, and the Mexican Image." Master's thesis, St. Mary's University, 1970.

Cowling, Annie. "The Confederate Cotton Trade With Mexico." Master's thesis, University of Texas, 1926.
Crews, James Robert. "Reconstruction in Brownsville, Texas." Master's thesis, Texas Tech University, 1969.
Dickeson, Sherrill L. "The Texas Cotton Trade during the Civil War." Master's thesis, Texas Tech University, 1967.
Douglas, James Ridley. "Juan Cortina: El Caudillo de la Frontera." Master's thesis, University of Texas, 1987.
Fielder, Bruce M. "The Mexican Connection: Confederate and Union Diplomacy on the Rio Grande, 1861–1865." Master's thesis, North Texas State University, 1978.
Gallegos, J. J. "Santiago Vidaurri: Regional Power, Trade, and Capital Formation in Northern Mexico." Copy courtesy of the author.
Graf, LeRoy P. "The Economic History of the Lower Rio Grande Valley, 1820–1875." Ph.D. diss., Harvard University, 1942.
Gray, Ronald Norman. "Edmund J. Davis: Radical Republican and Reconstruction Governor of Texas." Ph.D. diss., Texas Tech University, 1976.
Greer, Viola Ann. "Santiago Vidaurri, Cacique of Northern Mexico: His Relationship to Benito Juárez." Master's thesis, University of Texas at Austin, 1949.
Hildebrand, Walter W. "The History of Cameron County, Texas." Master's thesis, North Texas State College, 1950.
Hunter, John H. "Confederate Relations with the Mexican-French and with Maximilian during the Civil War Period." Brownsville, Texas, November 3, 1969.
Hunter, John Warren. "The Fall of Brownsville on the Rio Grande, November 1863." Center for American History. University of Texas at Austin.
Irby, James A. "Line of the Rio Grande: War and Trade on the Confederate Frontier, 1861–1865." Ph.D. diss., University of Georgia, 1969.
Kitchen, Carr P. "Mexican Depredations in the Lower Rio Grande Valley, 1835–1885." Master's thesis, Baylor University, 1933.
Levinson, Irving Walter. "Wars within War: Mexican Guerrillas, Domestic Elites, and the Americans, 1846–1848." Ph.D. diss., University of Houston, 2003.
Marcum Richard T. "Fort Brown, Texas: The History of a Border Post." Ph.D. diss., Texas Technological College, 1964.
McMillen, Quintellen. "Surveyor General: The Life and Times of José María Jesús Carvajal." Copy courtesy of the author.
Moretta, John. "The Scourge of the Rio Grande: José María Jesús Carbajal and the Filibustering Spirit in Texas, 1851–1853." Author's files.
"Reconstruction of Past Drought across the Coterminous United States from a Network of Climatically Sensitive Tree-Ring Data." National Oceanic and Atmospheric Administration, Washington, D.C.
Ribb, Richard Henry. "José Tomás Canales and the Texas Rangers: Myth, Identity, and Power in South Texas, 1900–1920." Ph.D. diss., University of Texas at Austin, 2001.
Riley, Denny. "Santos Benavides: His Influence on the Lower Rio Grande, 1823–1891." Ph.D. diss., Texas Christian University, 1976.
Salmon, Roberto Mario. "Don José San Ramón as Brownsville Capitalist, 1822–1879." Paper delivered at the annual meeting of the Texas State Historical Association, 1986.
Stuart, Ben C. "Texas Indian Fighters and Frontier Rangers: Their Organization and Some

of Their Noted Battles with an Account of the Battalion of 1874." Typed manuscript, Texas State Archives.

Thompson, James Heaven. "A Nineteenth Century History of Cameron County, Texas." Master's thesis, University of Texas, 1965.

Townsend, Stephen A. "The Rio Grande Expedition, 1863–1865." Ph.D. diss., University of North Texas, 2001.

———. "Steamboating on the Lower Rio Grande River." Master's thesis, Texas A&I University, 1989.

Valerio-Jimenéz, Omar Santiago. "'Indios Bárbaros,' Divorcees, and Flocks of Vampires: Identity and Nation on the Rio Grande, 1749–1894." Ph.D. diss., University of California at Los Angeles, 2001.

Walraven, Edward Lee. "Ambivalent Americans: Selected Spanish-Language Newspapers' Response to Anglo Domination in Texas, 1830–1910." Ph.D. diss., Texas A&M University, 1999.

Webster, Michael G. "Texan Manifest Destiny and the Mexican Border Conflict, 1865–1880." Ph.D. diss., Indiana University, 1972.

Index

Abilene, Tex., 217
Acapulco, Guerrero, 133
Aguilar, Gregorio, 269n68
Águilas, *See* Los Águilas
Agualeguas, N. L., 55
Ahuacatlán, Mex., 233
Alamo, Battle of, 34
Alamo (steamer), 138, 156–57
Albino Peña Ranch, *See* Rancho Albino Peña
Alderete, Concepcíon, 13
Amozoc, Puebla, 103
Ampudia, Pedro, 15
Alvarez, José Justo, 241
American G. I. Forum, 252
Anderson, Thomas McArthur, 209–10
Andrés, Florencio, 290n77
Anson, (steamer), 22
Antonia (gunboat), 164–65, 167–68
Arista, Mariano, 15–16
Arizona (steamer), 58
Ark (steamer), 137
Army of the North, 162
Arrocha, Juan J., 18, 196
Arroyo Colorado, Tex., 10–11, 32, 64, 72–73, 81, 208
Assembly of Notables, 106
Atascosa County, Tex., 65
Atascosa Rangers, 65
Augur, Christopher Colon, 209–10
Austin, Tex., 35, 48–49, 55, 61, 224
Austin Democratic Statesman, 227
Ávalos, Francisco, 22
Avery, Lucius, 181
Azcapotzalco, D.F., 230, 232, 241–45

Bacon, Nathaniel, 252
Bagdad Raid, 169–70, 285n100, 286n125
Bagdad, Tam., 107–108, 131, 138–39, 148, 155, 159, 162, 166–68, 180, 184, 201, 226, 229, 233
Bagwell, Charles, 286n125
Balcarcel, Blas, 132
Ballí de Young, Salomé, *See* Young, Salome Ballí de
Ballí, Jesus, 46
Ballí, Juan Solis, 202
Bancroft, Hubert Howe, 243, 245
Banks, Nathaniel P., 110, 118, 136, 145
Banquete, Tex., 60
Barcelona, Spain, 107
Barrera, Dimas, 71
Barthelow, Thomas Jefferson, 276n59
Barton, E. B., 29
Basel, Switz., 25
Basse, Elisha, 20, 31, 68
Bastrop, Tex., 35
Bazaine, Achille, 104, 133
Bee County, Tex., 216
Bee, Hamilton P., 110–13
Belden, Samuel A., 20, 43–44, 46, 51, 261n44
Belknap, William, 209–10, 233
Belle (steamboat), 153
Beltrán, Samuel, 159
Benavides, Basilio, 109
Benavides, Ramón, 269n68
Benavides, Refugio, 109
Benavides, Santos, 99–101, 110, 133, 135–36, 250
Berriozábal, Felipe, 189–92
Bexar County, Tex., 88
Beyer, Charles D., 222

Bigelow, Israel Bonoparte, 18, 21, 23, 29, 46, 54, 69, 114, 162n60
Bilbao, Spain, 27
Blanco, Miguel, 235–36
Blucher, Felix A., 147
Blue Party (Cameron County), 29–30
Boca del Río, Tam., *See* Bagdad, Tam.
Boca Chica, Tex., 144
Bonaparte, Louis Napoleon (Napoleon III), 103, 106
Bonaparte, Napoleon, 103
Boston, Mass., 107
Bourland Commission, 21
Bourland, William H., 21
Bonwill, C. E. H., 118–19, 125
Box, John, 78
Bracketville, Tex., 211
Brazos Island, Tex., 1, 26, 144
Brazos Santiago, Tex., 41, 48–51, 59, 68, 70, 88, 140–41, 147, 169, 176
Bremen, Ger., 107
Britton, Forbes, 91
Brown, Egbert Benson, 154–55
Brown, Jacob, 25
Brown, John, 61
Browne, James G., 20, 29, 38–39, 52, 69, 97
Brownsville, Tex., 2, 7, 9, 14, 19, 21, 25, 31, 34–35, 41, 45, 49, 51, 55, 59–62, 68, 70, 73, 84, 88, 90, 110, 112, 113, 116–17, 127, 135, 137, 140–41, 176, 188, 206, 211, 215, 220, 234
Brownsville American Flag, 28–30, 48, 50, 54, 68, 84, 89, 94
Brownsville Daily Ranchero, 180, 193, 222
Brownsville Expedition, 72
Brownsville Town Company, 32
Brownsville Sentinel, 216
Brownsville Tigers, 53–55, 57, 65
Buchanan, James, 49, 51, 58, 72, 90–92
Buena Vista, Battle of, 17
Buffalo Soldiers, 222
Burgos Mountains, Mex., 93–94
Burke, William, 213
Bush, Edward Geer, 211

Cabrera, Gerónimo, 52
Cabrera, Guadalupe, 52
Cabrera, Petra, 52
Cabrera, Tomás, 2, 41, 45, 52, 63, 92
Cadena, Santos, 55, 70
Calhoun, John Caldwell, 24
Callahan, Charles, 100
Callahan, Manuel, 5

Camargo, Tam., 8–10, 12, 16, 23, 39, 56, 77, 84, 99, 109, 129, 149, 151, 156–57, 159, 162, 166, 205, 213, 223, 225, 230, 232–33
Camargo (steamship), 153
Camarillo, Alberto, 3–4
Cameron County, Tex., 2, 3, 7, 9, 13, 19, 22–23, 29–31, 36, 39, 45, 51, 57, 67, 69, 70–71, 152, 172, 198–99, 202–203, 207, 209, 212, 216–17
Cameron County Democratic Party, 31
Campacuas Indians, 11
Campione, Alberto, *See* Champion, Albert
Camp Verde, Tex., 72
Campbell, Dolores, 58
Campbell, Francis M., 57–59, 69, 262n60
Canales, Antonio, 189
Canales, José T., 2, 251, 279n13, 300n127
Canales, Juan Treviño, 219–20
Canales, Modesto, 186
Canales, Servando, 141–43, 145, 162, 166, 170, 176, 183–84, 189–90, 196, 198, 220, 236–38, 288n19
Canales, Tristán, 176, 184, 189
Canby, Edward Richard Sprigg, 145
Cano, Nicolas, 71
Cantú, Ramó, 159
Capistrán, José Macedonio, 44, 46, 122, 127
Carbineros de de Tamaulipas, 298n81
Carlota (Marie Charlotte Leopoldine), 133, 158
Carolan, O. A., 46, 210
Carvajal, José María de Jesus, 22–23, 40, 44, 48, 52, 73, 102, 136–37, 148, 162–63, 166, 180–82, 191, 262n68, 285n100
Cárdenas, Dionisio, 207
Cárdenas, Octaviano, 124, 127
Carrillo, Antonio de Jesús García, 216
Carrizo (Zapata), Tex., 97, 100–101, 210
Carson, Cruse, 222
Cart War, 35
Casa Blanca, Tex., 72
Casa Mata (Matamoros), Tam., 147, 185–86, 231
Cass, Lewis, 35, 92–93, 265n154
Castillo, Pedro, 3–4
Catsel, Gabriel, 7, 33, 69, 260n16
Cavazos, Froilán, 269n68
Cavazos, Isidro, 69
Cavazos, María Josefa, 31
Cavazos, P. G., 290–91n80
Cavazos, Práxedis, 237, 243, 279n13, 297n64
Cavazos, Rafael García, 31
Cavazos, Sabás, 9, 13–14, 24, 32, 231, 237, 292n9

Index

Cavazos, Sarah Sada de, 279n13
Cavazos Ranch, Tex., 297n64
Céballos, José, 206
Celaya, Simón, 260n12
Centralists, 23
Cerda, Julián, 141–43
Cerralvo, N. L., 10, 23, 210
Champion, Albert, 26, 72, 212–13, 262n60
Champion, Felicítas, 69
Champion, Nicholas, 26, 212
Champion, Peter, 26, 69, 88, 212
Chapa, Francisco, 202
Chapa, Juan, 18
Chapultepec, D. F., 245, 247
Charco Escondido, N. L., 197
Charleston, S. C., 97
Chase, Franklin, 50, 288n25
Chavero, Ana, 283n48
Chicano Renaissance, 2–3
Chignahuapan, 194
Chiltipín Ranch, *See* Rancho Chiltipín
Chihuahua, State of, 132, 149, 181–82
China, N. L., 94, 122, 148, 151
Cipriano, Benito, 134
Cisneros, Florencio, 94
Cisneros, Tiburcio, 202
Ciudad Guerrero, Tam., *See* Guerrero
Ciudad Victoria, Tam., 45, 49, 55, 93, 129, 137, 160, 195, 222
Clareño, Tex., *See* Rancho Clareño
Clareño Massacre, 97–98, 108
Clark, Edward, 102
Clarksville, Tex., 61, 112, 167–68
Clay, Henry, 21
Cline, Henry, 71
Coahuila, State of, 23, 62, 114, 150
Cobos, José María, 114–17
Coke, Richard, 221, 224, 226, 230
Collins, Peter, 41
Colonel Benedict (steamboat), 180
Colonel Cross, (steamboat), 26
Colonel Holcomb (steamboat), 180, 288n25
Colorado County, Tex., 35
Colorado River, Tex., 18, 59–60
Comanches, 10, 91
Comisión Pesquisidora, 215–17
Committee of Public Safety (Brownsville), 48–52, 63
Comonfort, Ignacio, 103–106
Compromise of 1850, 21
Confederate District of Texas, 144
Contra-Guerrillas: Du Pin in command of, 136; defends Tuxpan, 136; seized Tampico, 136; skirmishing around Ciudad Victoria, 137; guards Mejía's rear, 138; on San Fernando River, 138; recruits Americans, 154; based at Ciudad Victoria and Matamoros, 160; in the Huasteca, 160; at Rio Blanco, 160; ambush of on Rio Grande, 165; attack on *Cortinistas* at San Fernando, 166, 171; recapture Bagdad; on parade in Matamoros, 175
Corona, Ramón, 191
Corpus Christi, Tex., 14, 36, 56, 59–60, 223–24
Corpus Christi Guards, 59
Corpus Christi Ranchero, 49, 59, 63, 68, 89, 96–98
Corpus Christi Weekly Caller, 245
Cortéz, Gregorio, 4
Cortéz, Rafaela, *See* Cortina, Rafaela
Cortina Brigade, 140–41
Cortina, María Dolores "Grande," 12, 255n32, 256n35
Cortina, María Estéfana: birth of, 13; death of, 192–93, 290n80; inherits portion of Espiritu Santo Grant, 27, land litigation of, 31
Cortina, Felicitas, 12
Cortina, Faustina, 13, 192, 256n35
Cortina, José Esteban, 9
Cortina, José Eusebio de Jesús, 9
Cortina, José María, 9, 11, 31, 46, 82, 85, 124, 129–30, 132, 137, 141, 148–49, 254n3, 262n68
Cortina, Juan Nepomuceno, scholarship and literature, of, 1–6; birth of, 7, 9; early life, 8–9; siblings, 10; in Indian wars, 11; in Matamoros National Guard, 12, 23; marriage of, 12–13; children, 13; in war with United States, 15–17; employee of Quartermaster Department, 17–18; alleged crimes, 18; concerns over loss of land, 20, 31–32; part of Separatists Movement, 20–21; in Merchants War, 22–23; disdain for Adolphus Glavecke, 27; indictment by grand jury, 28; in Cameron County politics, 29–31; shooting of Marshal Shears, 37–38; Brownsville Raid, 39–45; consequences of raid, 45, 48–53, 58–61; Rancho del Carmen *pronunciamiento,* 46–47; defeat of Brownsville Tigers, 54–55; *Cortinista* Army, 55–57; feared as abolitionist, 61–62; newspaper attacks on, 63–64; defeat of Texas Rangers on Palo Alto Prairie, 64–65; second *pronunciamiento,* 67–68; raids in Lower Rio Grande Valley, 69–72; United States Army

Cortina, Juan Nepomuceno (*cont.*)
offensive against, 73–77; defeat at Rio Grande City, 77–80; leads *Cortinistas* at La Bolsa, 83–85; Taylor-Navarro investigations of, 87–88; Governor Houston's reaction to, 91–93; retreat into Burgos Mountains, 93; fighting reactionaries in central Mexico, 95; leads Zapata County insurrection, 97–98; defeated at Carrizo, 98–101; inspires *Cortinistas* and *Zapatistas*, 108–110; collaborates with Federals, 110–11, 117–20, 133–35, 140–44, 152–53; inspires *Vidalistas*, 112–14; aids Cobos against Ruiz, 114–15; revolts against Cobos, 115; seizes power in Matamoros, 116; executes Vila and Cobos, 116; relations with Vidaurri, 119; defies Juárez, 120–22; harasses Confederates, 138–39; joins *Imperialistas* and gives up Matamoros, 145–47; reasserts loyalty to Liberals, 148; fights *Imperialistas*, 149–59; defeated at Rancho del Brazil, 159; war with contra-guerrillas, 159–62; helps drive Mejía from Matamoros, 163–71; in Tamaulipas struggle for power, 175–76, 181–86; Defeated at Rancho Sabanito, 177; routed at Palo Blanco, 177; attacks Canales, 186–89; at Querétaro, 191–92; in central Mexico, 193–95; suppresses Vargas Revolution, 195–96; failure to secure pardon, 198–99; orchestrates Texas cattle raids, 200–204, 207–209; Robb Commission investigates, 211–15; Comision Pesquisidora investigates, 215–18; alcalde of Matamoros, 219–22; Nuecestown Raid, 222–24; arrest by Lerdo government, 228–30; Santiago Tlatelolco imprisonment, 230–31; Azcapotzalco *pronunciamiento*, 232; support of Díaz and Plan de Tuxtepec, 233; besieges Matamoros, 233–34; defies Díaz, 236; arrested by Canales, 237–38; second Santiago Tlatelolco imprisonment, 238–41; at Azcapotzalco, 243–47; marriage to María de Jesus López, 241–42; Ford visits, 247; death of, 247, legacy of, 249–52

Cortina, María del Carmen, 9, 13, 192, 254n3
Cortina, María Dolores, 12–13, 255n32, 256n35
Cortina, Rafaela, 12, 156, 192, 236, 255n32, 256n35, 290n80
Cortina, Trinidad, 9, 255n15
Cortina War: Brownsville Raid, 43–45; Rancho del Carmen *pronunciamiento*, 46; *Cortinista* isolation of Brownsville, 48–50, 58–60; Brownsville Committee of Public Safety in, 53–54; widening of, 55–56; reaction in Texas to, 59–62; Cabrera hanging inflames, 63; defeat of Rangers on Palo Alto Prairie, 64; defeat of Rangers at Rancho del Carmen, 65; second Rancho del Carmen *pronunciamiento*, 67–68; *Cortinistas* raids in lower Valley, 68–71; United States Army in, 72–95; defeat of *Cortinistas* at La Ebonal, 73; Battle of Rio Grande City, 77–80; dispersal and regrouping of *Cortinistas*, 80–83; fighting at La Bolsa, 83; Rangers invasion of Mexico, 84–86; Governor Houston reaction to, 87; Taylor-Navarro Commission investigation of, 88–90; Knights of the Golden Circle in, 89–92; Duff Green's investigation of, 92–93; Robert E. Lee in, 93–94

Cortinistas: in Brownsville Raid, 40–45; defeat of Brownsville Tigers, 52–55; lynching of Cabrera inflames, 63–64; defeats Texas Rangers on Palo Alto Prairie, 64; defeats Rangers at Rancho del Carmen, 65; raids in Lower Rio Grande Valley, 68–71; defeat of at Rio Grande City, 77–80; at La Bolsa; defeats Ruiz, 122–27; defeated by *Imperialistas* at Rancho del Brazil, 159; war with Colonel Du Pin and contra-guerrillas, 159–62; hanging of Rómulo, 172; hanging of García, Vela, and Garza, 172–74; cattle raids in Texas, 200–209, Nuecestown Raid of, 222–24

Corvette (steamboat), 25
Cowen, Louis R., 283n48
Cox, Noah, 81, 102
Crawford, R. Clay, 167, 255n15
Crimean War, 103
Cristo, José Leonides, 220–22, 229
Croix, Tam., 195
Cross, John S., 28
Cross, Trueman, 258n94
Cumbres de Acultzingo, Vera Cruz, 103
Cummings, Frank, 43, 172

Dana, Napoleon Jackson Tecumseh, 122
Dashiell, D. H., 112
Daugherty, James, 292n9
Davis, Edmund J., 49, 111, 198
Davis, Henry Clay, 60, 63, 71–73, 77, 99, 102, 269n71, 275n32
Davis, Hilalria de Martinez, 78
Day, Henry Martyn, 138–41, 143–44
De Geofroy, L., 136, 144

Dean, Albert, 213
Defenders of the Monroe Doctrine, 136
Defensores de la Patria, 11, 15
De la Barra, Bernabé, 231
De la Fuente, Antonio, 50
De la Garza, José Saldivar, 10
De la Garza, Juan Antonio, 12
De la Garza, Juan José, 171, 182, 195
De la Garza, Martin Peña, 202
De la Luna, Juan, 18
De la Serna, Jesús, 117, 120, 122, 129
De León, Arnoldo, 4
De León, Jesús, 74
De León, Francisco, 149, 160, 162, 166, 168–69
Díaz, Agustín, 97
Díaz, Dario, 151
Díaz, Felix, 232
Díaz, Pedro, 97–98
Díaz, Porfirio, 104, 204, 231–32, 234, 236, 238–40, 243, 297n64
Dix, John James, 17–18
Dobie, J. Frank, 1–2, 214, 224
Dobie, Sterling Neblett, 214, 253n1
Doblado, Manuel, 133
Dodge City, Kansas, 217
Dodge, G. S., 285n100
Dogtown (Tilden), Tex.,
Domenech, Emmanuel H. D., 26
Dominguez, Manuel, 71
Donelson, John, 64, 96, 100
Dorr, Thomas, 242
Dougherty, Edward, 36, 50, 56
Douglas, James Ridley, 4
Drayton, Thomas F., 145
Du Pin, Charles Louis, 136, 138, 160–61, 171, 181, 280n35, 283n33
Duval County, Tex., 216, 221, 224
Dwyer, Joseph E., 224–25

Eagle Pass, Tex., 36, 135, 149–50, 212
Echazarreta, Miguel, 134, 143
Edinburg, Tex., 36, 70, 74, 77, 85, 208, 223
Elizabeth Street (Brownsville), 26, 34, 40–43, 48, 116
El Cerro de las Campanas, Queretaro, 191
El Guayalejo, Tam., 195
El Paso del Norte (Ciudad Juárez), Chihuahua, 133
El Sal del Rey, Tex., 7
Emperor Maximiliano - *see* Maximilian
Empress Carlota - *see* Carlota
Escandon, José de, 10

Escobedo, Mariano, 104, 162, 164–65, 170–71, 178–80, 186, 188, 191, 232
Esparza, Carlos, 212–13, 256n34, 292b9
Espinosa, Antonio, 54
Espíritu Santo Grant, Tex., 10, 13, 27, 31
Eugenia (steamer), 180
Everman (steamer), 289n34
Exploradores de la Fronera, 202, 298n81
Exploradores del Bravo, 144

Falcon, Blas María de la Garza, 9–10
Farías, Francisco Fuentes, 204
Farías, Policarpio, 202
Fernández, Florencio, 94
Ferrocarril Mexicano, 229
Fieles de Camargo, 298n81
Fieles de Bagdad, 298n81
Fieles de Cortina, 202
Finn, J. A., 48
Fish, Hamilton, 198, 210, 232–33
Fitzpatrick, Richard, 80
Flores, Julián, 71
Flores, Rosalio, 194
Flournoy, M. T., 151
Floyd, John B., 37, 58, 90–91
Ford, John S. "Rip", 8–9, 22, 23, 56, 61, 79, 82, 93, 99, 140, 144, 212, 231, 237, 243, 247
Forey, Élie Frédéric, 103–104
Fort Brown, Tex., 17, 19, 36, 40–41, 43, 48, 93, 109, 112–13, 118, 134, 137, 180, 204, 208–209, 226–27, 234
Fort Duncan, Tex., 36, 50, 154, 211
Fort Carlota (Bagdad), Tam., 175
Fort Clark, Tex., 50
Fort Guadalupe (Matamoros), Tam., 186
Fort Leavenworth, Kansas, 62
Fort Loreto (Puebla), Puebla, 103
Fort Matanzas (Matamoros), Tam., 165
Fort McIntosh, Tex., 36, 50
Fort Merrill, Tex., 72
Fort Monroe, Vir., 62
Fort Monterrey (Matamoros), Tam., 184, 186
Fort Paredes (Matamoros), Tam., 22, 188
Fort Sumter, S. C., 97
Fort San Fernando (Matamoros), Tam., 186–87
Fort Texas (Brown), Tex., 14, 25
Fort Xavier (Puebla), Puebla, 104
Foster, John W., 227, 230, 232, 235
Fountain, Albert B., 199
Fox, John, 46, 64, 262n60
Freeport, Tex., 186, 188

Frossard, C. V., 286n125
Fuentes, Baltazar, 233

Galindo, Ignacio, 216
Galván, Jeremiah, 8, 9, 25, 34, 51, 159, 261n44
Galveston Daily Civilian, 59
Galveston, Tex., 21, 68, 207
García, Antonio, Chapa, 202
García, Atanacio, 13
García, Benito, 212
García, Cleto, 84
García, Fabián, 198
García, Francisco, 256n35
García, Guadalupe, 82, 84, 89, 100, 129
García, Héctor, 251
García, Marcela, 36
García, Pedro, 71
García, Sabas, 207, 212–13, 217
García, Simon, 267n197
García, Vicente, 43, 172–74
García, Viviano, 43
Garibaldi, Giuseppe, 191
Garland, Rice, 21
Garrison, William Lloyd, 61
Garza, Alberto, 216
Garza, Basilio, 237
Garza, Catarino, 4
Garza, Florencio, 43, 172–74
Garza, Juan G., 99, 275n25
Garza, Juanita Gonzales, 258n87
Garza, Manuel, 202
Garza, Ramón, 134
Garza, Secundo, 269n68
Garza, Tomás, 195
General Sherman (steamer), 289n34
George, Jacob F., 70.
Getty, George, 172
Gholson, W.W., 165
Giddings, George, 143
Glavecke, Adolphus: at Cortina's wedding,13; close friend of Cortina,18; marriage to Concepción Ramirez, 27; in Mexican War, 27; blamed for death of Trueman Cross, 258n94; acquires Rancho San Pedro, 27; political influence in Cameron County, 27; feud with Cortina, 27–28; criminal accusations against, 28; has Cortina indicted, 28; indictment of, 261n87; posts bail for Alejo Vela, 261n42; foreman of grand jury in Shears shooting, 260n24; Cortina hatred of, 28; in land litigation, 32; Cortina threatens to kill, 39, 41, 43; during Brownsville Raid, 43–45, 261n44; account of Brownsville Raid, 261n44; as deputy sheriff, 52; capture of Cabrera, 52; Cortina challenges to combat, 55; with Brownsville Tigers, 63; guides Texas Rangers, 63; sends family to Matamoros, 68; correspondence with Scarborough, 88; testifies before Robb Commission, 212; Comisión Pesquisidora perjury charges against, 217–18; 1875 Navarro charges against, 258n87; attends banquet in Cortina's honor
Glavecke, Charles, 27
Glavecke, Gaspar, 27
Globe Hotel (Bagdad), Tam.,
Goldfinch, Charles W., 2, 300n127
Goliad County, Tex., 18, 35, 60, 216
Gómez, Francisco Valdez, 216
Gómez, Manuel, 189, 238
Gonzales, Tex., 61
Gonzales, Miguel, 71
Gonzales, Norberto, 262n60
Gonzales, Victor, 209
Goseascochea, Feliciana, 255n32
Goseascochea, José Manuel, 10
Goseascochea, María Estéfana, *See* Cortina, Estéfana
Graham, John, 68
Grampus (steamboat), 48
Grant, Ulysses S., 153–54m, 169,171, 209–10, 224, 226
Graves, Charles H., 189
Great Storm of 1867, 193
Green, Duff, 92–93
Grier, Thomas, 267n195
Guadalajara, Jalisco, 95, 133
Guadalupe County, Tex., 35
Guanajuato, State of, 146, 192
Guardia Nacional de Tamaulipas, *See* Tamaulipas National Guard
Guaymas, Sonora, 181
Guerra, Marcos, 262n60
Guerrero, Tam., 11, 22, 81, 98–100, 108–109, 135, 149, 209, 211, 233
Guias de Tamaulipas, 298n81
Gussettville, Tex., 60
Guzman, Fermín, 269n68

Hale and Allen, 31
Hall, George A., 225–26
Hamburg, Ger., 107
Hamilton, Alexander D., 221–22
Hamilton, Andrew Jackson, 135–36

Index

Hancock, John, 207
Hardeman, William P., 151
Harper's Ferry, Vir. (W.V.), 61
Harris, J.C., 58
Hatch, Edward, 222–23
Havana, Cuba, 101, 225–26
Hayes, Rutherford B., 239
Haynes, John L., 32, 62, 88, 89, 111–12, 118, 222, 265n157
Helena, Tex., 35
Heintzelman, Samuel Peter, 72–73, 76–77, 82, 84, 89, 260n32
Hemphill, John, 49
Henry, William Robertson, 272n149
Henry Dodge (revenue cutter), 51
Hernández, Apolinario, 212
Hernández, Jesús, 198
Hernández, Justo, 134
Hernández, Lucino, 269n60
Hernández, Rafaela, 268n35
Herron, Francis J., 124, 126, 133–35
Hidalgo County, Tex., 29, 36, 51, 56–57, 70, 101–102, 198, 202, 218, 223
Hinojosa, José María, 99, 275n25
Hinojosa, Mario G., 141
Hinojosa, Matías, 134
Hinojosa, Pedro, 164, 182, 197, 205, 219
Hinojosa, Rafael, 209
Hobsbaum, Eric, 4
Holquín, José María, 226
Hord, Robert H., 20, 32
Houston, Sam, 32, 78, 86–87, 89–93
Huasteca Region, Mex., 160, 175, 195
Hubbard, R. B., 227
Hugo, Victor, 191
Hunt, Henry, 94
Hunter, J. T., 63

Icamole (N. L.), Battle of, 232
Idar, Nicasio, 251
Iglesias, José, 134, 234
Immaculate Concepción Church, Brownsville, Tex., 13
Imperialistas: advance on Puebla, 103–104; defeat Liberals at San Lorenzo, 104; seize Buebla, 104; seize Mexico City, 104; seize San Luis Potosí, 131; Vidaurri joins, 131–32; occupy Guadalajara, 133; defeat Doblado at Matehuala, 133; capture Bagdad, 137–38, 140; defeat Cortina on San Fernando River, 138; enter Cortina joins, 147; Matamoros, 147; execute Vidal, 156–57; defeat Cortina at Rancho del Brazil, 159; decisively defeated at Santa Gertrudis, 178–80; evacuation of Matamoros and Bagdad, 180; surrender at Querétaro, 191
Independencia (steamer), 237
Indianola, Tex., 65, 88
Indianola Commercial Bulletin, 59
Indianola Courier, 60
Inez Huston (schooner), 226

Jalisco, State of, 196
Jenkins, Robert, 252
Jersey City, N. J., 221
Jiménez, Tam., 196
Johnson, Andrew, 154
Johnson, Benjamin Huber, 5
Johnson, Bob, 91
Johnson, James, 69
Johnson, M. T., 151
Johnson, Robert L., 43, 45–46
Johnson, William, 69
Joseph, Ferdinand Maximilian, *See* Maximilian
Juarez (gunboat), 229
Juárez, Benito, 3–4, 23, 95, 102–103, 106, 110, 115–16, 122–23, 127–29, 132, 148, 154–55, 160, 181, 195, 197, 198, 206
Juaristas: Cortina joins at Puebla, 102–103; defend and evacuate Puebla, 104; evacuate Mexico City, 104; evacuate San Luis Potosí, 131; evacuate Guadalajara, 133; defeated at Matehuala, 133; evacuate Ciudad Victoria and Monterrey, 137–38; guerrilla war with Du Pin in Tamaulipas and the Huasteca, 160–62; attack Matamoros, 162–65; defeat *Imperialistas* at Santa Gertrudis, 178–80; attack Tampico, 181; recapture Monterrey and Saltillo; force surrender of *Imperialistas* at Querétro, 191–92

Kahn, Henry, 41
Karankawa Indians, 255n25
Karnes County, Tex., 35, 64
Kelsey, John P., 71, 78, 197, 268n43
Kendall, George Wilkins, 48
Kenedy County, Tex., 224
Kenedy, Mifflin, 20, 25, 29, 48, 52–53, 59, 65, 70–71, 89, 106, 118, 157, 164, 208, 214, 217, 226
King, Clay, 151
King, Richard, 20, 29, 63, 70, 72, 89, 106, 118, 164, 212, 214, 226
King Ranch, 72, 207, 211

Kingsbury, Gilbert, 31
Kingsbury, Robert B., 47, 51, 68
Kinney, Henry Lawrence, 93
Kinney, Somers, 47, 68, 260n12
Kiowa Indians, 91
Knights of the Golden Circle, 22, 61, 89, 94
Know Nothing Party, 35

La Bolsa, Tam., *See* Rancho La Bolsa
La Bellone (gunboat), 156
La Burrita, Tam., 139, 143, 156
La Chura, Tex., 221
La Loba, *See* Plan de La Loba
La Florida, *See* Rancho La Florida
La Gloria, *See* Rancho La Gloria
La Grange, Tex., 18
Laborda, Julio, 124, 126
Lafragua, José María, 218, 227, 230
La Gran Liga Mexicinista, 251
Laguna de los Indios, Tam., 94
Lake Texcoco, Mex., 229
Langdon, Loomis Lyman, 65, 267n197
Lara, López de, 152
Laredo, Tex., 21 23, 36, 98–99, 135, 211–12
Larrache, Ramos, 150
Larralde, Carlos, 4
Las Cuevas, Tex., *See* Rancho Las Cuevas
Las Grullas, Tex., *See* Rancho Las Grullas
Las Norias, Tex., *See* Rancho Las Norias
Las Rucias, Tex., *See* Rancho Las Rucias
Latham, Frank W., 29, 46–47, 50–51
La Torrena, Tex., 213
Latrille, Charles, 103
Lavaca County, Tex., 216
Lee, Robert E., 86, 93–94
Lerdistas, 204, 231, 233–35
Linares, N. L., 233
Lincoln, Abraham, 102, 111, 135, 140
Lípan Apaches, 10–11
Literal, Jerry, 112
Littleton, John, 64
Live Oak County, Tex., 60, 64, 214
Liverpool, England, 106–107
Lo de Ovejo (Jalisco), Battle of, 197, 241
Lockridge, Samuel L., 61, 89, 266n173
Longoria, Donato, 202
Longoria, Guadalupe, 202
Longoria, Juan, 202, 262n60
Longoria, Leonardo, 202
Longoria, Matías, 44, 46
López, Albino , 109, 127
López, María de Jesús, 241–42, 245, 250

López, Miguel, 191
Los Águilas, 205, 220
Los Carbineros de Tamaulipas, *See* Carbineros de Tamaulipas
Los Exploradores de la Frontera, *See* Explorandores de la Frontier
Los Fieles de Bagdad, *See* Fieles de Bagdad
Los Fieles de Camargo, *See* Fieles de Camargo
Los Fresnos, Tex., 13, 256n36
Los Guias de Tamaulipas, *See* Guias de Tamaulipas
Los Indios, Tex., 69, 73
Los Rifleros de Bagdad, *See* Rifleros de Bagdad
Lovenskiold, Charles, 59, 265n157
Lugo, Longinos, 217
Lugo, Pedro, 217

McAllen, John, 212
McClusky, James B., 78
McCook, Alexander McDowell, 202–204, 206, 209, 212, 215
McCulloch, Ben, 90
McFadden, W. M., 64
McKay, William, 267n195
McLane, Robert, 50
McClernand, John A., 119, 135–36
McMurtry, Larry, 6
McNelly, Leander H., 224–26, 239
McWilliams, Carey, 3
Maggie Jane (schooner), 135
Magruder, John B., 120, 136, 150
Mallet, James M., 28
Maltby, Henry A., 59–60, 68, 152–53, 190, 198
Mariscal, Ignacio, 221
Market Plaza (Brownsville), 7, 24, 39, 63, 226
Márquez, Leonardo, 95, 104, 191
Martin, James, 69
Martínez, Hilaria de la Garza, *See* Davis, Hilaria de la Garza
Martínez, Pedro, 197
Mason, A. T., 18
Matagorda County, Tex., 35
Matagorda Island, Tex., 21
Matamoros, Tam., 8, 10, 14, 16, 22, 25, 34, 38–39, 44, 48, 51–52, 56, 68, 73, 82, 84, 94, 106, 112, 114–16, 120, 122, 125, 131, 133–36, 139, 143, 147, 153, 155, 158–59, 215, 220, 225–26, 232, 234, 243
Matamoros Daily Ranchero, *107, 152, 190*
Matamoros Eco de Ambas Fronterias, 233
Matamoros El Jaque, 191

Index 327

Matamoros El Mercurio, 11
Matamoros National Guard, 53
Matehuala, S. L. P., 133
Maxan, Nestor, 70
Maximilian, Joseph von Hapsburg, 106, 133, 146, 158, 166, 169, 175, 191, 290n74
Maxwell, James, 69
Mead, Fabius J., 211
Medrano, Enrique, 69
Mejía, Francisco, 132
Mejía, Enrique A., 168
Mejía, Ignacio, 194, 230
Mejía, Tomás, 131, 138, 145–49, 153–57, 162, 165–66, 169, 177–78, 181, 286n125, 288n27
Méndez, Juan N., 233
Merchants War, 23
Mesquital Lealeño, Tam., 109
Mexico City, D. F., 7, 17, 95, 114, 147, 192, 194, 198, 234–35, 237, 241, 245
Mexican Border Committee, 3, 45
Mexican War, 25–26, 34, 37
Mexico (steamer), 138
Mexico City El Monitor Republicano, 233, 238
Mexico City La Patria, 238
Mexico City Sufragio, 232
Mexico City Two Republics, 233
Michener, James A., 5
Mier, Tam., 11, 22, 55, 81, 99, 109–10, 129, 149, 151, 159, 178, 205, 232–33
Mier y Terán, Luis, 234
Milan, Francisco, 69, 213
Milstead, A.G., 69
Miller, George W., 226
Miller, Jacob, 69
Miller, James B., 21
Miller, W. A., 59–60
Miller Hotel (Brownsville), 26, 41
Millett, James, 69
Millett, Nicholas R., 267n195
Miramón, Miguel, 95, 114, 146, 191
Mireles, Pedro, 82
Mixquiahuala, Hidalgo, 194
Molina, Guillermo, 71
Molla, Dionicio, 269n68
Montejano, David, 4
Monterrey, N. L., 17, 68, 126, 129, 131–32, 138, 158, 178, 180–81, 205, 232
Montes, Jesús, 46, 261n42
Montreal, Canada, 144
Moore, Francis, 223
Moran, Victor, 269n68
Morel, Victor, 209, 213

Morelia, State of, 189
Morris, George, 41, 43, 45–46, 261n40
Morris, Luciana, 43
Móvil de Matamoros, 23
Muñoz, Juan, 209, 211
Murieta, Joaquin, 5
Murrah, Pendleton, 150–51
Mussett, John D., 97, 100

Natchitoches, La., 57
Navarro, José Ángel, 36, 88–90, 258n87, 272n138
Navarro, José Antonio, 88
Navarro, Ignacio, 134
Neale, William, 25, 29, 41, 56–57, 70
Neale, William Peter, 41–42, 45, 56
Nealeville, Tex., *See* Santa María
Negrete, Miguel, 148, 204, 241
Nelson, Thomas H., 204
Nelson, W. W., 31
Nepomuceno, Juan (Czech priest), 254
New Braunfels, Tex., 48
New Orleans, La., 47, 58, 61, 68, 84, 107, 109, 131, 133, 153, 170–71, 188, 235, 237
New Orleans Crescent, 175
New Orleans Daily Picayune, 48, 58, 60
New Orleans Daily True Delta, 59–60
New York City, N. Y., 107, 116
New York Herald, 107, 153, 155, 165, 167
New York Times, 215
Nickels, Peter, 70
Noakes, Thomas John, 60, 296n25
Nolan, Matthew, 64, 98, 265n157, 274n12
Nueces County, Tex., 64, 216, 221, 224–45
Nueces River, Tex., 21, 36, 49, 61, 68, 70, 72, 111, 193, 207
Nueces Strip, Tex., 16, 200, 216, 221, 223, 225, 230
Nuecestown, Tex., 223–24
Nuestra Señora Soledad de la Mota, Hacienda of, 202
Nuevo Laredo, Tam., 60, 62, 129, 135, 190, 195, 210–11, 233
Nuevo León, State of, 133, 159–60, 162, 175, 189, 196–97
Nuevo Santander, Province of, 10

Oaxaca, State of, 110, 123, 181, 204
O'Connell, Daniel, 232
O'Conner, Hugh, 69
O'Conner, Thomas, 214
Ochoa, Antonio, 97–99
Olguín, André, 159

Ord, Edward Otho Cresap, 227–28, 230, 233
Olvera, Rafael, 177, 179
Ortega, Jesús González, 17–71, 177, 194, 287n134, 289n35
Orteguistas, 170, 177
Osborn, Thomas O., 211

Padre Island, Tex., 59
Padrón, Anaclito, 212
Paisano (gunboat), 164
Palacios, Jesús, 171
Palacios, Miguel, 197, 204, 206
Palmito Ranch, Tex., 143
Palo Alto, Battle of, 36
Palo Alto House, 64
Palo Alto Prairie, Tex., 15–16, 53, 64, 226
Palo Blanco, *See* Rancho Palo Blanco
Panteón de Dolores, D. F., 245–46, 249
Parisot, Pierre Fourrier, 40, 107, 172
Parra, Emilio, 197
Parrat, Manuel, 228
Parsons, Mosby Monroe, 151
Passmento, Bartolo, 44
Pauda, Tómas, 156
Pease, Elisha M., 35
Peña, Albino, 162
Peña, Mandinio, 205
Peña, Miguel, 46, 262n67, 267n1
Peña, Rafael, 269n68
Phelps, Orlando C., 21
Pico de Orizaba, Mex., 229
Pierce, Leonard, Jr., 106, 117, 124, 126, 140–41, 171
Piedras Negras, Coa., 131, 150, 216
Piedras Pintas, Tex., 223
Pitner, Ernst, 178
Plan de Ayutla, 23
Plan de Tuxtepec, 231, 233, 236, 238
Plan de La Loba, 22–23
Plan de La Noria, 204–206, 231
Plan de San Diego, 5
Plaza de Independencia (Matamoros), 185
Plaza Hidalgo (Matamoros), 23, 39, 124, 136, 148, 164, 182, 186, 188, 219, 235
Point Isabel (Port Isabel), Tex., 14, 21, 25–26, 41, 46, 50–51, 68, 70–71, 96
Polk, James K., 14–15
Porfiristas, 204, 232–33, 235, 237
Portillo, Antonio, 53
Potrero del Espíritu Santo, *See* Espíritu Santo Grant

Powers, Stephen, 9, 20, 25, 29, 37, 48, 51–52, 56, 58, 89, 199
Pozo del Carmen, S. L. P., 95
Prince of Wales (steamboat), 169
Prisión Militar de Santiago Tlatelolco, D. F., *See* Santiago Tlatelolco
Puebla, City of, 103–104, 231
Puebla, State of, 194
Puerto del Indio, N. L., 232
Puente, José A., 140–41

Querétaro, City of, 146, 191–92, 290n74
Querétaro, State of, 189, 196
Quintero, José A., 109, 135
Quiroga, Julián, 205–206, 234

Ramireño, Tex. (Cameron County), 29–30, 40, 57
Ramírez, Jesús García, 110
Ramírez, Concepción, 27
Ramírez, Victor, 71
Ranchero (steamboat), 84, 165
Rancho Agua Negra, Tex., 69
Rancho Albercas, Tam., 218
Rancho Altravesada, Tam., 224
Rancho Anacintas Altos, Tex., 69, 134
Rancho Atascosa, Tex., 71
Rancho Barreta, 32
Rancho Bastón, Tex., 56–57, 70, 77, 82
Rancho Calabozo, Tex., 213
Rancho Canela, Tam., 212
Rancho Cantú, Tex., 71
Rancho Capote, Tex., 101
Rancho Carricitos, Tex., 15, 77
Rancho Chiltipín, 215
Rancho Clareño, Tex., 97–101, 109–110
Rancho Corral y Piedra, Tex., 224
Rancho Davis, Tex., *See* Rio Grande City
Rancho de los Sauses, Tex., 81
Rancho del Brazil, Tam., 159
Rancho del Carmen, Tex., 7, 13–19, 22–23, 27, 29, 30, 36–38, 45–47, 50–54, 57–58, 63, 65, 67, 69, 72–73, 93, 113, 153, 158, 176, 192, 198, 239, 256n36
Rancho El Mesquite, Tex., 224
Rancho Encantada, Tam., 212
Rancho Estero Grande, Tex., 225
Rancho Galveston, Tex., 69
Rancho Guadalupe, 202
Rancho La Blanca, Tex., 70
Rancho La Bolsa, Tex., 70, 102, 201, 209, 217

Rancho La Bolsa, Tam., 82, 84, 201, 271n105, 292n5
Rancho La Ebonal, Battle at, 73–74, 271n105
Rancho La Ebonal, Tex., 73, 250
Rancho La Florida, Tex., 26, 69
Rancho La Gloria, Tex., 26
Rancho La Grullas, Tex., 201, 222–23
Rancho La Mesa, Tam., 11, 85
Rancho La Mesteña, Tam., 202
Rancho La Unión, Tam., 228, 234
Rancho Laguna Tío Cano, Tex., 71
Rancho Las Norias, Tex., 11, 134
Rancho Las Cuevas, Tex., 77–78, 101, 109, 201, 214, 223
Rancho Las Rucias, Tex., 20, 29, 77, 201, 212, 220
Rancho Las Tranquilas, Tex., 217
Rancho Lopeño, Tex., 209
Rancho Los Diez, 222
Rancho Los Vibros, Tex., 81
Rancho Maguellitos, Tam., 202
Rancho Maguey, Tam., 85
Rancho Malahucea, 99
Rancho Mayelles, Tam., 28
Rancho Mogotes, Tam., 207
Rancho Naranja, Tam., 201
Rancho Nuevo, Tex., 201
Rancho Palito Blanco, Tam., 94, 177, 212–13, 234, 236, 256n35
Rancho Penascal, Tex., 224
Rancho Prietas, Tam., 201–201, 213
Rancho Quijano, Tam., 85
Rancho Relámpago, Tex., 36, 70
Rancho Rosairo, Tam., 162
Rancho Rosario, Tex., 268n35
Rancho Rucias, Tex., *See* Rancho Las Rucias
Rancho Sabinito, Tam., 50, 159, 177, 201
Rancho San José, Tex., 16–17, 23, 29–30, 50, 65, 97, 256n36
Rancho San Pedro, Tex., 27, 217
Rancho San Salvador de Tule, Tex., 70
Rancho Santa Cruz, Tam., 94
Rancho Santa Fe, 212
Rancho Santa Gertrudis, *See* King Ranch
Rancho Santa Rita, 212
Rancho Santa Rosa, Tex., 70
Rancho Sauz, Tex., 69
Rancho Soledad, 109
Rancho Soldadito, Tam., 195, 212
Rancho Solís, 222
Rancho Tahuachal, 202, 212
Rancho Tio Bueno, Tex., 69
Rancho Tulosa, 201
Rancho Viejo, Tex., 71, 84
Randall, A. M., 181
Rankin, Melinda, 150, 158
Rangers, *See* Texas Rangers
Redmond, Henry, 97–98, 100
Red Party, 29–30
Redmond's Ranch, Tex., 97–99
Reed, Arthur F., 167
Refugio, Tex., 9
Refugio County, Tex., 216
Rejón, Manuel G., 135
Republic of the Rio Grande, 22
Republic of the Sierra Madre, 61
Resaca de la Palma, Battle of, 16, 36
Revueltas, Ignacio, 233, 298n78
Reyburn, W. P., 261n44
Reyes, Clemente, 44
Reynosa, Tam., 22, 52, 55–56, 77, 84, 86, 94, 129, 149, 156, 159, 166, 189, 232
Reynosa Viejo, Tam., 102
Rhodes, Thaddeus M., 70, 212–13, 218, 269n64
Rifleros de Bagdad, 298n81
Ringgold Barracks, Tex., 36, 65, 77–78, 93, 109, 135, 189, 208–10, 222
Rio Bravo (gunboat), 234
Rio Grande (steamboat), 167
Rio Grande City, Battle of, 77–80
Rio Grande City, Tex., 3, 21–22, 32, 36, 59–60, 71, 77, 80–82, 86, 88, 96, 102, 118, 150, 190, 213, 222, 250, 269n67
Rio Grande Expedition, 116
Rio Grande, Territory of, 20–21
Rio Nueces, *See* Nueces River
Rio San Juan, Mex., 9
Rio Tula, Hidalgo, 194
Rio Verde, S. L. P., 162, 222
Rippy, J. Fred, 3
Robb, Thomas P., 211, 215
Robb Commission, 211–12, 216, 225
Robeson, George M., 227
Robinson, William, 78
Robles, Luis, 157
Rocha, Sóstines, 197, 204, 206
Rodriguez, J. M., 12
Rodríguez, Rafael, 159
Roma, Tex., 36, 79–81, 100, 102, 109, 190, 223, 245
Romero, Matías, 169
Rómulo, Evaristo, 172
Rosa, Cristobal, 169
Rosenbaum, Robert J., 4

Rosillo Massacre, 10
Rotonda de los Hombres Illustres (Mexico City),
Rudyville, Tex., 36, 56
Ruiz, Manuel, 110, 113–115, 117, 120, 122–24, 127, 129
Runnels, Richard Hardin, 49–50, 56, 62, 65, 74, 92, 270n80
Rurales, 175, 178, 217, 218, 236
Rusk, Thomas J., 21
Russell, Willliam H., 208

Sabine River, Tex., 60, 68, 92
St. Clair, William D., 167
Saliceo, Agustín, 216
Salinas, Ildefonso, 213
Saltillo, Coahuila, 17, 126, 129, 132, 181, 205
San Antonio Alamo Express, 62
San Antonio Daily Herald, 59, 61–62
San Antonio, Tex., 10, 49–50, 60, 91
San Antonio-El Paso Wagon Road, 36
San Antonio Ledger and Texan, 60
San Antonio River, Tex., 18
San Bartolo, Tex., 97–98m 100
San Diego, Tex., 211
San Fernando, Tam., 120, 122, 137–38, 166, 171, 190, 222
San Fernando Creek, Tex., 214
San Fernando River, Mex., 138
San Jacinto, Battle of, 34
San José, Tex., *See* Rancho San José
San Juan (steamer), 211
San Juan de Ulloa, Vera Cruz, 245
San Juan River, 10, 23, 149, 156, 205
San Lorenzo, Puebla, 104
San Luis Potosí, City of, 106, 120, 181
San Luis Potosí, State of, 95, 150, 160, 162, 192, 196, 233, 241
San Martín Grant, 27
San Patricio, Tex., 36, 72
San Patricio County, Tex., 101, 216
San Pedro, Tex., 297n64
San Román, José, 24–25, 27, 48, 159, 268n43
Sandoval, Jesús, 225
Santa Ana, La Iglesia de, 9
Santa Anna, Antonio Lopez de, 17, 23
Santa Gertrudis, Tam., Battle of, 178, 180, 186
Santa Gertrudis Creek, Tex., 214
Santa Gertrudis Ranch, Tex., *See* King Ranch
Santa Rosalia, Mex., 148, 162
Santa Rosalía, Tex., 29–30
Santa María, Tex., 25

Santa Rita, Tex., 18, 28
Santiago Tlatelolco, Prison of, 230–31, 238–39
Sárate, Polinar, 269n68
Sárate, Palmario, 269n68
Sauz, Tam., 196
Savage, Richard H., 211
Scarborough, Edwin B., 28–29, 56, 88
Schleicher, Gustav, 239
Schuhmacher, Luis, 286n125
Scott, Winfield, 45, 84
Sedgwick, Thomas D., 185, 188
Sedgwick's Bridge, 185
Seguin, Tex., 35, 61
Señorita (steamboat), 153, 283n25
Separatist Movement, 21–22
Serna, de la Jesús
Seward, William H., 21, 152, 154, 169, 191
Shays, Daniel, 252
Shears, Robert, 7, 24, 37–38, 41, 43, 45, 68, 89
Shelby, Joseph O., 150
Sheldon, Thomas C., 213
Sheridan, Philip H., 153–555, 169, 188, 227
Sherman, William T., 224, 227, 229
Sierra de San Miguel, Mex., 194
Sierra de Puebla, 194, 233
Sierra Gomas, N. L., 133
Sierra Gorda Imperial Infantry, 179
Sierra Gordo, Mex., 204
Sierra Madre Oriental, Mex., 104
Sierra de San Carlos, Tam., 102
Silva, José María, 119, 136–37
Slaughter, James, 147–48
Slidell, John, 59
Smillie, James, 19
Smith, Edmund Kirby, 150
Smith, L. B., 226
Smith, Peter, 151
Solís, Cecilio, 71
Solis, Estéfana, 26
Solís, Francisco, 70
Solís, Jesús, 70
Solís, Santiago, 71, 82
Sonora, State of, 132
Soto la Marina, Tam., 196
Southern Steamship Company, 58
Spears, N. P., 78
Specht, Franz, 214
Stansbury, R. N., 20–21
Stansbury's School House (Brownsville), 20–21
Stanton, Edwin, 188
Starr County, Tex., 77, 88, 198, 203, 222

Steele, Frederick, 150, 153, 157–59, 171
Steele, William, 224–25
Stillman, Charles, 18–20, 24, 26, 28–29, 32, 36, 41, 70, 89, 113
Stillman, Elizabeth, 113
Stillman, Frank D., 28
Stockman's Association of Western Texas, 208
Stoneman, George, 79, 93–94
Striker's Place, Tex., 69
Sub-District of the Rio Grande, 202
Sussex, England, 25
Suwanee (steamer), 289n34

Tagle, Elijio, 85
Tamaulipas (steamer), 289n34
Tamaulipas, State of, 10, 86, 115, 120, 128, 149, 159–60, 170, 175, 180, 186, 195, 198, 233, 238, 245
Tamaulipas Battalion, 136
Tamaulipas Brigade, 187, 194, 195
Tampacuas Indians, 11, 52, 55, 255n25
Tampico, Tam., 39, 45, 50, 86, 122–23, 137, 180–81, 229
Tapia, Santiago, 182
Taylor, Richard H., 88–90, 272n138
Taylor, Zachary, 17, 14–16, 25
Terrell, Alexander Watkins, 151–52
Texas Rangers, 2, 7–8, 50, 62, 73, 94, 96
Thomas, William D., 41, 71, 77, 212–13, 218, 260–61n32, 262n60, 294n69
Thompson, Jacob, 83
Thompson, William B., 53
Tijerina, Antonio, 27
Tijerina, Casimiro, 27
Tijerina, Dolores "Chica," 255n32
Tijerina, Feliciana Goseascochea, 27
Tijerina, Juan José, 13, 255n32
Tijerina, María Dolores "Grande," *See* Cortina, Dolores
Tijerina, Miguel, 39, 44–46, 52–53
Tobin, William Gerard, 2, 62–65, 74, 80, 84, 254n1
Toledo, Jesús, 231
Torrejón, Anastasio, 15
Torres Velásquez, Dimas de, 286n125
Townsend, E. D., 209
Treaty of Guadalupe-Hidalgo, 17, 19–20, 87, 202, 250
Treviño, Andres, 86, 102, 128, 132, 197, 230, 232–33, 235
Treviño, Felicítas, 27
Treviño, Francisco, 69

Treviño, Francisco Ballí, 25
Treviño, Gerónimo, 178–79, 188, 196, 205–206
Treviño, José, 126
Treviño, Francisco, 102
Treviño, Ignacio, 209, 211
Treviño, Justo, 56–57
Treviño, Manuel, 44, 204–205, 230
Treviño, María Concepción, 255n15
Tula, Hidalgo, 181, 222
Tumlinson, Peter. 65
Turner, Josiah, 69
Turner, Nat, 62
Tuxpan, Tam., 180, 229
Twiggs, David E., 36, 40, 49–50, 62, 72

United States Army: 1st Artillery, 72, 93; 1st Infantry, 72; 8th Infantry, 93; 10th Infantry, 25, 209, 211; 2nd Cavalry, 72, 93; 4th Cavalry, 185, 209; 9th Cavalry, 209, 222–23;
Uribe, Blas María, 97
Uribe, Fernando, 97
Uvalde County, Tex., 35, 211

Valle del Mezquital, 194
Vargas, Braulio, 195–96
Vela, Alejo, 43, 45, 261n42
Vela, Bacilio, 269n68
Vela, Cecilio, 218
Vela, Desiderio, 269n68
Vela, Isidro, 97–100
Vela, Juan, 43, 45, 172–74
Vela, Nepomuceno, 99
Vela, Pedro, 212, 214
Vela, Petra, 26
Vela, Santiago, 99
Velásquez, Ramón, 195
Valdéz, Fernando, 202
Veracruz, City of, 104, 229, 237, 245
Veracruz, State of, 160
Verbaum, Julius, 64
Veron, A., 140, 144
Victoria, Tex., 61, 207
Vidal, Adrián J., 112–13, 117–18, 156–57, 283n48
Vidal's Partisan Rangers, 117
Vidalistas, 113
Vidaurri, Santiago, 23, 101, 120, 122, 126, 129, 132–33, 135, 191, 278n98
Vila, Rómulo, 116
Villa Aldamá, N. L., 133
Villa de Santa Ana de Camargo, Tam., *See* Camargo
Villanueva, Tex., 55, 134

Villarreal, Gregorio, 212
Villarreal, Juan, 71, 99
Vino, Guillermo, 109
Viscaya, Spain, 10

Waco, Tex., 61
Wallace, Lew, 167, 285n100, 289n34
Walker, John G., 144–45
Walker Mounted Rifles, 59
Walker, William, 61
Ward, J. M., 69
War of the Reform, 102
Washington, D. C., 7, 48–49, 62, 91, 224, 234
Watrous, J. C., 31
Watson, A. F., 262n60
Waud, A. R., 181
Webb County, Tex., 100
Webb, Henry, 44
Webb, Walter Prescott, 2
Webster, Michael G., 4
Weitzel, Godfrey, 164, 166, 169
Werbiski, Alexander, 29, 44, 46–47, 262n60
West, Robert, 69
Weyss, John E., 19
White, Nathaniel, 69, 71
White's Ranch, Tex., 17, 143–44
Wild Horse Desert, Tex., 65, 72, 207, 223
Wilson, Thomas F., 200, 204, 208, 212, 231, 233–35, 239
Woodhouse, H. E., 48
Woodman, Lyman L., 2
Wright, Horatio Gouverneur, 170

Young, Salome Balli de, 70
Young, Elliott, 5
Yturria, Francisco, 24, 27, 29, 44, 46, 48, 89, 156, 262n12, 262n60

Zacatecas, State of, 40, 114, 206
Zambrano, Juan A., 170
Zamora, Teodoro, 56, 74, 99, 101–102, 190
Zampano, Trinidad, 97
Zapata, Antonio, 97, 209
Zapata County, Tex., 96–100, 108–109, 211
Zapata, Tex., *See* Carrizo
Zapata, Octaviano, 108–10
Zapatistas, 109
Zaragosa, Ignacio, 103
Zepeda, Francisco, 86
Zona Libre, 23

ISBN-13: 978-1-58544-592-9
ISBN-10: 1-58544-592-4

www.ingramcontent.com/pod-product-compliance
Lightning Source LLC
Chambersburg PA
CBHW020352080526
44584CB00014B/992